SIKH SOLDIER
VOLUME FOUR
Warriors and Generals

Shaheed Baba Deep Singh Ji (1684-1757).

NARINDAR SINGH DHESI

With the assistance of:
GRAHAM WATKINS B.Sc. (Hons)

Published by

The Naval & Military Press Ltd
Unit 10 Ridgewood Industrial Park,
Uckfield, East Sussex,
TN22 5QE England
Tel: + 44 (0) 1825 749494
Fax: + 44 (0) 1825 765701
www.naval – military- press.com

Copyright: Narindar Singh Dhesi

Banda Singh Bahadur

DEDICATION

To those gallant Generals and stalwart Warriors, whose heroic deeds continue to inspire Sikhs the world over.

The Ghorchurras!
(Mounted Warriors)
Rise to Power!

CONTENTS

Dedication	3
Illustrations	5
Acknowledgements	6
Foreword	7
Introduction	8
The Sikhs	9
The Sardars	14
The Cis-Satluj Sardars	53
Maharajah Ranjit Singh	72
Ranjit Singh's Generals	83
Generals in the Anglo – Sikh wars	105
Indian Army	123
The Generals	130
Indian Navy	217
The Admirals	221
Indian Air Force	241
The Marshals	244
Royal Air Force	271
Sikh Governors	275
Prominent Sardars	286
Man on a Mission	298
Sikh Diaspora	300
Sources	315
Index	317

ILLUSTRATIONS

Shaheed Baba Deep Singh Ji	1
Banda Singh Bahadur	2
The Ghorchurras	3
Maharajah Ranjit Singh	5
General Harbakhsh Singh	5
General Jagjit Singh Arora	5
Marshal of the Air, Arjan Singh	6
Rear Admiral Kirpal Singh	6
Vice Admiral Harinder Singh	7

Maharajah Ranjit Singh

General Harbakhsh Singh

General Jagjit Singh Arora

ACKNOWLEGEMENT

I must express my warmest thanks and respects to Vice Admiral Harinder Singh, (Retd) for editing the chapter on the Indian Navy, for providing profiles of some naval officers and finally writing the foreword to this volume. May you always stay in *"Chardi Kala"*

Thanks to Mr. Harjinder Singh Kanwal for providing me the profile of Lieutenant Colonel Gurcharan Singh Chana of Kenya armed forces.

Thanks to Mr. Diljit Singh Bahra for providing the profile on Colonel Tarlochan Singh Marwaha of British armed forces.

Thanks to the handful of Generals who provided me with their profiles!

Final thanks to Major General AJS Sandhu for providing the profile of his father Lieutenant General Jaswant, and that of Lieutenant General Prem Singh Gyani.

My special thanks to my family, Beverley, Surindar, Jodh, Jassa and Sher who have borne the brunt of my 'Sikh Attacks'!

And my final thanks to long-suffering Hon. Prof. Graham Watkins, who helped to make the manuscript ready for publication.

Arjan Singh 'Marshal of Air'

Rear Admiral Kirpal Singh

FOREWORD

The order of the Khalsa, enshrined by Guru Gobind Singh, transformed a lowly man, otherwise an insignificant creature of poor and oppressed society, into a bold Sikh warrior. Narindar Singh Dhesi profiles the Sikh warriors that rose to power and then established and served the Sikh Empire, leading us through to its fall. Having illustrated the Sikh Sardars and Generals who fought and fell in the Anglo-Sikh Wars, he goes on to depict the senior Sikh military leaders of all the armed services of the Indian Armed Forces, as well as the Sikh military officers of the Sikh Diaspora. The structure of this work is not that of conventional narrative history. The individual chapters are organized around selected topics. It is best considered as a set of essays that together offer us a view into the profiles of the Sikh military leaders.

A well-researched and well-written book, this is a worthy sequel to the author's earlier publications on the Sikh soldiery.

Vice Admiral Harinder Singh, (Retd) PVSM, AVSM
Indian Navy

INTRODUCTION

Sikhism began as a peaceful religion, and tolerance always remained one of its fundamental tenets. However, religious persecution led to the development of a martial ethos that was enshrined by Guru Gobind Singh in the Order of the Khalsa. As Vice Admiral Harinder Singh states in the Foreword 'The order of the Khalsa transformed a lowly man, otherwise an insignificant creature of poor and oppressed society, into a bold warrior'. In 1708, the Sikh warriors, led by Banda Bahadur, shook the foundations of the Mughal Empire by setting up the first Sikh state in the Punjab. He and his comrades were eventually defeated and executed. After a long exile the warriors regrouped and fought against the Mughals and the Afghans, eventually resulting in the establishment of a number of small republics called Misls (autonomous confederacies) and later in the formation of the Sikh Empire. The boundaries of the Sikh Empire stretched from Tibet to Afghanistan and from Kashmir to Satluj in the south and included the regions of Punjab, NWFP, Kashmir, Jammu, and Ladakh. The formal start of the Sikh Empire began with the coronation of Ranjit Singh in 1801, creating a unified political state, with a galaxy of Sardars and Generals. All the Sardars who were affiliated with Maharaja Ranjit Singh were nobility with usually long and prestigious family martial histories. After Maharaja Ranjit Singh's death in 1839, the empire was severely weakened by internal divisions and political mismanagement. This opportunity was used by the British to precipitate the Anglo-Sikh Wars. A series of betrayals of the Sikhs by some prominent leaders and generals in the army led to its downfall. The Sikh Empire was finally dissolved after a series of the hardest fought wars against the British in 1849. The formidable Sikh soldier then went soldiering to the far corners of the British Empire. Almost every battlefield, in the two World Wars and before, where Indian soldiers participated in the fighting under the British, has witnessed their valour and many a legend has been woven around their name. When India gained independence and was partitioned in 1947, the exodus of Muslim troops resulted in the raising of the proportion of Sikhs in the army dramatically to thirty percent, although they comprised only two percent of the Indian population. A host of Sikh soldiers have risen to the highest ranks in all the armed services of their motherland and in the countries where their ancestors had taken military service. Whilst it is impossible to record and profile every Sikh Sardar and General, this is a token attempt to hopefully salute the few!

N.S.Dhesi

THE SIKHS

The Sikh homeland, the Punjab, is a very fertile region in northwest India. In 1947, the Punjab was partitioned between British India's successor states, India and Pakistan. Over the centuries many invading armies had poured in great cascades through the mountain passes of the North West Frontier of India, to raid, conquer and rule the fertile plains of the Punjab. As a result the Punjabi people were a mixture of Aryans, Persians, Greeks, Scythians, and the warriors from central Asia–the Bactrians, the Kushans, and the Huns. They had settled in Punjab, married local women and were absorbed into the local communities, worshiping a pantheon of Hindu gods. Prophet Mohammad established the religion of Islam in the desert wastes of Arabia. His followers, at the point of a sword, furiously and with great enthusiasm carried the Islamic banner to Syria, Egypt, Iran, Sudan, North Africa and southern Spain. In 712 AD, one of his followers, Mohammad Bin Qasim, stormed through the Bolan Pass to Baluchistan, overran Sindh and captured Multan in the Punjab. The Muslims went on to conquer Delhi and establish the Delhi Sultanate. The Delhi Sultanate was maintained by different Turco-Afghan clans. This was essentially an armed occupation, sustained by a constant influx of Muslims from across the mountains of North West India and Central Asia. At all times during the establishment and consolidation of Muslim rule, there was conflict, chaos, and political upheaval throughout the Punjab. In 1525, Babbar the Chaghatai Turk, the Mongol descendent of Genghis Khan and Tamerlane, invaded the Punjab. He plundered Lahore and defeated the Sultan's army with great slaughter. As he advanced on Delhi, Sultan Ibrahim Lodhi offered him battle at Panipat. With his seasoned soldiers and strong artillery, Babbar defeated and killed Ibrahim Lodhi and went on to lay the foundation of the Mughal Empire. At the time the Mughals established their rule, the people of the Punjab were sharply divided into separate religious societies. One, the Muslim, was an occupational army constantly sustained by fresh influx of Turkic and Afghan tribes, which practiced fanaticism and intolerance. The other, the Hindu, was rooted in idol worship, meaningless rituals and the degradation of caste.

Sikhs

Meantime a remarkable people had emerged in the Punjab. They believed in the faith of Guru Nanak (Guru means a spiritual teacher and a guide). The chief doctrines preached by Guru Nanak were 'The Unity of God, Brotherhood of Man, Rejection of Caste and the futility of Idol Worship'. His followers became known as Sikhs.

The Sikhs

Guru Nanak,

Guru Nanak (1469-1539) was one of the greatest religious innovators of all time and the founder of the Sikh religion. Nanak's religious ideas drew on both Hindu and Islamic thought, but are far more than just a synthesis. Nanak was an original spiritual thinker and expressed his thoughts in extraordinary poetry that forms the basis of Sikh scripture. He was born about 40 miles from Lahore (now in Pakistan) in 1469, into a Hindu family. Nanak soon showed an advanced interest in religion and studied Islam and Hinduism extensively. He learnt the alphabet from a Hindu Pandit, and Persian and Arabic from a Muslim mullah. As a child he demonstrated great ability as a poet and philosopher. Nanak continued to demonstrate a radical spiritual streak, arguing with local holy men and sages, both Hindu and Muslim that external things like pilgrimages, penances, and poverty were of far less spiritual importance than internal changes to the individual's soul. He was inspired by a powerful spiritual experience that gave him a vision of the true nature of God, and confirmed his idea that the way to spiritual growth was through meditation and through living in a way that reflected the presence of the divine within each human being. He worked for a while as an accountant but while still quite young decided to devote himself to spiritual matters. In 1496, Nanak set out on a set of spiritual journeys through India, Tibet and Arabia that lasted nearly 30 years. He studied and debated with the learned men he met along the way and as his ideas took shape he began to teach a new route to spiritual fulfilment and the good life. The last part of his life was spent at Kartarpur in the Punjab, where he was joined by many disciples attracted by his teachings. In 1499 he announced his mission by declaring: 'There is no Hindu, there is no Mussalman.' Nanak was a strict, uncompromising monotheist. He defined God, calling Him the Sat Kartar, meaning the 'True Creator'; Truth was Godhood. The most famous teachings attributed to Guru Nanak are that there is only one God, and that all human beings can have direct access to God with no need of rituals or priests. His most radical social teachings denounced the caste system and taught that everyone is equal, regardless of caste or gender. The succeeding gurus nurtured Nanak's mission with great organising ability, energy and devotion. They moulded the Sikhs into a distinct community with their own language, literature, religious beliefs and institutions, culminating in the Order of the Khalsa.

The Sikhs

Guru Hargobind

Guru Hargobind, sixth Sikh Guru, developed a strong army and gave the Sikh religion its military character, in accord with the instructions of his father, Guru Arjan (1563–1606). Guru Arjan was the first Sikh martyr, who had been executed on the order of the Mughal Emperor Jahangir, on his refusal to convert to the Muslim religion. Up to the time of Hargobind, the Sikh religion had been passive. At his succession ceremony, Hargobind is believed to have defiantly borne two swords, symbolizing his twin authority as temporal (Miri) and spiritual (Piri) head of the community. He also devoted much time to military training and the martial arts, becoming an expert swordsman, wrestler and rider. Despite the Mughal opposition, Hargobind built up his army and fortified his cities. In 1609 he built at Amritsar the Akal Takht ("Throne of God"), a temple and assembly hall combined, where both spiritual and temporal matters pertaining to the Sikh nation could be resolved. He built a fort near Amritsar and named it Lohgarh. Deftly he instilled the will to fight and established high morale in his followers. The Mughal emperor Jahangir viewed the build-up of Sikh power as a threat and had Guru Hargobind jailed in the fortress of Gwalior. During the years Guru Hargobind remained a prisoner, the Sikh devotion to him only intensified. Finally, the emperor, apparently seeking the favour of the Sikhs as possible allies against the Indian states still defying Mughal rule, set the Guru free. Hargobind followed his former militant course, recognizing that a clash with Mughal power was coming. After Jahangir's death (1627) the new Mughal emperor, Shah Jahan, persecuted the Sikh community in earnest. The Sikhs under Hargobind defeated Shah Jahan's armies four times, crushing the myth of Mughal invincibility.* To the Sikh ideals of his predecessor, Guru Hargobind added another: the right and duty of the Sikhs to defend their faith by the sword if necessary. Shortly before his death, Guru Hargobind appointed his grandson, Har Rai, his successor. Guru Nanak had stressed the need for practicing religious beliefs based on truthful living and a respect for human rights rather than on meaningless rites. Guru Hargobind's emphasis on martial arts to resist tyranny and oppression by despot rulers nearly completed the identity of Sikhs as a 'people.'

- After this says Cunningham: "the Sikhs were in little danger of relapsing into the limited merit or utility of monks and mendicants" (J.D. Cunningham)

The Sikhs

Guru Gobind Singh

At the martyrdom of Tegh Bahadur, his son Gobind succeeded to the Guruship. To save the faith and the infant community from annihilation, he decided to transform the Sikhs into a fierce military brotherhood. In 1699, he created the Order of the Khalsa (the pure). He summoned the Sikhs to the city of Anandpur and baptised them into the fold of the Khalsa. The Guru administered them *Khande-da–Amrit* (Baptism of the Sword). This symbolised their rebirth in the Order of the Khalsa. Henceforth their profession was to wield the sword in the cause of their faith. They formed the nucleus of a fighting fraternity and were given new names with the surname Singh – Lion. They were to observe five Ks, Kesh (unshorn hair), to carry a Kangha (a comb in the hair), to wear Kacha (military pants), to wear a Kara (a steel bracelet) and always carry a Kirpan (a Sabre). The orchard of the Sikh faith needed the thorny hedge of armed men for its protection. The Singhs of the Khalsa were the orchard and the hedge rolled into one, ever willing to wield the sword in righteous cause. When Guru Gobind Singh created the Order of the Khalsa, he laid the foundations of the Sikh military might by setting up a tradition of reckless valour, which became the distinguishing feature of Sikh soldiery. They came to believe in the triumph of their cause as an article of faith, and like their Guru asked for no nobler end than a death on the battlefield.

> O Lord, with clasped hands this boon I crave,
> Let me never shun the righteous task,
> Let me be fearless when I go battle,
> Give me faith that victory will be mine,
> Give me power to sing Thy praise,
> And when time comes to end my life,
> Let me fall in mighty strife.

Guru Gobind Singh fought many desperate unequal battles against the Mughals. Two of his sons died in the fighting and Nawab Wazir Khan, the Mughal Governor of Sirhind, executed the two younger ones. Guru Gobind Singh himself was stabbed to death by one of his own Muslim retainers.

What Guru Gobind Singh had succeeded in doing was to ". . . teach the sparrow to hunt the hawk and one man to have the courage to fight a legion."

(Khushwant Singh)

The Sikhs

By Dr. Harinder Kaur Sekhon

With the creation of Khalsa on the Baisakhi day (first day of the second solar month of Baisakhi, considered auspicious to begin harvesting of the crop) of 1699 by Guru Gobind Singh, Sikhism underwent a major transformation. The Khalsa was created to instil a fresh spirit of courage and confidence among the Guru's followers. Here women were an integral part of the celebrations. They were baptised and initiated into the Khalsa fold without discrimination. The Amrit (holy water) for baptism was prepared by Mata Sahib Kaur, wife of Guru Gobind Singh. This was a high and rare honour extended to her since in other religious beliefs the association of women in ecclesiastical affairs was viewed with extreme disdain. At the time of taking Amrit a man was given the name "Singh" (lion) and women added "Kaur" (princess) to their names. The suffix "Kaur" is of immense significance as a woman was recognised as an individual who need not take her husband's name after marriage. She could use the word "Kaur" after her name from birth to death. The word 'Kaur" is derived from the word "Kanwar" - the son of a king. This explanation of Bhai Kahan Singh in the Mahankosh is symbolically significant. Apart from equality in socio-religious affairs, Sikh women could participate in political matters as well, including leading an army into battle. This gave women in Sikhism a sense of enormous self-confidence. Guru Gobind Singh's widow Mata Sundari played a key role in Sikh history for forty momentous years. She issued Hukamnamas (decrees) to the Khalsa giving directions at a critical juncture and successfully guided the destiny of the Sikh against both the Afghan invaders and various claimants to the "Guruship". Maharaja Ranjit Singh owed much of his success to the astute statesmanship and diplomacy of his mother-in-law, Rani Sada Kaur. She has been called "the ladder by which Ranjit Singh climbed to greatness in his early years". She accompanied him on his triumphant capture of Lahore in 1799 and urged Ranjit Singh to proclaim himself the Maharaja of Punjab. The house of Patiala too produced some exceptional ladies during the eighteenth Century. The most celebrated of them was Rani Sahib Kaur who personally led her forces into battle and defeated the Maratha Holkar in 1793.

An important aspect of the rights conferred on women in the Sikh faith was that they did not have to fight for their rightful place in Sikh society: they were given their due voluntarily because of the enlightened ideals of the Gurus.

THE SARDARS

Banda Singh Bahadur

Banda Singh Bahadur was an eighteenth century Sikh warrior who for the first time seized territory for the Khalsa and paved the way for the ultimate conquest of the Punjab by them. He learned yoga from Yogi Aughar Nath at Nasik, and after his death; he left Nasik and established a monastery of his own at Nanded. Here he had an encounter with Guru Gobind Singh who happened to visit his hermitage on 3RD September 1708. At the end of the visit, he fell at Guru Gobind Singh's feet, pronouncing himself to be his Banda or slave. Guru Gobind Singh escorted him to his own camp, and administered to him the vows of the Khalsa and gave him the name of Banda Singh. Guru Gobind Singh blessed him and bestowed upon him a drum, a banner and five arrows as emblems of Guru's authority. He was ordered to challenge the Imperial authority in the Punjab. Accompanied by five Sikhs, Binod Singh, Kahan Singh, Baj Singh, Daya Singh and Ram Singh, he set out towards the Punjab, determined to chastise the tyrannical Mughal faujdar of Sirhind. As he reached the Punjab, Sikhs began to rally round his standard. On 26TH November 1709, Banda Singh attacked Samana, the native town of Jalal ud Din, the executioner of Guru Tegh Bahadur, and the two executioners who had volunteered to behead Guru Gobind Singh's two young sons, at Sirhind. After the sack of Samana, Banda Singh occupied Ghuram, Thaska, Shahabad and Mustafa Bad. The town of Kapuri, whose faujdar, Qadam ud Din, was notorious for his debaucheries and persecution of Hindus and Sikhs, was razed to the ground. Next came the turn of Sadhaura, whose chief, Usman Khan, had not only oppressed the Hindus but had also tortured to death the Muslim saint, Sayyid Budhu Shah, for having helped Guru Gobind Singh in the battle of Bhangani. Banda Singh then took a long circuitous route awaiting Sikhs from the Doaba and Majha areas to join his force before he attacked Sirhind, where two of Guru Gobind Singh's sons had met with a cruel fate at the hands of Wazir Khan, the Mughal satrap. Wazir Khan was killed in the battle of Chappar Chiri on 12TH May 1710, and on 14TH May the city of Sirhind was captured and given over to plunder. Baj Singh, one of Banda Singh's companions, was appointed governor of Sirhind. Banda Singh was now the virtual master of territories between the Yamuna and the Satluj. He made the old Fort of Mukhlis Garh, in the safety of the Himalayas, his headquarters, renaming it Lohgarh. Soon Banda Singh assumed the style of royalty and introduced a new calendar dating from his capture of Sirhind.

The Sardars

Banda Singh Bahadur (Cont.)

He had new coins struck in the name of Guru Nanak and Guru Gobind Singh. The inscription on his seal contained the word deg (the kettle in Guru Ka Langar signifying charity) and Tegh (the sword of the Khalsa signifying victory). Banda Singh's rule, though short lived, had a far-reaching impact on the history of the Punjab. Banda Singh abolished the Zamindari system and made the tillers masters of the land by conferring upon them proprietary rights. He was liberal in his treatment of Hindus and Muslims, many of whom joined the Sikh faith and took up arms under him. In the summer of 1710, Banda Singh crossed the Yamuna and seized Saharanpur but he had to return to the Punjab, without making any further conquest in the Gangetic valley. In the Punjab, he took Batala and Kalanaur, marched towards Lahore, while a contingent proceeded to occupy the city and parganah of Pathankot. Seized with terror, Sayyid Aslam, the governor of Lahore, shut himself up in the Fort. Cries of jihad or religious war against the Sikhs proved of little avail and Banda Singh inflicted a crushing defeat upon the gathered host at the village of Bharoval. Except for the city of Lahore, the whole of Majha and Riarki had fallen into his hands. On 3RD October 1710, he occupied Rahon in the Jalandhar Doab. Banda Singh's increasing influence roused the ire of the Mughal emperor Bahadur Shah, who came northwards from the Deccan, and commanded the governors of Delhi and Oudh and other Mughal officers to punish the Sikhs. The order he issued on 10TH December 1710 was a general warrant for the faujdars to kill the worshippers of Nanak, i.e. Sikhs, wherever found. Even in the face of this edict for wholesale destruction of the Sikhs, Banda Singh maintained towards the Muslims generally an attitude of tolerance. A report submitted to Emperor Bahadur Shah stated that as many as five thousand Muslims of the neighbourhood of Kalanaur and Batala had joined Banda Singh and that they were allowed the fullest liberty to shout their religious call, azan, and recite khutba and namaz, in the army of the Sikhs and that they were properly looked after and fed. In 1710, a massive imperial force drove the Sikhs from Sirhind and other places to take shelter in the Fort of Lohgarh. Here Banda Singh was closely invested by sixty thousand cavalry and infantry. For want of provisions, the Sikhs were reduced to rigorous straits. On the night of 10TH December 1710, Banda Singh made a desperate bid to escape and hacked his way out of the imperial cordon.

The Sardars

Banda Singh Bahadur (Cont.)

Banda Singh was far from vanquished and, within a fortnight of his escape from Lohgarh, he began to send out commands exhorting the people to carry on the fight. He ransacked the state of Bilaspur. Mandi, Kulu, and Chamba submitted to his authority of their own accord. In June 1711, as he descended towards the plains he was engaged in an action at Bahrampur near Jammu, in which the Mughal troops were worsted. Banda Singh was, however, forced in the end to retreat into the hills. After the death, on 28TH February 1712, of Emperor Bahadur Shah, the war of succession for the imperial throne and the disturbed state of affairs in Delhi brought Banda Singh some respite, but Farrukhsiyar who ascended the throne of Delhi in 1713 accelerated the campaign against the Sikhs. They were hounded out of the plains where Banda Singh had reoccupied Sadhaura and Lohgarh. Their main column, led by Banda Singh, was subjected to a most stringent siege at the village of Gurdas Nangal, about six kilometers from Gurdaspur. The supplies having run out, the Sikhs suffered great hardship and lived on animal flesh which they had to eat raw owing to lack of firewood.

For eight long months, the garrison resisted the siege under gruesome conditions. The royal armies at last broke through and captured Banda Singh and his famished companions on 7TH December 1715. They were at first taken to and paraded in the streets of Lahore and then sent to Delhi where they arrived on 27TH February 1716. The cavalcade to the imperial capital was a grisly sight. Besides 740 prisoners in heavy chains, it comprised seven hundred cartloads of the heads of the Sikhs with another 2,000 stuck upon pikes. By the emperor's order, Banda Singh and some two dozen leading Sikhs were imprisoned in the Fort, while the remaining 694 were made over to the Kotwal, Sarbrah Khan, to be executed at the Kotwali Chabutra at the rate of a hundred a day. Then Banda Singh Bahadur and his remaining companions were taken to the tomb of Khwaja Qutb ud Din Bakhdyar Kaki, near the Qutb Minar. There he was offered the choice between Islam and death. Upon his refusal to renounce his faith, his four year old son, Ajai Singh, was hacked to pieces before his eyes. He himself was subjected to the harshest torments. His eyes were pulled out and hands and feet chopped off. His flesh was torn with red-hot pincers and finally his body was cut up limb by limb. This occurred on 9TH June 1716.

The Sardars

Misldari System

Misldari system was a political relationship as well as of land tenure, which came into being with the rise of Sikh power in the eighteenth century Punjab. The Sikh warriors who, since the execution of Banda Singh Bahadur in 1716, had lived precariously as small guerilla bands, had by the middle of the century grouped themselves into eleven main divisions and started acquiring territory as **Misls (Misl generally refers to the sovereign states of the Sikh Confederacy).** Under the Misldari system, the chief or Sardar of each Misl could allot land to a member of his own Misl, or even to an outsider, not as a grant Jagir, but as a share of the territory in the conquest of which the latter was an equal partner. Sometimes the subordinate Misldars or commanders occupied territory on their own, but continued to accept the Sardar of the Misl as their chief. The Misldars were independent in the management of their respective territories. They could pass it to a member of the parent Misl, but not to an outsider. Their relationship with the Sardar of the parent Misl remained that of subordinates, but only for the purpose of the offence and defence against outsiders. Again, occupation of territory only entitled them to a share in the produce. The Misldars, like the jagirdars, could not interfere with the traditional proprietary or occupancy rights of the tillers of the land. Misldari was a transient phenomenon. With the emergence of the Sikh kingdom under Maharaja Ranjit Singh in the early decades of the nineteenth century absorbing most of the Misls, the system became redundant. Many of the Misldars, however, took service under Maharaja Ranjit Singh, who allowed them to keep the whole or part of their past holdings Jagirs but not as permanent or independent freeholds.

Sardar

Sardar, meaning holder of headship, is honorific, signifying an officer of rank, a general or chief of a tribe or organization. Sikhs adopted Sardar for the leaders of their Jathas or bands fighting against Afghan invaders under Ahmad Shah Durrani. With the expansion of the fighting force of the Sikhs under the Misls the number of Sikh Sardars multiplied. During the reign of Maharaja Ranjit Singh and his successors, Sardar came to be used as an appellation for all Sikhs in general having Singh as their common surname, although officially Sardar was a coveted title conferred on generals or civil officers of rank.

The Sardars

Nawab Kapur Singh,

Nawab Kapur Singh was an eighteenth century Sikh hero who was founder of the Dal Khalsa (Sikh Army). He was born in 1697 in a peasant family of Virk in the village of Kaloke, now in Sheikhupura district of Pakistan. His father's name was Dalip Singh. When Kapur Singh was of the age to bear arms, he seized the village of Faizullahpur, near Amritsar, renamed it Singhpura and started living there. For this reason he is also known to history as Kapur Singh Faizullpuria and the principality he founded as Faizullpuria or Singhpuria Misl or Chieftaincy. Kapur Singh was eleven years old at the time of Guru Gobind Singh's death and nineteen when Banda Singh Bahadur and his companions were tortured to death in Delhi. He had thus passed his early life in an atmosphere charged with the fervour of faith and sacrifice. Side by side with religious discipline, Kapur Singh practised manly exercises like horse riding and swordsmanship. In 1721, he received the vows of Khalsa initiation at the hands of Bhai Mani Singh, a pious and learned Sikh of that time, at a large gathering of Sikhs held at Amritsar on the occasion of the Diwali festival. Kapur Singh's physical prowess and spirit of boldness proved valuable assets in those days of high adventure, and he soon gained a position of eminence among his people, who were then engaged in a desperate struggle for survival. When Zakariya Khan became the governor of Lahore in 1726, he adopted rigorous measures against the Sikhs. Kapur Singh led a band of warriors, who, with a view to paralyzing the administration and obtaining food for their companions, were forced to seek shelter in remote hills and forests. From these retreats they attacked government treasuries and caravans while moving from one place to another. Such was the effect of these depredations that the Delhi government, in 1733, at the instance of Zakariya Khan, decided to lift the quarantine forced upon the Sikhs and made an offer of a grant to them. Subeg Singh, a Sikh resident of Jambar, near Lahore, who was for a time a police inspector of the city under Mughal authority, was entrusted with the task of negotiating peace with the Khalsa. He reached Amritsar and offered the Sikhs, assembled there on the occasion of the Baisakhi festival, on behalf of the government the title of Nawab and a jagir consisting of Parganahs of Dlpalpur, Kariganval and Jhabal. After the Sikhs accepted the offer, Kapur Singh, humbly swinging a handfan over the assembly, was unanimously chosen to be honoured with the title of Nawab.

The Sardars

Nawab Kapur Singh (Cont.)

During the respite thus secured, Kapur Singh gave attention to reorganizing the Sikh force which he divided into two sections, the Buddha Dal, army of the elderly, and the Taruna Dal, army of the young. The former, under the charge of Nawab Kapur Singh, was entrusted with the task of looking after the holy places, preaching the Guru's word and administering the vows of the Khalsa to Sikhs, while the latter was the more active division whose function was to fight in times of emergency. As Taruna Dal grew in strength, Nawab Kapur Singh further split it into five parts, each with a separate centre and its own banner and drums. The detente with the Mughals did not last long and before the harvest season of 1735, Zakariya Khan sent a force and occupied the jagir. The Buddha Dal being driven away towards the Malva, Nawab Kapur Singh continued his missionary and military activities in the Cis-Satluj parts. He conquered the territory of Sunam and made it over to Ala Singh, the Phulkari chief, who had received rites of initiation from him. Nawab Kapur Singh led the Buddha Dal right up to the vicinity of Delhi, vanquishing, on the way, the chieftains of Jhajjar, Dadri, Dojana and Pataudi. Overrunning Faridabad, Balabhgarh and Gurgaori in the parganah of Delhi, the Dal returned to the village of Thikrivala in the Malva. When in 1739, Nadir Shah was returning to Persia after a hearty plunder of Delhi and the Punjab, Nawab Kapur Singh swooped down upon his rearguard, near Akhnur on the river Chenab, and rescued a number of innocent Hindu girls who were being abducted, and restored them to their parents. On the occasion of Baisakhi (29TH March) of 1748, when Sikhs were able to assemble at Amritsar after a long interval, a new force known as the Dal Khalsa was constituted at the instance of Nawab Kapur Singh. Different Jathas of the Sikhs, whose number had already touched sixty five, were leagued together into eleven main associations, each with a separate banner, a stable, a kitchen and a leader but acting under one supreme commander binding each group with the other group and also with the whole Panth. Kapur Singh surrendered his authority to Jassa Singh Ahluwalia who was, at his suggestion, chosen the supreme commander of the Dal Khalsa. Nawab Kapur Singh died on 7TH October 1753 and was cremated in the premises of Gurdwara Baba Atal at Amritsar.

The Sardars

Ahluwalia, Jassa Singh, Sardar

Jassa Singh Ahluwalia was founder of the Ahluwalia Misl, remnants of which lasted until recent years in the form of the princely state of Kapurthala. He was born the son of Badar Singh at the village of Ahlu, near Lahore, on 3RD May 1718. Since his father had died when he was barely five years of age, he was taken by his mother to Delhi where he grew up under the care of Mata Sundari, widow of Guru Gobind Singh. On the eve of his return to the Punjab in 1729, Mata Sundari bestowed upon him a sword, a mace, a shield, a bow and a quiver full of arrows, a dress and a silver staff predicting that he would rise to eminence. On his arrival in the Punjab, Jassa Singh joined, at Kartarpur, the Jatha or military band of (Nawab) Kapur Singh, who was deeply impressed by the young man's courage and ambition. When during his first invasion of the Punjab in January 1748, Ahmad Shah Durrani moved southwards from Lahore, the Sikh Sardars under Nawab Kapur Singh and Jassa Singh Ahluwalia caused him much harassment at Nur di Sarai and Vaoroval. Jassa Singh was one of the leading Sardars who two months later defeated a strong Mughal force commanded by Salabal Khan in an action at Amritsar. On the Baisakhi of 1748, a general assembly of Sikhs was convened at Amritsar which resolved to consolidate the sixty-five roving Sikh Jathas into one command called Dal Khalsa under Jassa Singh. Its eleven subdivisions were called Misls; the twelfth Misl Phulkari traced a separate origin. Persecution by the ruling Mughal authority meanwhile became more virulent. Under Mir Mannu, Subahdar of Lahore from 1748 to 1753, numerous punitive detachments roamed the country to hunt out the Sikhs. After the death on 7TH October 1753 of Nawab Kapur Singh, Jassa Singh started seizing villages and towns in .the Punjab thrown into confusion with the passing away of Mir Mannu in November 1753 and established the system of Rakhi (protection) or tax received for the security provided. The Dal Khalsa, under Jassa Singh, routed, in April 1754 an Afghan force from Lahore which had laid siege to Amritsar. In 1757, Jassa Singh struck and defeated the rearguard of Taimur Shah whom his father, Ahmad Shah, had appointed governor of Lahore and who was marching towards the city after sacking Kanarpur. In response to the request of Adina Beg, who, after his dismissal from the governorship of Lahore, was attacked by the Durranis from Lahore under Murad Khan and Buland Khan, Jassa Singh came to his rescue and defeated the Durranis at Mahalpur, in the Jalandhar Doab.

The Sardars

Ahluwalia, Jassa Singh, Sardar (Cont.)

The Dal Khalsa, led by Jassa Singh and other Sardars, took a decisive part in reinstalling, in April 1758, Adina Beg in Lahore. In October 1759, Ahmad Shah Durrani crossed the Indus and invaded northern India for the fifth time. For 15 months he was occupied subjugating the Marathas and the Jats of Bharalpur. On 17TH January 1761, he finally defeated the Marathas at Panipat. During this period the Dal Khalsa established its authority in the Malva and Majha regions, exacted Rakhi and levied nazranas (tribute) on Mughal as well as on Afghan satraps. The Sikhs, under the leadership of Jassa Singh, made a surprise attack on the Shah's force near Amritsar in March 1761 and rescued 2,200 women captives whom the invader was carrying in his train as slaves. A combined force of Sukkarchakkia, Kanhaiya and Bhangi Sardars worsted the troops of Khwaja Ubaid Khan, the Afghan governor of Lahore, near Gujrariwala in September 1761, victorious Sikhs pursuing him to the walls of Lahore. The city was besieged and occupied by the Sikhs without any resistance. Jassa Singh Ahluwalia was proclaimed King of Lahore with the title of Sultan ul Qaum (King of the Nation). A coin was issued in the name of Guru Nanak and Guru Gobind Singh commemorating the Sikh victory. On hearing the news of the fall of Lahore, Ahmad Shah Durrani hastened towards the Punjab. This was in 1762, his sixth incursion into India. The Sikhs retired to the south of the Satluj. The Shah sent orders to all his faujdars in the Punjab to join forces with Zain Khan, the governor of Sirhind. He set out from Lahore with a mammoth army estimated at 150,000 strong, and covering a distance of about 250 km in fewer than 36 hours reached Malerkotla on 5TH February. The Dal Khalsa, under the leadership of Sardars such as Jassa Singh, Shiam Singh and Charhat Singh Sukkarchakkia lay encamped at Kup, 9 km from Malerkotla. In the battle which followed about 25,000 Sikhs (figure given in the Persian source Tahmds Ndmah) were killed, Jassa Singh Ahluwalia sustaining twenty-two wounds on his body. The battle of Kup is still remembered in Sikh history as Vadda Ghallughara or the Major Holocaust. Returning to Lahore, Ahmad Shah marched to Amritsar and had the Holy Harimandar blown up with gunpowder. Under the shadow of the carnage at Kup and the disaster at Amritsar, Jassa Singh, with the remnants of the Dal Khalsa, was waiting for his opportunity. While the Shah was still in Lahore, he fell upon Sirhind on 17TH May 1762, and exacted nazranas from Zain Khan, the faujdar.

The Sardars

Ahluwalia, Jassa Singh, Sardar (Cont.)

In April 1763, Jassa Singh marched into the Jalandhar Doab and, after defeating the faujdar, Sadat Khan, occupied Kathgarh and Garhsharikar. The Bhangis and the Sukkarchakkias joined Jassa Singh, and their combined force defeated the Afghan commander, Jalian Khan, near Sialkot, in November 1763. The Dal Khalsa was again active and the Kanhaiya, Ramgarhia, Bhangi and Sukkarchakkia forces assembled under the command of Jassa Singh at Ropar. They occupied Kurali and Morinda, and attacked Sirhind on 14TH January 1764. The Afghan faujdar, Zain Khan, was killed and the town laid waste. On 17TH April 1765, Sikhs reoccupied Lahore. When in 1765, the Durrani came again, he was obliged to be conciliatory and he wrote to Jassa Singh and other Sardars seeking an agreement with regard to the future political setup in the Punjab, but the Sardars spurned his overtures. Jassa Singh and the Dal Khalsa now had time to consolidate their conquests. The Indian empire of the Durranis lay in ruins. Najib ud Daulah, alarmed at the growing influence of the Sikhs, resigned, and Emperor Shah Alam opened correspondence with Jassa Singh and other Sikh chiefs with a view to securing his Trans Yamuna territories against their raids. The new Wazir of the emperor, Abdul Ahad Khan, who had led an imperial force against Raja Amar Singh of Patiala in 1779, was beaten back by Jassa Singh. He returned the entire tribute collected from the Sikhs and paid Rs 700,000 as an indemnity to the Dal Khalsa. As a leader of the Dal Khalsa, Jassa Singh had organized the Sikh militarily, overthrown Afghan power in northern India and won from the Mughal emperor the right for Sikhs to rule independently over territories they had wrested from the Afghans. The Subedar of Sirhind came under the Phulkari chiefs; Lahore, the capital of the Punjab, was given over to the Bhangis; the Jalandhar Doab was parcelled out among several of the misls; and the foundations of the Ahluwalia principality laid firmly at Kapurthala. Besides his leadership in the military and political spheres, Jassa Singh was widely revered for his deeply religious and pious character. It was considered especially meritorious to receive Amrit, the Sikh rites, at his hands. Maharaja Amar Singh of Patiala was among those who sought him to administer to them the vows of initiation. Jassa Singh died on 20TH October 1783 at the age of 65 and a Samadh or cenotaph in his honour stands in the precincts of Gurdwara Baba Atal, near the Golden Temple at Amritsar.

The Sardars

Ahluwalia, Fateh Singh, Sardar

Jassa Singh Ahluwalia died in 1783. He had no son and was succeeded by his second cousin, Bhag Singh, who died in 1801. Fateh Singh, the son of Bhag Singh, succeeded to command the Misl. He was the chosen companion of Maharaja Ranjit Singh, with whom, in 1802, he exchanged turbans in a permanent bond of brotherhood. He held military command in the Bhimbar, Rajauri and Bahawalpur expeditions. In 1806, Fateh Singh acted as the plenipotentiary of Ranjit Singh and signed the first Anglo-Sikh treaty with Lord Lake at the time when the Maratha chief, Jaswant Rao Holkar, had sought shelter in the Punjab. Fateh Singh took part in almost all the early campaigns of Ranjit Singh; Kasur (1802-03), Malwa (1806-08), Kangra (1809), Haidru (1813), Multan (1818), Kashmir (1819) and Mankera (1821). Close association with the ruler of Lahore brought Fateh Singh ample rewards. The Maharaja had bestowed upon him the districts of Dakha, Kot, Jagraon, Talwandi, Naraingarh and Raipur after his Malwa campaigns. Fateh Singh possessed extensive territories on both sides of the Satluj yielding annual revenue of 176,000 rupees in 1808; in 1836, his territories were estimated to be worth 1,600,000 rupees annually. The cordiality between the two chiefs was strained by Fateh Singh's direct communications with the British over the question of the Bhirog and Kotla chieftainships, the construction by him of a strong citadel at Isru and his constant pleas for British protection. Feeling unsafe at Lahore, Fateh Singh fled across the river in 1825 to his Cis - Satluj territory and sought British protection. Ranjit Singh promptly seized his Trans-Satluj possessions, but showed willingness to forgive him if he returned to Lahore. The rift between the Ahluwalia chief and the Maharaja of Lahore was, however, soon repaired. Fateh Singh returned to Lahore in 1827, and the Maharaja received him with honour restoring to him all his possessions. Later in his life, Fateh Singh lived at Kapurthala where he died in October 1836. On his death in 1837, Maharajah Ranjit Singh annexed his Trans-Satluj territory except the Kapurthala state, to the expanding Sikh Kingdom.

The Sardars

Ahluwalia, Nihal Singh, Sardar

Nihal Singh Ahluwalia, son of Fateh Singh Ahluwalia, succeeded to the Ahluwalia chieftaincy on the death in 1936 of his father. In his youth he was a favourite of Maharajah Ranjit Singh and was recipient of the towns of Nur Mahal and Kalal Majra and other occasional bounties. In the first Anglo-Sikh war, his sympathies lay with the Khalsa Durbar. In spite of treaty obligations with the British, he afforded them little assistance. On the contrary, the Ahluwalia troops, cavalry, infantry, and artillery, fought on the side of the Sikhs both at Badhowal and Aliwal. He was penalised by the British by the confiscation of his territories south of the River Satluj. The Jalandhar Doab estates were maintained and evolved into the Sikh Princely state of Kapurthala. Nihal Singh died on 13TH September 1852. The descendants of Fateh Singh ruled Kapurthala state for more than a century until it merged with the Patiala and East Punjab Union (PEPSU) in 1948 after the British withdrew from India.

Ali Singh, Sardar

Sardar Ali Singh, a native of the village of Salaudi, near Sirhind, was in the service of Wazir Khan, the Mughal faujdar of Sirhind. According to Ratan Singh Bhangu, Prachin Panth Prakash, Wazir Khan, on learning of Banda Singh's advance from the South towards the Punjab under the orders of Guru Gobind Singh, called Ali Singh to his presence and taunted him with the remark that another Guru of theirs had appeared and that he should join him and bring him to Sirhind to be despatched like the previous Guru's sons. Ali Singh took his comment as an insult and tried to leave the Khan's service. On learning this, Wazir Khan put him into prison from where he escaped and joined Banda Singh's ranks. Ali Singh took part in battles fought at Samana and Sadhaura. In the battle of Sirhind fought on 12TH May 1710 at the nearby village of Chappar Chiri, he was one of the commanders of the Malva Sikhs. After the sack of Sirhind, he was appointed deputy governor of the town under Baj Singh. Ali Singh was captured in Lohgarh in 1715, while defending the fortress against the Mughal onslaught and was put to death in Delhi in June 1716 with Banda Singh Bahadur and his men seized in Gurdas Nangal.

The Sardars

Baghel Singh, Sardar

Baghel Singh, who succeeded in 1765 Karora Singh as leader of the Karor Singhia misi or chiefship, is celebrated in Sikh history as the vanquisher of Mughal Delhi. A Dhaliwal Jatt, Baghel Singh arose from the village of Jhabal, in Amritsar district, to become a formidable force in the Cis-Satluj region. According to Syed Muhammad Latif, he had under him 12,000 fighting men. As well as being a soldier, he was adept in political negotiation and was able to win over many an adversary to his side. The Mughals, the Ruhilas, the Marathas and the English sought his friendship. In the wake of the decay of Mughal authority in the Punjab, owing to Ahmad Shah Durranis successive invasions during the latter half of the eighteenth century, the Sikhs began extending their influence. Baghel Singh took possession of portions of the Jalandhar Doab and established himself at Hariana, near Hoshiarpur. Soon after the Sikh conquest of Sirhind in January 1764, he extended his arms towards Karnal, occupying a number of villages including Chhalaudi, which he later made his headquarters. In February 1764, Sikhs in a body of 40,000 under the command of Baghel Singh and other leading Sardars crossed the Yamuna and captured Saharanpur. In April 1775, Baghel Singh with two other Sardars, Rai Singh Bhangi and Tara Singh Ghaiba, crossed the Yamuna to occupy that country, then ruled by Zabita Khan, son and successor of Najib ud-Daulah. Zabita Khan in desperation offered Baghel Singh large sums of money and proposed an alliance jointly to plunder the crown lands. The combined forces of Sikhs and Ruhilas looted villages around the present site of New Delhi. In March 1776, they defeated the imperial forces near Muzaffar Nagar. The whole of the Yamuna Gangetic Doab was now at their mercy. When in the autumn of 1779, a large Mughal army under the command of Prince Farkhanda Bakht and Wazir Abdul Ahad Khan led an expedition against the Cis-Satluj Sikhs, Baghel Singh along with Rai Singh of Buna and Bhanga Singh of Thanesar, joined hands with the imperial forces at Karnal and encircled Patiala. Raja Amar Singh visited Baghel Singh in his camp at the village of Lahal and made peace with him and had his son. Sahib Singh, receive the rites of Khalsa initiation at his hands. Meanwhile, Amar Singh had invited Trans Satluj Sikhs for help. Baghel Singh out-witted his imperial allies who sought safety in flight, suffering heavy losses.

The Sardars

Baghel Singh, Sardar (Cont.)

When in April 1781, Mirza Shafi, a close relative of the Mughal prime minister, captured the Sikh military post at Indri, 10 km south of Ladva, Baghel Singh retaliated by attacking Khalil Beg Khan of Shahabad, who surrendered with 300 horse, 800 foot and 2 pieces of cannon. When on 11TH March 1783, Sikhs entered the Red Fort in Delhi and occupied the Diwani-Am, the Mughal emperor, Shah Alam II made a settlement with them, agreeing to allow Baghel Singh to raise Gurdwaras (Temples) on Sikh historical sites in the city and realize six annas in a rupee (37.5%) of all the octroi duties in the capital. Baghel Singh stayed in Sabzi Mandi, with 4000 troops and took charge of the police station in Chandni Chowk. He located seven sites connected with the lives of the Gurus and had shrines raised thereon within the space of eight months, from April to November 1783. Gurdwara Sis Gary marked the spot in the main Mughal Street of Chandni Chowk where Guru Tegh Bahadur had been executed under the fiat of the emperor and Gurdwara Rikabganj, near modern-day Parliament House, where the body was cremated. Bangla Sahib and Bala Sahib commemorated the Eighth Guru, Guru Har Krishan. Three other Gurdwaras built were at Majnu ka Tilla, Moti Bagh and Telivara. Baghel Singh died probably in 1802, at Hariana, in present day Hoshiarpur district. A Samadh enshrining the memory of one of the more picturesque Misl Sardars still stands in the town.

Baj Singh, Sardar

Baj Singh, a Bal Jatt, was a native of Mirpur Patti, a village in Amritsar district of the Punjab. A devoted Sikh, Baj Singh had received the rites of initiation at the hands of Guru Gobind Singh himself. He accompanied the Guru to the Deccan in 1708 and was one of the five Sikhs sent by him to the Punjab with Banda Singh Bahadur. He took part in all of Banda Singh's major campaigns. For his fearlessness in battle, he came to be known as Baj Bahadur (Bahadur, lit. Brave). In the battle of Sirhind fought at Chappar Chiri in May 1710, Baj Singh was in command of the right wing of Banda Singh`s army. He faced Nawab Wazir Khan in the battle, striking his horse down with a lance. As the battle was won, Baj Singh was named administrator of the town. Baj Singh was captured at Gurdas Nangal in December 1715 and taken to Delhi, where he was executed in June 1716 along with Banda Singh and his other companions.

The Sardars

Bedi, Ram Singh, Sardar

Ram Singh Bedi, a Nihang warrior, was the son of Bhai Faqir Chand, of the village of Kotia in Sialkot district, now in Pakistan. The family claimed direct descent from Guru Nanak. Ram Singh took Amrit or vows by the double edged sword, thus entering the fold of the Khalsa. Tall and hefty of build and trained in the martial arts as well as in sacred learning, and always carrying on his person a quintet of weapons, he became a legendary hero in the region. At the end of November 1796, Shah Zaman, grandson of Ahmad Shah Durrani, invaded India at the head of a host of 30,000 men, his third incursion into the country. The Sikh chiefs, following their time tested strategy of avoiding pitched battles against numerically superior forces, retired towards Amritsar, allowing the Shah to advance unopposed to Lahore, which he entered on 3RD January 1797. Soon after, however, the news of the rebellion in Herat by his brother, Prince Mahmud, compelled him to go back, leaving a force of 12,000 under his general, Ahmad Khan Barakzai, better known as Shahanchi Khan, to keep the Punjab under occupation. The Sikh Sardars resorted to their usual tactics and kept preying upon the retreating Afghan columns right into the territory across the River Jehlum. Ram Singh, at the head of a small band of irregulars, took part in these operations. Shahanchi Khan, planning to surprise the returning Sikhs, advanced from Lahore, intercepted some of the troops under the young Sukkarchakkia chief, Ranjit Singh, at Ramnagar and besieged them. The Sikhs fighting back desperately forced Shahanchi Khan to raise the siege and retire towards Gujrat. Ram Singh and his band of warriors overtook his column on the way. In the skirmish that ensued, Ram Singh Bedi fell fighting near the village of Paropi, where a memorial was later raised in his honour. Shahanchi Khan was also killed soon after in the main battle that took place a few kilometres east of Gujrat.

Bhangi Chajja Singh, **Sardar**

The founder of the Bhangi Jatha (band), Chajja Singh, a Jat, was a native of Panjvar village, about eighteen miles from Amritsar. He received Sikh baptism of Amrit at the hands of Guru Gobind Singh, and fought in many battles under him. The Bhangi Jatha is said to have its name from its founder's addiction to bhang - an intoxicating preparation of hemp. After Chajja Singh's death, Bhuma Singh became his successor.

The Sardars

Bhanga Singh, *Sardar*

Bhanga Singh, a prominent Sardar of the Karorsinghia Misl, seized in January 1764 after the fall of Sirhind, the parganah of Pehova along the bed of the River Saraswati, 22 km west of Thanesar. Later he captured Thanesar leaving Pehova in the possession of his brother, Bhag Singh. Bhanga Singh and Bhag Singh commanded a force of 750 horse and 250 foot. In January 1786, Bhanga Singh, along with other Sikh chiefs, entered the Ganga Doab at the head of 5,000 horse and ravaged Meerut, Hapur and Garh Mukteshvar. In April 1789, Mahadji Scindia, regent of the Mughal empire, confirmed Bhanga Singh's right to Rakhi (protection) some of the areas under his influence. In January 1791, Bhanga Singh advanced up to Anupshahar, a British cantonment on the Gariga under the charge of Lieutenant Colonel Robert Stuart. He captured the Colonel and brought him to Thanesar, where he was confined for nine months in the fort before his release in October 1791 at the intercession of Lord Cornwallis, the British governor general, and some Sikh and Mughal chiefs and on payment of sixty thousand rupees as ransom. In 1795 Bhanga Singh captured Karnal and in 1799 he helped Raja Bhag Singh of Jind against the attack of the Irish adventurer, George Thomas. Bhanga Singh joined hands with Lord Lake in attacking Delhi in September 1803 and was granted some additional territory. In 1806 he accompanied Maharaja Ranjit Singh on his return journey from Thanesar to the Satluj and received from him a village in jagir in Talwandi parganah between Moga and Ferozepore. Sir Lepel Griffin has described Bhanga Singh as a man "of a most savage and untameable character," and as "the fiercest and most feared of all the Cis-Satluj chiefs." Bhanga Singh died in 1815.

Bhangi, Bhuma Singh, Sardar

Bhuma Singh commanded a body of about 300 men and was one of 25 roving bands of the Sikhs. He rose to prominence during Nadir Shah's invasion of India in 1739. Bhuma Singh lost his life fighting against the Mughals in the Chhota Ghallughara (Small Holocaust) in 1746 near Kahnuvan, in Gurdaspur. Bhuma Singh's nephew and adopted son Hari Singh succeeded him to the leadership of the Bhangi Jatha.

The Sardars

Bhangi, Hari Singh, Sardar

Sardar Hari Singh Bhangi was the founder of the Bhangi Misl. He vastly increased the power and influence of the Bhangi Misl, which began to be ranked as the strongest among its peers. He created an army of 20,000 dashing youths, captured Parijvar in the Tarn Taran parganah and established his headquarters first at Sohal and then at Gilvali, both in present day Amritsar district. Lastly, he set himself up at Amritsar where he established a residential area with a market known as Katra Hari Singh, and started constructing a fort called Qila Bhangian. Hari Singh constantly harassed the Afghan invader, Ahmad Shah Durrani, during his invasions into India. A few months after the massacre of the Sikhs at Kup, near Malerkotla, in what is known in Sikh history as the Vadda Ghallughara or the Great Holocaust (February 1762), Hari Singh attacked Khwaja Sayyid Khan at Kot, and seized a large quantity of arms. In 1763, along with the Kanhaiyas and Ramgarhias, he sacked the Afghan stronghold of Kasur. In 1764, he ravaged Bahawalpur and Multan. Crossing the River Indus, he realized tribute from Baluchi chiefs in the districts of Muzaffargarh, Dera Ghazi Khan and Dera Ismail Khan. On his way back home, he reduced Jharig, Chiniot and Sialkot. When Baba Ala Singh of Patiala submitted to the authority of Ahmad Shah Durrani in March 1765 accepting certain concessions from him, Hari Singh marched upon Patiala to chastise him. Hari Singh was killed in this campaign, allegedly owing to the conspiracy of those who had been jealous of his growing influence.

Bhangi, Jhanda Singh, Sardar

Sardar Jhanda Singh succeeded his father, Hari Singh, to the leadership of the Bhangi principality upon his death in 1765. Under Jhanda Singh, the power and prestige of the Bhangi Misl rapidly increased. In 1766, he challenged both Shuja` Khan, Afghan governor of Multan, and Mubarak Khan, the ruler of Bahawalpur. As a result of the battle that followed, the holy town of Pakpattan was declared to be the line of demarcation between the Bhangi territories and those belonging to the Muslim chiefs. In 1772, Jhanda Singh attacked Multan once again, and drove out the Nawab. Multan became a Khalsa territory and the city was parcelled out between Jhanda Singh and his commander, Lahina Singh. Jhanda Singh then went on to sack Jharig, Khushab, Mankera and Kala Bagh. He also attacked the stronghold of Chattha Jatts at Rasulnagar, later known as Ramnagar.

The Sardars

Bhangi, Jhanda Singh, Sardar (Cont.)
He seized from there the Zamzarna gun, which later became famous as Bhangian di Top, i.e. the gun of the Bhangis, and carried it to Amritsar. Jhanda Singh completed at Amritsar the fort of the Bhangis begun by his father, Hari Singh. He also laid out a garden there and erected another Katra or bazaar named after him. Towards the end of his career, Jhanda Singh was involved in constant warfare and feud with the other Sikh chiefs. He was killed in 1774 when embroiled in a battle with the Kanhaiyas and the Sukkarchakkias at Jammu.

Bhangi, Ganda Singh, Sardar
On the death of Jhanda Singh, his younger brother Ganda Singh succeeded to the headship of the Bhangi Misl. Earlier he had participated in all the activities with Jhanda Singh. He was brave and as daring as his elder brother and father. He had taken active part in the campaigns of Bahawalpur, Multan, Central Punjab and Western Punjab. At the death of Ganda Singh he was succeeded by his minor son, Desa Singh. Desa Singh was killed in action against Mahan Singh Sukarchakia in 1782.

Bhangi, Gulab Singh, Sardar
Desa was succeeded by his son Gulab Singh. Gulab Singh possessed a body of 600 cavalry. In an emergency he could raise a force of 4,000 cavalry and 2,000 infantry. He defeated the Pathan chiefs of Kasur Nizam-ud-din and Qutab-ud-din and made them his tributaries. Gulab Singh died in the jungles of Bhasin in 1800 as a result of hard drinking and debauchery.

Bhangi, Jodh Singh, Sardar
Sardar Jodh Singh possessed the Parganahs of Wazirabad, Ghaniwala, Gharathal, Jagdeo, Karial, Mitranwali, Saurian and Talwandi Musa Khan containing about 500 villages. He was a brave warrior and powerful chief. In 1797 he joined the Sikh chiefs against the Pathans of Kasur. In 1802, Jodh Singh thwarted Ranjit Singh's designs on his estates. Jodh Singh died in 1809. Maharajah Ranjit Singh immediately seized all the lands of Jodh Singh to the expanding Sikh Kingdom.

The Sardars

Bhangi, Lahna Singh, Sardar

Lahna Singh was one of the triumvirates who ruled over Lahore for more than 30 years before its occupation by Ranjit Singh. The most spectacular achievement of Lahna Singh, in collaboration with Gujjar Singh and Sobha Singh, was the capture of Lahore from the Afghan nominees, Kabuli Mall. He enjoyed complete obedience and respect of the subjects. When in December 1766, Ahmad Shah Durrani invaded Lahore and Lahna Singh retired towards Kasur, the Muslim citizens of Lahore pleaded before the Shah to confirm Lahna Singh in the governorship of the Punjab. To this end, the Durrani actually invited Lahna Singh, but the latter declined the proposal. He returned to the Shah the fruit he had sent him, saying that such delicacies were meant for royalty alone. The Sikhs, he told the messenger, lived on parched gram. Of this he gave a quantity to the messenger to be presented to Ahmad Shah on his behalf. Lahna Singh occupied Lahore as soon as the Shah left for Afghanistan. Lahna Singh retained a permanent body of 3,000 cavalry and 2,000 infantry and in an emergency he could muster a force of 7,000 horse and 4,000 foot. His territory yielded about 15 lakhs of rupees annually. Lahna Singh died in September, 1797.

Bhangi, Karam Singh Dullu, Sardar

Sardar Karam Singh Dullu, an eighteenth century Bhangi Sardar, was the chief of Jhang district, along the River Chenab. He commanded about 2,000 cavalry and 1,000 infantry as a permanent force, and could on occasions muster 6,000 horse and 3,000 foot. He had eight strong forts in his territory. Karam Singh had seized this territory from Sials, a warlike Muslim tribe.

Chuhar Singh, Sardar

Sardar Chuhar Singh was a close relation of the Bhangi Sardar, Rai Singh, the conqueror of Jagadhari and Dialgarh. He received the Jarauli area as his share of the spoils after the sack of Sirhind in January 1764. He retained ten villages for himself and made over the rest to his deputies. Returning to Amritsar, he held charge of the Shahid Bunga for many years. He acquired considerable territory on either side of the River Ravi, and was considered one of the most powerful Sardars of his day. He placed his younger son, Mohar Singh, in charge of the village of Jarauli, while Karam Singh the elder, subsequently succeeded to the family estates north of the Satluj. Karam Singh died in 1808.

The Sardars

Bhangi, Gujar Singh, Sardar

Sardar Gujar Singh Bhangi, one of the triumvirates who ruled over Lahore for thirty years before its occupation by Ranjit Singh, was the son of a cultivator of very modest means, Natha Singh. Strong and well built, Gujar Singh received the vows of the Khalsa at the hands of his maternal grandfather Gurbaksh Singh Rorarivala, who presented him with a horse and recruited him a member of his band. As Gurbaksh Singh was growing old, he made Gujar Singh head of his band. Soon the band was united to the force of Hari Singh, head of the Bhangi Misl. Gujjar Singh set out on a career of conquest and plunder. In 1765, along with Lahina Singh, adopted son of Gurbaksh Singh, and Sobha Singh, an associate of Jai Singh Kanhaiya, he captured Lahore, from the Afghans. As Lahina Singh was senior in relationship, being his maternal uncle, Gujar Singh allowed Lahina Singh to take possession of the city and the fort, himself occupying the eastern part of the city, then a jungle. Gujjar Singh erected a mud fortress and invited people to settle there. He sank wells to supply water. A mosque was built for Muslims. The area, the site of the present day railway station of Lahore, still bears his name and is known as Qila Gujjar Singh. Gujjar Singh next captured Eminabad, Wazirabad, Sodhra and about 150 villages in Gujrariwala district. He then took Gujrat from Sultan Mubarak Khan whom he defeated under the walls of the city in December 1765, capturing both the city and the adjoining country, and making Gujrat his headquarters. Next year, he overran Jammu, seized Islamgarh, Purichh, Dev Batala and extended his territory as far as the Bhimbar hills in the north and the Majha country in the south. During Ahmad Shah Durrani's eighth invasion, Gujjar Singh along with other Sikh Sardars offered him strong opposition. In January 1767, when Durrani chief Jahan Khan reached Amritsar at the head of 15,000 troops, the Sikh Sardars routed the Afghan horde. Soon afterwards Gujar Singh laid siege to the famous fort of Rohtas, held by the Gakkhars, with the assistance of Charhat Singh Sukkarchakkia, who was on the most amicable terms with him and who gave his daughter, Raj Kaur, in marriage to his son, Sahib Singh. Gujar Singh subjugated the warlike tribes in the northwestern Punjab and occupied portions of Pothohar, Rawalpindi and Hasan Abdal. He died at Lahore in 1788.

The Sardars

Sahib Singh, Sardar

Sahib Singh, son of Gujar Singh of the Bhangi Misl, was married to Raj Kaur, daughter of Charhat Singh Sukkarchakkia, the grandfather of Maharaja Ranjit Singh. On the eve of the first invasion in 1794, of Shah Zaman, grandson of Ahmad Shah Durrani, it was estimated that Sahib Singh's state yielded an annual revenue of thirteen lakh rupees. He owned twelve forts and had a body of 2,000 horses in permanent employ, besides a big gun called Shah Pasand. In June 1797, Sahib Singh joined Ranjit Singh in his campaign against Hashmat Khan, the chief of the Chattha tribe, whose possessions lay on the left bank of the River Chenab. At the time of the last invasion of Shah Zaman in 1798, Sahib Singh, along with Ranjit Singh, attacked him with 500 horses. On the withdrawal of Shah Zaman from the Punjab in January 1799, Sahib Singh, under instruction from Ranjit Singh, led a force towards Kashmir and in 1806 accompanied him on his expedition into the Cis-Satluj region. As his own position became vulnerable in consequence of the hostility of the surrounding Sikh chiefs, Ranjit Singh ended Sahib Singh's authority by annexing his country. In 1810, the Maharaja, upon the intercession of Mai Lachhmi, mother of Sahib Singh, granted him a Jagir worth one lakh of rupees, which he held until his death the following year. On Sahib Singh's death, Maharaja Ranjit Singh married by the customary rite of Chadar Dalna, two of the former's wives, Daya Kaur and Ratan Kaur, who were real sisters, celebrated for their beauty. Daya Kaur gave birth to princes Kashmira Singh and Pashaura Singh and Ratan Kaur gave birth to Prince Multana Singh.

Bota Singh, Sardar

In 1739, Zakariya Khan, the Mughal governor of Punjab, launched an all out campaign of persecution of Sikhs. Thousands of Sikhs were murdered. Cartloads of their heads were taken to Lahore for obtaining rewards from the governor, Zakariya Khan. In the days of dire persecution, Bota Singh along with many fellow Sikhs had sought the safety of jungles. At nightfall, Bota Singh would come out of his hiding place and visit some human habitations in search of food. Occasionally he would come to Amritsar by night to have a dip in the holy tank, spending the day in the wilderness around Tarn Taran. One day he was noticed by some people who thought he was a Sikh. But one of the party said that he was not a Sikh, for had he been one he would not conceal himself thus.

The Sardars

Bota Singh, Sardar
The taunt cut Bota Singh to the quick. Accompanied by his companion Garja Singh, and with a bamboo club in his hand, he took up position on the grand trunk road, near Sarai Nur ud Din, near Tarn Taran. To announce his presence and proclaim the sovereignty of the Khalsa, he started collecting toll from the passers-by. **None dared to refuse the demand and nobody reported it to the government. Bota Singh's aim in collecting the toll was to prove to Zakariya Khan that in spite of all his efforts to exterminate Sikhs, they were very much in existence.The Governor was highly incensed and sent a force of one hundred horsemen to arrest them. But, the two Sikhs refused to surrender and died fighting after nearly wiping out the Mughal force. Their only weapons were big sticks cut from kikkar trees.** This happened in 1739.

Dasaundha Singh, Sardar
Dasaundha Singh, founder of the Nishananvali Misl, was the son of Chaudhari Sahib Rai belonging to the village of Mansur, in Ferozepore district of the Punjab. He received pahul, the Khalsa initiatory rites at the hands of Diwan Durbara Singh, a prominent Sikh leader of the post Banda Singh period. By 1734, Dasaundha Singh was a leading figure in the Taruna Dal. At the time of the formation of the Dal Khalsa in 1748, he was proclaimed the leader of the Nishananvali Misl. The Nishananvali Misl, was kept as a reserve force at Amritsar, and used to act as standard bearers of the Khalsa army. In January 1764, after the conquest of Sirhind, Dasaundha Singh took possession of Singharivala in Ferozepore district, Sahneval, Sarai Lashkari Khan, Doraha, Amioh, Zira and Ambala. At the latter, he established his headquarters. He was killed in May 1767 at Meerut in a sudden attack by Jahan Khan and Zabita Khan.

Fateh Singh, Sardar
Fateh Singh, an army commander under Banda Singh Bahadur, was appointed administrator of Samana after the town was occupied by the Sikhs in 1709. Fateh Singh participated in several of Banda Singh's battles against the Mughal rulers. In the battle of Sirhind fought at the nearby village of Chappar Chiri, Fateh Singh killed Nawab Wazir Khan, the faujdar of Sirhind. He was taken prisoner at Lohgarh in December 1715 and was executed in Delhi in June 1716 along with Banda Singh and his other companions.

The Sardars

Gulab Singh, Sardar

Gulab Singh, impressed with Banda Singh's armed victories, joined him as a soldier. He took part in various battles under his command. In the siege of Lohgarh in December 1715, Gulab Singh decided to sacrifice his life to save the life of Banda Singh. Since he had a striking physical resemblance with him, he dressed himself in his fine garments and seated himself in his place. Banda Singh made his way through the imperial camp in the disguise of a Mughal soldier and fled towards Nahan in the mountains. When on the morning of 11TH December the royal troops entered the fortress, they took Gulab Singh for Banda Singh and made him a prisoner. There were great rejoicings, but soon it was discovered that the real Banda Singh had in fact escaped. Gulab Singh was put in an iron cage and sent to Delhi where he was executed on 9TH June 1716 along with Banda Singh and the last batch of his men captured at Gurdas Nangal.

Gulab Singh, Sardar

Gulab Singh, founder of the Dallewalia clan, was born at the village of Dallewalia, near Dera Baba Nanak on the left bank of the River Ravi, 50 km northeast of Amritsar. In his younger days, he ran a grocery shop in his village and was known as Gulaba Khatri. Having heard tales of heroism of the Sikhs, he came to Amritsar, waited upon Nawab Kapur Singh, and volunteered to become a Sikh. He was advised to grow long hair, practice horsemanship, archery and the use of sword and to come again after a year. Gulaba returned home, won over a small number of young men as companions and commenced a career of adventure. He came to Amritsar on the occasion of Diwali accompanied by his band, many of whom were on horseback. Nawab Kapur Singh was highly impressed and, administering initiatory rites to him, named him Gulab Singh. At the formation of the Dal Khalsa in 1748, Gulab Singh, who had already fought bravely against Nadir Shah in 1739 and in the Chhota Ghallughara in 1746, was declared the head of the Dallewalia Misl. Later the Dallewalia and the Nishanarivali Misls were stationed at Amritsar to protect the holy city. In 1757 when Ahmad Shah Durrani was returning homeward laden with the booty from Delhi, Mathura and Agra, Gulab Singh made frequent night attacks on his baggage train. At the fords of Ravi and Chenab, Gulab Singh with several other Sikh Sardars captured a large number of Afghan horses. Commanding a Jatha of 400 men, Gulab Singh plundered Panipat, Rohtak, Harisi and Hissar. Gulab Singh died fighting, in 1759, against Ambo Khan of Kalanaur, 27 km west of Gurdaspur

The Sardars

Ghaiba, Tara Singh, Sardar

Tara Singh Ghaiba succeeded Gulab Singh as head of the Dallewalia Misl. Tara Singh proved to be an able leader and a fearless fighter. One of his first exploits was to attack a detachment of Ahmad Shah Durrani's army and rob it of its horses and arms. In 1760, he crossed the Satluj and seized the towns of Dharamkote and Fatehgarh. On his return to the Doab, he took Sarai Dakkani from the Afghan chief Saif-ud-Din of Jalandhar and marched eastwards seizing the country around Rahon. He made Rahon his headquarters. He next captured Nakodar from Manj Rajputs and several other villages on the right side of the Satluj, including Mahatpur and Kot Badal Khan. In 1763, Tara Singh joined the Bhangi, Ramgharia and Kanhaiya Sardars against the Pathan Nawab of Kasur, sacking and plundering the town. He joined other Sikh Sardars in laying siege to Sirhind and razing it to the ground after defeating its Faujdars Zain Khan. The Dallewalia Misl under Tara Singh held a major portion of the upper Jalandhar Doab, and the northern portions of Ambala and Ludhiana, with some portions of Ferozepore. Dharam Singh of the Dallewalia Misl captured Kohlan and a cluster of villages, in the centre of which he founded the village of Dharamsinghwala, where he set up his permanent headquarters while Saunda Singh captured Tihala and Khanna. Tara Singh became a close friend and associate of Maharajah Ranjit Singh, and took part in his early campaigns. He died in 1807 at the age of 90.

Haqiqat Singh, Sardar

Haqiqat Singh, emerging as an independent chief, occupied Kalanaur, Kahngarh, Adalatgarh, Pathankot and several other villages. In 1760, he destroyed Churiarivala and founded another village naming it Sangatpura and constructed a fort at Fatehgarh. Haqiqat Singh died in 1782 and his only son Jaimal Singh, then a minor, succeeded to his estates. Haqiqat Singh's granddaughter, Chand Kaur, was married to Prince Kharak Singh, eldest son of Maharaja Ranjit Singh. Jaimal Singh died in 1812, leaving no heirs. His estates were merged into the Sikh Kingdom.

The Sardars

Jai Singh, Sardar

Sardar Jai Singh was founder of the Kanhaiya Misl. It is commonly believed that the name of the band, Kanhaiya, was derived from the name of Jai Singh's village, Kahna, although another explanation connects it with the Sardars own handsome appearance which earned him the epithet (Kahn) Kanhaiya. Jai Singh seized a part of Riarki comprising the district of Gurdaspur and upper portions of Amritsar. His first headquarters were at his wife's village, Sohian, 15 km from Amritsar, from where he shifted to Batala and thence to Mukerian. His territories lay on both sides of the rivers Beas and Ravi. A contemporary Muslim historian, Qazi Nur Muhammad, wrote in 1765 that Jai Singh Kanhaiya had extended his territory up to Parol, about 70 km southeast of Jammu, and that he worked in collaboration with Jassa Singh Ramgarhia, both sharing between them the territory of Batala. The hill chiefs of Nurpur, Datarpur and Siba became Jai Singh's tributaries. In 1774, Jai Singh built a katra or bazaar at Amritsar called Katra Kanhaiya. In October 1778, with the help of Mahan Singh Sukkarchakkia and Jassa Singh Ahluwalia, he drove away Jassa Singh Ramgarhia to the desert region of Hansi and Hissar. In 1781, Jai Singh and his associate, Haqiqat Singh, led an expedition to Jammu and received a sum of three lakh of rupees as a tribute from Brij Raj Dev of Jammu. Jai Singh died in 1793 at the age of 81. Control of the Kanhaiya Misl passed into the hands of his daughter-in-law, Sada Kaur, his son, Gurbaksh Singh, having predeceased him.

Karora Singh, Sardar

At the formation of the Dal Khalsa in March, 1748, Karora Singh, from the village of Barki in the district of Lahore, headed the Karorasinghia Misl. Karora Singh generally confined his activities to the tract lying south of the Kangra hills in Hoshiarpur district. In 1759, at the death of Adina Beg Khan, Karora Singh killed Adina's Diwan Bishambhar Mall, and seized considerable territory, including places such as Hoshiarpur, Hariana, Sham Chaurasi, Basis, Shamsabad, Banbell, Bahadurpur and the Talwan territory. The Talwan territory extended from the Ghorewala in the east to Shahkot in the west. It contained 360 villages, and was held by Mahmud Khan. He possessed a few hundred troopers of his own, but considered it advisable to submit to the rising tide of Sikh power. Karora Singh was killed at Taraori, near Karnal, fighting against the Nawab of Kunjpura in 1761.

The Sardars

Khushal Singh, Sardar

Nawab Kapur Singh was succeeded by his son Khushal Singh. He added a number of places and Parganahs such as Bahrampur and Nurpur to his estate. After the death of Adina Beg Khan, the faujdar of Jalandhar Doab, Khushal Singh along with Jassa Singh Ahluwalia, attacked his Diwan Bishambhar Mall in 1759, and captured Jalandhar and several adjoining areas. Khushal Singh made Jalandhar his capital. Khushal Singh posted 150 horsemen and 50 footmen at Marawali and 750 horsemen and 250 footmen under Mahan Singh at Jalandhar. He captured the Parganahs of Haibatpur and Patti from the Pathan chief of Kasur and placed these under the charge of his son, Budh Singh. At the time of the conquest of Sirhind by Sikhs in January 1764, Khushal Singh acquired Bharatgarh, Machhali, Ghanauli, Manauli and several other villages as his share of the booty. Along with other Sikh Sardars he kept making guerrilla attacks upon the invading Afghan hordes of Ahmed Shah Durrani whenever he could. Khushal Singh and Raja Amar Singh of Patiala seized from the Nawab of Raikot 23 villages around Chhat and Bannu which remained under their joint control for several years. Khushal Singh built a Bazaar at Amritsar called Katra Singhpurian, now known as Bazaar Kaserian. Khushal Singh died in 1795.

Lang, Hari Singh, Sardar

Hari Singh Lang (lame) of Dallewalia clan seized a large tract of land on both sides of the River Satluj, at the foot of the Shivalik hills. He captured the Parganahs of Awankot, Korali, Rupar, Siaba, and Siswan. He took possession of the fort of Khizarabad which was built by Chaudhry Tek Chand. He seized Parganahs of Bahrampur, Chanderi and Saradat from the Raja of Bilaspur. The Raja of Jaswan purchased peace by surrendering one half of the revenue of Manaswal. He annexed Chamkaur by expelling Sodhi Nahar Singh who had acquired it in 1764, and captured ten villages of Budh Singh Singhpuria. Hari Singh possessed 106 villages. He commanded 1,500 horsemen and 500 footmen. He died in 1793.

The Sardars

Mahtab Singh, Sardar

Punjab had gone through an era of Sikh persecution under the Mughal governor of Lahore, Zakariya Khan, from 1726 to 1745. The Sikhs had taken refuge in the deserts of the Rajputana. Mehtab Singh had taken up employment under the ruler of Bikaner. In 1740, the governor of Lahore put Massa Ranghar or Musalul Khan, a Chaudhary of Mandiala in charge of the Harmandir Sahib (Golden Temple). Sikhs were not allowed to visit the Harmandir Sahib or to take a dip in the holy waters of its tank (Sarovar). Massa Ranghar persecuted the Sikhs and looted the shops and homes of Hindus. He watched the dancing girls perform, drank alcohol and smoked hookah inside the Harmander Sahib. Two residents of Amritsar Tej Ram, a Hindu and Bulaka Singh took this news to a band of Khalsa in the deserts of Bikaner under the leadership of Sardar Sham Singh. Tej Ram and Bulaka Singh narrated their stories to the congregation of Sikhs. After listening Sardar Mehtab Singh volunteered to bring Massa Ranghars head back to Bikaner. Another Sikh, Sardar Sukha Singh of Mari Kamboki also stood up and asked to accompany Mehtab Singh. Both of the Sikhs disguised themselves as landlords (Choudhries) bringing revenue to Amritsar. They rode across the desert and reached Damdama Sahib at Talwandi Sabo near Bhatinda. They filled up bags of broken pottery pieces and made them look as if they are full of coins. On August 11TH, 1740, they dressed up as landlords from Patti and entered the city of Amritsar. They reached the Harmandir Sahib and tied their horses to the berry tree and went inside the Harmandir Sahib carrying the bags. Massa Ranghar was smoking the hookah and watching the dancing girls. The Sikhs threw the bags under Massa's bed and said that they had come to pay the revenue. Massa bent downwards to have a look at the bags. Mehtab Singh immediately took his sword and slashed it at Massa's neck and instantly severed his head. Sukha Singh finished off the guards of Massa Ranghar. They put Massa's head in a bag and rode their horses back to Talwandi Sabo the same evening. The next day they reached Bikaner and presented Massa Ranghars head on a spear to the congregation of Sikhs. In 1745, Bhai Mehtab Singh heard the news of the arrest and torture of Bhai Taru Singh. He decided to surrender himself voluntarily to die beside Bhai Taru Singh. In June 1745, Bhai Mehtab Singh was ordered by the governor of Lahore, to be tortured until death and was martyred on the rotating wheels of nails.

The Sardars

Milkha Singh Thehpuria, Sardar

Sardar Milkha Singh Thehpuria was one of the most notable Sardars attached to the Bhangi Misl. He was a powerful Sikh chief during the latter half of the eighteenth century. Abandoning his native place, Kaleke, near Kasur; he founded the village of Thehpur in Lahore district. He took possession of a number of villages in the vicinity of Thehpur, and in Gujrat and Gujrariwala districts. Not content with these possessions, he marched northward and seized Rawalpindi, then an insignificant place inhabited by Rawal mendicants. Milkha Singh fixed his headquarters there, building new houses and fortifying the town. Rawalpindi, being on the highway into India, was a vulnerable possession exposed to attacks of Afghan invaders, but Milkha Singh held his own. He conquered a tract around Rawalpindi worth several lakhs of rupees a year and had won the esteem of the warlike tribes of Hazara. He had adopted the cognomen of Thehpuria from the village he had founded, but in the north he was known as Milkha Singh Pindiwala. Maharaja Ranjit Singh, whom Milkha Singh had joined in his early expeditions, called him Babaji, i.e. the revered grandfather. Milkha Singh died in 1804. Jivan Singh, his only son, who succeeded to his father's estates, fought in the Maharaja's Kashmir campaign in 1814, and died the next year. The force which Milkha Singh and Jivan Singh had maintained was transferred to the service of the Sikh State and placed under Sardar Atar Singh Sandharivalia, bearing the name of Dhera Pindiwala.

Mohar Singh, Sardar

Sardar Mohar Singh **was** a prominent leader of the Nishananvali Misl. He added Ambala and Zira to the territories he had inherited and soon became an influential figure among the Cis-Satluj chiefs. In 1785, Mahadji Scindia, regent of the Mughal Empire, decided to win over the Sikhs by a treaty of friendship, and sent Amba ji Ingle to start negotiations. The Sikhs deputed Mohar Singh and Dulcha Singh, of the Karorsinghia Misl, as their representatives, first to meet Amba ji Ingle and then Mahadji Scindia, at Malhura. As a result of these parleys a treaty was signed by Mohar Singh and Dulcha Singh with Mahadji Scindia on 9TH May 1785. At the time of departure they were given robes of honour, necklaces of pearls and horses. Mohar Singh died at Ambala in 1785 in a feud with Gurbaksh Singh of Morinda.

The Sardars

Nakai, Hira Singh, Sardar
Hira Singh was the founder of Nakai Misl. In 1731, he received the initiatory rites of the Khalsa at the hands of the celebrated Bhai Mani Singh, and took to the adventurous and daring way of life of the Sikhs of those days. Hira Singh had taken to arms while still very young. He led a band of notoriously brave young men, on great plundering raids. He was part of the Khalsa, when the Sikhs sacked Kasur in 1763 and conquered Sirhind in 1764. Hira Singh occupied Bahirval, Chunlan, Dlpalpur, Jambar, Jethupur, Kanganval and Khudian establishing his headquarters at Chunian. In 1767, he led out an expedition to Pakpattan, but was killed in the action that took place.

Nakai, Ran Singh, Sardar
Ran Singh, who succeeded Hira Singh, considerably increased the power and influence of the Nakais. The territory under his control comprised Chunlan; part of Kasur, Sharakpur, and Cugera and, at one time, Kot Kamalia. Ran Singh had a force of 2,000 horsemen, with camel swivels and a few guns. His headquarters were at Bahirval in Lahore district. Ran Singh died in 1781 and was succeeded by his eldest son Bhagvan Singh, whose sister, Raj Kaur, was married to Maharaja Ranjit Singh. His younger brother, Gian Singh, who died in 1807 leaving a son, Kahn Singh, succeeded Bhagvan Singh. Ranjit Singh granted Kahn Singh a Jagir of 15,000 rupees per annum and seized all the possessions of the family.

Nakai, Kamar Singh, Sardar
The other branch of the Nakai Misl was founded at Sayyidwala near Kot Kamalia. Its leader was Kamar Singh. Kamar Singh subdued the independent tribes living on both sides of the Ravi such as Kathias, Kharals, and other robber clans. To keep these lawless tribes under control he built five forts at Chittavatni, Dhaulri, Harappa, Kamalia and Killianwala. He divided his possessions into two districts, Satghara and Sayyidwala. Kamar Singh was a great Sardar. He conquered Kot Kamalia from Muhammad Yar Khan and Ahmad Yar Khan. Kamar Singh died in 1780.

The Sardars

Nakai, Budh Singh, Sardar
In 1783 a terrible famine broke out in Northern India. A member of the Nakai Misl, Sardar Budh Singh, out of compassion, sold all his property. He purchased grain and gave it away in charity - a fixed quantity of it to every starving person, without any consideration of caste, creed or religion. As a matter of fact a large part of his benevolence benefited the poor Muslims. In 1803 Ranjit Singh seized all the Nakai territories, and this Misl came to an end. The survivors of the Misl were pensioned off with an annual Jagir. Nakai became a prominent last name among several families. Many Nakai Sardars were converted to Islam, lured by the women, power and money. A former Chief Minister of Punjab, Arif Nakais grandfather was born as a Sikh but got converted to Islam.

Nirmala, Karam Singh, Sardar
Sardar Karam Singh Nirmala, nephew of Himmat Singh of the Nishanarivali Misl, had captured Shahabad Markanda and Ismailabad in January 1764 after the sack of Sirhind. On Himmat Singh`s death without issue in 1771, Karam Singh succeeded him in the leadership of the Nishanarivali Misl. Karam Singh commanded a force of 750 horse and 250 foot. In January 1786, Karam Singh and others plundered the Ganga Doab. Again in April 1790, a body of 12,000 Sikhs led by Karam Singh ravaged Ganga Doab including Hapur and Aligarh, 57 km from Delhi. Karam Singh sent his vakil to Mahadeo Scindia, regent of the Mughal Empire, demanding more grants of lands in the Doab. After some time Scindia granted to Karam Singh, Shikarpur in jagir and the title of Sardar under the royal seal. Karam Singh`s son, Kharak Singh, was married to Prem Kaur, daughter of Raja Sahib Singh of Patiala.

Rai Singh, Sardar
Rai Singh, son of Lakhmir Singh of Amritsar and a leader of the Bhangi family, captured, together with his brother Bagh Singh, 204 villages around Buria after the sack of Sirhind by the Sikhs in January 1764. Eighty-four of these villages including Jagadhari and Dialgarh fell to the share of Rai Singh. Jagadhari had been completely ruined by Nadir Shah. Rai Singh invited traders and artisans to settle there and they turned it into a flourishing town. Rai Singh also controlled Haridvar and received considerable income from the city at the time of fairs and festivals. The state of Garhwal was tributary to him as well.

The Sardars

Raja, Bhup Singh,

Little is known about his life except that in 1808-09, along with Deva Singh, Bhup Singh was in possession of Ropar and its adjacent districts including Khyrabad and Mianpur, a tract covering 115 villages with estimated annual revenue of Rs 53,000. He was grandson of Sardar Hari Singh of Dallewalia Misl, who had taken possession, around 1763, of a large territory including Ropar, Sialba, Khyrabad and Kurali. In 1792, one year before he died, Hari Singh divided his possessions between his two surviving sons, Charhat Singh and Deva Singh, the former getting Ropar and the latter Sialba. Bhup Singh was the son and successor of Charhat Singh, who might have died during the former's minority. This explains the reference to Deva Singh being the co-ruler at Ropar in lists prepared in 1809 by Lieutenant Colonel D. Ochterlony and Lieutenant F.S. White of the East India Company. According to these lists, Ropar was under Maharaja Ranjit Singh. It came under British protection as a result of the treaty of Amritsar (25TH April 1809), which limited Ranjit Singh`s authority, mainly to territories north of the River Satluj. The chief of Ropar, Bhup Singh, was removed as prisoner and his whole estate was confiscated in 1846 in consequence of his opposing the British during the first Anglo-Sikh war. Raja Bhup Singh is remembered as a just ruler and as a pious Sikh who constructed Gurdwara Dehra Baba Gurditta Ji at Kiratpur and Gurdwara Gurugarh Sahib at Ropar. At the latter Gurdwara he had started a Langar, or free kitchen, which remained open round the clock, for which reason, the shrine is still known as Gurdwara Sada Varat (where Langar is open all the time to serve food to whoever comes).

Ram Singh, Sardar

Ram Singh, a Bal Jatt of the village of Mirpur Patti in Amritsar district of the Punjab, was the younger brother of Baj Singh, who was appointed governor of the town of Sirhind after it was occupied by Banda Singh Bahadur in May 1710. Ram Singh had received the rites of the Khalsa at the hands of Guru Gobind Singh, and was one of the five Sikhs who had accompanied Banda Singh from Nanded to the Punjab in 1709. He took part in various campaigns launched by Banda Singh. In May 1710, he was appointed administrator of Thanesar. He fought battles against Firoz Khan Mevati at Arnim, Taraori, Thanesar and Shahabad. He was taken prisoner in the siege of Gurdas Nangal and sent to Delhi where he was executed along with Banda Singh and his other companions in June 1716.

The Sardars

Ramgarhia, Jassa Singh, Sardar

Jassa Singh Ramgarhia was founder of the Ramgarhia Misl and one of the prominent military leaders of the Sikhs in the second half of the eighteenth century. He was born in 1723 at Tchogill, a village 20 km east of Lahore. His grandfather, Hardas Singh (d. 1716) had received pahul, the vows of the Khalsa, at the hands of Guru Gobind Singh and had fought in the campaigns of Banda Singh Bahadur. His father, Bhagvan Singh was killed in a fight against Nadir Shah during his invasion of India in 1739. Young Jassa Singh then joined the Jatha of Nand Singh Sarighania and learnt the art of warfare at an early age. In 1745, he was deputed to settle terms with Adina Beg, the faujdar of the Jalandhar Doab, who was harassing the Sikhs under instructions from Nawab Zakariya Khan, the Mughal governor of Lahore. The faujdar, Adina Beg, prevailed upon Jassa Singh to accept office under him, with a minor command of a regiment consisting of 100 Sikhs and 60 Hindus. The Sikhs were greatly annoyed at the conduct of their envoy, but Jassa Singh did not remain with Adina Beg for long. When in October 1748, the Sikhs gathered at Amritsar to celebrate the festival of Diwali, Mir Mannu, and the new provincial governor, marched upon the city to expel the Sikhs. The Sikhs disappeared into the neighbouring jungle, but 500 of them took shelter within their newly built fortress, Ram Rauni, and defied the Mughal force. The mud fortress was besieged and skirmishes continued for four months in which two hundred Sikhs lost their lives. The survivors requested Jassa Singh to come to their rescue. Jassa Singh left Adina Beg, and made an appeal to Kaura Mall, the Diwan of Lahore and a Sahajdhari Sikh, to save the Sikhs from destruction. At the Diwan's intercession, Mir Mannu raised the siege, though the fortress of Ram Rauni was completely destroyed. Mir Mannu's death in November 1753 plunged the Punjab into anarchy. The Sikhs again emerged into the open and decided to rebuild the Ram Rauni fort. Jassa Singh was assigned to this task and with the help of his contingent; he reconstructed the fortress and named it Ramgarh. Since then Jassa Singh, earlier known as Tchogill after the name of his village, began to be called Ramgarhia in appreciation of the work done by him. In April 1758, Adina Beg became governor of the Punjab. He sent a strong force under Mirza Bakhsh to clear the forests in which Sikhs had taken shelter. A large number of them including Jassa Singh Ramgarhia, Jai Singh Kanhaiya and Amar Singh Kirigra, fled to Amritsar and took shelter in the fortress. Ramgarh was besieged.

The Sardars

Ramgarhia, Jassa Singh, Sardar (Cont.)

Jassa Singh and Jai Singh made numerous sallies killing a large number of the besiegers, but were ultimately forced to evacuate. After Adina Beg's death in September 1758, the roving bands of the Sikhs returned. Jassa Singh Ramgarhia and Jai Singh Kanhaiya united and within a short time they seized large slices of territory in four out of the five Doabs; they occupied the fertile tract called Riarki to the north of Amritsar, embracing the district of Gurdaspur. Within a decade Jassa Singh became one of the leading figures of the Dal Khalsa. In 1770, he led plundering expeditions into the hills. The local Rajas sought safety in submission and Jassa Singh collected a tribute of 200,000 rupees from the Kangra states. He built a fort at Talvara on the left bank of the Beas and stationed his brother, Mali Singh, with 4,000 horses, in the fort. Jassa Singh Ramgarhia along with other Sikh Sardars fought many a pitched battle against the Afghan invader, Ahmad Shah Durrani. As the Afghan threat receded, the Sikh Sardars began fighting among themselves. The Ramgarhia Kanhaiya cleavage over their adjoining territories in the districts of Gurdaspur and Hoshiarpur widened. In the battle of Dinanagar in 1775, Jassa Singh Ramgarhia joined the Bhangi Sardars against the forces of the Kanhaiyas and the Sukkarchakkias. Soon a rift appeared between Jassa Singh Ramgarhia and Jassa Singh Ahluvalia when the latter wrested Zahura, a Ramgarhia territory, and conferred it upon Baghel Singh KarorSirighia. Jassa Singh Ramgarhia and Jassa Singh Ahluvalia became sworn enemies of each other. Jai Singh Kanhaiya joined Jassa Singh Ahluvalia and the Ramgarhia Sardar had to flee the Punjab. Driven out of the Punjab, Jassa Singh became a soldier of fortune. Jassa Singh took possession of Hissar and raised a large body of irregular horse, his depredations extending to the gates of Delhi and its suburbs and into the Gangetic Doab. Jassa Singh and other Sikh chiefs conquered Delhi and entered the Red Fort. Jassa Singh Ahluvalia ascended the throne on 11TH March 1783, but Jassa Singh Ramgarhia challenged his right to do so, at which the Ahluvalia chief vacated the royal seat. Jassa Singh Ramgarhia then invaded Meerut and levied an annual tribute of 10,000 rupees on the Nawab. Soon a body of 30,000 horse and foot under him and Karam Singh crossed into Saharanpur district, ravaging it freely. After the death of Jassa Singh Ahluvalia in October 1783, there were further fissures in the Dal Khalsa. Jai Singh Kanhaiya and Maha Singh Sukkarchakkia fell out.

The Sardars

Ramgarhia, Jassa Singh, Sardar (Cont.)

Maha Singh won over to his side Raja Sansar Chand of Kangra and invited Jassa Singh Ramgarhia to come back to the Punjab and make a bid to recover his lost possessions. Jassa Singh Ramgarhia returned to the Punjab and allied himself with the Sukkarchakkias in order to destroy his old foe, Jai Singh Kanhaiya. Together they marched upon the Kanhaiya citadel of Batala in 1787. Jai Singh was defeated and his son Gurbaksh Singh killed. Jassa Singh recovered all his lost territories and set himself up at Batala, which he fortified by a thick wall. At the height of his power, Jassa Singh's territory in the Ban Doab included Batala, Kalanaur, Dinanagar, Sri Hargobindpur, Shahpur Kandl, Gurdaspur, Qadiari, Gliuman, Matteval, and in the Jalandhar Doab, Urmur Tanda, Sarih, Miani, Garhdivala and Zahura. In the hills Kangra, Nurpur, Mandi and Chamba paid him a tribute of two lakh of rupees. Jassa Singh died on 20TH April 1803 at the age of 80.

Ramgarhia, Jodh Singh, Sardar

Jodh Singh Ramgarhia, soldier and feudatory chief was the eldest son of Jassa Singh Ramgarhia. Ranjit Singh bound himself in a pledge of friendship with Jodh Singh Ramgarhia before the Guru Granth Sahib at Durbar Sahib, Amritsar. The Maharaja had great reverence for him and used to call him Babaji. He was always seated next to the Maharaja in the royal Durbar. Jodh Singh was Ranjit Singh's ally in his earlier campaigns. In 1802, he helped him to seize Amritsar from the Bhangis. In 1807, he accompanied the Maharaja to Kasur with all his force against Qutb ud Din, who surrendered after a month's resistance. Jodh Singh was a deeply religious person. He built the Ramgarhia Bunga on the Golden Temple premises, and supplied pieces of perforated marble that served as parapets on both sides of the causeway leading to the sanctuary. He also brought many pieces of mosaic work from Delhi and Agra. He built the first two storeys of Baba Atal, the loftiest building in Amritsar, near the Golden Temple. Jodh Singh died at Amritsar in August 1815.

The Sardars

Sahib Singh Bedi, Baba

Sahib Singh Bedi, Baba, tenth in direct descent from Guru Nanak, was much revered for his piety as well as for his martial prowess. He was born at Dera Baba Nanak, Gurdaspur district in April 1756. Around 1770, his parents Baba Ajit Singh and Mata Sarupan Devi, shifted from Dera Baba Nanak to Una, a town now in Himachal Pradesh in the Sivalik foothills, where the family held extensive Jagirs. As a young boy, Sahib Singh studied the Sikh sacred texts and had training in the use of arms. On the death of his father in Calcutta in 1773, Sahib Singh succeeded to the ancestral estate. He became widely reputed for his religious learning and devotees flocked to his magnificently built fortress at Una to listen to his discourses. A charisma grew around his person and it was considered a signal honour to receive pahul or the Sikh initiatory rite at his hands. At the same time, he became the arbiter of political feuds among the Misldars, and then engaged in occupying territories in parts of the Punjab. The Sardars settled upon him grants of lands and he came to acquire great influence in the Jalandhar Doab and the Majha region. In 1794, he led a punitive campaign against the Afghan ruler, Ata Ullah Khan, of Malerkotla. Tara Singh Ghaiba, Baghel Singh and Bhanga Singh of Thanesar joined forces with him in this expedition. But Patiala, Nabha, Jind and Kalsia troops intervened on behalf of `Ata Ullah Khan and Sahib Singh withdrew after receiving a war indemnity. In 1798, helped by the forces of Tara Singh, Gurdit Singh and Jodh Singh, he attacked Rai Iliyas, of Raikot, about 40 km from Ludhiana. He occupied Jagraon, Dakha and Badhowal, and then advanced towards Ludhiana and Mansuran and took both these places. A Gurdwara in the village of Akhara (Ludhiana district) commemorates his victory. During Shah Zaman's invasion of northern India (1796), Sahib Singh spearheaded Sikh resistance. When on 7TH July 1799, the young Sukkarchakkia chief Ranjit Singh took possession of Lahore, Sahib Singh threw his weight on his side and helped him to vanquish Gulab Singh Bhangi in the battle of Bhasin in March 1800. At the time of Ranjit Singh`s coronation at Lahore on 11TH April 1801, Baba Sahib Singh placed the tilak or mark of sovereignty on his forehead. In 1807, he helped to settle a longstanding dispute between the rulers of Nabha and Patiala. He travelled extensively in the Pothohar, Majha and Malva regions and wherever he went people thronged in large numbers to see him and to pay homage to him. Baba Sahib Singh died at Una on 17TH July 1834.

The Sardars

Shahid, Baba Dip Singh

Baba Dip Singh Shahid was founder of the Shahid Misl as well as of the Damdama Taksal or Damdama school of Sikh learning. Baba Dip Singh was born in 1682, the son of Bhai Bhagat and Mai Jiuni, a Sikh couple living in Pahuvind, a village 40 km southwest of Amritsar. He received the vows of the Khalsa at Anandpur where he stayed for some time to study the sacred texts under Bhai Mani Singh. He rejoined Guru Gobind Singh at Talwandi Sabo in 1706 and, after the latter's departure for the South, stayed on there to look after the sacred shrine, Damdama Sahib. At the head of a small group of warriors, he joined Banda Singh Bahadur in his campaign against the Mughal authority, but left him in 1714, retiring to Damdama Sahib at Talwandi Sabo with his band of warriors, he resumed his study and teaching of the Scripture and training in martial skills. In 1726, he had four copies of the Guru Granth Sahib made from the recension prepared earlier by Bhai Mani Singh under the supervision of Guru Gobind Singh during their stay at Damdama Sahib. In 1732, he went to the rescue of Sardar Ala Singh who had been besieged in Barnala by Manjh and Bhatti Rajputs in collaboration with the faujdar of Jalandhar and the Nawab of Malerkotla. In 1733, when the Mughal governor of Lahore sought peace with the Sikhs offering them a Nawab ship and a jagir, Dip Singh and his Jatha or fighting band joined Nawab Kapur Singh at Amritsar to form a joint Sikh force, the Dal Khalsa, which was soon divided for administrative convenience into Buddha Dal and Taruna Dal, the latter being further split into five Jathas. Dip Singh, now reverently called Baba, was given the command of one of these Jathas which in 1748 were redesignated misls. It came to be known as Shahid Misl after its founder met with the death of a martyr (Shahid, in Punjabi).The Misls soon established their authority over different regions under Rakhi system, which meant collection of a portion of the revenue of the region for guaranteeing peace, protection and security. Shahid Misl had its sphere of influence south of the River Satluj and Dip Singh`s headquarters remained at Talwandi Sabo. The tower in which he lived still stands next to the Takht Sri Damdama Sahib and is known as Burj Baba Dip Singh Shahid. During his fourth invasion of India in the winter of 1756-57, Ahmad Shah Durrani annexed the Punjab to the Afghan dominions and appointed his son, Taimur, viceroy at Lahore, with the veteran general, Jahan Khan, as his deputy. Jahan Khan invested Amritsar in May 1757, razed the Sikh fortress of Ram Rauni and filled up the sacred pool.

The Sardars

Shahid, Baba Dip Singh (Cont.)

As the news of this desecration reached Dip Singh, he set out with his Jatha towards the Holy City. Many Sikhs joined him on the way so that when he arrived at Tarn Taran he had at his command a force of 5,000 men. Jahan Khan's troops lay in wait for them near Gohlvar village, 8 km ahead. They barred their way and a fierce action took place. Dip Singh suffered grave injury near Ramsar, yet such was the firmness of his resolve to reach the holy precincts that he carried on the battle until he fell dead in the close vicinity of the Harimandar. This was on 11TH November 1757. A legend grew that it was Baba Dip Singh`s headless body holding his severed head on his left hand and wielding his Khanda, double edged sword, with his right hand that had fought on until he had redeemed his pledge to liberate the holy shrine.

Shahid, Karam Singh, Sardar

Karam Singh was a leading figure in the Shahid clan of Sandhu Jatts of the village of Marahka in Sheikhupura district, now in Pakistan. He was a grandson of Baba Dip Singh, the martyr. In January 1764, at the conquest of Sirhind province by the Sikhs, he seized a number of villages in the Parganahs of Kesari and Shahzadpur in Ambala district, yielding about a lakh of rupees annually. Karam Singh made Shahzadpur his headquarters, but he lived for most of the time at Talwandi Sabo (Damdama Sahib), in Bhatinda district. In 1773, Karam Singh overran a large tract of land belonging to Zabita Khan Ruhila in the upper Gangetic Doab. He captured a number of villages in Saharanpur district. Karam Singh died in 1784.

Sukarchakia, Buddha Singh, Sardar

Buddha Singh, great-great-grandfather of Maharajah Ranjit Singh, was a founder of the Sukarchakia Misl. One of his ancestors, Bhara Mall, who lived in the village of Sukkarchakk in Gujranwala district, now in Pakistan, had been initiated into the Sikh faith by the Seventh Guru, Guru Har Rai. Buddha Singh received baptism at the hands of Guru Gobind Singh himself and fought in battles under him and under Banda Singh Bahadur. He constructed a big house at Sukkarchakk and acquired considerable influence in those turbulent times. He was elected the village Chaudhari or chief. He was a daring horseman, and there were many legends current about his adventures on his favourite piebald mare called Desi. It is said that on the back of Desi, he swam across the Ravi, Chenab and Jehlum rivers as many as fifty times. The dauntless warrior had on his body scars of scores of wounds by sword, spear and gun. He died in 1718.

The Sardars

Sukarchakia, Nodh Singh, Sardar

Budha Singh had two sons, Nodh Singh and Chanda Singh. Nodh Singh remained with his father at Surkarchak. Chanda Singh settled at Sindhanwalia in Sialkot district, and was called Sindhanwalia. Nodh Singh served under Nawab Kapur Singh. In 1745 Nodh Singh was the leader of one of twenty-five bands of Sikh warriors. In 1748 Nodh Singh became head of the Sukarchakia Misl. Nodh Singh was killed in 1752 on a pillaging expedition.

Sukarchakia, Charhat Singh, Sardar

Charhat Singh took to arms while still very young and attacked Eminabad, killing the faujdar and plundering the town. He next captured Wazirabad. His most significant victory was at Sialkot, where in August 1761 he besieged Ahmad Shah Durrani's general, Nur ud Din Bamezai. He pressed the Afghan general hard and forced him to flee the town. He had now to face Khwaja Ubaid Khan, the Afghan governor of Lahore, who marched upon Gujranwala to chastise him. The town was besieged, but Charhat Singh fought with courage and surprised the besieger by his night sallies. In the meantime, other Sikh Sardars, under the leadership of Jassa Singh Ahluwalia, came to his rescue. Ubaid Khan was forced to retreat, leaving behind siege guns, ammunition and stores. In the Vadda Ghallughara or Great Holocaust of 5TH February 1762, when the Sikhs were involved in a pitched battle with Ahmad Shah Durrani, Charhat Singh fought with great skill and courage. No sooner had Ahmad Shah returned to Afghanistan than the Sikhs reappeared all over the Punjab. Charhat Singh and the Bhangi Sardars sacked Kasur in April 1763. In November 1763 he engaged at Sialkot the Shah's commander-in-chief, Jahan Khan, who had been especially sent to punish the Sikhs, and inflicted upon him a severe defeat. The Shah, who came out himself, was forced to return home harassed by the pursuing Sikh bands. Charhat Singh swept across the Rachna and Chaj Doabs and reached Rohtas. The Afghan commander of the fort, Sarfaraz Khan, offered stiff resistance, but was overcome near Attock. Charhat Singh defeated Sarbuland Khan, governor of Kashmir, who was on his way to meet the Afghan ruler at Lahore. He followed these victories with the occupation of a large portion of the Dhanni and Pothohar areas. He then took Pind Dadan Khan, and built a fort there. The Salt Range of Kheora and Miani was the next to fall to him. Charhat Singh was fatally wounded by the bursting of his own gun in 1770.

The Sardars

Sukarchakia, Mahan Singh, Sardar

Mahan Singh, son of Charhat Singh of Sukkarchakkia Misl, was young in years when his father died. During his minority, his mother, Mai Desan, carried on the administration, with the help of her brothers. As soon as he came of age, Mahan Singh embarked upon a career of conquest. He took the fort of Rohtas back from Nur-ud-Din Bamezai. Aided by Jai Singh Kanhaiya, he advanced upon Rasulnagar. The powerful Chattha chief, Pir Muhammad, offered him stiff resistance, but was at last overcome. The town was occupied and renamed Ramnagar. As Mahan Singh returned from his victorious campaign, he received the news of a son having been born to him on 13TH November 1780. He named his son Ranjit Singh, Victor in War, and celebrated the event with great rejoicing. Continuing his campaign of conquest, Mahan Singh took Pindi Bhattian, Sahival, Isa Khel and Jhang. He then seized Kotli Loharari, in the neighbourhood of Sialkot. In 1782, he, like his father, got involved in the affairs of Jammu. Taking advantage of the internecine feud between the Jammu brothers, he plundered the town, collecting a huge booty. Mahan Singh fell seriously ill with dysentery, and died in April 1790.

Sukha Singh, Sardar

Sukha Singh had heard with great fascination stories of Sikhs' daring and sacrifice in those days of fierce persecution and joined the Jatha or band of Sardar Shiam Singh. Once taking up the challenge thrown by Qazi `Abdul Rahman, the Kotwal of Amritsar, to the Sikhs to come, if they dared, for a dip in their holy pool, Sukha Singh went to Amritsar in broad daylight, made his ablutions and, loudly declaring who he was, rode away to the safety of the woods. An immediate pursuit led by the infuriated Qazi resulted in an encounter with the Sikhs in which the Qazi himself was killed. Sukha Singh accompanied Mahtab Singh to Amritsar in August 1740 to chastise the notorious Masse Khan Rarighar, the successor of the Qazi `Abdul Rahman as Kotwal. This further enhanced Sukha Singh's popularity among the Khalsa and he soon became the leader of a separate Jatha of his own. Early in 1746, he and Sardar Jassa Singh Ahluwalia pushed northwards and entered the Emlnabad territory in Gujranwala district where they were attacked by the local Jagirdar, Jaspat Rai, brother of Lakhpat Rai, the Diwan of Yahiya Khan, the governor of Lahore. Jaspat Rai was killed in the encounter. This led to the vengeful Lakhpat Rai's relentless campaign against the Sikhs ending on 1ST May 1746 in what is known in Sikh history as a Ghallughara or holocaust.

The Sardars

Sukha Singh, Sardar (Cont.)

During this fateful battle, Sukha Singh's leg was fractured by a direct hit from an enemy swivel. He immediately tied his leg to his saddle with his own turban and continued to fight and lead his men across the Rivers Ravi, Beas and Satluj. It was three days later, after he had taken the survivors of the Ghallughara to the safety of the sandy desert of Malva that he got his injury properly dressed. Early in 1752, as Sukha Singh and his Jatha lay in the forest along the River Ravi north of Lahore, Ahmad Shah Durrani came out leading his third invasion into India and camped at Shahdara preparatory to an attack on the Punjab capital. Sukha Singh, out on a foraging expedition north of the river, encountered a strong body of enemy troops. A fierce action took place in which Sukha Singh and his men died fighting to a man. This was sometime during the first half of January 1752.

Wazlrabadia, Jodh Singh, Sardar

Jodh Singh Wazlrabadia was a powerful Sikh chief. He possessed the Parganahs; of Wazirabad, Karial, Mitranwali and Talwandi Musa Khan, comprising about 500 villages. At the siege of Sodhra in 1792, Jodh Singh is said to have betrayed Maha Singh. Sahib Singh, who was besieged in the fort, was short of powder, and his surrender was certain. But Jodh Singh, who feared that Maha Singh would become too powerful were Sahib Singh to give in, supplied the latter with ammunition. Mahar Singh had been dangerously ill throughout the siege, and this treachery hastened his end. The action of Jodh Singh is said to have been the cause of Ranjit Singh's hostility towards him. But when Ranjit Singh found that the Wazirabad chief was too strong for him, he endeavoured to gain by stratagem what he was unable to take by force. He invited Jodh Singh to Lahore, but the latter brought with him a large force. This Ranjit Singh desired him to send back which he, too proud to show fear, did, and arrived at Lahore with only 200 picked men. Next day he attended court, leaving his escort outside. He was received by Ranjit Singh with the greatest courtesy. Suddenly however the Maharaja arose from his seat and made a sign to his attendants to seize the Sardar. Jodh Singh drew his sword and dared them to attack him, for, as he declared, he did not know how to flee. Ranjit Singh loved a brave man. He became Jodh Singh's admirer and dismissed him with honour and rich gifts. Jodh Singh died in 1809.

THE CIS-SATLUJ SARDARS

The Cis-Satluj Sardars did not serve under the banner of the Dal Khalsa. They were expelled from Sikh Confederacy and Dal Khalsa for making alliances with the enemy (Afghans), betraying and attacking other Sikh Misls. As they came to maturity at the decline of the Mughal power, they faced the ambitions of the lion of the Punjab; Maharajah Ranjit Singh. Cis-Satluj states were saved from annihilation by the arrival of the British. The Cis-Satluj Sikhs were familiar with the concept of Imperial authority and willingly accepted the British protection. The active British influence in Cis-Satluj was visible when Cis-Satluj Sardars approached the British Government for seeking protection against the rising power of Maharaja Ranjit Singh. There is no doubt that Ranjit Singh was very moderate towards the Cis-Satluj Rajas and he was never hesitant to solve their intricate problems whenever such situations occurred. But, in due course, with the rising power of Ranjit Singh, they became suspicious of his designs and hence sought British protection. Accordingly, the leaders of the Cis-Satluj Sikh states, including the rulers of Patiala, Nabha and Jind decided in a conclave to send a deputation to the British Resident in Delhi, Mr. Seton. Consequently, a delegation consisting of the Raja of Jind, Bhag Singh, Bhai Lal Singh of Kaithal the Diwan of Patiala, Sardar Chain Singh and the confidential agent of Nabha Ghulam Hussain, was despatched to Delhi and presented their memorandum to the British Resident on 1st April 1809. They pledged their loyalty to every succeeding power in Delhi and formally sought protection of the British. The British were very glad to entertain their offer and accordingly took them under their protection. The Maharajah realised the power of the British, and signed a treaty of friendship with them on 25th April 1809. The Maharaja agreed not to carry his military exploits in the Cis-Satluj territories. Thus the hope of the Maharaja to unite the whole Sikh nation met with a disaster. The Cis-Satluj Misls emerged as the Sikh Princely States in British India. However, with the secure borders at Satluj he was able to extend and secure his kingdom.

In 1948 the Sikh Princely States of Cis-Satluj signed the Instrument of Accession with the Independent India, thus facilitating the process of national integration and the loss of their independent status.

The Cis-Satluj Sardars

Ala Singh, Raja

Ala Singh was a Sikh Misl leader who became the first ruling chief of Patiala. He was born in 1691 at Phul, in present day Bhatinda district of the Punjab, the third son of Bhai Ram Singh. Ala Singh's career of conquest began soon after the execution of Banda Singh Bahadur in 1716 when central Punjab lay in utter confusion. Ala Singh was living at Phul about 40 km from Bhatinda. He gathered around him a band of dashing and daring young men. In 1722, he set up his headquarters at Barnala and his territory comprised 30 odd villages. At Barnala, Ala Singh defeated in 1731 Rai Kalha of Raikot, an influential chief with a large force at his command. Aided by roving bands of the Dal Khalsa (Sikh army), he ransacked and annexed several villages belonging to the Bhattis. He also founded several new villages such as Chhajali, Dirba, Laungoval and Sheron. For a period Ala Singh remained in the custody of Ali Muhammad Khan Ruhila, Mughal governor of Sirhind from 1745-48, and was released only when the latter fled his capital at the approach, in February 1748, of the Afghan invader Ahmad Shah Durrani. In the battle fought on 11TH March 1748, near Manupur, northwest of Sirhind, between the Mughals and Ahmad Shah Durrani, Ala Singh sided with the former. He cut off Durrani's supplies and captured his camels and horses. In 1749, Ala Singh defeated and repulsed Farid Khan, a Rajput chieftain. Three years later, Ala Singh captured the district of Sanaur with its eighty four villages. In 1763 Baba Ala Singh laid the foundation of the Patiala fort known as Qila Mubarak, around which the present city of Patiala developed. In the Vadda Ghallughara or Great Carnage of February 1762, Ala Singh remained neutral. Ahmad Shah punished him with the devastation of the town of Barnala. Ala Singh took the Pahul in 1732 at the hands of Nawab Kapur Singh, leader of the Dal Khalsa. He was an ally of Jassa Singh Ahluwalia in the attack on Sirhind in 1764. Later he purchased this town from Bhai Buddha Singh, to whom it had been assigned by the Khalsa. On 29TH March 1761, Ahmad Shah Durrani had already recognized by a written decree the sovereignty of Ala Singh over the territories held by him. At the time of his seventh invasion of India, he confirmed him in the government of Sirhind (1765) and granted him the title of Raja, with the robes of honour as well as with a drum and a banner as insignia of royalty. Ala Singh died on 7Th August 1765 at Patiala and was cremated in the fort, now inside the city.

The Cis-Satluj Sardars

Amar Singh, Raja

In 1765, Amar Singh succeeded his grandfather, Ala Singh, to the throne of Patiala. In 1766, he captured Payal and Isru from the Kotla Afghans, with the help of Trans Satluj Sikhs under Jassa Singh Ahluwalia, from whom he had received the rites of Khalsa baptism. Payal was annexed to Patiala state, while Isru was given to Jassa Singh Ahluwalia. Ahmad Shah Durrani's invasion of the country in 1767 proved very beneficial to the rising power of Amar Singh, who sent his vakils to the Shah with presents. The Shah granted him the subahdari (governorship) of Sirhind with the title of Rajai Rajgan. He was also given a flag and a drum as insignia of absolute authority. He paid a lakh of rupees to the Shah to secure the release of several thousand Hindus taken captive in the vicinity of Mathura and Saharanpur. He issued coins in the name of Ahmad Shah. In 1768, Amar Singh marched against, Gharib Das of Mani Majra who, after the death of Ala Singh, had captured the fort and district of Pinjore. Amar Singh, helped by the hill rulers of Hindur, Kahlur and Nahan, defeated Gharib Das and captured the Pinjore fort. Gharib Das was, however, not fully reduced to submission. Raja Amar Singh marched against him again in 1778. Gharib Das paid a large sum of money to the Patiala chief and retained control of his territory. Amar Singh next attacked the fort of Kot Kapura, killing Jodh Singh, the local chief, in the battle. In 1771, he occupied the district of Bhatinda subduing Sukhchain Singh to whom the Fort of Gobindgarh, commanding the town, belonged. Three years later, he reduced Saifabad, a strong fort 7 km to the northeast of Patiala. In 1774, he occupied the Bhatti country lying south of Patiala. Fatehbad, Sirsa and the fort of Rania now passed into his hands. In 1777 he overran Faridkot and Kot Kapura but did not attempt to annex them. In 1779, he frustrated the designs of Abdul Ahad Khan against Sikh territories in the Malva. He received help from Jassa Singh Ahluwalia, Jassa Singh Ramgarhia, Tara Singh Ghaiba and Jodh Singh, of Wazirabad, and repulsed the Mughal expedition at the village of Ghuram. By his extensive conquests and by the shrewd political alliances he made with the rulers of Nahan and Bikaner, and with the Misldari Sardars, Amar Singh had made Patiala the most powerful state between the Yamuna and the Satluj. Raja Amar Singh died at Patiala on 5TH February 1782 in the prime of his youth.

The Cis-Satluj Sardars

Sahib Singh, Raja

Sahib Singh was born on 18TH August 1773 to Raja Amar Singh and Rani Raj Kaur. He ascended the throne of Patiala after his father's death in February 1781. In 1787 he was married, at Amritsar, to Ratan Kaur, daughter of Ganda Singh, the Bhangi chief. Five years later, he contracted a second marriage, with As Kaur, daughter of Gurdas Singh Chattha. During his minority, Bibi Rajinder Kaur, the aunt of the Raja, managed the affairs of the state. Even when he assumed ruling powers, Sahib Singh, was guided and helped by his sister, Sahib Kaur, who by her strong leadership saved the state in 1794 from usurpation by the Marathas. After Sahib Kaur's death the real power passed into the hands of Rani As Kaur, the Raja's wife. Raja Sahib Singh died at Patiala on 26TH March 1813. It was during his rule that the state came under British protection.

Karam Singh, Maharaja

Karam Singh (1798-1845), who ascended the throne of Patiala on 30Th June 1813, was born on 16TH October 1798 at Patiala, the son of Raja Sahib Singh and Rani As Kaur. He was married to Rup Kaur, daughter of Bhariga Singh of Thanesar. Maharaja Karam Singh helped the British in 1814 in checking Gurkha incursions into the Punjab hills and secured in return a large tract in the Himalayan foothills. He was an able ruler and a devout Sikh. He had shrines built in honour of the Gurus at many historical sites within his state and outside, making endowments for their maintenance. Maharaja Karam Singh died at Patiala on 23RD December 1845.

Narinder Singh, Maharaja

Narinder Singh (1824-1862), succeeded his father, Maharaja Karam Singh, to the Patiala throne on 18TH January 1846. After the annexation of the Sikh State of Lahore to the British dominions in March 1849, the Patiala ruler was generally acknowledged as a spokesman for the Sikh community. Maharaja Narinder Singh cemented his alliance with the British by his ready support of guns, carriage, loans and troops during the uprising of 1857. He was invested with the Order of the Star of India on 6TH November 1861 and, in 1862, he was made a member of the Viceroy's Legislative Council. Narinder Singh died at Patiala on 13TH November 1862 after a short illness and was succeeded by his ten year old son, Mohinder Singh.

The Cis- Satluj Sardars

Mohinder Singh, Maharaja
Mohinder (1852-1876), was born at Patiala on 16TH September 1852, the son of Maharaja Narinder Singh. He ascended the Patiala throne on 29TH January 1862 at the age of ten. The young Maharaja was fairly well educated and enlightened. He sponsored several works of public utility. A project he helped with a handsome contribution of 150,000 rupees was the construction of the Sirhind canal. The canal, opened in 1882, irrigated large areas of Patiala, Nabha and Jind as well as those of Ludhiana and Ferozepore districts in the British territory. Maharaja Mohinder Singh made a donation of seventy thousand rupees to the University College at Lahore, paid a lakh of rupees for the relief of the famine stricken people of Bengal, and founded in 1875 the Mohindra College at Patiala for the promotion of higher education in the state. This college, the oldest in the north-western region of India, and initially affiliated to Calcutta University, imparted education without charging any fees right up to the postgraduate stage and attracted students from distant parts of the country. Maharaja Mohinder Singh died at Patiala on 12TH April 1876. His work was continued by his son Rajinder Singh, who ascended the throne of Patiala after his father's death and died in November 1900 at the age of 28.

Bhupinder Singh, Maharaja
Bhupinder Singh, Knight Grand Commander of the Order of the Star of India, Knight Grand Commander of the Order of the Indian Empire, Knight of the Order of the British Empire, ruler of the Sikh state of Patiala, was one of the most colourful and influential Indian princes of the interwar years. Tall, robust, dashingly handsome, he was to the British the personification of the Punjabi martial races, a veritable "flower of Oriental aristocracy." In his own eyes, and in the eyes of many of his coreligionists, he was the temporal leader of Sikhism. Born on 12TH October 1891, Bhupinder Singh was only ten years old when the premature death of his father, Maharaja Sir Rajinder Singh, catapulted him into the public arena. He started ruling in his own right in 1909, and was invested with full powers on 3RD November 1910. However, the outbreak of war in 1914 was the first real turning point in Bhupinder Singh's career. Prior to 1914 Patiala had been just one of many medium sized states, having no special claims to distinction. During the war, under Bhupinder Singh's leadership, the state established itself as favoured ally of the British by contributing lavishly in men, money and materials to the imperial cause.

The Cis- Satluj Sardars

Bhupinder Singh, Maharaja (Cont.)

The Maharaja took a personal role in the war effort as Honorary Lieutenant Colonel of 1ST Ludhiana Sikhs. These earned Bhupinder Singh a clutch of imperial decorations, a seat at the Imperial War Conference of 1918, an appointment as Honorary Aide de Camp to the King Emperor and later an appointment as an Indian delegate to the League of Nations. Bhupinder Singh began to see himself as a future leader of the princely order and as a power broker in Sikh affairs. He was also a lavish patron of sport, endowing a gymnasium in London for use by Indian students and several cricket grounds in India. One of these, at Chail, the Patiala summer residence, 7,000 feet up in the foothills of the Himalayas, remains the highest playing field in the world. Bhupinder Singh beautified the city of Patiala by endowing it with new palace buildings, gardens and metalled roads. He established a High Court, numerous hospitals and schools and a beautiful Secretariat. He was Chancellor and Chief Patron of the Sikhs' premier educational institution the Khalsa College at Amritsar. Sapped by overindulgence, he died at Patiala, ostensibly from heart failure, on 22ND March 1938.

Maharaja Yadvinder Singh

Maharajah Yadvinder Singh (1913-1974), Grand Commander of the Indian Empire, Companion of the British Empire, Doctor of Laws from Banares and Punjab Universities, was the last hereditary ruler of the Indian princely state of Patiala. Born on 7TH January 1913 during the high noon of the British Raj, he lived to see India become an independent democratic republic. He was the premier ruling prince in the Punjab. Prominent in sports, courageous in war, persuasive in diplomacy, knowledgeable in botany and agriculture, modern India's nearest, equivalent to ideal renaissance man. Yadvinder Singh's early life was moulded by his rank and environment. Son of Maharaja Bhupinder Singh, one of the most prominent of India's 600 odd ruling princes, Yadvinder Singh was brought up in a luxurious atmosphere. At the suggestion of the local British Resident, Bhupinder Singh sent his son, while still a young boy, to the Atchison College at Lahore. There he received a solid all-round education, acquired valuable habits of inquiry and self discipline, and distinguished himself on the cricket field. In 1930, after completing his education, he accompanied his father to the first Round Table Conference in London.

The Cis- Satluj Sardars

Maharaja Yadvinder Singh (Cont.)

He spent some time at the Punjab Police School, Phillaur, and acquired some training in revenue work back in Patiala. At his majority, in 1931, he was made Superintendent of Police for Patiala district, graduating two years later to the rank of Inspector General. In 1933, he was appointed the Chancellor of Khalsa College, Amritsar, and he held this position for a number of years. Seconded in 1935 to a crack Sikh unit of the Indian Army, he did valuable work helping in reconstruction after the terrible Quetta earthquake and earned a glowing tribute from the military authorities. Yadvinder Singh's public activities were, however, overshadowed by his sporting achievements. Patiala had always been synonymous with Indian cricket, boasting at Chail, the Maharaja's summer residence, the highest ground in the world. Encouraged to play the game by his father, who had captained India on the tour of England, Yadvinder Singh rapidly blossomed into a fine all-round player. He donned Indian colours in 1934 when he was selected to play against England. However, cricket was far from his only athletic accomplishment. Supple of limb and reaching almost 6' 4" when fully grown, he had no difficulty adapting successfully to a variety of games: he climbed, ran, played hockey, was north Indian tennis champion, and led the Patiala polo team. In his devotion to sport, he had followed in the footsteps of his father. In 1928, Bhupinder Singh had been elected Founder-President of the Indian Olympic Association, formed after India had won its first gold medal in the hockey competition at the IXth Olympiad in Amsterdam. On Bhupinder Singh's death in 1938, the members of the Association chose the son to replace the father. Yadvinder Singh continued as President until 1960, when he stepped down in favour of his brother, Bhalendra Singh. During his 22 year term, he cemented India's connection with the international Olympic movement, fostered the establishment of branches of the Association in several provinces and encouraged the formation of national federations for individual Olympic sports. 1938 was indeed a momentous year for the young prince. It was clouded, of course, by his father's death; but on the brighter side it saw his election to the Presidency of the Olympic Association. He became the ruler of a kingdom of 5,932 square miles having a population of nearly two million. In the year of his accession was also solemnized his marriage to Mohinder Kaur, daughter of a Patiala nobleman, Harchand Singh Jeji.

The Cis-Satluj Sardars

Maharaja Yadvinder Singh (Cont.)

On the outbreak of World War II in 1939, Maharaja Yadvinder Singh founded the Khalsa Defence of India League. Sikh enlistment to the Army was accelerated by the efforts of the Maharaja, who himself went to the Italian theatre of war and to the Middle East and Malaya. His support of the war effort was rewarded in 1944 by an honorary appointment as Lieutenant Colonel in the Indian army. Viceroy Lord Wavell, who described Yadvinder Singh as "one of the best of the princes, really interested in managing his state on progressive lines," caused him to be appointed an aide-de-camp to the British King and supported his election as Chancellor of the Chamber of Princes in March 1946. The Maharaja became a leading figure in the politics of the Indian princes. When after the failure of the Cripps Mission in 1942, the British Government sent to India the Cabinet Mission under the leadership of Lord Patrick Lawrence; the Maharaja of Patiala led a Princes' Delegation to the Mission. He was also a Member of the Negotiations Committee of the Princes which, under the Cabinet Mission Plan, was to negotiate with the representatives of British India the terms on which the states would accede to the Indian Union. Patiala was also one of the first princely states to decide on 13TH March 1947 to participate in the Constituent Assembly and to send up its representatives as members. On 1ST August 1947, twenty two rulers of states, with Maharaja Yadvinder Singh leading, signified their decision to accede to the Indian Union and others followed in quick succession. In May 1948 he gave his assent to the merger of Patiala with seven other Punjab states to constitute what came to be known as the Patiala and East Punjab States Union (PEPSU). When the decision to partition the Punjab was announced, Yadvinder Singh went to Viceroy Mountbatten and pleaded with him to fix the boundary on the basis of landed and religious property rather than population, thereby preserving the central Punjab as a Sikh homeland. Mountbatten refused, and the Radcliff Commission opted for a line which left many Sikhs and Sikh shrines in Pakistan. Yadvinder Singh then took his case to Sardar Patel, urging that the rehabilitation of the Sikhs should be made a priority of government policy. Sikh refugees should be fully compensated for their losses, and the community as a whole assured of its rightful place in the polity of India through the incorporation of suitable provisions in the new Constitution. In subsequent letters to the Sardar, he enjoined the Government to open negotiations with Pakistan for the return of Sikh religious records and the preservation of untended Gurdwaras.

The Cis- Satluj Sardars
Maharaja Yadvinder Singh (Cont.)

In November 1956, in accordance with the recommendations of the States Reorganization Commission, PEPSU was merged with East Punjab and Yadvinder Singh, who had been Rajpramukh of the state since its inception, found himself for the first time in his adult life without a fulltime occupation. But soon thereafter Prime Minister Jawaharlal Nehru sent him to New York as a Member of the Indian Delegation to the 11TH session of the United Nations General Assembly. In 1958, Yadvinder Singh represented India in Paris at the 10th annual conference of UNESCO, and in 1959, 1961, 1962, 1963, 1967 and 1969 he led the Indian team at meetings of the UN Food and Agricultural Organization (FAO) a task for which the horticultural knowledgeable Maharaja was well suited. In 1960, the Government made him Chairman of the newly created Indian Council of Sports, a body designed to oversee the whole sporting sphere and advise on the allocation of public money to sports teams and facilities. In 1965, the Lal Bahadur Shastri Government appointed him to the prestigious post of Indian Ambassador in Rome, where he served until 1967. The decade 1956-1966 was a relatively quiet and relaxed period in Yadvinder Singh's life, much of it spent abroad. As a diplomat he shunned public forums, preferring to exercise his considerable personal charm in private informal gatherings. In February 1967 elections were held for the Punjab legislature; Yadvinder Singh decided to stand as an Independent Candidate, and was voted in by a handsome majority. His short parliamentary career was over as he soon realized that he was unfit for the role of a professional politician. He continued, however, to involve himself closely in Sikh affairs. He was chosen President of the Guru Gobind Singh Foundation as well as of the Guru Nanak Foundation. Throughout the latter part of 1969, Yadvinder Singh continued his association with FAO and the Council of Sports and in 1970 took on a new role as Chairman of the Indian Horticulture Development Council. In 1971, Yadvinder Singh took up his second and last permanent diplomatic posting at The Hague in the Netherlands. Three years later, on 17TH June 1974, he suffered a severe heart attack and died. He was 61 years of age. His body was flown to India and was cremated with full State Honours on 21ST June at Patiala in the family crematorium, the Shahi Samadhari.

The Cis-Satluj Sardars

Gajpat Singh, Raja

Gajpat Singh (1738-1789), founder of the Sikh state of Jind, was born on 15TH April 1738, the second son of Sukhchain Singh, who was the younger brother of Gurdit Singh, an ancestor of the ruling family of Nabha. In 1755, at the age of seventeen, Gajpat Singh seized a large tract of country including Jind and Safidori. In 1764, he joined the Khalsa Dal under Jassa Singh Ahluwalia and took part in the conquest of Sirhind. He then overran Panipat and Karnal. In 1766, he made Jind his capital. Unlike other Sikh chiefs, he continued to acknowledge the Mughal authority in Delhi and paid revenue to the Emperor. He obtained the title of Raja under a royal decree from Emperor Shah Alam II in February 1772. Gajpat Singh was constantly at war with the Nabha chief, and seized his territories Amioh, Bhadsori and Sarigrur in 1774. Raja Amar Singh of Patiala and other Sikh chiefs compelled him to return the first two to Nabha, but Gajpat Singh retained Sarigrur which eventually became the capital of the Jind state. In 1774, Raja Gajpat Singh's daughter, Raj Kaur, was married to Mahar Singh of the Sukkarchakkia Misl. Raj Kaur became the mother of Maharaja Ranjit Singh. Raja Gajpat Singh was a strong ally of Raja Amar Singh of Patiala. He accompanied the Patiala chief on many of his expeditions, joining him in his incursions upon Sialba and Meerut. In 1789, while engaged in an expedition against refractory villages near Ambala, Gajpat Singh fell ill and was carried to Safidori where he died on 11TH November 1789.

Bhag Singh, Raja

Bhag Singh (1760-1819), succeeded his father, Gajpat Singh, to the throne of Jind state in 1789. Like his father, he was also a close ally of Patiala and joined them in 1794 against the Marathas. He was mainly responsible for checking the advance of George Thomas towards Sikh territories and later on of General Perron of the Maratha service. He maintained friendly relations with the British and accompanied Lord Lake to the River Beas in pursuit of Jaswant Rao Holkar. He was deputed by the British General to persuade his nephew, Maharaja Ranjit Singh, not to espouse the hopeless Maratha cause. Bhag Singh's mediation in behalf of the British helped pave the way for the first Anglo Sikh treaty of 1806. He gained in territory both from the British and Maharaja Ranjit Singh. Ludhiana, later acquired by the British for establishing a political agency, once belonged to him. Raja Bhag Singh died in 1819 and was succeeded by his son Fateh Singh.

The Cis- Satluj Sardars

Sarup Singh, Raja

Raja Fateh Singh of Jind died in 1822 and was succeeded by Sangat Singh who died in 1834. At the death of Sangat Singh, Raja Sarup Singh succeeded to the Jind throne. Sarup Singh was very tall and handsome. Sir Lepel Griffin writes in his The Rajas of the Punjab: "In person and presence he was eminently princely and the stalwart Sikh race could hardly show a taller or stronger man. Clad in armour, as he loved to be, at the head of his troops there was perhaps no other prince in India who bore himself so gallantly and looked so true a soldier." Sarup Singh had cordial relations with the British and his loyalty to them during the Anglo Sikh wars and the uprising of 1857 was rewarded with the grant of territories, the right of adoption in case of failure of direct heirs and other concessions. He was granted Dadri in Haryana and thirteen villages near Sahgrur, a house in Delhi and an eleven gun salute. He introduced many reforms in his state on the British model, particularly concerning revenue and police administration. Raja Sarup Singh died on 26th January 1864, and was succeeded by his son, Raghbir Singh.

Raghbir Singh, Raja

Raghbir Singh (1834-1887), son of Raja Sarup Singh, ascended the throne of Jind on 31st March 1864 after the death of his father. He was an able and enlightened ruler, indefatigable in his efforts to promote the prosperity of his people. He built the town of Sarigrur on the model of the Rajput city of Jaipur. He helped the British with men and money during the second Afghan war (1878-80) and was rewarded with the title of Rajai Rajgan in perpetuity. Raja Raghbir Singh died in 1887, and was succeeded by his grandson, Ranbir Singh, as his only son, Balbir Singh, had predeceased him.

Ranbir Singh, Maharaja

Ranbir Singh (1879-1948), son of Balbir Singh and a grandson of Raja Raghbir Singh, was born at Sangrur on 11th October 1879. He ascended the gaddi of Jind state in 1887 and was invested with ruling powers in 1899. Deaf from a relatively early age, Maharaja Ranbir Singh lived until 1948 and witnessed fifty momentous years from his throne. He died on 1st April 1948, and was succeeded by his son, Rajbir Singh, during whose time Jind state joined the Patiala and East Punjab States Union (PEPSU).

The Cis- Satluj Sardars

Hamir Singh, Raja

Gurdit Singh had occupied large tracts of land, during the struggle and expulsion of the Afghans from the Punjab. His grandson Hamir Singh was a brave and energetic chief and added largely to his possessions. He founded the town of Nabha in 1755. In 1764, he joined Ala Singh of Patiala and the Dal Khalsa in the conquest of Sirhind, when Zin Khan, the Muhammadan Governor was slain and received the Parganahs of Amioh as his share of spoils. He conquered Rori from Rahimdad Khan in 1776. Hamir Singh was the first chief of Nabha who established a mint, which may be accepted as sign of his complete independence. Hamir Singh died in 1783.

Jasvant Singh, Raja

Jasvant Singh succeeded his father, Raja Hamir Singh, to the throne of Nabha in 1783 at the age of eight, under the guardianship of his stepmother, Mai Deso, a very resourceful and energetic woman. In 1790, after the death of Mai Deso, he assumed the reins of government into his own hands. Jasvant Singh conducted protracted campaigns, first against Jind and then against Patiala, to regain disputed territory for his state. His feud with Jind ended in 1789 with the death of the Jind chief, Gajpat Singh. With the help of General Perron of the Maratha service, he succeeded in checking the advance of the Irish adventurer, George Thomas. In 1804, he entered into alliance with Lord Lake against Jasvant Rao Holkar. In 1805, Raja Jasvant Singh, in company with Raja Bhag Singh of Jind, appealed to Maharaja Ranjit Singh to arbitrate his dispute with Patiala and though the dispute was not resolved, Jasvant Singh was able to extend his territory with grants from Ranjit Singh. Despite these favours, Jasvant Singh joined hands with the other Satluj princes in seeking and accepting British protection in 1809. Jasvant Singh helped the British in the Gurkha war in 1814 as well as in the Kabul campaign in 1838. Raja Jasvant Sirigli was a popular prince much loved by his subjects. Writing about him, Sir David Ochterlony, British diplomat and soldier, said, "Jaswant Singh is one of the principal Sirdars under our protection and by far superior in manner, management, and understanding to any of them I have yet seen." Sir Lepel Griffin considered him "the nearest approach to the civilised among the whole set of rude barons." Raja Jasvant Sirigli died at Nabha on 22ND May 1840.

The Cis- Satluj Sardars

Hira Singh, Maharajah
Maharaja Jasvant Singh of Nabha died in 1840 and was succeeded by his son Devinder Singh. In 1845, during the Anglo - Sikh war, Devinder Singh withheld supplies from the British, and as punishment was deposed in 1846 (died in confinement in 1865). Devinder's son, Bharpur Singh, had been installed as the Maharaja in 1847. Bharpur Singh died in 1863, leaving no heir. The younger brother of Bharpur Singh, Bhagwan Singh, was installed in 1864 but later died in 1871 without heirs. Hira Singh, born on 19TH December 1843, ascended the throne of Nabha state on 10TH August 1877 after Raja Bhagvan Singh, who had died issueless and without adopting an heir. Hira Singh ruled for forty years and did much for the welfare of the people of the state and of the Sikhs in general. He despatched contingents of troops to fight in most of the major frontier campaigns and was duly rewarded by the British with many honours, including the titles of Rajai Rajgan and Maharaja. Maharaja Hira Singh provided funds for the establishment of the Khalsa Printing Press at Lahore, supported the Khalsa College at Amritsar and promoted the reformist (Anand) form of Sikh marriage. He also patronised Max Arthur Macauliffe who was then engaged in his monumental work 'The Sikh Religion'. Maharaja Hira Singh was one of the ablest of Nabha rulers: wise, liberal and pious. Legends about his justice and munificence are still current in the countryside. He died at Nabha on 25TH December 1911 and was succeeded by his son, Ripudaman Singh.

Ripudaman Singh, Maharaja
Ripudaman Singh was in France when the news reached him of his father's death on 25TH December 1911. He came back to India, and ascended the throne of Nabha on 24TH January 1912. Under British pressure he signed a letter of voluntary abdication on 7TH July 1923, and the British government formally deposed him on 9TH July 1923. He was sent to Dehra Dun on an annual pension of Rs 300,000. He was removed from Dehra Dun in 1926 to Kodaikanal, in the far South. He remained unbent and unrepentant. Early in 1927 he went on pilgrimage to Sri Abichalnagar Hazur Sahib, Nanded, where he took the Khalsa pahul and was renamed Gurcharan Singh. He died at Kodaikanal on 13^{Th} December 1942. His son Prince Pratap Singh was proclaimed ruler of Nabha and the state was placed under a British administration. In 1948 Nabha State joined the Patiala and East Punjab States Union (PEPSU).

The Cis-Satluj Sardars

Nihal Singh, Raja

Nihal Singh, son of Fateh Singh Ahluwalia, succeeded to the Ahluwalia chieftaincy on the death of his father in 1836. In his youth he was favourite of Maharajah Ranjit Singh and was recipient of the towns of Nur Mahal and Kalal Majra and other occasional bounties. In the first Anglo-Sikh war, his sympathies lay with the Khalsa Durbar. In spite of treaty obligations with the British, he afforded them little assistance. On the contrary, the Ahluwalia troops, cavalry, infantry, and artillery, fought on the side of the Sikhs both at Badhowal and Aliwal. He was penalised by the British by the confiscation of his Cis-Satluj territories. Nihal Singh died on 13TH September 1852.

Randhir Singh, Maharaja

Randhir Singh was like his great grandfather, Jassa Singh Ahluwalia; his reign was marked with daily aggrandizement of his power and influence and of his very attractive qualities. The estates of Fatehbad, which were the ancestral patrimony of the Ahluwalia dynasty, were resumed by the British government after the demise of Raja Nihal Singh, like similar life – tenure Jagirs of other Sardars. But Maharaja Randhir Singh received them back from the British Government after his meritorious conduct in the Sepoy Mutiny of 1857, when he led a contingent to Oudh which did good service. He also received a grant of land in Oudh, 700 m² in extent, yielding a gross rental of 89,000 Rupees. In Oudh, however, he exercised no sovereign powers, occupying only the status of a large landholder, with the title of Raja-i-Rajagan. In the Punjab his estate evolved into a British protected Princely state of Kapurthala, and the state's forces were put at British disposal. The Kapurthala state forces went on to serve in Afghanistan 1878-79, and Punjab Frontier 1897-98. During the First World War they fought against the Germans in East Africa and then in Afghanistan in 1919. During the Second World War the Kapurthala forces served against the Japanese in Malaya. The descendants of Jassa Singh Ahluwalia ruled Kapurthala state for more than a century until it merged with the Patiala and East Punjab Union (PEPSU) in 1948 after the British withdrew from India.

The Cis-Satluj Sardars

Kapur Singh, Sardar

Sardar Kapur Singh an ancestor of the Faridkot ruling house was born the son of Lala in 1628. He succeeded in 1643 his uncle, Bhallan, to the chaudhanat or headship of the Brar Jatts. He was a brave and able man. He consolidated his possessions winning many victories over Bhatti and other tribes in his neighbourhood. He at first resided at Panj Grain, but subsequently founded Sarlivala, now a deserted place near Bagiana, which he soon abandoned for a new site, Kot Kapura, named after himself, which he is said to have founded in 1661 at the suggestion of Bhatti Bhagatu, a holy man who was an ancestor of the Kaithal family. The reputation for justice and benevolence which Kapura enjoyed induced many immigrants to settle in Kot Kapura, which soon became a place of considerable importance. During his long life, Kapur Singh had the rare honour of serving Guru Har Rai and Guru Gobind Singh during their travels in his part of the country. It is said that he received the rites of Sikh initiation at the hands of Guru Gobind Singh who bestowed upon him a sword and shield, still preserved in the family. In 1708, at the age of eighty, Kapur Singh was treacherously assassinated by his old rival Isa Khan, a Manjh Rajput, with whom he had a longstanding feud and who, in turn, fell at the hands of his revengeful sons, Sukhia, Sema and Mukhia

Harindar Singh, Raja

Faridkot was captured in 1803 by Ranjit Singh, but was one of the Cis-Satluj states that came under British protection after the 1809 Treaty of Amritsar and the state's forces were put at British disposal. During the Sikh wars in 1845, Raja Pahar Singh aided the British, and was rewarded with an increase of territory. Faridkot forces aided the British in suppressing the Sepoy Mutiny in 1857. They went on to serve in East Africa and in France and Flanders during the First World War. During the Second World War, they fought against the Japanese in Burma. The state forces were absorbed into the Indian Army in 1948. The Princely state of Faridkot merged with the Patiala and East Punjab Union (PEPSU) in 1948 after the British withdrew from India.

The last Ruler of Faridkot was HH Farzand-i-sadaat Nishan Hazrat-i-kaisar-i-hind Raja Sir Harindar Singh Brar Bans Bahadur.

The Cis- Satluj Sardars

Desu Singh, Bhai

Bhai Gurbaksh Singh was a close associate of Ala Singh of Patiala and had carved for himself some territories around Sirhind and Kaithal, besides his ancestral possessions in several villages around Bhuchcho, near Bhatinda. After his death in 1764, Desu Singh became head of the clan. Desu Singh marched on Kaithal and defeating Bikh Baksh and Nihmat Khan, two brothers in possession of Kaithal, established himself there as an independent chief sometime between 1764 and 1768. He began further to extend his territories and seized the town of Thanesar with one of its two forts. Bhai Desu Singh fell out with Raja Amar Singh, of Patiala, in 1778, because he did not support the Raja in his punitive action against Hari Singh, of Sialba, who had been friendly with the Kaithal chief. After dealing with the Sialba chief, Raja Amar Singh sent a force against Kaithal, too, but an attack was averted by the intercession of some of the Bhai brothers. Bhai Desu Singh died at Kaithal in 1781.

Lal Singh, Sardar

At the death of Desu Singh, Sardar Lal Singh, became chieftain of the Kaithal clan. He was regarded as the most powerful of the Cis-Satluj Sardars at the time of the British advance northwards, in 1809, after the Raja of Patiala. He was a very able man, though utterly untrustworthy, and so violent and unscrupulous the English authorities had the greatest difficulty in persuading him to maintain anything like order in his territories. He acquired immense tracts of country by plundering his neighbours on all sides, and he succeeded in regaining possession of much coveted Thanesar after he had been kept out of possession for many years by his old enemy Bhanga Singh. He waited on General Ochterlony and having offered his assistance in the Gurkha War, was liberally treated, and was allowed to retain the territories of Chausatha and Gohana, under condition of furnishing 500 Sowars, for whose support eight additional villages were set apart. He joined the British in the pursuit of Jaswant Rao Holkar up to the Satluj border, and received a sanad acknowledging his services in connection with the treaty made on that occasion with Maharajah Ranjit Singh. In 1819, the Government allowed him to succeed to the share of the estate held by Mai Bhagbari, the widow of his first cousin Karam Singh. Partab Singh the elder son and then the younger son, Udai succeeded, but on the death of the latter without issue in 1843, the whole of the Kaithal estate lapsed to the British Government.

The Cis-Satluj Sardars

Gurbaksh Singh, Raja

Gurbaksh Singh was a Sandhu Jatt, belonging to the village of Kalsia in Lahore district. He received Sikh initiatory rites at the hands of the revered Bhai Mani Singh at Amritsar in the time of Nawab Zakariya Khan of Lahore. As a mark of mutual friendliness, he exchanged turbans with Karora Singh, the Karorasinghia Misl chief, and participated in several expeditions of the Dal Khalsa. At the time of the conquest of Sirhind in January 1764, he seized the parganah of Chhachhrauli, now in Jagadhari tahsll of Haryana, comprising 114 villages, and founded an independent principality called Kalsia after the name of his native village. He went on to capture Bambeli parganah in Hoshiarpur district and collected immense wealth from different places in Haryana and Rajasthan. Some of his villages had been seized by Raja Amar Singh of Patiala which he later recovered. Gurbaksh Singh died in 1785.

Jodh Singh, Raja

Jodh Singh son of Gurbaksh Singh succeeded him as head of the Kalsia principality. Jodh Singh by his great abilities and personal daring managed to secure the lands north of Ambala, consisting of the territories of Basi, Chhachhrauli and Chirak. At the height of his power, Jodh Singh's possessions is said to have yielded over five lakhs rupees annually. He considered himself the equal of the leading Phulkian chiefs, and was frequently at war with Nabha and Patiala. Raja Sahib Singh of Patiala was happy to give his daughter in marriage to his second son, Hari Singh, and thus secure the alliance of a most troublesome neighbour. When Maharaja Ranjit Singh attacked and occupied Naraingarh in the Shivalik in 1807, Jodh Singh was with him. In recognition of his services, Ranjit Singh presented him territories of Badala, Kameri and Chhabbal. Jodh Singh died in Multan, where he had been left in command of the troops after the siege of 1818. After his death, his son Sobha Singh assumed charge of Kalsia state and held it till his death in 1858. When Lahna Singh, his successor assumed power, the Kalsia territory was intact as a British protectorate. After Lahna Singh came Ranjit Singh Kalsia, then his son Ravi Sher Singh and finally Ravi Karan Singh. The Kalsia rajas held their estate till 1947 when it was merged with the Indian Union.

The Cis- Satluj Sardars

Churhr Singh, Sardar

Churhr Singh succeeded to the Chieftainship of the Bhadour Clan in 1773. This Chief was the most famous of all the Bhadour stock, and his prowess and energy added much to his ancestral possessions, and the fame of "Churhr Singh Ke Bar"; his victories over the Brars, and his charity to the poor, are still sung in many ballads, by the village bards. He was acknowledged arbiter in all disputes; people preferred their complaints before him, and he punished offenders severely. For all this Churhr Singh was the most notorious robber on the border; cattle-lifting was not named in the code of offences which he punished. In the year 1799, Churhr Singh was appointed Chaudhari and collector of revenue in the Pihora and Bhadour districts, by Timur Shah, who in that year had invaded India, desiring to recover some of the authority possessed by his father Ahmad Shah. After the death of Raja Amar Singh of Patiala and the succession of the weak minded Sahib Singh, the Bhadour Chief began to extend his possessions at the expense of Patiala State. He seized ninety villages in the neighbourhood of Bhadour, many of which he subsequently lost; attacked the Maler Kotla Afghans, whose villages were redeemed by Patiala giving certain others in exchange, and even gained for a time possession of the district of Barnala. But in the midst of his successes, treachery put an end to his life. On his road from Barnala he remained to rest at the village of Ghanne and was invited by a Brar of the name Sujjan to sleep in a small Burj or tower for the night. Churhr Singh, who was accompanied by his brother Dal Singh, suspected nothing; but their deceitful host, having drugged their liquor and seeing them in a deep sleep, surrounded the tower with armed men, and piling brushwood against the walls and doors, set it on fire. Awoken by the heat and noise and finding all exits barred, the two brothers mounted to the roof, from which they shot arrows at their enemies till the roof fell in and both perished in the flames. This happened in 1793.

Churhr Singh's sons Bir Singh and Dip Singh were alive when the British power felt its way up to the south bank of the river Satluj, and the Sardars claimed to deal direct with the British. This was objected to by Patiala, as Patiala claimed supremacy over the Bhadour Sardars. In 1858, Patiala supremacy was recognised as a reward for loyal services rendered in the years of the Sepoy Mutiny. All the rights of the Paramount Power were then yielded to Patiala. The decision was naturally distasteful to the Bhadour Sardars, as they were reduced to the level of ordinary Jagirdars.

The Cis- Satluj Sardars

Jai Singh, Sardar

Sardar Jai Singh, a Jatt Sikh of Majha living near the village of Atari in Amritsar district, joined hands with the Nishananvali Misl in its invasion of the Cis-Satluj tracts, fighting in the battle of Sirhind (1764) and assisting in the seizure of Ambala, Shahabad, Lidhrari, Amioh and Sarai Lashkar Khan. He obtained 34 villages as his share around Lidhrari and Kharar. Shortly afterwards Jai Singh suffered defeat with his associates at the hands of Ahmad Shah Durrani and had to take refuge in the hilly country north of Ambala. Raja Amar Singh of Patiala annexed his seven villages around Kharar. A serious discord erupted as Jai Singh found himself strong enough to claim his possessions. Eventually a compromise was arrived at, Patiala agreeing to surrender four of the villages. Jai Singh's daughter was married to Raja Jasvant Singh of Nabha. Jai Singh died in 1784. His son, Charhat Singh, who succeeded him, accepted British protection in 1809. He accompanied General Ochterlony's force into the Simla hill country in the campaign against the Nepal General, Amar Singh Thapa, in 1814, and gave good help in the matter of carriage and supplies. On his death the family was obliged to place themselves under the protection of the Nabha Chief.

Rai Singh, Sardar

Sardar Rai Singh, one of the leaders of the Karorsinghia Misl, was the son of Matab Singh of Mirarikot in Amritsar district, the avenger of the sacrilege perpetrated by Masse Khan, the Muslim chieftain, who had occupied the holy Harimandar and converted it into a place of revelry. Rai Singh was nursed back to health by the village elder, Natha Khahira, when he as a small child was grievously wounded and left as dead by an imperial force that had come in search of his father. As Rai Singh grew up, he joined the Jatha or band of Shiam Singh of Nari, a commander of the Karor Singhia, who gave him his daughter in marriage. At the conquest of Sirhind by the Sikhs in January 1764, Rai Singh occupied a number of villages in Samala of Ludhiana district. Rai Singh built a mud fort at Mirarikot where he lived until his death in 1809.

MAHARAJA RANJIT SINGH

Ranjit Singh (1780-1839), Maharaja of the Punjab, popularly called Shere Punjab, i.e. the Lion of the Punjab, was the most colourful, the most powerful and yet the most endearing figure in the history of the Sikhs. He ruled over a domain extending from the Khaibar Pass in the west to the River Satluj in the east, from the northern extremity of Kashmir to the deserts of Sindh in the south, comprising the provinces of Lahore, Multan, Peshawar and Kashmir, and their dependencies. Rising from a family of little political consequence and commanding no more than a small band of fighting horsemen, he was the first Indian in a thousand years to stem the tide of invasions from the northwest frontier and to carry his flag into the homeland of the traditional conquerors of Hindustan. Born on 13TH November 1780 at Gujranwala, now in Pakistan, Ranjit Singh was the only son of Mahar Singh Sukkarchakkia and Raj Kaur, daughter of Raja Gajpat Singh of Jind. He was given the name of Buddh Singh, which, in commemoration of an armed victory his father had won, was changed into Ranjit (Victor in Battle) Singh. An attack of smallpox during infancy deprived Ranjit Singh of the sight of his left eye. He attended no school and spent most of his time riding and in chase. He developed a passionate love for horses and had his first encounter with steel at the age of ten when he fought beside his father against the Bhangi chieftains. Ranjit Singh had lost his father soon after. Since he showed little interest in administrating the estates he had inherited, his mother and his late father's manager, looked after them until his maternal uncle, Dal Singh, and his mother in law, Sada Kaur, took over the management. In 1796 Ranjit Singh had married Mahitab Kaur, daughter of Sada Kaur, head of the Kanhaiya Misl. Sada Kaur had given him active support during the early part of his career of battles and conquests. Shah Zaman, the King of Kabul and a grandson of Ahmad Shah Durrani, made several frantic efforts to re-establish the Durrani power in India. In the autumn of 1796, he occupied the city of Lahore, but he had to retire to his country in January 1797 leaving behind his general Ahmad Shah Shaharichibashi as his deputy with 12,000 soldiers to deal with the Sikhs. The Sikhs followed the Shah all the way across the Jehlum and deprived him of much of his baggage. Shaharichi Khan, as the Afghan general was generally called by the Sikhs, planned to take the returning Sikhs by surprise and intercepted them near Ramnagar, but was killed in the battle that followed and his force was completely routed. Ranjit Singh distinguished himself in battle and his reputation rose from that of an obscure Sikh chieftain to the hero of the Punjab.

Maharaja Ranjit Singh

The humiliation of this defeat rankled in Shah Zaman's mind and, as soon as he had settled his domestic problems, he once more descended upon the Punjab, in the autumn of 1798. Ranjit Singh made no resistance and let the Shah occupy Lahore without opposition. On 27TH November 1798 Ranjit Singh retired to Amritsar to collect a Sikh force. With these men he defeated a detachment of Afghans despatched by the Shah and forced them to retire to Lahore. He followed them and encircled the capital. He cut off the Afghans' supply lines and burnt the standing crops in the neighbouring countryside. Ranjit Singh at this time thrice rushed upon the Samman Burj of the Fort with a small force, fired some shots, killed and wounded a number of the Afghans, and challenged the Shah to a hand-to-hand fight. But as there was no response from the other side, Ranjit Singh had to return without a trial of strength with the Durrani. There was news of fresh trouble in Afghanistan which led Shah Zaman again to turn his footsteps towards his home country. On 7TH July 1799, Ranjit Singh drove the Bhangi rulers out of Lahore and became master of the capital. The populace, largely consisting of Muslims and Hindus, welcomed him as their redeemer. Shah Zaman tried to regain diplomatically what he had failed to do militarily and proposed to invest Ranjit Singh with a title. Ranjit Singh accepted the compliment, and in return presented the Shah with some cannon the Afghans had lost during their retreat from the Punjab. On Baisakhi day, 12TH April 1801, Sahib Singh Bedi, a pious Sikh in direct descent from Guru Nanak, applied the ceremonial saffron mark to Ranjit Singh's forehead and proclaimed him Maharaja of the Punjab. For the coronation ceremonies Ranjit Singh refused to wear any emblems of royalty or sit on a throne. He continued to hold Durbar seated cross-legged in his chair as before. He had his coins struck in the name of the Guru, and did not lend them his effigy or name. The seal of the government likewise bore no reference to him. Despite the many sonorous titles, officials and others used for him, the one by which he preferred to be addressed was the plain Singh Sahib. Nor was the government related to him or to his family. It was Sarkar Khalsa ji, Government of the Honoured Khalsa; the court was known as Durbar Khalsa ji. Yet his intention was not to establish a Sikh theocracy, but a State in which all people, Muslims, Hindus and Sikhs, would enjoy equal rights and opportunities. His council of ministers consisted of men belonging to all those different communities. His army, though its nucleus remained Sikh, had large contingents of Muslims, mainly in the artillery.

Maharaja Ranjit Singh

Although punctilious in the observance of Sikh ritual, he joined his Muslim subjects in their religious celebrations as he joined his Hindu subjects at their festivals. The first task to which Ranjit Singh now applied himself was to bring the entire Punjab under his control. His closest collaborators in this were his mother in law, Sada Kaur, and Fateh Singh, chief of the Ahluwalias, with whom he had ceremonially exchanged turbans to mark their fraternal relationship. Their combined forces levied tribute on the Zamindars of Dhanni Pothohar and on the Afghan rulers of Kasur and Multan. The most significant achievement was the taking in 1802 of Amritsar, the chief trading centre of the Punjab and the holy city of the Sikhs. Amritsar was divided among a dozen families. The combined force of Ranjit Singh, Sada Kaur and Fateh Singh Ahluwalia reduced them one after the other and also captured the powerful fort of Gobindgarh. Equally valuable was the procurement of the services of Akali Phula Singh, a fearless and outspoken soldier who was destined to play a crucial role in several of Ranjit Singh's military campaigns. Ranjit Singh received a great welcome from the people of Amritsar. After paying homage at the Harimandar Sahib, he ordered the Temple to be rebuilt in marble and its domes to be covered with gold leaf. The capture of Amritsar added spiritual sanction to Ranjit Singh's temporal powers. He sent emissaries to the independent principalities in the province exhorting them to declare allegiance to the Sarkar Khalsa ji. At the same time he began to reorganize his army. First to feel the impact of the new army was Ahmad Khan Sial of Jhang, Punjab's premier breeder of horses. Ahmad Khan was defeated and reinstated as a vassal of the Lahore Durbar. Thus encouraged, Ranjit Singh carried out extensive reorganization of his army. Several new commanders came to the fore; Hari Singh Nalwa, Hukma Singh Chimni, Fateh Singh Kaliarivala, and Desa Singh Majithia. Heavy artillery was raised under a Muslim, Chaudhari Ghaus Khan. Ranjit Singh made it a daily practice to watch his troops at drill and manoeuvres. After the conquest of Jhang, the Maharaja was moving towards Multan when the news of the arrival of the Maratha fugitive Jasvant Rao Holkar in the Punjab reached him. Holkar was being pursued by Lord Lake, the British commander, who had come as far as the River Beas. Ranjit Singh hurried back to Amritsar where a meeting of the Sarbatt Khalsa, comprising the leading Sardars, was convened to decide by gurmatas or common resolution how to treat the Maratha chief and his pursuers.

Maharaja Ranjit Singh

The Maharaja could ill afford to make the Punjab a theatre of war between two foreign armies, especially when his own position was not yet secure. He therefore decided to have the issue settled by negotiations. He was eventually able to bring about reconciliation between the British and the Maratha chief and have all the latter's territories beyond Delhi restored to him. At the same time a treaty was entered into, on 1ST January 1806, between Lord Lake and the Sikh chiefs by which the Maharaja and Fateh Singh Ahluwalia agreed to "cause Jaswant Rao Holkar to remove with his army to the distance of 30 coss from Amritsar and... never hereafter hold any further connection with him," while Lord Lake undertook that so long as the conditions of this treaty were observed "the British armies shall never enter the territories of the said chieftains, nor will the British government form any plans for the seizure or the sequestration of their possessions or property." In the autumn of 1806, Ranjit Singh crossed the Satluj and toured the Malwa country receiving tribute from several Sardars, including Tara Singh Ghaiba, head of the Dallewalia Misl. He also settled a dispute which had arisen between the chiefs of Nabha and Patiala. On his way back to Lahore, the Maharaja was invited by Raja Sansar Chand of Kangra to help him expel the Gurkhas who had invaded his domains. Ranjit Singh marched up to Javalamukhi, at which the Gurkhas withdrew from the valley. In February 1807, Ranjit Singh's troops attacked Kasur whose chief, Nawab Qutb udDin, had failed to pay tribute. After a month of fierce fighting, the town was captured. Qutb ud Din was caught while fleeing the fort, but Ranjit Singh set him at liberty and made over to him as jagir some villages on the left bank of the River Satluj. A domestic quarrel between Raja Sahib Singh of Patiala on the one hand and his wife Rani As Kaur and the heir apparent Karam Singh on the other, gave Ranjit Singh another opportunity to cross over into the Malwa region. He settled the dispute in the Patiala family and once more took tribute from other Cis-Satluj chieftains. On his way back to his capital, he took Naraingarh from the Raja of Sirmur and, on the death of the head of the Dallewalia Misl, incorporated his estates into his kingdom. Another notable acquisition was the fort of Sheikhupura, near Lahore. It is clear that by the autumn of 1808 Ranjit Singh had made up his mind to subjugate the entire Cis-Satluj region, and, but for the arrival of the British mission in 1808 and continuing British interest in the area, his dream of uniting all the Sikhs under his supremacy would have been realized.

Maharaja Ranjit Singh

The British mission to the court of Ranjit Singh was the outcome of a supposed threat of French invasion under Napoleon Bonaparte. Later its primary object apparently became the reduction of Ranjit Singh's power. The British decided to extend their protection to the Sikh principalities south of the River Satluj, and demanded surrender of all conquests made by Ranjit Singh in this region subsequent to the arrival of the British mission at his court. Negotiations between the two powers led to the signing of a treaty of mutual friendship at Amritsar on 25TH April 1809. The treaty provided that the British government would count the Lahore Durbar among the most honourable powers and would in no way interfere with the Sikh ruler's dominions to the north of the Satluj. It however fixed the southern limit of his kingdom and barred further extension of Sikh frontier in that direction. Yet the establishment of peace and friendship between the two powers left Ranjit Singh free to pursue a course of conquest in the north and beyond the River Indus unhampered and to consolidate his power in the central and southern Punjab. One of the Maharaja's more decisive campaigns lay towards the northeastern hills. The incursion of the Gurkhas under Amar Singh Thapa into the Kangra valley made Raja Sansar Chand seek once again the help of Ranjit Singh, who himself led out an army. He defeated the Gurkhas at Ganesh Ghati on 24TH December 1809. He occupied Kangra Fort and held a royal Durbar, which was attended by the hill chiefs of Chamba, Nurpur, Kotia, Shahpur, Guler, Kahlur, Mandi, Suket and Kulu. Desa Singh Majithia was appointed governor of Kangra. On his return to his capital, Ranjit Singh launched expeditions to subdue scattered chiefships which still kept up a show of independence. The estates of the Singhpuria and of the Bhangis at Gujrat were confiscated. The Baluch tribes round Khushab and Sahival were tamed. Other territories seized were Jalandhar, Tarn Tarn, Jammu, Mandi, and Suket, the salt mines of Kheora, Daska and Halloval. Ranjit Singh did not spare his kinsmen and the estates of the Nakais and the Kanhaiyas were likewise reduced to fiefdoms. Ranjit Singh's major conquests began with the occupation of Multan in 1818. In 1819 Kashmir was annexed. He conquered Peshawar, Dera Ghazi Khan, Dera Ismail Khan, Hazara, Kohat, Tonk and Bannu in quick succession, but was, at first, content to rule these regions through the local Muhammadan chieftains, who acknowledged his over-lordship and paid tribute. He seized Peshawar in 1818, but gave it first to Jahandad Khan, then in 1923 to Yar Muhammad Khan and finally, in 1830, to Sultan Muhammad Khan as a feudatory.

Maharaja Ranjit Singh

Ranjit Singh conquered Dera Ghazi Khan in 1820, but gave it to the Nawab of Bahawalpur to govern. From Sultan Muhammad Khan of Peshawar, Ranjit Singh used to receive an annual tribute, while he kept one of Khan's children as a hostage in his court as a guarantee of good conduct. He subjugated Dera Ismail Khan in 1821, but gave it to the dispossessed Mankera ruler, Hafiz Muhammad Khan, as a tributary to Lahore. The neighbouring districts were made tributary in 1822 but not directly annexed. However, after the disturbances created by the fanatical Sayyid Ahmad Barelavi were quelled, there was a change in Ranjit Singh's policy regarding his Trans-Indus territories. Dera Ghazi Khan was brought under direct control in 1831, Peshawar in 1834; Tonk, Bannu and Dera Ismail Khan were annexed between 1832 and 1836. In the northwest the boundaries of the Sikh kingdom now extended into the base of the Yuzufzai territory, northeast of Peshawar, and up to Fatehgarh, a fort near the Khaibar Pass. In the southwest, it touched the undefined borders of Sindh beyond Rojhan and Mitlhankot, the junction of the rivers Satluj and Indus. Among the four major provinces comprising the Sikh kingdom, Lahore, where the central government was located, included the entire Majha country and the major cities of Lahore and Amritsar. The province of Multan included the dependencies all along the east bank of the River Indus, and the districts of Jhang, Dera Ismail Khan, Dera Ghazi Khan, Muzaffargarh and Leiah. The province of Peshawar comprised the valley of Peshawar and its dependencies across the River Indus and in the Yuzufzai region. The province of Kashmir included the whole valley of Kashmir, Muzaffarabad, Ladakh and Gilgit. There were besides tributary states in the hills, among them Bilaspur, Suket, Chamba, Rajauri, Ladakh and Iskardu. Some of the territories farmed out were Mandi, Kulu, Jasvan, and Kangra. Kutlehar, Siba, Nurpur, Haripur, Datarpur, Basohli, Chhachh, Hazara, Rawalpindi, Hasan Abdal, Dhanni, Katas, Chakval, Tonk, Bannu, Mankera, Ramnagar, Mittha Tiwana, Bhera, Khushab, Pind Dadan Khan, Gujrat, Wazirabad, Sialkot, the Jalandhar Doab and Sheikhupura. Besides, Ranjit Singh held large territories in the Cis-Satluj region. The administration of Maharaja Ranjit Singh may be described as a personalized military despotism based on popular will. Designated as the Sarkar Khalsa, it was an absolute centralized monarchy, but liberal and benevolent. Its chief merit was religious moderation and practical efficiency. Though based on military might and sustained by successive victories, it was extremely popular.

Maharaja Ranjit Singh

As absolute monarch, Ranjit Singh enjoyed great power which he wielded unhampered for the common-wellbeing of all his subjects, Hindu, Sikh, Muhammadan and others. For the purpose of provincial administration, the kingdom was roughly divided into four principal provinces, Lahore, Peshawar, Multan and Kashmir. The hill principalities and territories conquered from the Sardars paid tribute direct to the State. Ranjit Singh created an army which, at the zenith of his power, was a formidable force. Its overall strength was almost 100,000 men, cavalry strength of 30,000 horses and a field artillery of 288 guns. It was a favourite of Ranjit Singh's and he nursed it with great care with one third of his entire revenue. The army of Ranjit Singh was of two categories: regular and irregular, with four major divisions, viz. infantry, cavalry, artillery and Fauji Khas or the special brigade. It also contained a turbulent though highly valiant wing, the Akal Sena, a body of irregular horse of the reckless Akali warriors numbering 4,000. The crude military system inherited from Sikh Misls was reorganized by Ranjit Singh by building up both infantry and artillery as separate divisions. Although Ranjit Singh had been introducing new methods of fighting in his army by copying whatever he could from the practices prevalent in the forces of the East India Company, it was not until 1822 that he decided to modernize it along European lines. The court of Maharaja Ranjit Singh represented unparalleled Oriental pageantry, ostentation and brilliance. The Maharaja was usually dressed in simple white; he wore no crown or ornaments, but a single string of pearls around his waist and on special occasions, the famous Kohinoor diamond on his arm. He was surrounded by magnificently dressed, fine looking ministers, Sardars, courtiers and civil and military officials. Only a few were privileged to sit on chairs in the Durbar; a severe court discipline and etiquette were observed and none could speak unless addressed. His looks contributed little to his popularity; he was of short stature, of swarthy complexion and his face was pockmarked. The loss of one eye gave him an appearance of ungainliness. Yet he was possessed of great bodily vigour and activity. He grew up a fine soldier and his energies were directed towards war and conquest. His illiteracy was counterbalanced by a sharp inquisitive mind and a subtle genius and intuition with which he had mastered statecraft. He possessed a sharp intellect, a prodigiously retentive memory and an imaginative mind. An inherent quality of kindness was a marked aspect of his disposition. He was a humane despot; in his life he never wantonly inflicted either capital punishment or mutilation.

Maharaja Ranjit Singh

He always treated his fallen foe with deliberate kindness, and seldom imbued his hands in blood. In the words of Baron Charles Hugel, "Never perhaps was so large an empire founded by one man with so little criminality." Ranjit Singh was a devout Sikh. He considered himself a humble servant of the Guru. An inscription over the entrance of the central shrine at Amritsar reads: `The Great Guru in His wisdom looked upon Maharaja Ranjit Singh as his chief servitor and Sikh and, in his benevolence, bestowed upon him the privilege of serving the temple." He frequently visited the Golden Temple and would devoutly take a dip in the holy tank and make costly offerings to the temple. Some of his offerings still preserved, included a bejewelled gold canopy originally presented to him by the Nizam of Hyderabad. (They were destroyed by the Indian Army, during the operation Bluestar in June 1984) In May 1836, Ranjit Singh issued an order to all members of the Sikh royalty and aristocracy to make nazars or offerings at the Golden Temple. Ranjit Singh`s court reflected the liberal pattern of his State. Amongst the first family to rise to prominence in Ranjit Singh`s court were the Bokharis, sons of Ghulam Mohi ud Din of Lahore. Being of a Sufi persuasion they were known as Faqirs. The eldest, Faqir `Aziz ud Din, was closest to the Maharaja and advised him on external affairs. His two brothers, Nur ud Din and Imam ud Din also held important positions in the Durbar. Khushal Chand, a Brahman from Meerut, known after his conversion as Khushal Singh, became chamberlain. His nephew, Tej Singh, rose to be a general in the Sikh army. When Khushal Singh fell from the Maharaja's favour, his place was taken by Dhian Singh Dogra of Jammu. Dhian Singh`s son, Hira Singh, became a great favourite and the Maharaja treated him like his own son. The Dogra family remained the most powerful in the counsels of the Durbar.

This family of Brahmins exerted a baleful influence which Ranjit Singh was never able to shake off. It was one of the rare instances of Ranjit Singh misjudging the quality of the men he employed; Tej Singh played a traitorous role during the Anglo-Sikh wars. (Khushwant Singh)

There were no forced conversions in Ranjit Singh`s time. The Muslim women he married, Morari, Gul Bahar Begam, and others, retained their faith. His Hindu wives likewise continued to worship their own gods. He spent great sums on the repairs of Muslim places of worship. This attitude won him the loyalty of all his subjects. Ranjit Singh, the beau ideal of his people, died of paralysis at Lahore on 27TH June 1839.

Maharaja Ranjit Singh

The Army of Maharaja Ranjit Singh

Army of Maharaja Ranjit Singh, a formidable military machine that helped the Maharaja carve out an extensive kingdom and maintain it amid hostile and ambitious neighbours, was itself the creation of his own genius. His inheritance was but a scanty force which, in the manner of the Sikh Misldari days, comprised almost solely horsemen, without any regular training or organization. Everyone brought his own horse and whatever weapon he could afford or acquire. What held these troopers together was their personal loyalty to the leader. The tactics followed were those of the guerrilla warfare. The system had stood the Khalsa in good stead during the turbulent and anarchic eighteenth century, but was unsuited to the needs of the changed times and to Ranjit Singh's ambition to establish a secure rule. Early in his career, he had watched how the British troops with their systematic training and their discipline, had vanquished Indian forces vastly superior in numbers. He had also realized how crucial in warfare was a well drilled infantry as well as artillery. In 1802, soon after his occupation of Amritsar, he engaged some deserters from the army of the East India Company to train his own platoons of infantry. These troops were soon tested during the short campaign against Ahmad Khan Sial of Jharig and the Zamindars of Uchch during the winter of 1803-04. Ranjit Singh gave equal importance to artillery which had, till his time, been limited to the use of Zambureks or swivels only. He increased the number of guns. The casting of guns of larger calibre, as well as the manufacture of ammunition, was undertaken on a large scale. Artillery was further classified according to its mode of traction, which was generally determined by the size of the guns. In 1804, this arm had been bifurcated into Topkhana Kalan, heavy artillery and Topkhana Khurd, light artillery. Zambureks or swivels, usually carried on camels, were attached to infantry units. Horse drawn artillery was introduced in 1810. During the same year, a special artillery corps, known as Topkhana Khas or Topkhana Mubarak, was formed as the royal reserve under Ghaus Muhammad Khan. Topkhana Jinsi, literally personal artillery (reserve), was a mixed corps with batteries of gavi, bullock-driven, aspi, horse-driven, fill, elephant-driven, guns and the Aobobs or howitzers. Topkhana Aspi or horse-driven artillery consisted of batteries for attachment to divisions of irregular army. Zambureks or camel swivels and ghubaras or mortars were organized into deras or camps subdivided into batteries. Batteries were subdivided into sections of two guns each, with provision for even a single gun functioning as a subunit.

Maharaja Ranjit Singh

The Army of Maharaja Ranjit Singh (Cont.)

The entire field army was divided into faujia'in or regular army, Faujibeqava'id or irregular army and Jagirdari Fauj or feudal levies. Fauji Beqava'id forming a larger bulk consisted of Deras of Ghorchurras, or irregular cavalry grouped into divisions, each under one of the many distinguished generals such as Hari Singh Nalwa, Fateh Singh Ahluwalia and Fateh Singh Kalianvala. Ranjit Singh himself was the supreme commander. He also led some expeditions personally. The crack brigade of Akali under their famous leader, Phula Singh, was virtually an autonomous formation pressed into service when needed by the Maharaja through his personal influence and tact. Standard deployment at the commencement of a battle was guns in the centre and slightly forward of the rest of the force, infantry a little behind and also covering the flanks of artillery, and cavalry on the extreme flanks. The battle usually commenced with artillery barrage. Regular troops wore distinctive uniforms prescribed for each arm. Cavalrymen were dressed in red jackets (French grey for lancers), long blue trousers with a red stripe, and crimson turbans. Woollen jackets were used during winter. The regiments were armed with varying combinations of weapons sword/sabres and carbines and matchlocks or lances. Infantry was clad in scarlet jacket/coat, white trousers with black belts and pouches. The Ghorchurras or the irregular cavalry had no uniform laid down for them; yet they turned out remarkably well, as testified by Baron Hugel, a Prussian noble, who visited Maharaja Ranjit Singh in 1836 and inspected a cavalry parade. "I never beheld," he wrote of a troop of Ghorchurras, neither "a finer nor a more remarkably striking body of men. Each one was dressed differently and yet so much in the same fashion that they all looked in perfect keeping." Recruitment to the army was on a purely voluntary basis. There was no class composition on the basis of religion or nationality, nor was there a prescribed age limit for enrolment or retirement. Physical fitness and loyalty to the State were the essential conditions. Similarly, bravery in the field and efficiency in the performance of duty were the only considerations for promotion and reward, which were also extended to the sons of those who died in action. A well defined system of reward and punishment was enforced to maintain discipline and morale.

Maharaja Ranjit Singh

The Army at the death of Maharajah Ranjit Singh in 1839

Commander in Chief:
The Maharajah Ranjit Singh

Irregular Cavalry;
Ghorchurra Khas Dehra
Sham Singh Attariwala Dehra
Gurmukh Singh Lamba Dehra
Sandhanwalia's Dehra
Ardalyan Derah
Pindiwala Dehra
Attariwala Dehra
Mul Raja Dehra
The Dogra Dehra Na
Naulakha Dehra
Khas Dehra

Regular Infantry;
Fauj-I-Khas Brigade
Colonel Amir Singh Man's Brigade
Tej Singh's Brigade
Dhonkal Singh's Brigade
Misar Sukh Raj's Brigade
Court's Brigade
Colonel Gulab Singh's Brigade

Note;
Each Brigade averaged 4 Battalions one Cavalry Regiment and one Artillery Battery.

31 Regular Battalions
Several Independent Companies

Regular Cavalry;
1ST Dragoon Regiment
2ND Lancers (Dragoon Regiment)
Gurmukh Singh Rajman
Hira Singh Rajman
Mehtab Singh Rajman
Horse Grenadier Rajman
Ram Rajman
Three other Rajmans

Irregular Infantry;
Garrison Infantry
Personal Guards
Constabulary

Artillery;
Horse Artillery "Aspis"
Siege Trains "Jinsi"
Total: 14 Batteries "Jinsi"
192 Guns "Aspis"
Garrison Artillery (100)
Zambureks (500)

Jagirdari;
Feudal Infantry (30 Battalions)
Feudal Horse (11,800)
Feudal Artillery (50 Zambureks)

Sources: Bajwa

RANJIT SINGH'S GENERALS

Amar Singh Majithia, Governor
Amar Singh Majithia called Amar Singh Kalan (senior) to distinguish him from his namesake Amar Singh Khurd (junior) was from the village of Majitha. He took part in many an early campaign under Maharajah Ranjit Singh. He was appointed governor of Hazara in 1820. While engaged in curbing the activities of the turbulent and unruly Afghan tribes, he was treacherously killed in an ambush. Amar Singh was a fine bowman and the local tribesmen to this day point to a large tree pierced through by an arrow which, they say, came from the bow of Amar Singh.

Amar Singh Majithia, Commander
Known as Amar Singh Khurd (junior) to distinguish him from his namesake Amar Singh Kalan (senior) was a Jagirdar and military commander under Maharajah Ranjit Singh. He was placed in the Derah Khas, a regiment of irregular cavalry composed of the sons of the Sikh nobility. The young Amar Singh distinguished himself in the siege of Multan in 1818 and in the Kashmir campaign the following year. In 1834, he accompanied the army under Prince Nau Nihal Singh and General Hari Singh Nalwa to Peshawar, when the province was formally annexed to the Sikh kingdom. He was employed on outpost duty in this campaign and had many a fierce encounter with the Afghans. He fought with distinction in the battle of Jamrud (30TH April 1837). Being a celebrated marksman, he was chosen in 1846 to instruct the young Maharajah Duleep Singh in shooting. In the year following, he left the Punjab on a pilgrimage to Haridvar, and died there in 1848.

Atar Singh Sandhanvalia, Sardar
Atar Singh Sandhanvalia was collateral of Maharajah Ranjit Singh. After the direct descendants of the Maharajah, he, as the eldest of the Sandhanvalia family, stood close to the throne. A daring soldier, he took part in several Trans Indus campaigns in Peshawar and Hazara. After the death of General Hari Singh Nalwa, he was considered to be the "champion of the Khalsa." At Ranjit Singh`s death he refused to swear fealty to heir Kharak Singh. When in May 1844, Kanvar Pashaura Singh and Kanvar Kashmira Singh revolted; he raised a small force and joined them at Naurarigabad after crossing the Satluj, near Harike. A Sikh force 20,000 strong under Mian Labh Singh and General Gulab Singh crossed the Satluj and surrounded the Derah of Bhai Bir Singh Naurangabadi.

Ranjit Singh's Generals

Atar Singh Sandhanvalia, Sardar (Cont.)
However, the Lahore commanders, respecting the sanctity of Bhai Bir Singh, repaired to his camp to bring about an amicable settlement. As negotiations were in progress, Atar Singh flew into a rage and fatally stabbed General Gulab Singh with his dagger. The attendants of the General instantly fell upon Atar Singh and hacked him to pieces. This was in May 1844.

Bachittar Singh Malvai, Sardar
Bachittar Singh Malvai, joined the army of Ranjit Singh in about 1827, and served first at Bahawalpur. When Peshawar was occupied by the Sikhs in 1834, Bachittar Singh was sent to Shabkadr, where a new cantonment had been laid out and a fort built by Chatar Singh Attariwala. He was there when, in April 1837, the Afghan army attacked the post and the fort of Jamrud. In January 1839, Bachittar Singh accompanied the Sikh forces escorting Shahzada Taimur, son of Shah Shuja, to Peshawar. He died in 1840.

Budh Singh Sandhanvalia, Commander
Budh Singh Sandhanvalia, a Jagirdar, was son of Amir Singh Sandhanvalia, his two brothers being the more famous, Lahina Singh Sandhanvalia and Atar Singh Sandhanvalia. Budh Singh entered the Maharajah Ranjit Singh's service in 1811. The first independent command he held was at Bahawalpur where he had been sent to collect tax arrears. In 1821, he captured the forts of Maujgarh and Jamgarh and received Jagirs in reward from the Maharajah. Later, he was sent to the Jammu hills in command of two regiments of infantry and one of cavalry. He also commanded a Sikh force in the battle of Tin in 1823. Not long afterwards, he fell from favour and, to keep him away from Lahore, the Maharajah gave him the Peshawar command and sent him into the Yuzufzai country against Khalifa Sayyid Ahmad, then preaching jihad against the Sikhs. Budh Singh fought against the Khalifa and inflicted such a crushing defeat on him that it took him two years to recover his forces sufficiently to do battle again. After this victory Budh Singh returned to Lahore, where he was received with much honour. A few months later, at the close of 1827, he died of cholera.

Ranjit Singh's Generals

Desa Singh Majithia, General

Desa Singh Majithia, an army general and civil administrator, was the son of Naudh Singh, a feudal retainer under Amar Singh Bagga of the Kanhaiya Misl. When Naudh Singh died in 1788, Desa Singh succeeded to the family estates. He served Budh Singh Bagga, successor of Amar Singh Bagga, for a number of years before joining Ranjit Singh's army. In 1804, Desa Singh was made a commander of 400 Sowars. He served the Maharajah in many of his early campaigns. In August 1809, he was appointed commandant of the Fort of Kangra after Ranjit Singh had occupied it by driving away the Gurkha general, Amar Singh Thapa. In 1811, he was charged with reducing the Fort of Kotia, halfway between Kangra and Nurpur. Soon after he was made the Nazim (administrator) of Kangra and hill districts of Chamba, Nurpur, Kotia, Shahpur, Jasrota, Basohli, Mankot, Jasvan, Siba, Guler, Mandi, Suket, Kulu and Datarpur. Desa Singh made the hill region his home and married a Kangra girl, to whom was born a son, Ranjodh Singh. Desa Singh participated in the campaigns launched to capture Multan (1818), Kashmir (1819) and Naushera (1823).He commanded great influence at the Sikh court and was the recipient of several titles and Jagirs. For a few years he served as the Nazim of Amritsar and its adjoining territories, with management of the Golden Temple as his special charge. He was often sent to receive and look after foreign dignitaries visiting the court. He established in the hill territories a mild and humane administration. The Guler style of Sikh painting, with the ten Sikh Gurus and the Maharajah and his courtiers as its main themes, developed during his time. Desa Singh died in 1832, and was succeeded in all his estates and honours by his eldest son, Lahina Singh Majithia.

Gurmukh Singh, Sardar

Gurmukh Singh, son of Fateh Singh, belonged to the village of Turig, near Amritsar. In 1816, he joined Maharajah Ranjit Singh's army. In 1823 he was given command of 100 horses and placed under Desa Singh Majithia. Gurmukh Singh served as commandant in the Ramgarhia Brigade and took part in several battles including those of Multan (1818), Kashmir (1819), Mankera (1821) and Peshawar (1822). He also fought in the first Anglo Sikh war of 1846 in which his brother, Nidhan Singh, was killed. Gurmukh Singh died in 1870.

Ranjit Singh's Generals

Dhanna Singh Malvai, Commander

Dhanna Singh Malvai, soldier and Jagirdar under Maharajah Ranjit Singh, belonged to the village of Maur in Nabha territory. Mall Singh, Dhanna Singh's father, was the first in the family to be initiated a Sikh. He left his village about 1760 and entered the service of Charhat Singh Sukkarchakkia as a Sowar. He was killed in a campaign in the northwest of India. His son, Dhanna Singh, left Maur in 1793 and took up service with Sahib Singh Bhangi of Gujrat. About the year 1800, he enlisted in the force of Fateh Singh Kalianvala as a trooper, and soon obtained an independent command. He fought in the Kalianvala contingent in Pindi Bhattiari and Kasur campaigns. On the death, in 1807, of Fateh Singh Kalianvala at Naraingarh in Ambala district, Dhanna Singh entered the service of Maharajah Ranjit Singh. In 1810, he fought against Fateh Khan of Sahival, receiving a wound in the face. He was one of the agents sent by Ranjit Singh to Wazir Fateh Khan of Kabul to arrange an interview between the two, which took place in December 1812 at Jehlum. In July 1813, he fought in the battle of Attock, when Fateh Khan Barakzai was defeated by the Khalsa army of Maharajah Ranjit Singh. He accompanied the detachment of Dal Singh Naherna in the first expedition against Kashmir. He distinguished himself in the siege of Multan in 1818, the jewelled sword and shield of the defending Nawab, Muzaffar Khan, falling into his hands. In 1819, he took part in the final Kashmir expedition and in 1821 in the siege of Mankera. He was present at the capture of Jehangira Fort and at the battle of Teri in 1823, and remained on duty for some time in the Peshawar district, under the command of Budh Singh Sandhanvalia and Prince Kharak Singh. In 1837, he took part in the battle of Jamrud. Dhanna Singh enjoyed great esteem in the Maharajah's court. There were few Sardars whose influence was greater or whose advice was better regarded. He was sent on some political embassies and was a member of the mission which called on Lord William Bentinck at Shimla in April 1832. He was granted several Jagirs by the Maharajah, who also secured him at his request his ancestral village, Maur, in 1819. Dhanna Singh died in May 1843.

Ranjit Singh's Generals

Divan Singh Ramgharia, Sardar

Divan Singh Ramgharia was a soldier and a Jagirdar. He was son of Tara Singh and nephew of Jassa Singh, the famous Ramgarhia Sardar. As a young man he built a fort near Qadian and named it Thakargarh. With a garrison of 1400 horsemen, he fixed his residence in it. When on the death in 1816 of his cousin, Jodh Singh, there was a dispute about the family estate and as Maharajah Ranjit Singh tried to intervene, he panicked and fled to Patiala. He met with a friendly reception there, but was forced to leave the city. Eventually, he submitted to Maharajah Ranjit Singh and was granted a handsome jagir. He was sent in command of about 1,000 men to Baramula cantonment in Kashmir, a difficult hill post on the road to Srinagar. He remained on duty in Baramula cantonment until his death in 1834.

Fateh Singh Kalianvala, Sardar

Fateh Singh Kalianvala was the son of Jassa Singh and grandson of Jaimal Singh. Jaimal Singh was a Sandhu Jatt and the first in the family to embrace the Sikh faith. He was a resident of Kala village in Amritsar district. He joined the troops of the Sukkarchakkia chiefs, Charhat Singh and Mahan Singh, and fought against the Chatthas inhabiting the northern part of Gujranwala district. In one of the skirmishes with the Chatthas he lost both of his sons, Jai Singh and Jassa Singh. Fateh Singh entered the service of Maharajah Ranjit Singh in 1797, and rapidly rose in the favour of his master. He was a brave and skilful soldier and took part in almost every campaign undertaken by the Maharajah during his early career. He fought against Ghulam Muhammad Khan Chattha and against Jodh Singh of Wazirabad. He was with the Maharajah at the time of the capture of the city of Lahore in 1799. He participated in the Kasur (1801) and Jhang (1806) campaigns. Fateh Singh conquered Chiniot and, when Jhang was taken in 1806 from Ahmad Khan Sial, the district was leased to him. When towards the close of 1806, Qutb-ud-Din Khan of Kasur raised the banner of revolt, Fateh Singh Kalianvala was sent against him. In 1807, when Ranjit Singh besieged the fort of Naraingarh, Fateh Singh was in immediate command and assaulted the fort. He was repulsed and mortally wounded and died on 25TH October, 1807.

Ranjit Singh's Generals

Fateh Singh Man, Commander

Fateh Singh Man had entered the service of the Maharajah as a trooper, and took part in several campaigns, including those of Multan (1818) and Kashmir (1819). He rose to be a Commandant. He served mostly in the northwest frontier region, across the Indus. After Maharajah Ranjit Singh's death, he became an active partisan of Kanvar Nau Nihal Singh and Wazir Dhyan Singh. In the courtly intrigue following the death of Maharajah Kharak Singh and Kanvar Nau Nihal Singh, Fateh Singh Man aligned himself with the faction supporting Ram Chand Kaur against Sher Singh. The faction comprised Sandhanvalia Sardars, the Jammu brothers, and the Bhais. However, the accession of Sher Singh to the throne on 20TH January 1841 broke up the faction supporting Chand Kaur. Fateh Singh submitted to Maharajah Sher Singh and saved his Jagirs and command. He continued thereafter to serve in the Sikh army, retaining his influence at the court. The army Panchayats deputed Fateh Singh to Jammu to negotiate with Raja Gulab Singh the surrender of Hira Singh's treasure, which the Dogra chief had carted away to his capital. Gulab Singh paid Rs 400,000 and promised to surrender the treasure at an early date. The Lahore deputation left Jammu but was waylaid outside the town by Gulab Singh's troops and Fateh Singh Man was killed on 28TH February 1845.

Gulab Singh Pahuvindia, General

Gulab Singh Pahuvindia, a general in the Sikh army, was the son of Karam Singh, who along with his three brothers had taken possession of the country between the rivers Satluj and Beas in the latter half of the eighteenth century. Karam Singh's brothers dying heirless, the estate passed on to his only son Gulab Singh. When in 1806 Maharajah Ranjit Singh took possession of the Doab, Gulab Singh entered his service as an adjutant of an infantry regiment, soon becoming commandant. After the capture of Multan in 1818, he was promoted colonel and took part in various actions that took place against the Afghans in the Peshawar valley. In 1826, he was given command of 3 infantry and 2 cavalry regiments with a troop of artillery. In 1839, he was promoted to the rank of general and in 1847 appointed governor of Peshawar. During the second Anglo-Sikh war, General Gulab Singh and his son Colonel Ala Singh were kept under restraint by the Sikh troops for their sympathy with the British. After the annexation of the Punjab, the British rewarded him, confirming him in his Jagirs worth 17,500 rupees. General Gulab Singh died in 1854.

Ranjit Singh's Generals

Gurmukh Singh Lamma, Commander

Gurmukh Singh Lamma, a commander in Maharajah Ranjit Singh`s army, born in 1772, was of humble origin. His father, Pardhan Singh, being a money-changer in the small town of Khiva, situated on the right bank of the River Jehlum. Lamma in Punjabi means tall, but the cognomen Lamma was not conferred on Gurmukh Singh on account of his height, for he was of middle stature, but from his taking command of the contingent of Mohar Singh Lamma, who was exceptionally tall.

In the summer of 1780, as Maha Singh Sukkarchakkia was passing through the town on his return from an expedition in the neighbourhood of Find Dadan Khan, Gurmukh Singh, then a boy of eight years, joined his camp. He was the childhood companion of his son, Ranjit Singh. During the early years of Ranjit Singh`s power, wealth and honours were showered on Gurmukh Singh liberally. He was with Ranjit Singh at the capture of Lahore in July 1799, and was then made paymaster of the forces and put in charge of the treasury. Gurmukh Singh fought in most of the campaigns undertaken by the Maharajah. He fought at Kasur where he commanded 2,000 troops, at Jharig and Sialkot, and against the Gurkhas in 1809. The next year he took part in the siege of Multan, and in attacks on Sahival and Khushab. He commanded a division in the battle of Attock in 1813 and fought in Kashmir. Fifteen times he was wounded in battle: eight times by musket balls, thrice by sword cuts, thrice by spear thrusts, and once by an arrow. For his services Gurmukh Singh was munificently rewarded by his master. Before the capture of Lahore, he received in jagir Pindi Lala and Shahidarivala and afterwards Diriga and Ratto. After the conquest of Kasur in 1807, he received Jagirs in the Kasur area. When Nar Singh Cheliarivala died in 1806, his troops were placed under Gurmukh Singh and a large portion of his estates also. At one time Gurmukh Singh`s estates amounted to three and a half lakh of rupees, but the envy of the Dogras, Gulab Singh and Dhyan Singh, destroyed both his power and wealth. In August 1847, Gurmukh Singh was appointed along with Bur Singh of Mukcriari to take charge of Maharani Jind Kaur, confined at Sheikhupura. His son Atar Singh (d. 1880) held Jagirs at Naushera in Shahpur and Pindi Lala, Ghakk Basava, Doburji and Qila Atar Singh in Gujrat.

Ranjit Singh's Generals

Hari Singh Nalwa, General

Hari Singh Nalwa, celebrated general of Maharajah Ranjit Singh, was born in April 1791, at Gujranwala, now in Pakistan, to Gurdial Singh, an Uppal Sikh. The family originally came from Majitha, near Amritsar. His grandfather, Hardas Singh, had been killed fighting against Ahmad Shah Durrani in 1762. His father, Gurdial Singh, had taken part in many of the campaigns of the Sukkarchakkias Charhat Singh and Maha Singh. Hari Singh was hardly 7 years of age when his father died. His mother, Dharam Kaur, had to move to her parental home to live under the care of her brothers. There Hari Singh learnt Punjabi and Persian and trained in the manly arts of riding, musketry and swordsmanship. Dharam Kaur returned to Gujranwala when her son was about 13 years old. In 1805, Hari Singh participated in a recruitment test for service in the Sikh army and so impressed Maharajah Ranjit Singh with his skill at various drills that he was given appointment as a personal attendant. Not long after, he received the commission with a command of 800 horse and foot. This rapid promotion was owed to an incident in which he had cloven with sword the head of a tiger which had seized him. From that day he came to be known as Baghmar, the tiger killer, and earned the title of Nalwa. Hari Singh was commander of a regiment at the time of the Maharajah's final attack on Kasur in 1807 and gave evidence of his prowess on the field of battle. He was rewarded with a handsome Jagir. In the years 1809-10 he participated in the Sialkot, Sahival and Khushab expeditions and in four (1810, 1816, 1817 and 1818) of Ranjit Singh's seven campaigns against Multan. He fought in the battle of Attock in 1813 as second in command to Diwan Mohkam Chand, and in Kashmir in 1814 and 1819. Kashmir was occupied and, in 1820, Hari Singh was appointed its governor in succession to Diwan Moti Ram. He restored order in the turbulent areas, and reorganized civil administration. The territory was divided into Parganahs, each under a collector, and thanas each under a Thanedar. The habitual criminals were bound down and robbers infesting the forests were suppressed. Construction of forts at Uri and Muzaffarabad and Gurdwaras at Matan and Baramula was undertaken and work was started on laying out a spacious garden on the bank of the River Jhelum. To alleviate the misery of the people in the wake of the unprecedented floods of 1821, he took measures to provide prompt relief.

Ranjit Singh's Generals

Hari Singh Nalwa (Cont.)

In 1834, Hari Singh finally took Peshawar and annexed it to the Sikh dominions. Towards the end of 1836, Hari Singh Nalwa attacked and captured the small, though very strategic, fortified Misha Khel Khyber village of Jamrud, situated on the south-side of a range of mountains at the mouth of the Khyber pass. With the conquest of Jamrud, the frontier of the Sikh Empire now bordered the frontier of Afghanistan. This Sikh victory at Jamrud was followed by the resounding defeat of the Yuzufzai chief, Fatteh Khan of Panjtar. The Afghans were constantly waiting for an opportunity to eject the Sikhs from their territories. The opportunity arrived on the preparations of Prince Nau Nihal Singh's wedding at Lahore. Maharajah Ranjit Singh had recalled the cream of the Khalsa forces to the wedding: only a token force was retained to guard the passes. General Hari Singh Nalwa was sick and bedridden at Peshawar. Sardar Maha Singh, with a garrison of 600 manned the fort at Jamrud. Dost Muhammad despatched twenty five thousand Afghans and Pathans with 18 heavy guns to reduce the Jamrud fort. The Afghans laid siege and started pounding the fort with heavy artillery. As the walls were being, reduced to rubble, the Khalsa returned the fire, killing about 500 Afghans. Urgent appeals were made to Hari Singh Nalwa at Peshawar for assistance. Nalwa rose from his sick bed and advanced on Jamrud with 6,000 foot, 1,000 regular cavalry, 3,000 irregulars and 20 pieces of cannon. The Khalsa bombarded and drove the Afghan army into the plains, then charged them and compelled them to retreat. At their retreat, the Khalsa started plundering the Afghans and were in turn charged by a fresh Afghan force, suffering heavy casualties. As Nalwa led by the front, he was fatally wounded. He asked his death to be kept secret until the arrival of the Maharajah. Sardar Maha Singh took charge of the Khalsa and drove the Afghans back. This was followed by another engagement, when Akbar Khan engaged the Sikhs with a fresh force. The Afghans were driven back to the hills abandoning their guns. The Sikhs pursued them through the Khaibar Pass and decimated them. The remnants and Akbar Khan fled away to Kabul. There was a heavy price to pay that day. The Khalsa lost 6,000 men and the Afghans, who outnumbered them, left about 11,000 dead on the blood-drenched fields. The greatest loss was the death of Nalwa, the most dashing of the Khalsa generals

Ranjit Singh's Generals

Hukma Singh Chimni, Commander

Hukma Singh Chimni was a commander cum-civil administrator under Maharajah Ranjit Singh. He was the son of Ram Singh of Bhera, who was the first one in the family to take the vows of the Khalsa, and who entered the service of the Sukkarchakkia Misl under Charhat Singh as a trooper. After the death of his father, Hukma Singh was admitted into Ranjit Singh`s army and took part in the Kasur expedition of 1807. He soon won the favour of the Maharajah by his valour, particularly in the reduction of the Kanhaiya citadel of Pathankot in 1808, and in the seizure of Sialkot in the same year. The energy and alacrity of Hukma Singh won from the Maharajah the affectionate epithet of Chimni. "Chimna" in Punjabi signifies both a man of small stature and a little bird, swift and strong of wing. The nickname fitted Hukma Singh, who was short of stature, but very virile and active. Hukma Singh was created a Sardar and was made the governor of Ramnagar on a salary of Rs 2,000 per month. He also became the controller of customs and salt mine duties. He was assigned a jagir worth 60,000 rupees annually. Hukma Singh took part in the battle of Haidru, 8 km from the Fort of Attock, in 1813, when the Sikhs defeated the Kabul Wazir, Fateh Khan. As Yar Muhammad Khan, the Afghan governor of Peshawar, made an attempt to reoccupy Attock, Hukma Singh drove the Afghan army from the fortress and plundered the retreating host. In 1818, Maharajah Ranjit Singh appointed Hukma Singh as the governor of Attock and Hazara. Hukma Singh was primarily a soldier, and there were few of the Maharajah's campaigns in which he did not participate. He was well rewarded for his skill and bravery, **and, at one time, held Jagirs amounting to upwards of three lakhs of rupees.** Maharajah Ranjit Singh had dispatched Hukma Singh Chimni to annex Jammu in the year 1808. Gulab Singh Dogra had joined in the battle and due to the resistance put forward by him and his group, against the Sikh forces they were forced to withdraw to Saidgarh. Eventually, however, Maharajah Ranjit Singh was able to annex Jammu to his empire. Nevertheless, Bhai Hukma Singh was greatly impressed by the fighting abilities of Gulab Singh and subsequently informed Maharajah Ranjit Singh about him. Ranjit Singh allowed Gulab Singh Dogra to join his army. At the death of Ranjit Singh and the ensuing conflict with the British, Gulab Singh played a treacherous role in the fall of the Sikh Kingdom

Ranjit Singh's Generals

Hukam Singh Malvai, **Sardar**

Hukam Singh Malvai was a soldier and Jagirdar during the reign of Maharajah Ranjit Singh. He was the son of Dhanna Singh Malvai, an important official of the Sikh kingdom. Like his father, Hukam Singh served the Lahore Durbar. In January 1839, along with his brother Bachittar Singh, he escorted Shahzada Taimur to Peshawar. In 1841, after Maharajah Sher Singh had ascended the throne, Hukam Singh was sent to Kulu to capture the fugitives, Lahina Singh Sandhanvalia and Kehar Singh Sandhanvalia. For his valuable services he was granted a handsome increase in his jagir. Hukam Singh was killed in the battle of Sobraon during the Anglo Sikh war in February 1846.

Javala Singh Padhania, Sardar

Javala Singh Padhania, Alias Lakhdata, a Sandhu Jatt of the village of Padhania, in Lahore district, was a military commander. His father, Mit Singh had joined service under Maha Singh Sukkarchakkia and continued to serve under his son Maharajah Ranjit Singh, taking part in several of his military campaigns. Sohan Lal Suri, the official Lahore diarist, lists Javala Singh, among the principal Sardars of Maharajah Ranjit Singh. Javala Singh took part in the Maharajah's Malva campaign of 1807 and in expeditions of Multan (1818), Kashmir (1819) and Mankera (1821). He was put in charge of the fortress of Attock, which with a handful of troops, he successfully guarded against Afghan onslaughts. In 1829, Javala Singh suffered a stroke of paralysis and retired from active service. A brave soldier, he was a man of generous disposition. There are many stories of his generosity towards faqirs, Brahmans and indigent persons. It is recorded that he rescued from custody Diwan Baisakha Singh, by paying his entire fine of over one lakh of rupees, where after he came to be known as Lakhdata (dispenser of lakhs or millions). Javala Singh was married to the elder sister of Maharani Jind Kaur. He laid out an extensive garden midway between Lahore and the Badami Bagh, which became the Maharajah's favourite resort. He often held his court there and received foreign dignitaries. Javala Singh died in 1835.

Ranjit Singh's Generals

Jawand Singh Mokal, Sardar

Jawand Singh Mokal was a soldier and courtier of Maharajah Ranjit Singh. His father, Thakur Singh, held a minor command under Maharajah Ranjit Singh. Jawand Singh joined the Sikh army as a trooper and took part in the battle fought near Attock, in July 1813. The same year he fought in the battle of Haidru, in which the Sikhs worsted the Wazir of Kabul, Fateh Khan. For his gallantry in the battle he was assigned jagir worth Rs 30,000 annually in Gujrat district. He also took part in the expeditions of Multan (1818) and Kashmir (1819). His fortune rose quickly, and he became a Sardar and companion of the Maharajah. Jawand Singh, along with his troops, was in the entourage of the Maharajah at the Ropar meeting in 1831. His sons, Bela Singh and Gurmukh Singh, inherited the jagir. The former, with 200 horses, took part in the first Anglo Sikh war. He was wounded at Sobraon and washed away in the River Satluj. Bela Singh's son, Surjan Singh, fought in the second Anglo Sikh war. His jagir was confiscated by the British

Jhanda Singh Butaua, Commander

Jhanda Singh Butaua son of Sham Singh was a Jagirdar and military commander under Maharajah Ranjit Singh. He saw military service in Punch where Diwan Dhanpat Rai and Mir Baz Khan had been giving trouble, and was then ordered to Hazara. He accompanied the Maharajah in the campaign of 1821-22 when Mankera and Derah Ismail Khan were taken, and received for his gallantry valuable presents. He remained mostly on the frontier, in Chhachh, Peshawar and Hazara. He was a man of energy and ability, and the Maharajah gave him charge, under Sardar Hari Singh Nalwa, of this most unruly part of the country. In 1836, Jhanda Singh accompanied Prince Nau Nihal Singh on his Derajat expedition. During part of the Kabul campaign, he was governor of the Attock Fort. Prime Minister Jowahir Singh made Jhanda Singh an Adalati, or chief justice of Lahore, in conjunction with Diwan Hakim Rai, and he held this office until 1846. In 1847, he was sent to Hazara as Naib Nazim, or deputy governor, under Chatar Singh Attariwala.

Ranjit Singh's Generals

Jivan Singh, Colonel
Jivan Singh joined the army of Maharajah Ranjit Singh and was placed under Prince Kharak Singh. He first saw active service in Kashmir where he was wounded. For the bravery he displayed in the Tonk campaign, he was appointed to the adjutancy of the Sher Dil Paltan. He again went on active service in 1841 in Kashmir, where he lost his younger brother, Kishan Singh. For his services in the campaign, he was promoted to the command of the regiment. Shortly after the return of the regiment to Lahore, Jivan Singh was sent with it to Amritsar to guard the Darbar Sahib. On the occupation of the Punjab by the British, the regiment was taken over by them and it formed the nucleus of 19TH Punjab Infantry. Jivan Singh was confirmed in the position of commandant, with the rank of Colonel. Jivan Singh died at Amritsar in 1851.

Jodh Singh Rosa, Commander
Jodh Singh Rosa had joined service in the time of the Maharajah's grandfather, Charhat Singh. After the death of Charhat Singh, Jodh Singh retained his appointment at Gujranwala under Maha Singh and Ranjit Singh, and in 1799, he accompanied the latter to Lahore, when the city was captured. Jodh Singh served under Ranjit Singh in the Kasur, Pindi Bhattiari and Jharig campaigns, in the last of which he obtained, for his bravery, a jagir in Jharig district. He was shortly afterwards severely wounded at the siege of Chiniot. Jodh Singh was killed in 1819 during the Kashmir campaign. He had seven sons, all of whom served the Sikh Durbar in various capacities. Three of his sons Daya Singh, Divan Singh and Mardan Singh were killed in action at Ferozeshah on 21ST December 1845 while fighting against the British in the first Anglo Sikh war.

Jodh Singh, Commandant
From 1813 to 1825 Jodh Singh served with the Ghorchurras (special light cavalry) of Sardar Jodh Singh Sowariarivala. In 1831, he participated in Prince Sher Singh's successful campaign against Sayyid Ahmad Khan. In 1834 Jodh Singh became a trooper in Raja Hira Singh's Derah (army unit) and achieved the rank of commandant in 1836; he remained with the same unit until 1848. After the British formally annexed the Punjab in March 1849, Jodh Singh remained at Amritsar and entered government service. Jodh Singh retired from government service in 1862. He passed away in 1864.

Ranjit Singh's Generals

Lahina Singh, Sardar

Lahina Singh, a military commander, came from a Sodhi Khatri family of Gharjakh, a village adjacent to the town of Gujranwala (now in Pakistan). His grandfather, Panjab Singh, was a trooper in the regiment of Sardar Fateh Singh Kalianvala, a general in the army of Maharajah Ranjit Singh. After Fateh Singh`s death in 1807 in the battle of Naraingarh, Panjab Singh left his regiment to join another directly under Ranjit Singh`s command, where he rose in rank and was given a jagir. His son, Kahn Singh, was given the command of 500 horses and a jagir worth 15,000 rupees a year. He remained in the service of the Maharajah for nine years and was dismissed on account of some discrepancies discovered in his accounts. Kahn Singh then served successively under Hari Singh Nalwa, Atar Singh Sandhanvalia and Colonel Mihan Singh, the governor of Kashmir. Lahina Singh was the youngest of the three sons of Kahn Singh and Kishan Kaur. As he grew up, he joined army service under Ajit Singh Sandhanvalia. He married Chand Kaur, daughter of Hari Singh Nalwa. Lahina Singh was present in Jamrud Fort at the time of Hari Singh Nalwa's death. Lahina Singh`s family (including Kahn Singh and his other sons) continued to receive royal patronage until the murder of Maharajah Sher Singh in September 1843. Raja Hira Singh, who then came into power, confiscated the jagir and threw Lahina Singh and his elder brother, Fateh Singh, into prison. Lahina Singh managed to escape and sought asylum in the Derah of Baba Bir Singh of Naurangabad. The family was restored to their former position after the fall of Hira Singh in December 1844. Kahn Singh was killed during the first Anglo Sikh war, and the family jagir was restricted to annual revenue of 2,910 rupees. After the annexation of the Punjab to British dominions, the jagir was resumed by the government and pensions in cash were granted to different members of the family. Lahina Singh`s share was 360 rupees per annum. At the request of his mother in law, Mat Desari, he retired to live with the latter in Sardar Hari Singh`s haveli or mansion in the heart of Gujranwala town. There, under the influence of a holy man, Baba Ratan Singh, he turned to spiritual pursuit adopting a simple way of life, and came to be known as Sant Lahina Singh. He died at Gujranwala in 1893.

Ranjit Singh's Generals

Lahina Singh Majithia, Commander
Lahina Singh Majithia was commander, civil and military administrator, and one of the principal Sardars of the Sikh court. Of all the Majithias associated with the ruling family of Lahore, Lahina Singh was the ablest and most ingenious. He succeeded his father Desa Singh in 1832 as the Nazim (governor) of Kangra and the hill districts, with the title of Qaisar ul-Iqtidar. Earlier, he had served the Maharajah in various capacities. He commanded 2 battalions of infantry, a Topkhana of 10 light and field guns, and 1,500 horses. At the death of Ranjit Singh and feeling insecure at Lahore, he left the Punjab for Banares where he died in 1854.

Mahan Singh, Sardar
Sardar Mahan Singh came to Lahore from Jammu at a very early age to seek his fortune in the Sikh capital. Maharajah Ranjit Singh, who was struck by his skill and courage on a hunting expedition when Mahan Singh unassisted had killed a leopard with his sword, gave him an appointment in the army under Hari Singh Nalwa. Young Mahan Singh fought in several campaigns with gallantry, and at the last siege of Multan in 1818 was twice wounded. He also served in Kashmir and Peshawar. He was in charge of the Fort of Jamrud as Qiladar in April 1837 when the Afghan army attacked it in force. He held out bravely against enormous odds until Hari Singh himself arrived from Peshawar to fight the memorable battle in which he fell. Even after the death of his patron, Mahan Singh continued to enjoy the favour of the Maharajah who, in 1839, gave him a jagir worth Rs 37,000 of which Rs 12,000 was personal and Rs 25,000 for the service of 100 Sowars. He retained this estate throughout the reigns of Maharajahs Kharak Singh and Sher Singh. Mahan Singh was murdered by his own men in 1844.

Sadhu Singh, Akali,
Sadhu Singh was known for his daring exploits during the final Sikh assault on Multan in 1818. On 2ND June, when the fort wall was breached by cannonading, Akali Sadhu Singh accompanied by a few of his companions rushed through the breach and closed in on the Afghan defenders. The old Nawab and his sons donned the green garb and with drawn swords "came out to answer the call of the angel of death." Nawab Muzaffar Khan, his two sons and a nephew were killed and so were Sadhu Singh and his men. But the citadel was captured by the Sikhs.

Ranjit Singh's Generals

Meva Singh Majithia, Commander

Meva Singh Majithia was an artillery commander in the Sikh army. His regiment was called Topkhana Meva Singh, consisting of 10 light and 10 field guns and 1,014 men. In December 1844, Meva Singh was nominated a member of the council constituted by Maharani Jind Kaur to run the administration of the Punjab. He commanded the Lahore Durbar force dispatched to Jammu in February 1845 for the chastisement of Raja Gulab Singh. Of all the Majithia Sardars connected with the Sikh court; Meva Singh was the only one who took the part of the Dogras. It was through his intervention and that of Sardar Chatar Singh Attariwala that milder terms were given to Raja Gulab Singh, whose forces were routed by Ranjodh Singh Majithia at Akhnur in March 1845. Meva Singh pleaded with skill and vigour before the Khalsa Council for the restoration of Gulab Singh`s power and territories. Sikh or British records have little to tell of Meva Singh after 1845.

Mihan Singh, Governor

Mihan Singh was governor of Kashmir from 1834 to 1841. He had taken part in numerous military operations under Maharajah Ranjit Singh and his successors. As governor of Kashmir, he ordered a free assessment of the land in the province. He also had his Tarikhi Kashmir, which was a document of much historical and economic importance, compiled. Soon after Maharajah Sher Singh`s accession, two battalions of the Sikh army in Kashmir revolted and on 17TH April 1841 assassinated Mihan Singh at his residence in Srinagar.

Mit Singh Padhania, Commander

Mit Singh entered the service of the Sukkarchakkia Misl under Maha Singh, who assigned to him a Jagir worth Rs 12,000 annually. In 1804, in Ranjit Singh`s reign, he had command of 500 horse. He took part in Ranjit Singh`s occupation of Lahore (1799) and distinguished himself in the Kasur (1807) and Kashmir (1814) expeditions. He was killed in action during the retreat of the Sikh forces from Kashmir in 1814. Ranjit Singh assigned to his son, Javala Singh, additional estates worth Rs.125, 000 in Haripur Guler, in Kangra district.

Ranjit Singh's Generals

Milkha Singh Thehpuria, *Sardar*

Milkha Singh Thehpuria was a powerful Sikh chief during the latter half of the eighteenth century. He founded the village of Thehpur in Lahore district and took possession of a number of villages in its vicinity and in Gujrat and Gujranwala districts. Not content with these possessions, he marched northward and seized Rawalpindi. Milkha Singh fixed his headquarters there, building new houses and fortifying the town. Rawalpindi, being on the highway into India, was a vulnerable possession exposed to attacks by Afghan invaders, but Milkha Singh held his own. He conquered a tract around Rawalpindi and had won the esteem of the warlike tribes of Hazara. He had adopted the cognomen of Thehpuria from the village he had founded, but in the north he was known as Milkha Singh Pindiwala. Milkha Singh died in 1804. Jiwan Singh, his only son, who succeeded to his father's estates, fought in the Maharajah's Kashmir campaign in 1814, and died the next year. The force which Milkha Singh and Jiwan Singh had maintained was transferred to the service of the Sikh State and placed under Sardar Atar Singh Sandhawalia, bearing the name of Derah Pindiwala.

Suba Singh, *General*

Nahar Singh, founder of the family, is said to have crossed the Beas in 1759 and seized several villages in the Phillaur Tehsil of the Jullunder Doab. He became rich and built a handsome Bunga or rest-house close to the Durbar Sahib at Amritsar, which is still owned by his descendants, and known by his name. His son Diwan Singh and grandson Dalel Singh were killed in Maharajah Ranjit Singh's service. Budh Singh and Fateh Singh, sons of Dalel Singh, were allowed a third share in assignment valued at Rs. 30,000, made by the Maharajah under the usual conditions of service. Several members of the family held high military appointments and distinguished themselves on various occasions. Sardar Singh was a General in the Sikh Army, and met his death during the assault on the Multan fort.

Ranjit Singh's Generals

Nidhan Singh Panjhattha, Commander

Nidhan Singh Panjhattha was a military commander and Jagirdar under Maharajah Ranjit Singh. He acquired the epithet Parijhattha, the "five handed," for his gallantry in the battle of Ten Hill (1823). He single-handed made five Pathans prisoners and captured their weapons. This act of valour earned him the title of Panjhattha. In every battle, Nidhan Singh was among the first to advance and the last to retreat, and his body was covered all over with the marks of his courage. His great grand father, Dulcha Singh, had been in the service of Raja Ranjit Deo of Jammu, and his grandfather, Ram Dat Singh, is said to have served the Sukkarchakkia family under Maha Singh. Ram Singh, Nidhan Singh`s father, joined the service of Maharajah Ranjit Singh in 1798, and took part in the occupation of Lahore by Ranjit Singh in 1799. Nidhan Singh himself joined as a Sowar in the Sikh irregular horse. He distinguished himself in the battle of Jaharigira (1823), under General Hari Singh Nalwa and Prince Sher Singh. The Afghan force, defeated in the battle, retreated towards Ten hills, west of Attock. Muhammad `Azim Khan, the Amir of Afghanistan, reinforcing it marched upon Nowshera. A strong detachment of Sikh troops under Nidhan Singh Parijhattha and Maha Singh Akali was posted behind the Teri hills, but it suffered a reverse in the fierce action which followed. Akali Phula Singh made a headlong charge against the enemy and was killed. Nidhan Singh valiantly held out, rallying his troops till the battalions kept in reserve by the Maharajah came to his rescue and routed the Afghans. Nidhan Singh was a member of the Sikh goodwill mission which called on Lord William Bentinck in Shimla in 1831. In 1834, he joined Kanvar Nau Nihal Singh and Sardar Hari Singh Nalwa in their expedition to Peshawar. Peshawar was occupied by the Sikhs and Nidhan Singh`s troops were stationed there under the command of Sardar Hari Singh Nalwa. Nidhan Singh also took part in the battle of Jamrud in 1837. He died in May 1839.

Sangat Singh Saini, General

Sardar Sangat Singh Saini was a distinguished and highly ranked General in the Khalsa army under Maharajah Ranjit Singh. It is said that the Maharajah was so impressed with his contributions in the military campaigns that he granted him a fief. The town Sangatpura in district Gurdaspur is named after this illustrious Saini General.

Ranjit Singh's Generals

Nihal Singh Attariwala, Sardar

Nihal Singh was a soldier and courtier in the service of Maharajah Ranjit Singh. The Attariwalas were Sidhu Jats, settled at Tibba, a mound between Lahore and Amritsar, where Gauhar Singh built a house which, because of its imposing façade, came to be called Atari, in Punjabi a house with a high elevation. This was the origin of the name of the family and of the village that grew around the house. Gauhar Singh joined in those days of high adventure the Jatha of Sardar Gurbaksh Singh Roranvala and in 1737 took under Rakhi or protection a number of villages around Atari. Later he joined the Bhangi Misl under Gujjar Singh and acquired a military command and a Jagir. His son Nihal Singh served under Sahib Singh Bhangi and took part in the campaign against the Afghans. He won special distinction fighting in 1798 against Ahmad Khan Shahanbchibashi, one of the generals of Zaman Shah Durrani. With the Bhangis, he confronted Ranjit Singh at Bhasin in 1800, but later took up service under him. From 1801 to 1817, he participated in most of the Maharajah's military expeditions, including those of Kashmir and Multan. In 1803, he was assigned a Jagir worth 50,000 rupees annually at Sukkho in Pothohar and in 1807 he was put in charge of Kasur after the defeat and expulsion of its Pathan ruler, Qutb ud Din. He accompanied Maharajah Ranjit Singh in the first two of his campaigns across the Satluj in 1806-07. Nihal Singh was known for his loyalty and devotion to the person of Maharajah Ranjit Singh. He died of serious ailment around 1818.

Nihal Singh Sodhi, Sardar

Nihal Singh, son of Megh Singh, entered Maharajah Ranjit Singh's army in 1819. Five years later, he was made commandant of 100 horsemen in the Charyari corps. He fought for Maharajah Sher Singh during the siege of Lahore in January 1841. Under Sher Singh's successor, Nihal Singh was sent in command of 1,000 horse to administer the area of Dhanni, which was in a state of insurrection. He shot the leader of the insurgents dead and by his vigour and severity soon reduced the country to submission. After Raja Hira Singh's death, Nihal Singh was sent to Shahpur district to keep the tribes of the bar in order and in 1847, after the first Anglo Sikh war, he was made an addlati or judge. A few months later he was transferred to Jalandhar in the same capacity. After the annexation of the Punjab by the British, Nihal Singh was assigned to civil duties. He restored order in the region between Jehlum and Attock. Nihal Singh died in 1859.

Ranjit Singh's Generals

Phula Singh, Akali

Phula Singh Akali, Sikh hero and an eminent religious figure of the time of Maharajah Ranjit Singh, was born in 1761 at the village of Shihari, now in ruins, about 5 km west of Miinak, in present day Sarigrur district of the Punjab. His father, Ishar Singh, an associate of the Nishananvali Misl, died in 1762 fighting Ahmad Shah Durrani in Vadda Ghallughara, the Great Carnage, leaving his infant son to the care of Baba Narain Singh, who belonged to the Shahid Misl. Baba Narain Singh brought him up and instructed him in the Sikh texts as well as in the methods of warfare. He also administered to him the initiatory vows of Khanda di pahul. As he grew up, Phula Singh joined the Jatha of Baba Narain Singh at Anandpur and took part in many an expedition. After the death of Baba Narain Singh, he was elected leader of the Jatha. In the midst of soldierly occupation, Phula Singh showed concern about the manner in which the Sikh shrines were being administered, and denounced some of the prevalent usage. In January 1802, when Maharajah Ranjit Singh, attacked Amritsar to wrest control of the city from the Bhangis, Phula Singh mediated between the clashing groups and averted bloodshed. He took charge of the holy shrines there and began levying charges on the Sardars and officials of the Sikh court for their maintenance. As provost of the Takht Akal Bunga, he once imposed punishment on Maharajah Ranjit Singh for infraction of the Sikh code. Phula Singh's Akalis distrusted the foreigners, Afghans as well as Feringhees. In 1809, they were involved in an attack on the Muhammadan escort of Charles Metcalf, the British envoy to the court of Ranjit Singh. The same year Lieutenant F.S, White, a British officer, who was proceeding through the Sikh country with 80 troopers to survey the Cis-Satluj region on the authority of the Phulkian chiefs, was challenged by Akali Phula Singh's Jatha at Pattok. Timely intervention by the Nabha chief saved the life of Lieutenant White. Maharajah Ranjit Singh appointed Phula Singh commander of the Akali troops in his service. These troops, not fully subservient to the Maharajah's authority, were the most daring in his service. In February 1807, Akali Phula Singh and his Jatha fought valiantly at Kasur and helped the Lahore forces subjugate the Pathan governor, Qutb ud Din Khan. As a reward, the Maharajah gave Phula Singh's force regular barracks at Amritsar, which later developed into the headquarters of the Nihang sect and became known as Akalian di Chhauni or the Akali Cantonment.

Ranjit Singh's Generals

Phula Singh, Akali (Cont.)

In 1816, when Ranjit Singh`s armies made their sixth attack upon Multan, Phula Singh led a storming party of his Akali zealots. The Akalis fought with reckless courage and took the Fort in the final assault they launched in 1818. Phula Singh and his band of Akalis also participated in the Peshawar (1818) and Kashmir (1819) campaigns. In January 1823, Amir Muhammad `Azim Khan marched from Kabul with a strong host, bent upon occupying Peshawar and chastising the Sikhs. A Sikh army under Prince Kharak Singh rapidly moved northwards and converged on Naushera, midway between Attock and Peshawar. In the fierce action fought at Naushera, the Akali contingent, 1500 strong, made a desperate charge and was soon in the thick of the battle. Suddenly, Phula Singh`s horse was struck by a bullet and died. Phula Singh was also hurt, but he shifted on to an elephant and pressed forward. The Afghan militia made him their main target and he fell under a heavy shower of bullets. Although Phula Singh and most of his men had been killed, the battle was won and the Afghans had to flee Naushera. Akali Phula Singh had met with a hero's death on 14TH March 1823. He was cremated at Persia, 6 km east of Naushera, with full military honours. A Samadh was built on the site and the Maharajah attached to it a jagir for its maintenance. Another monument in Akali Phula Singh`s honour stands at Amritsar in the form of Burj Baba Phula Singh.

Shamir Singh Thethar

Shamir Singh Thethar, soldier and a minor commander in the service of Maharajah Ranjit Singh. He was the son of Prem Singh, of the village of Thethar, near Lahore, and brother of Lakha Singh along with whom he entered the service of Sukkarchakkias. Shamir Singh fought in the battle of Rasulnagar in 1778-79 under Mahan Singh, who had joined hands with Jai Singh, of the Kanhaiya Misl, against Pir Muhammad Khan Chattha. To recover the famous cannon Zamzama, which the Bhangi chief Jhanda Singh had left with Pir Muhammad Khan, the Sikh chiefs attacked Rasulnagar. It is claimed that Shamir Singh killed the Chattha chief with a musket shot during the siege. Shamir Singh built the Fort of Gobindgarh at Amritsar at Maharajah Ranjit Singh`s order and became its first Qiladar (commandant). He served in the expedition of Kasur (1807). In 1819, the Maharajah appointed him the Thanedar of Nurpur. He held a jagir in Gujranwala. He died in 1824.

Ranjit Singh's Generals

Charyari Sowars

Charyari Sowars was the name given to an irregular cavalry regiment in Sikh times. It owed its origin to four friends, or Char (four) friends, who were seen together all the time. Their names were: Bhup Singh Sidhu, Jit Singh, Ram Singh Saddozai and Hardas Singh Bania. They were all young men of the same age, very handsome, well built and always elegantly dressed. Maharajah Ranjit Singh became very fond of the foursome and employed them as soldiers. He was so impressed by their bearing that he gave them fine horses to ride and created a regiment named Charyari Sowars after them. The force grew in strength under the patronage of the Maharajah. It was placed under the command of Raja Suchet Singh, who was always splendidly turned out and was known as the dandy of the Punjab. He was assigned a Derah, i.e. Camp, near the Shalimar Gardens at Lahore. The Khalsa Durbar Records, as well as the `Umdatut Twarikh, includes it amongst the seventeen Derahs of the Ghorchurras of different sizes under the name of the Derah Naulakkha or the Derah Charyari. The Derah consisted of a number of squadrons of varying strength. Each horseman wore a velvet coat, a shirt of mail and a steel helmet; the horses were bedecked with metal capped peacock plumes. The recruitment was voluntary. The troops were seldom paid a salary, though provision was made for their food, uniform and equipment.

They owned their own horses and were under no feudal obligations. The Charyari force was a fine body of horse, richly clad and mounted, strutting pompously on all ceremonial occasions during Ranjit Singh`s reign. After the death of the Maharajah, it became involved in partisan feuds. It took the part of Rani Chand Kaur when, in January 1841, Sher Singh invested the Lahore Fort. Later, Sher Singh won over the Charyari Sowars, who, with Raja Dhian Singh, joined his standard. But they deserted the Maharajah to support his Mukhtiar or attorney, Jawala Singh, who had revolted against his master. The Charyari force sided with Raja Hira Singh in the fight with Atar Singh Sandhanvalia, who had taken shelter with Bhai Bir Singh of Naurangabad. On 18TH December 1844, Raja Hira Singh discharged about five hundred men of the Charyari force. That was the end of this colourful and picturesque regiment.

GENERALS IN THE ANGLO-SIKH WARS

Maharajah Ranjit Singh had created and consolidated the most awesome military muscle ever seen in India and became king of an Empire extending from Tibet to the deserts of Sindh, and from the Khyber Pass to the Satluj. It was near-anarchical conditions that overtook the Lahore court after the death of Maharaja Ranjit Singh in June 1839. The British, by then firmly installed in Ferozepore at the Sikh frontier, about 70 km from Lahore, the Sikh capital, were watching the happenings across the border with more than neighbour's interest. They had been extremely farsighted in their expansion of India and wanted to extend their power to the continent's natural border, the North West Frontier. After the fall of Delhi, the British had a standoff against Maharajah Ranjit Singh, who was seeking to expand the Sikh State. The British checked this by taking the Cis-Satluj territories under their protection. They also checked the Sikh State's expansion towards Sindh and the sea by taking the Amirs of Sindh under their protection. Additionally, the Anglo-Sikh treaty blocked the State's expansion towards Afghanistan. They had practically boxed in the Sikh Kingdom and had made no secret of their intention to destroy the Sikh Kingdom and annex the Punjab to the British Empire. With the turmoil in the Punjab, and their under-estimation of the fighting qualities of the Sikh soldier, the British started massing their armies; the largest force ever assembled in India, on the Kingdom's borders. The total number of British troops around Punjab was 86,023 men and 116 guns. In addition to the concentration of troops on the border, an elaborate supply depot was set up by the British at Basslan, near Raikot, in Ludhiana district. The Sikh ranks, alerted to the danger of a British offensive, started their own preparations. Yet the army panches or regimental representatives, who had taken over the affairs of the Lahore forces into their own hands, were at this time maintaining a wonderful order at Lahore and almost puritanical discipline in the military republic. However, the emergence of the army Panchayats as a new centre of power greatly perturbed the British authority, who termed it as "unholy alliance between the republican army and the Durbar." In this process the Sikh army had indeed been transformed. It had now assumed the role of the Khalsa. The morale of the Khalsa was extremely high. The Sikh soldier was extremely brave and had always carried everything before him. However, the Khalsa were led by traitors. The two principal generals, Lal Singh and Tej Singh, were not Sikhs, but Brahmin Hindus, and were not committed to the cause for which they were fighting.

Generals in the Anglo Sikh Wars

"A powerful, well-trained, and confident Sikh army prepared for war under the leadership of a Commander-in-Chief under orders from a Vizier, and watched from the sidelines by a powerful and clever chieftain. All three men dedicated to the defeat of the army they lead, and secretly informing their British opponents of that fact!" (Donald Featherstone)

Traitors on the field and traitors at court commanded the Khalsa armies; their main aim was the destruction of the Khalsa on the British bayonets. Thus with ignominious treachery and deceit were sold the lives of the valiant soldiers of the Khalsa by their rulers, and thus was fought the First Anglo-Sikh War.

The British Generals, although they had had the co-operation of the Sikh commanders, had won the war at enormous cost. They duly paid tribute to the Khalsa soldiery. Commander in Chief General Gough paid tribute to the gallantry of the Sikhs: "Policy precluded me publicly recording my sentiments on the splendid gallantry of our fallen foe, or record the acts of heroism displayed, not only individually, but almost collectively, by Sikh Sardars and the army." The British government became the guardian of the young Maharajah Dalip Singh, and the Punjab became a British protectorate. The Khalsa was restricted to 20,000 infantry and 12,000 cavalry, and was crushed as a military power. However, the Governor General Lord Dalhousie wrote: "The task before me is the utter destruction and prostration of the Sikh power, the subversion of its dynasty, and the subjection of its people. This must be done promptly, fully and finally."

The district of Multan was a tributary of the Sikh Kingdom, and the revolt of the Hindu governor of Multan provided the excuse for the British annexation of the Punjab. As the remnants of the Khalsa rallied around the city of Multan, the British declared war on the Sikh Nation! The British invading forces deployed at various points in the Punjab were a staggering total of 104,666 men, comprising of 61,366 Regular British Army, 5,300 Lahore Army, 38,000 Irregular troops, plus 13,542 Cavalry, 123 Field guns and 22 Heavy guns.

At the conclusion of the First Anglo-Sikh War, the British had methodically destroyed the military power of the Sikhs. The soldiers had been disarmed, disbanded and dispersed. The pride of the Khalsa, the guns, were dismantled and taken away.

Generals in the Anglo Sikh Wars

The Second Anglo-Sikh war, which resulted in the abrogation of the Sikh kingdom of the Punjab, was virtually a campaign by the victors of the first Anglo-Sikh war. Since then the de facto rulers of the State finally overcame the resistance of some of the Sardars, who chafed at the defeat in the earlier war which, they believed, had been lost owing to treachery on the part of the commanders and not to any lack of fighting qualities of the Sikh army. It marked also the fulfilment of the imperialist ambition of the new governor-general, Lord Dalhousie, to carry forward the British flag up to the natural boundary of India on the northwest. The new regime confronted a rebellion in the Sikh province of Multan, which it utilized as an excuse for the annexation of the Punjab. The British Resident at Lahore increased the levy payable by the Multan governor, Diwan Mul Raj, who appointed General Kahn Singh Man in his place and sent him to Multan along with two British officers P.A. Vans Agnew and William Anderson, to take charge of Multan. The party arrived at Multan on 18TH April 1848, and the Diwan vacated the Fort and made over the keys to the representatives of the Lahore Durbar. Diwan's soldiers rebelled at the takeover and the British officers were set upon in their camp and killed, which started the Multan outbreak. Some soldiers of the Lahore escort deserted their officers and joined Mul Raj's army. Lord Dalhousie received the news at Lahore on 21ST April, but delayed any action and allowed the Multan rebellion to spread for five months. The Sikh army was but a shadow of the colossal military machine of Maharajah Ranjit Singh. The total force the Sikhs could muster was 23,000; these were the various contingents from Hazara, Peshawar, Tank, Bannu, Kohat and Attock, including 10,000 Irregulars. The major battle of the Second Sikh War was fought near Chillianwala. When darkness fell the British left the battlefield and fell back on the village of Chillianwala. During the battle of Chillianwala the British casualties amounted to 2,446 men, with 132 officers killed and 4 guns lost. Chillianwala was the worst defeat the British had suffered in their annals of Indian warfare. However, re-enforced with fresh forces, they turned defeat into victory at the battle of Gujarat. The observers who watched the Sikh surrender greatly admired the bearing of the Sikh soldiers, who still carried themselves with pride. They were tired and hungry, but their spirit was by no means broken. The Punjab was annexed to British India, the Sikh Kingdom ended, and Maharajah Dalip Singh was pensioned off to England.

Generals in the Anglo Sikh Wars

Lal Singh, Raja

Lal Singh, son of Misr Jassa Mall, a Brahman shopkeeper of Sanghoi, in Jehlum district in West Punjab, entered the service of the Sikh Durbar in 1832. He rose to power during the heyday of Wazir Hira Singh Dogra's authority, when he was given a minor military command. He increased his influence by winning the favour of those in power. To this end, he engineered, in 1843, the murder of Beli Ram, his own benefactor, and Bhai Gurmukh Singh. By his beguiling manner he won the confidence of Maharani Jind Kaur and became her closest adviser. In December 1844, he was appointed a member of the Council of Regency under her. He was made Wazir on 8TH November 1845 after the assassination of Jawahar Singh. As Wazir and as a commander, Lal Singh proved disloyal to the Sikh Durbar in the Anglo Sikh war of 1845-46. He in fact acted in conformity with the secret instructions received from the British officials. He supplied military information to Captain Peter Nicholson, at Ferozepore. Two divisions of Sikh troops under his command remained entrenched at Ferozeshah without attacking a small British garrison at Ferozepore. Brigadier Litter's garrison at Ferozepore was thus allowed to escape from there and form junction with Lord Gough`s army at Ferozeshah. After the reverse at Ferozeshah, Lal Singh fled to Lahore and offered to the Council of the Khalsa to relinquish his office. He was relieved of the office of Wazir, but no change in the military command was made. On the eve of battle of Sobraon (10TH February 1846), Lal Singh sent to Captain Nicholson a map of the Sikh entrenchments. During the battle, he kept his artillery battalions and the dreaded Ghorchurra Cavalry away from the battlefield. He himself retired to Lahore. After the war, he was suitably rewarded by the British. He was confirmed as Wazir of the State of Lahore under the Resident, Henry Lawrence. He, however, lost British patronage when it came to light that he had sent written instructions to Shaikh Imam Ud Din, the governor of Kashmir, to thwart the occupation by Gulab Singh of the valley, bought by him from the British on 16TH March 1846. Lal Singh was tried by a Court of Inquiry and found guilty. He was removed from his high office and expelled from the Punjab with a pension of 12,000 rupees per annum. He was sent to Agra and then to Dehra Dun, where he died in 1866.

Generals in the Anglo Sikh Wars

Tej Singh, Raja

Tej Singh, a Gaur Brahman of Meerut district, was born in 1799. His original name was Tej Ram. He was a nephew of Jemadar Khushal Singh, a dignitary of the Sikh kingdom. He took up service at the Sikh court in 1812. He made rapid progress in the army cadre, becoming a general in 1818. He served in all the three Kashmir expeditions of 1813, 1814 and 1819, and took a leading part in reducing Mankera, Leiah and the Derajat. He was a divisional commander in the Peshawar campaign of 1823 and fought in the battle of Ten Hill. In 1831, he had under his command twenty-two battalions of the regular Sikh army. On the eve of the Anglo-Sikh war of 1845-46, Tej Singh was appointed commander in chief of the Sikh army. His conduct during this war and during the one following was, however, marked by duplicity. He established secret liaison with the British and desired their victory rather than that of the army he led. Two divisions under his command hovered around Ferozepore when that strategic town could have been stormed and the small British garrison destroyed. At the fiercely fought battle of Ferozeshah (21ST December 1845), he kept his army away from the battlefield. When the action was over, he appeared with his army on the morning of 22ND December and drove straight into the shattered British lines. But suddenly his guns ceased to fire. He abandoned the field and took the road to Lahore. At Sobraon (10TH February 1846), he advised the brave Sikh general, Sham Singh Attariwala, to leave the battlefield. The latter continued the battle determined to fight to the end, but Tej Singh and Commander Lal Singh fled hastily even as the contest hung in the balance. As the battle went in favour of the British, Tej Singh cut out the retreat of the Sikh army by sinking the bridge of boats and the tete de pont constructed in front of it. At the end of the war, he made an offer of Rs. 2,500,000 to Lord Hardinge to buy for himself an independent kingdom like Gulab Singh had done. However, he retained his position of pre-eminence in the new setup. He was nominated president of the council of Regency in December 1846, and was allowed to continue as commander in chief of the Sikh army. He was created Raja of Sialkot in August 1847. At the time of the annexation of the Punjab, he was guaranteed the enjoyment of all the privileges and rights which he possessed under the Sikh government. During the uprising of 1857, he raised Sikh cavalry regiments to aid the British. His scattered Jagirs were consolidated and he received the new title Raja of Batala. He died on 4TH December 1862.

Generals in the Anglo Sikh Wars

Ajit Singh, Raja

Ajit Singh, Raja, ruler of Ladva, was born the son of Gurdit Singh, who had acquired territory around Thanesar after the conquest by Sikhs in 1764 of the Mughal province of Sirhind. Gurdit Singh belonged to the same clan as Ranjit Singh. He originally came from the village of Vein Poin, about 15 km south of Amritsar, and was a member of the Karorsinghia Misl or confederacy. In addition to his other acquisitions, Gurdit Singh received in Jagir from Maharaja Ranjit Singh the village of Badhowal, near Ludhiana. After Gurdit Singh's death, Ajit Singh succeeded him and became the ruler of the Ladva state. Ajit Singh, like his father, continued to be an ally of Ranjit Singh in his campaigns of conquest and received favours from him. He built a bridge over the River Saraswati at Thanesar, and received the title of Raja from Lord Auckland, the British governor general of India. In the first Anglo-Sikh war, Ajit Singh fought on the side of the Sikhs against the British. Along with Ranjodh Singh Majithia he crossed the Satluj at Phillaur with a force of 8,000 men and 70 guns. In rapid marches Ajit Singh and Ranjodh Singh seized the forts of Fatehgarh, Dharamkote, and Badhowal, and stole into Ludhiana cantonment, setting many of the barracks on fire. In the action fought on 21ST January 1846 at Badhowal, Sir Henry Smith's column was attacked and more than 200 of his men were slain. But Ajit Singh suffered a defeat in the action fought in Aliwal after a week and fled the battlefield. Ajit Singh's estates were confiscated by the British in 1846 and he was arrested and detained at Allahabad. He, however, contrived to escape after killing his keeper and after long wanderings is supposed to have died in Kashmir.

Arjan Singh, Commander

Arjan Singh was born at Rarighar Nangal, in Gurdaspur district. He was a military commander under Maharajah Ranjit Singh. In 1845, on the eve of the first Anglo Sikh war, he was given the command of four infantry regiments, one regiment of cavalry, and a troop of horse artillery, with which force he served at the battle of Sobraon. In 1848, he accompanied Raja Sher Singh Attariwala to Multan, and became an ally in his rebellion. His followers, hearing this, rebelled too and defended the fort of Rarighar Nangal successfully against two companies of the Lahore troops. After the annexation of the Punjab by the British, the estates of Arjan Singh were confiscated. Arjan Singh died in 1859.

Generals in the Anglo Sikh Wars

Atar Singh Kalianvala, Commander

Atar Singh Kalianvala, soldier and feudatory chief, was a military commander under Maharaja Ranjit Singh. Atar Singh's ancestors belonged to the village of Karial, in Sheikhupura district, now in Pakistan. His great great grandfather, Sahib Singh, had been given a jagir by Charhat Singh Sukkarchakkia. Sahib Singh's son, Hukumat Singh, and grandson, Kaur Singh, had served in the Sukkarchakkia Misl. Kaur Singh's son, Dal Singh, served Ranjit Singh in Kasur, Multan, Kashmir and Derah Ismail Khan campaigns. His son, Atar Singh served in Peshawar under the command of Prince Nau Nihal Singh. During the reign of Maharaja Sher Singh, he was given Pindi Gheb and Miroval in Jagirs, valued at over a lakh of rupees, subject to the service of two hundred horses. Atar Singh was made Adalati (chief justice) of Lahore and the surrounding districts, and received command of the Pindiwala irregular cavalry which had been first raised by Milkha Singh Pindiwala. He took part in the first Anglo Sikh war. After the treaty of Bharoval, he was appointed a member of the Council of Regency formed in December 1846, which position he retained till the annexation of the Punjab (1849). Atar Singh died in December 1851.

Bikram Singh Bedi, Baba

Bikram Singh Bedi was the third and youngest son of Sahib Singh Bedi of Una, a lineal descendant of Guru Nanak. On Sahib Singh's death in 1834, Bikram Singh succeeded to his father's Jagirs and position as preceptor to the royal family of Lahore. Baba Bikram Singh vehemently opposed the stationing of British troops at Lahore after the Anglo Sikh war of 1845-46. After the annexation of the Doab in 1846, the British dispossessed him of arms, and reduced his Jagirs. He, however, started organizing an armed opposition to the British in the hilly areas of the Sivaliks. He sent his emissaries to Diwan Mul Raj of Multan and Sardar Chatar Singh Attariwala, the governor of Hazara, who had raised the banner of revolt against the British. In December 1848, he crossed the Beas at Sri Hargobindpur and joined forces with Raja Sher Singh Attariwala and fought the British in the battles of Chillianwala (13TH January 1849) and Gujrat (21ST February 1849). He surrendered to the British along with the Attariwala Sardars at Rawalpindi in March 1849. He was interned at Amritsar where he died in 1863.

Generals in the Anglo Sikh Wars

Buddh Singh Man, General

Buddh Singh Man entered the service of Maharajah Ranjit Singh in 1816 and rose to command a cavalry troop. Later, he was promoted a colonel. Eventually he commanded four regiments of infantry, one regiment of cavalry, and two troops of artillery. He commanded a division of the Sikh army during the first Anglo-Sikh war. He continued in the service of the Lahore Durbar after the reorganization of the Sikh army under the treaty of Lahore (1846). During the second Anglo-Sikh war he remained with the British, though the troops under his command had deserted him and joined Chatar Singh Attariwala. He fought the Sikhs at Margalla Pass, was wounded and taken prisoner. He secured his release after the battle of Gujrat (21ST February 1849) He died in 1856.

Chatar Singh Attariwala, Sardar

Chatar Singh was appointed governor of Peshawar in August 1846. He was transferred to Hazara, where as the governor of the province he came into conflict with the overbearing Assistant British Resident, Captain James Abbott. Since the Multan outbreak in April 1848, James Abbott had alleged that a conspiracy was being hatched by Chatar Singh, to subvert British power in the Punjab. He charged him with high treason, and leading the local chiefs and large numbers of Muslim levies, he marched on Haripur to expel the Sikh governor. At this juncture Commodore Canora, an artillery officer in the Sikh service, who was in secret communication with Captain Abbott, refused to move his battery, and was consequently shot down at Chatar Singh`s orders. Under the orders of the British Resident at Lahore this Hazara incident was investigated by Captain Nicholson, who in his enquiry report not only exonerated Chatar Singh, but also justified the defensive measures he had taken to save the besieged capital of Hazara from Abbott's Muhammadan mercenaries. Resident Frederick Currie, notwithstanding Nicholson's report, issued orders which amounted to Chatar Singh`s virtual dismissal and the confiscation of his Jagirs, which drove him to open defiance. The Hazara revolt now escalated into hostilities between the British and the Sikhs, which led to the 2ND Anglo-Sikh war. After their defeat at Gujrat on 21ST February 1849, Chatar Singh was imprisoned at Allahabad from where he was removed to Fort William at Calcutta, where he died on 27TH December 1855.

Generals in the Anglo Sikh Wars

Chet Singh, Commander

Chet Singh was a military commander, engineer and a kardar, i.e. a revenue officer, under Maharaja Ranjit Singh. In 1831 he became engineer in charge for constructing a bridge over the River Satluj for the Ropar meeting between Maharaja Ranjit Singh and Governor General William Bentinck. Earlier in 1833 he was appointed kardar of the Cis-Satluj estates of the Maharaja. In 1835, he was deputed to Anandpur to settle the dispute between the local Sodhi factions. Chet Singh was on guard duty near the gate on the fateful evening (5TH November 1840) when its archway fell upon Kanvar Nau Nihal Singh returning from the funeral of his father, Maharaja Kharak Singh. During the first Anglo Sikh war, Chet Singh commanded the Ropar division along the western bank of the Satluj. In the second Anglo Sikh war, he fought in the battle of Ramnagar (22ND November 1848) when he was taken prisoner by the British.

Fateh Singh, Commandant

Fateh Singh was a soldier in the Sikh army and was attached to his father's contingent, wherein he remained until 1827 when he was placed in the Ghorchurra Kalan regiment. In 1834, he accompanied Maharaja Ranjit Singh to Peshawar and, in 1840, he was sent, under Arjan Singh Ranghar Nanglia, to Mandi and Kulu where a rebellion had broken out. After the death of Raja Hira Singh in December 1844, Fateh Singh was ordered to Rajauri and Punch to put down an insurrection there. During the first Anglo Sikh war (1845-46), Fateh Singh remained in Lahore with General Gulab Singh Pahuvindia, assigned to protecting the minor Maharaja Duleep Singh. Soon after the war, he was appointed commandant of the Suraj Mukhti corps. He served throughout the Multan campaign of 1848. After the annexation of the Punjab, he joined the police. Fateh Singh died in 1875.

Harsa Singh, General

Harsa Singh, was a soldier in the Khalsa army, and commanded one of the regiments of the French brigade. He had the rank of general under Maharaja Sher Singh. In 1848, he fought on the side of Diwan Mul Raj at Multan. He was deprived of his Jagirs by the British after the Punjab was annexed in 1849. During the uprising of 1857, he enlisted in 11TH Bengal Lancers as a Risaldar. He retired in 1860 with the title of Sardar. Harsa Singh died at Amritsar in 1887.

Generals in the Anglo Sikh Wars

Ganda Singh, Commander
Ganda Singh of Butala was a soldier in the Sikh army. Early in his career he was assigned by Maharaja Ranjit Singh to Prince Sher Singh's troops. Ganda Singh's father, Dharam Singh, had also served in the Sikh army and taken part in several battles, including those of Multan, Kashmir and Peshawar. Ganda Singh remained the favourite of Prince Sher Singh, who granted him a jagir worth 3,000 rupees from his own estates. He fought in the Prince's Yuzufzai and Kulu campaigns and held both civil and military appointments under him when he was the Nazim of Kashmir. He afterwards served at Naushera and Bannu. When Sher Singh ascended the throne, he conferred upon Ganda Singh several Jagirs around Butala, and appointed him to the command of the Orderly Derah. He was with the Maharaja when the latter was assassinated in September 1843, and was severely wounded in the endeavor to save his life. Ganda Singh was killed in December 1845 in the battle of Ferozeshah

Hukam Singh Malvai, **Sardar**
Hukam Singh Malvai was a soldier and Jagirdar in the service of Maharajah Ranjit Singh. He was the son of Dhanna Singh Malvai, an important official of the Sikh kingdom. In January 1839, along with his brother Bachittar Singh, he escorted Shahzada Taimur to Peshawar. In 1841, after Maharaja Sher Singh had ascended the throne, Hukam Singh was sent to Kulu to capture the fugitives, Lahina Singh Sandhanvalia and Kehar Singh Sandhanvalia. For his valuable services he was granted a handsome increase in his jagir. Hukam Singh was killed in the battle of Sobraon in February 1846.

Bela Singh Mokal, **Sardar**
Jawand Singh joined the Sikh army as a trooper and took part in the battle fought near Attock, in July 1813. The same year he fought in the battle of Haidru in which the Sikhs worsted the Wazir of Kabul, Fateh Khan. For his gallantry in the battle he was assigned jagir worth Rs 30,000 annually in Gujrat district. He also took part in the expeditions of Multan (1818) and Kashmir (1819). His fortune rose quickly, and he became a Sardar and companion of the Maharaja. His son, Bela Singh with 200 horses, took part in the first Anglo Sikh war. He was wounded at Sobraon and washed away in the River Satluj. Bela Singh's son, Surjan Singh, fought and died in the second Anglo-Sikh war.

Generals in the Anglo Sikh Wars

Jivan Singh Chhachhi, *Commander*

Jivan Singh Chhachhi, son of Uttam Singh, a Kohli Khatri, was a military commander in the Sikh army. His father and grandfather had also served under Maharaja Ranjit Singh. Jivan Singh's contingent, consisting of sixty-five horse, five Zambureks or camel swivels, and a kettledrum, was known all along the north-western frontier for its swift movement. He served at Bannu, Tonk, Mittha Tiwana, Peshawar and Jamrud. For about eight years, he was stationed at Derah Ismail Khan where he had to face the hostility of the border tribes. He took part in the two Anglo Sikh wars. He died on 22ND September 1852.

Jawahar Singh Nalwa, Sardar

Sardar Jawahar Singh Nalwa, son of the celebrated general, Hari Singh Nalwa, joined the Sikh army in 1832 and was sent to Jehangira, a military post on the northwest frontier. Two years later he was posted to Peshawar, where he took part in numerous campaigns against the Afghans up to the time of his father's death at Jamrud in April 1837. During the second Anglo Sikh war, he joined Sher Singh's forces and fought against the British with great gallantry at Chillianwala, leading a desperate charge of irregular cavalry, which had nearly proved decisive. In 1857, Jawahar Singh was appointed Risaldar in 1st Sikh Cavalry raised by the British after the abrogation of Sikh rule. He saw action at Lucknow, Kanpur and at several other places. In 1859, he was rewarded with Jagirs for his services and, in 1862, was made an honorary magistrate at Gujrariwala. Jawahar Singh died in 1877.

Jodh Singh, Colonel

Jodh Singh was a colonel in the army of Maharaja Ranjit Singh. He was son of Jai Singh, a descendant of the Man family of Mughal Chakk. Jodh Singh was appointed headman of twenty-two villages. His grandfather, Sarja Singh, was an ally of Charhat Singh Sukkarchakkia. The Man family achieved great honour and influence under Maharaja Ranjit Singh and almost twenty-two members of the family held trustworthy military posts in the Sikh army. During the Anglo Sikh war of 1848-49, Jodh Singh fought against the British and consequently the Jagirs of this branch of the family were confiscated by the British government. Jodh Singh was, however, granted a pension by the British. He died in 1874.

Generals in the Anglo Sikh Wars

Kahn Singh Rosa, Colonel

Kahn Singh Rosa was appointed Jemadar in the Dragoons corps of the Sikh army in 1822. The following year he was made a Risaldar in the same regiment. In 1829, he was appointed commandant in the Khas Paltan, or Life Guards. He served with his regiment in Kulu and Mandi in the hills. He was severely wounded in the chest by a musket shot in the attack on Raja Suchet Singh in March 1844. In 1848, Kahn Singh was posted at Peshawar as colonel of the Dragoons. He was one of the first to join the uprising against the British. A man of great bravery and an admirable cavalry officer, his influence with the army was great. Throughout the second Anglo Sikh war, he fought stubbornly against the British. After the annexation of the Punjab, Kahn Singh`s Jagir was confiscated, though he was granted a pension. Kahn Singh died in June 1864.

Kahn Singh Majithia, General

Kahn Singh Majithia, son of Amar Singh Majithia, served as a general in the Sikh army in the second Anglo Sikh war. During Maharaja Ranjit Singh`s reign, Kahn Singh was a minor military officer, when he is said to have killed a lion with his sword while out hunting with the Maharaja in 1831. In 1838 he was an officer in the Ghorchurra Khas. He was commandant of the Sikh force at Peshawar in 1848, when his troops marched out of Peshawar to join Chatar Singh and Sher Singh; Kahn Singh fought the British both at Chillianwala and Gujrat. He died in 1853 at Majitha, his ancestral village.

Kahn Singh Man, General

Kahn Singh Man, was appointed commandant of Maharaja Ranjit Singh`s bodyguard at a comparatively young age. He took part in several campaigns under the Maharaja, rising to the rank of general in 1836, commanding four regiments of infantry and a 10 gun section of artillery. In 1846, after the first Anglo Sikh war, Kahn Singh was sent at the head of an expedition against Shaikh Imam Ud Din, the rebellions governor of Kashmir. He succeeded in bringing Imam Ud Din a prisoner to Lahore, without having to fire a shot. In March 1848, General Kahn Singh was appointed governor of Multan, to replace Diwan Mul Raj who had resigned. However, Diwan Mul Raj rebelled and imprisoned Kahn Singh and his minor son, Vasava Singh. When the British army bombarded the Fort, both father and son perished in the prison on 30TH December 1848.

Generals in the Anglo Sikh Wars

Kahn Singh, Sardar
Kahn Singh, joined Maharaja Ranjit Singh's army and was sent to Pindi Gheb in command of 500 horse. Kahn Singh accompanied Hari Singh Nalwa on his numerous expeditions. He fought in the campaign against the Yuzufzai tribes on the northwest frontier in 1831. He took part in the campaign of 1837, in which the great general Hari Singh Nalwa was killed. Kahn Singh died fighting at Sobraon during the first Anglo Sikh war.

Lal Singh Moranvala, General
General Lal Singh Moranvala was a member of the Council of Regency constituted by Maharani Jind Kaur in December 1844. During the first Anglo Sikh war, Lal Singh Moranvala saw action in the battle of Alival (28TH January 1846) under the command of Ranjodh Singh Majithia. In 1848, he was appointed chief justice of the Sindh Sagar Doab. During the Hazara revolt of 1848 he showed sympathies with Chatar Singh Attariwala, occupied Wazirabad, joined Raja Sher Singh along with his troops and fought against the British. He took part in the battles of Ramnagar (22ND November 1848), Chillianwala (13TH January 1849), and Gujrat (21ST February 1849).

Mahitab Singh Majithia. General
Mahitab Singh started his career as a Subadar in the Irregular Sikh Cavalry of Maharaja Ranjit Singh. In 1831, he was promoted Colonel and posted as commandant of Sikh troops stationed at Amritsar. He served in the Peshawar campaign in 1834, and, in 1839, in the campaign against the Afridis and other trans-Indus tribes. In 1841, Maharaja Sher Singh made him a General and gave him command of the Sikh troops stationed at Peshawar. In 1844, General Mahitab Singh commanded four battalions of infantry, one regiment of cavalry, and a top khana, light artillery. Under the regency of Maharani Jind Kaur, he was nominated (December 1844) a member of the Khalsa Supreme Council. In March 1845, General Mahitab Singh proceeded with his troops to Bhimbar, where the chief, Raja Faiz Talab Khan, had joined Prince Pashaura Singh who had risen in revolt. General Mahitab Singh defeated the Bhimbar chief, and soon afterwards Pashaura Singh capitulated to his troops at Sialkot. Mahitab Singh fought in the 1ST Anglo Sikh war against the British. During the 2ND Anglo-Sikh war he led the Durbar's troops against Raja Sher Singh Attariwala. He died in 1865.

Generals in the Anglo Sikh Wars

Man Singh, Sardar

Man Singh was a soldier in Maharaja Ranjit Singh's army. He took part in the capture of Peshawar (1834) and then entered Raja Hira Singh's brigade as a cavalry adjutant. He fought against the British in the first Anglo Sikh war at Mudki, Ferozeshah and Sobraon. After the hostilities ceased, he was stationed at Lahore in command of a troop of fifty horses. In 1848, he was sent to Amritsar. After the second Anglo Sikh war his troop was disbanded and he retired on a pension. Man Singh died in 1892.

Nahar Singh, Sardar

Nahar Singh, joined Maharaja Ranjit Singh's service in 1803. He joined the expedition against Hafiz Ahmad Khan of Jhang, resulting in the imprisonment of that chief. He served in the first campaign of Multan and then in both the Kashmir expeditions. He fought in the battle of Teri in 1823 and served under the command of Hari Singh Nalwa, and participated in the fighting against the Mazaris of Mitlhankot in 1835. He was appointed commander of the Mulrajia Regiment, and was deputed against the insurgents who had ravaged the country in the neighbourhood of Gujrat and had looted the shrine of Ker Sahib, a place of sanctity for the Sikhs. During the first Anglo Sikh war (1845-46) Nahar Singh had served under Ranjodh Singh Majithia. Nahar Singh died in 1866

Ram Singh Chhapevala, Commander

Ram Singh Chhapevala was a man of note who fought in the battles of Ramnagar, Chillianwala and Gujrat during the second Anglo Sikh war of 1848-49. Under Maharaja Sher Singh, Ram Singh received various military commands. In 1847, Ram Singh was sent in command of some irregular horse to Bannu, under Shamsher Singh Sandhanvalia, who was in command of the Sikh force sent by the Lahore Durbar to help Lieutenant Herbert Edwardes settle the disturbed district. Ram Singh was instrumental in arousing the Sikh force stationed in Dalip Garh Fort at Bannu to rebellion in 1848. The force headed by Ram Singh marched on to join Raja Sher Singh against the British. Ram Singh showed his worth by fighting bravely at Ramnagar (22ND November 1848), Chillianwala (13TH January 1849) and at Gujrat (21ST February 1849). He fell in the last-named battle.

Generals in the Anglo Sikh Wars

Ranjodh Singh Majithia, Commander

Ranjodh Singh Majithia was the governor of Hazara and the commander of Durbar troops in 1844. He was called to lead Sikh military operations against Jasrota, to forestall the machinations of Raja Gulab Singh Dogra of Jammu. The fortress was reduced and Gulab Singh obliged to surrender. In the first Anglo Sikh war, Ranjodh Singh commanded a division of the Khalsa army with 70 guns. He entered the Jalandhar Doab, and having joined his forces with the Ladva chief, seriously threatened Ludhiana. He had a skirmish at Badhowal, 11 km on the road to Jagraori, with Major General Harry Smith, who had hastened to the relief of Ludhiana, on 21ST January 1846. Outnumbered, the British general was chary of giving battle. He made a detour to the right, and hastily retreated towards Ludhiana. Ranjodh Singh`s artillery opened up a cannonade on the retiring British force. A portion of it was worsted, with 77 men taken prisoner. General Smith was however able to save Ludhiana, but the Sikhs claimed a victory at Badhowal. Ranjodh Singh marched on Jagraori in order to cut off British communications with Ferozepore. He took part in the battle of Aliwal on 28TH January 1846. After the treaty of Bharoval, Ranjodh Singh was made a member of the Council of Regency. In 1848, he was arrested following interception of his correspondence with Diwan Mul Raj of Multan, but was released after the war. Ranjodh Singh Majithia died in 1872.

Ratan Singh Man, General

Ratan Singh Man was a general in the Sikh army. He joined military service as a trooper and rose to be an adjutant. He served under Hari Singh Nalwa in Kashmir and Hazara and was, in 1821, severely wounded at Marigli in the Kashmir hills, where Hari Singh was besieging a strong fort defended by the hill men. For his services in this campaign, he received the command of a regiment. Ratan Singh accompanied Sardar Sham Singh`s contingent to Kulu and Mandi, where he was engaged for nearly two years in reducing the hill tribes to submission. He took part in the expedition against Gulab Singh Dogra and the conquest of Jasrota. In December 1844, Gulab Singh had invested Jasrota, expelled the Sikh garrison, and carried away the treasure and crown jewels hidden there by Wazir Hira Singh. General Ratan Singh retrieved State property and secured the surrender of Jasrota. General Ratan Singh fought in the First and Second Anglo Sikh wars. The general died in 1857.

Generals in the Anglo Sikh Wars

Sham Singh, Attariwala, Sardar

Sham Singh Attariwala, a general in the Sikh army, was the grandson of Sardar Gauhar Singh, who had embraced Sikhism in the early days of Sikh political ascendancy and joined the Jatha or band of Gurbaksh Singh of Roranvala. He soon established his rakhior protection over an area around Atari, a village he had founded some 16 miles from Amritsar. His son, Nihal Singh, was known for his martial prowess and for his personal loyalty to Maharaja Ranjit Singh. Nihal Singh`s son, Sham Singh, entered the service of the Maharaja in 1817 and, in 1818, took part in the military campaigns of Peshawar, Attock and Multan. He also fought in Kashmir in 1819. He led Sikh forces against Sayyid Ahmad of Bareilly, who had during the years 1826-31 carried on in the Trans-Indus region a relentless crusade against the Sikhs. Sayyid Ahmad was overcome and killed on 6TH May 1831, along with his chief Lieutenant, Muhammad Ismail. At the Durbar, Sham Singh Attariwala acted on occasions as Chief of Protocol. In that capacity, he received Sir Alexander Burnes when he had in July 1831 brought from the King of England presents of horses and a carriage for the Maharaja. He was charged with protocol duties at the Ropar meeting in October 1831 between Lord William Bentinck, the Governor General of India, and Maharaja Ranjit Singh, as also at the Ferozepore meeting in November 1838 between the Maharaja and Lord Auckland. Sham Singh`s influence at the court was further enhanced by the marriage of his daughter, Bibi Nanaki, to Maharaja Ranjit Singh`s grandson, Prince Nau Nihal Singh. In the cold season of 1844, Sham Singh led a punitive expedition to Jammu against Raja Gulab Singh and secured the surrender of Jasrota. His troops led the insurrection against Dogra dominance in Lahore, which ended in the assassination of Hira Singh and his favourite, Pandit Jalla. For his influence over the Khalsa army and for his qualities of courage and forthrightness, Sham Singh was nominated to the council of regency set up by Maharani Jind Kaur on 22ND December 1844, for the minor sovereign Maharaja Duleep Singh. At the outbreak of the first Anglo-Sikh war, Sham Singh was at Karkalla, south of the Sikh frontier, for the wedding of his second son, Kahn Singh. As he heard the news, he rushed back to the Punjab. The defeat of the Sikh forces at Ferozeshah led the Queen Mother, Maharani Jind Kaur, to summon him from Atari. Sham Singh immediately repaired to Lahore. He chided the commanders, Misr Tej Singh and Misr Lal Singh, who had fled the field, and himself crossed the Satluj swearing an oath on the Guru Granth Sahib that he would lay down his life rather than return in defeat.

Generals in the Anglo Sikh Wars

Sham Singh, Attariwala, Sardar (Cont.)

The battle was joined at Sobraon on 10TH February 1846. Dressed in white and riding his white steed, the grey bearded Sardar Sham Singh moved from column to column calling upon his men to fight to the last.

As the battle was in a critical stage, Misr Tej Singh fled across the Satluj and sank a part of the bridge of boats after him. Sham Singh, far from disheartened by this, rushed into the thick of the battle. He made a desperate charge along with his fifty men against the advancing enemy. Within minutes he was overpowered and he fell to the ground dead. In the evening as the battle was over, his servants swam from across the river to recover the body. On 12TH February 1846, Sham Singh was cremated outside his village. A Samadh raised on the site now honours his memory.

Sher Singh Attariwala, Raja

Sher Singh Attariwala, provincial governor under Maharaja Duleep Singh of Lahore, was the son of Chatar Singh Attariwala. He was appointed governor of Peshawar in October 1845, and recalled in August 1846 to Lahore, where he was nominated a member of the Council of Regency. He was created Raja in November 1847. In April 1848, Raja Sher Singh commanded the Lahore Durbar troops sent out to Multan by the British Resident to quell the rebellion by Diwan Mul Raj. But on hearing of the humiliation his father, Chatar Singh, who was governor of Hazara, had suffered at the hands of Captain James Abbott, the Assistant Resident, and sore at the British refusal to permit the marriage of his sister who had been betrothed to Maharaja Duleep Singh, Sher Singh left the British camp and went over to Mul Raj along with the Durbar troops. He moved northwards to join his father, Chatar Singh, at Hazara. Sher Singh's action set into motion a chain of events which set the whole of the Punjab ablaze. From across the Ravi and from the Sind Sagar Doab multitudes of disbanded Khalsa soldiers swelled his ranks. Overnight, he became a leader of Sikh resistance. He proclaimed himself a Servant of the Khalsa and that of the sovereign, and called upon the people to rise in arms and expel the British from their country. Simultaneously, the rising in the north under his father, Chatar Singh Attariwala, gained popular support. The Sikh contingents at Bannu, Kohat, Tonk, Peshawar and Attock revolted and joined him. On the other hand, without a formal declaration of war, the British commander in chief .Lord Sir Hugh Gough crossed the Ravi on 16TH November 1848, with 24,000 men and 65 guns.

Generals in the Anglo Sikh Wars

Sher Singh Attariwala, Raja (Cont.)

Sher Singh fought the British at Ramnagar on 22ND November 1848, defeating Brigadier General Campbell's 3RD Infantry Division. The force under his command fought another action on 3RD December at Sadullapur, engaging the British division commanded by General Thackwell, and crossed over to the left bank of the river. Soon afterwards he joined his father, Chatar Singh, and together they worsted the British at Chillianwala on 13TH January 1849 but in the last action at Gujrat on 21ST February 1849 they suffered a heavy defeat. Both Chattar Singh and Sher Singh fled towards Jehlum, pursued by General Gilbert. On 14TH March, Sher Singh surrendered to the British commander at Rawalpindi. The Punjab was annexed to the British dominions and Sher Singh, along with his father, was detained at Atari and then imprisoned at Allahabad. They were later transferred to Fort William at Calcutta from where they were released in January 1854. Raja Sher Singh died at Banares in 1858.

Surat Singh Majithia, Sardar

Surat Singh Majithia was a soldier, commander and notable Sardar of the Sikh Durbar. Details of his early career and of his service under Maharaja Ranjit Singh are scanty. Surat Singh was commandant of the Sikh battalion posted at Peshawar during the first Anglo Sikh war. After the peace settlement of 1846, he was retained in the Sikh army by British Resident Sir Henry Lawrence, and posted to Lahore. He fell foul of Wazir Lal Singh, who became his enemy and ordered the reduction of his jagir. Surat Singh played a prominent role in events leading to the Sikh national rising against the British in 1848. He commanded 2,000 men in the division sent under Sher Singh Attariwala to Multan, to quell Diwan Mul Raj's revolt. In September 1848 he, as well as Sher Singh`s troops, joined the rebels. His appeal to the Khalsa troops in the name of their sovereign, Duleep Singh, and his call to arms against the Feringhees brought an immediate response. Many disbanded Sikh soldiers, religious leaders and laymen joined the standard of revolt. Mul Raj's troops deserted and rallied round him. He moved northwards, plundered Chiniot and Jhang and fought the British at Sadullapur, Chillianwala and Gujrat along with Sher Singh`s force, which had swelled to 12,000 men and 28 guns. At Sadullapur, 6 km from the town of Ramnagar, at a principal ford on the River Jehlum, the Sikhs nullified General Thackwell`s manoeuvre against their flank and safely crossed the river to join Chatar Singh's force. At Gujrat, the force under Surat Singh was the last to yield. He died in 1881.

INDIAN ARMY

When India was partitioned in 1947, the exodus of Muslim troops resulted in the raising of the proportion of Sikhs in the army dramatically to 30 percent. This predominance irked those in the ruling party who inherited the mantle of the Raj. The home minister Sardar Vallabhbhai Patel vowed to cut down the Sikhs strength in the army in line with their population. Patel is also believed to have decreed that no Sikh shall be appointed Chief of the Army Staff. There is no denying the fact that, despite five decades of republican democracy, India has had several outstanding Sikh Generals but never a be-turbaned Chief of Army Staff, until General Joginder Jaswant Singh assumed charge of the Indian Army, as the 22ND Chief of Army Staff, on 31ST January 2005, followed by General Bikram Singh on 31ST May 2012.

Indo-Pakistani War of 1947

Almost immediately after independence, tensions between India and Pakistan began to boil over. Upon the Maharaja of Kashmir's reluctance to accede to either India or Pakistan, an impatient Pakistan sponsored a 'tribal' invasion of parts of Kashmir. The men also included Pakistan army regulars. Soon after, Pakistan sent in its troops to annex the state. In spite of a determined effort by the Jammu and Kashmir state forces and by the initially inducted Indian troops, the enemy reached the outskirts of Srinagar on November 20TH and the fall of the capital city was imminent. On November 21ST, reports came in of a concentration of around 3,000 enemy troops on the outskirts of Srinagar at Shalateng, just 4 miles from the city centre, preparing to attack the city. Colonel Harbakhsh Singh, then Second-in-Command of the newly inducted 161ST Brigade was given the task of conducting the battle. He attacked Shalateng on November 22ND with two Infantry Battalions, 1ST Sikh and 1ST (Para) Kumaon with a troop of armoured cars of 7TH Cavalry and, in a brilliantly planned and executed operation, routed the enemy leaving 472 enemy dead on the field. The threat to Srinagar was now over. If the capital city had fallen, it would have been one of the greatest disasters in Indian history. Promoted to command 163RD Brigade, his was one of the two Brigades launched by General Thimmaya, then in command of Sri Division (later 19TH Division), on May 17TH, 1948, to clear the enemy out of the Jhelum valley, up to Muzaffarabad and Domel. The 161ST Brigade under Brigadier L.P Sen was on the Jhelum axis, and the second in a flanking move by his 163RD Brigade over the Nasta Chun Pass to Tithwal and beyond.

Indian Army

Indo-Pakistani War of 1947 (Cont.)

Brigadier Harbakhsh Singh's offensive, as discussed by General Birdwood in his book, A Continent Decides, was a triumph. "Pakistan's situation was now grim, and had India only used air supply more aggressively to maintain the impetus of this outflanking success, her forces would so severely have threatened Muzaffarabad as to force a Pakistani withdrawal from the whole of the northern sector. Luckily for Pakistan, they paused". Tithwal fell on May 23RD. In six days, Brigadier Harbakhsh Singh had, in a lightning move, secured all territory starting from Handwara to the Kishanganga over the Nasta Chun Pass and Tithwal after fighting aggressive battles. An intense war was waged across the state and former comrades found themselves fighting each other. Both sides made some territorial gains and also suffered significant losses. An uneasy UN sponsored peace returned by the end of 1948 with Indian and Pakistani soldiers facing each other directly on the Line of Control, which has since divided Indian from Pakistani-held Kashmir. In October 1948, Pakistani troops launched an attack with the objective of capturing Richmar Gali to the south of Tithwal and occupying Nastachur Pass to the east of Tithwal. Lance Naik Karam Singh was commanding a forward outpost in the Richmar Gali area. During the initial attacks, all the bunkers in the platoon area were destroyed by heavy enemy shelling. Communications with his Commander were also cut off, hence Karam Singh was unable to update his situation or ask for reinforcements. Although wounded, he brought back two injured comrades to the frontline with the help of another man to the main company position and defended Richmar Gali. Twice wounded by the fifth enemy attack, Lance Naik Karam Singh refused evacuation and continued to hold on to the first-line trenches. When enemy soldiers secured a position close to the frontline, Karam Singh jumped out of his trench and bayoneted the two intruders to death. This bold action so demoralized the enemy that they broke off the attack. In all, the outpost was attacked eight times that day and the Sikhs repulsed the enemy every time. For his outstanding role in the battle of Tithwal, Karam Singh was awarded the highest wartime Gallantry Award 'Param Vir Chakra' at Richmar Gali in Jammu and Kashmir on 13TH October 1948.

Indian Army

Goa, Daman and Diu Operation (1961)

Even though the British and French vacated all their colonial possessions in the Indian subcontinent, Goa, Daman and Diu remained under Portuguese control. In 1961, after repeated Portuguese refusals to negotiate towards leaving, New Delhi ordered a small contingent of its troops to invade the Portuguese territories and secure them. It was called Operation Vijay. Unable to withstand the assault, Portugal signed a truce with India and gave up its control over the small territories, which formally became part of the Indian Union.

The Indo-China Conflict- 1962

Since 1959 Indian Police posts had been pushed forward into territory claimed by the Chinese Government. Small scale clashes broke out as India insisted the border ran along the "traditional" watershed, in effect the McMahon Line, which China disputed. In 1962 Indian soldiers were ordered to move to the Thagla ridge near the border between Bhutan and Arunachal Pradesh, which formed part of the watershed, but was some three miles to the north of the McMahon line. Tensions rose further when New Delhi discovered that the Chinese had constructed a road through Aksai Chin which India claimed. In September 1962 Chinese troops made a surprising attack on the Indian soldiers from the ridge. On October 12TH, Nehru gave orders for the Chinese to be expelled from Aksai Chin. On October 20TH, Chinese soldiers attacked India in both the North-West and North-East parts of the border, entering the disputed Aksai Chin region along with Arunachal Pradesh in numbers. China then called on the Indian Government to negotiate. With no peaceful agreement between the two countries, China unilaterally withdrew their troops from the territory they had occupied. The major reason for the Indian defeat was that the executive didn't involve the Indian Air Force to annihilate the Chinese aggression and transport lines. As a result the Chinese victory was due to sheer number rather than military superiority.[1]

---

[1] Subedar Joginder Singh was awarded the highest wartime Gallantry Award 'Param Vir Chakra' fighting against the Chinese at Bumla Axis on the North East Frontier on 23RD October 1962.

Indian Army

Indo-Pakistani War of 1965

A second confrontation with Pakistan took stand in 1965, largely over Kashmir. Pakistani dictator General Ayub Khan launched Operation Gibraltar in August 1965, believing an Indian leadership still recovering from the 1962 war with China would be unable to deal effectively with such a military thrust. It proved to be a serious miscalculation for Ayub. India responded almost immediately with Armoured Regiments being deployed to both counter enemy intrusions and strike across the border. Initially, the Indian Army met with considerable success in the northern sector. After launching prolonged artillery barrages against Pakistan, India was able to capture three important mountain positions in Kashmir. The Indian Army had made considerable in roads into Pakistan. India had its largest haul of Pakistani tanks when the offensive of Pakistan's 1ST Armoured Division was blunted at the Battle of Assal Uttar on September 10TH. The battle was so fierce and intense that at the end of the war, the Fourth Indian Division .a.k.a. "The Fighting Fourth" had captured about 97 tanks, destroyed and damaged or intact condition. This included 72 Patton tanks and 25 Chafees and Shermans. 32 of the 97 tanks, including 28 Pattons, were in running condition. Indian losses in Khem Karan were 32 tanks. Roughly about fifteen of them were captured by the Pakistan Army, mostly Sherman tanks. Pakistan launched Operation Grand Slam on September 1ST, invading the Chamb-Jaurian sector. In retaliation, the Indian Army's 15TH Infantry Division crossed the International Border on the Western Front on September 6TH. By the end of the war, it was estimated that Pakistan lost nearly 300 tanks destroyed. India had more than 150 tanks in its hands as war trophies and it is not unsafe to assume that more tanks were destroyed, that were in Pakistani territory, both by army as well as air action. Indian losses were less than half at 128 tanks destroyed. About 40 tanks would have fallen into Pakistani hands, most of them vintage AMX-13s from Chamb and Shermans from Khem Karan. [2]

---

[2] See the profile of Lieutenant General Harbakhsh Singh on page 90. He refused orders to retreat, annihilated the Pakistani attacking force and saved the Punjab falling into Pakistani hands.

Indian Army

Indo-Pakistani War of 1965
"Sikh War with Pakistan!"

I have read in the recent past some Indian journalist calling 1965 the "Sikh War with Pakistan." I always wondered why this respected journalist called it a Sikh War and not India's war. If analysed, this war was wholly fought by Sikh Generals. Almost all Senior Commanders in the Western Sector and Punjab sector were Sikhs. Lieutenant General Harbakhsh Singh, with his Chief of Staff, Major-General Joginder Singh, commanded the entire Western zone and was, as such, the principal architect of India's victory. Involved with planning at the army headquarters was another Sikh General, Major-General Narinder Singh. Lieutenant General Joginder Singh Dhillon, a brilliant tactician, with Brigadier Parkash Singh Grewal, and Artillery Commander, Brigadier S.S. Kalha, commanded the troops operating in the Punjab and parts of Rajasthan. Major-General Niranjan Prasad was replaced midbattle by Major-General Mohindar Singh as Division Commander in the Amritsar sector, the other Division Commander, in the Khem Karan sector, being Major-General Gurbaksh Singh. North of the Ravi, Major-General Rajinder Singh 'Sparrow', commanding an Armoured Division in a lightning push into Pakistan, his Centurion tanks humbled Pakistan's prestigious American gifted Pattons and Chaffees. The Khem Karan sector, too, was turned into what came to be known as the graveyard of the Pakistani Patton tanks. South of the Satluj, Brigadier Bant Singh, commanding an independent Sikh Brigade Group, defended stoutly an extensive border covering the entire Ferozepore and Ganga Nagar districts. To the North in Kashmir Major Ranjit Singh Dayal, later Lieutenant General - led his troops up the impenetrable Haji Pir Pass and captured it, inflicting a devastating blow on the enemy control in the area. Both at Hussainiwala and Fazilka, Sikh Battalion Commanders held fast to their positions despite intensely heavy shelling by Pakistan artillery. The Indian Air Force, with many heroic Sikh pilots under the command of the Sikh Air Chief Marshal, Arjan Singh, made devastating strikes and surprised military experts the world over by decisively outpacing a far superior, i.e. better equipped, Pakistani Air force.

Indian Army

Bangladesh Liberation War, 1971

The Indo-Pakistani conflict was sparked by the Bangladesh Liberation war, a conflict between the traditionally dominant West Pakistanis and the majority East Pakistanis. The Bangladesh Liberation war was ignited after the 1970 Pakistani election, in which the East Pakistani Awami League won 167 of 169 seats in East Pakistan and secured a simple majority in the 313-seat lower house of the Majlis-e-Shoora (Parliament of Pakistan). Awami League leader Sheikh Mujibur Rahman presented his credentials to the President of Pakistan and claimed the right to form the Government. After the leader of the Pakistan Peoples Party, Zulfikar Ali Bhutto, refused to yield the premiership of Pakistan to Mujibur Rahman, President Yahya Khan called the military, dominated by West Pakistanis to suppress dissent. Wary of the growing involvement of India, the Pakistan Air Force (PAF) launched a pre-emptive strike on India. The attack was modelled on the Israeli Air Force's Operation Focus during the Six-Day War. However, the plan failed to achieve the desired success and was seen as an open act of unprovoked aggression against the Indians. Indian Prime Minister Indira Gandhi declared war on Pakistan in aid of the Mukti Bahini, (Bengal Liberation Army) she ordered an immediate mobilisation of troops and launched the full-scale invasion of East Pakistan. This marked the official start of the Indo-Pakistani War. Three Indian corps were involved in the invasion of East Pakistan. They were supported by nearly three Brigades of Mukti Bahini fighting alongside them, and many more fighting irregularly. This was far superior to the Pakistani army of three divisions. The Indians quickly overran the country, bypassing heavily defended strongholds. Pakistani forces were unable to effectively counter the Indian attack, as they had been deployed in small units around the border to counter guerrilla attacks by the Mukti Bahini. Unable to defend Dhaka, the Pakistanis surrendered on 16TH December 1971. The Instrument of Surrender was signed at Ramna Race Course in Dhaka on December 16TH, 1971, by Lieutenant General Jagjit Singh Arora, General Officer Commanding in Chief of Eastern Command of the Indian Army and Lieutenant General A.A.K. Niazi, Commander of Pakistani forces, as the formal act of surrender of all Pakistani forces.

*During the 1971 Indo-Pak conflict, Flying officer Nirmal Jit Singh Sekhon was awarded India's highest Gallantry Award, the Param Vir Chakra. He is the only Officer of the Indian Air Force ever to be awarded this award.

Indian Army

Siachen Conflict, 1984

Prior to the 1980s, neither India nor Pakistan maintained any permanent military presence in the Siachen region. However, Pakistan began conducting and allowing a series of mountaineering expeditions to the glacier beginning in the 1950s. By the early 1980s, the Government of Pakistan was granting special expedition permits to mountaineers and United States Army maps deliberately showed Siachen as a part of Pakistan. India, possibly irked by these developments, launched a military operation in April 1984. The entire Kumaon Regiment of the Indian Army was airlifted to the glacier. Pakistani forces responded quickly and clashes between the two followed. The Indian Army secured the strategic Sia La and Bilafond La Mountain passes and by 1985, more than 1,000 square miles (2,600 km) of territory, 'claimed' by Pakistan, was under Indian control. The Indian Army continues to control all of the Siachen Glacier and its tributary glaciers. Pakistan made several unsuccessful attempts to regain control over Siachen. In late 1987, Pakistan mobilised about 8,000 troops and garrisoned them near Khapalu, aiming to capture Bilafond La. However, they were repulsed by Indian Army personnel guarding Bilafond. During the battle, about 23 Indian soldiers lost their lives while more than 150 Pakistani troops perished. Further unsuccessful attempts to reclaim positions were launched by Pakistan in 1990, 1995, 1996.

Kargil conflict, 1999

Pakistani paramilitary forces and Kashmiri insurgents in mid-1999 captured deserted, but strategic, Himalayan heights in the Kargil district of India. These had been vacated by the Indian army during the onset of the inhospitable winter and were supposed to be re-occupied in spring. The regular Pakistani troops who took control of these areas received important support, both in the form of arms and supplies, from Pakistan. Once the scale of the Pakistani incursion was realised, the Indian Army quickly mobilised about 200,000 troops and Operation Meghdoot was launched. Two months into the conflict, Indian troops had slowly retaken most of the ridges they had previously abandoned. The Indian Army launched its final attacks in the last week of July; as soon as the Drass sub sector had been cleared of Pakistani forces, the fighting ceased on 26TH July. By the end of the war, India had resumed control of all territory south and east of the Line of Control, as was established in July 1972 per the Shimla Accord.

THE GENERALS

Amarjit Singh, Major General

Major General Amarjit Singh is an Additional Director General of NCC Gujarat, Dadra Nagar Haveli, Daman, Diu and a Member of the Board of Governance. He is an Alumnus of the National Defence Academy Khadakvasla and was commissioned into the Corps of Signals of the Indian Army in June 1979. He is also an Alumnus of the Defence Services Staff College and the College of Defence Management, Master of Defence Studies from the Madras University, Master of Management Studies from Osmania University and Master of Technology in Computer Engineering from the Indian Institute of Technology Kharagpur. He was Brigadier in Charge Administration and Deputy Chief Instructor (Logistics) at the Military College of Telecommunication Engineering, Mhow and also officiated as its Chief Instructor. Major General Amarjit Singh has been an Instructor at the Military College of Telecommunication Engineering, Mhow. He has worked on strategic planning and simulation with the National Security Council Secretariat and the National Defence College. He was appointed as Director Perspective Planning (Operations Research and Systems Analysis) at Army Headquarters. In 2004, he led the Indian Delegation at the 10TH meeting of Working Party 8F of the International Telecommunication Union (ITU). He was appointed as Director Systems and Joint Communications Electronic Staff at Headquarters Integrated Defence Staff. As Chief Signal Officer of a Corps in the Eastern Sector, he was responsible for the design and execution of the entire information systems capability of the Indian Army in North Bengal and Sikkim. He has experience in the area of conflict management, having been a Military Observer with the United Nations Mission in Mozambique and a Military Mission Officer in the Department of Peace Keeping Operations at the United Nations headquarters in New York. He has also experience in counter insurgency, mountain warfare and desert warfare at various levels of command and staff and was the Commanding Officer of a Headquarters Counter Insurgency Force Signal Regiment from 1999 to 2002. During his career of 33 years, Major General Amarjit Singh has held a number of prestigious Command and Staff appointments and attended all competitive training courses.

The Generals

Atma Singh, Major General

Major General Atma Singh, after receiving his commission from Officer Training at Sandhurst, joined the 2ND Battalion, 1ST Punjab Regiment. He was involved in extensive military operations on the North-West Frontier Province and Waziristan. With the outbreak of the Second World War, many raiding gangs, at the instigation of the Faqir of Ipi, said to be subsidized by Germany and Italy, became active in Waziristan and all military traffic had to be strongly escorted. During the Second World War, with surprising rapidity and masterly skill, the Japanese had pushed back the Allied Forces in Burma to the Indian border. It was not only essential to stop the Japanese from invading India, but also imperative to regain Burma. The 2ND Battalion was mobilised in February, 1942 as a part of 47TH Brigade and joined 14TH Indian Division on April 5TH. In October, 1942, 14TH Division mounted offensive operations against the Japanese in the first Arakan campaign and captured Donbaik and Hitzwe. Atma Singh, with the Battalion, was in the vanguard of defeating the Japanese in Burma. He ended the war as a Lieutenant Colonel. Immediately after the Independence of India he was rushed to Jammu and Kashmir, to contain the Pakistani aggression. At the partition of the Indian Subcontinent, Kashmir being a Muslim-dominant state was considered a natural part of Pakistan, which had made Islam the basis of its modern nationality. The Army Headquarters of Pakistan planned the main invasion plan, code-named Operation Gulmarg. According to Operation Gulmarg, every Pathan tribe was required to enlist at least one Lashkar of 1,000 tribesmen. These Lashkars were to be concentrated at Baftnu, Wana, Peshawar, Kohat, Thal and Nowshera by the first week of September 1947. The Brigade Commanders at these places were to issue arms, ammunition and some essential clothing items. Each Lashkar was also to be provided with a Major, a Captain and ten JCOs of the regular Pakistan Army. The entire force was to be commanded by Major General Akbar Khan, who was given the code name Tariq. When the first wave of tribal warriors from Pakistan invaded the Kashmir Valley on 22ND October 1947, the kingdom of Jammu and Kashmir had not acceded to either Pakistan or India. Therefore, taking the plea that it was an internal matter, India refused to send in its troops to the Valley. However, when Maharaja Hari Singh signed the Instrument of Accession with the Indian Government on the evening of 26TH October 1947, Jammu and Kashmir became an integral part of the Indian Dominion legally, morally and constitutionally.

The Generals

Atma Singh, Major General (Cont.)

Now was the time to react to the tribal invasion, which India did commendably, considering the short notice given to its Military Commanders. On October 27TH, 1947, the Indian Army entered Kashmir to flush out the intruders from Kashmir. Nearly one hundred planes were pressed into service to bring troops and arms in Leh and Ladakh. The Indian soldiers fought the war at the height of 23900 feet. Lieutenant General Kalwant Singh was in overall command and ordered, now Major General Atma Singh, to the relief of Poonch. Operation Easy was aimed at establishing the final link-up with Poonch, which had proved to be difficult throughout most of 1948. An attempt to link up with Poonch could be made either from the south, namely, via Thana Mandi or Rajauri, or from the north via the Haji Pir Pass. Major General Atma Singh was ordered to plan for a link-up accordingly. Major General Atma Singh was further ordered to carry out Phase I (secure Pir Badesar) by October 8TH; commence Phase II (demonstrate north of Thana Mandi) by October 10TH; and concentrate in Rajauri the required force for Operation Easy by October 16TH. On October 9TH, Major General Atma Singh finalised and implemented his orders. The main operation was to commence on about October 19TH with 5TH Brigade advancing from Rajauri and securing Pir Kalewa ridge. Lieutenant Colonel Jagjit Singh's Column was then to pass through, moving from south of Thana Mandi to secure a firm base in the area around. Major General Atma Singh now detailed 19TH Brigade Group to capture Point 5732 with a view to exploit Jhhika Gali, an enemy stronghold barring the way to Mendhar and also captured its objective at 0620 hours. Then the exploitation began. The link-up with Poonch in November 1948 was a notable performance. The enemy ring round Poonch was broken and attempts to force the Poonch garrison to surrender were finally frustrated. Operation Easy resulted in the capture of 800 square miles (2,100 km^2) of territory. Large numbers of refugees, including 10,000 Muslims were able to get away and obtain relief from the State Administration. India brought the matter before the United Nations. Under the supervision of the United Nations, the cease-fire was implemented on January 1ST, 1949.

Atma Singh retired from the Army with the rank of Major General.

The Generals

Ardaman Jit Singh Sandhu, Major General

Major General Ardaman Jit Singh Sandhu, more commonly known by the nickname 'Abdo', is the third generation of a military family. His Grandfather, Subedar Sohan Singh had distinguished himself during the First World War, earning three Gallantry Awards for displaying exceptional bravery. One of the Certificates was signed by none other than Sir Winston Churchill, who was the then Secretary of State for War. His Father, Lieutenant General Jaswant Singh, who rose to the rank of Vice Chief, had the rare and singular honour of fighting in three full scale wars, as well as a very intense insurgency in North East India. Amongst the twelve of the family who joined the Army, one became a Lieutenant General, one a Major General and two rose to become Brigadiers. In fact during the 1971 Indo-Pakistan War, six members (including four brothers!) of the family were involved in active combat in the Western and Eastern fronts.

Ardaman Jit Singh Sandhu did his schooling in the famous Lawrence School, Sanawar. After appearing in the Senior Cambridge Examination, he decided to continue the martial traditions of the family and joined the National Defence Academy, Khadakvasla, and later the Indian Military Academy, Dehra Dun. He was commissioned into the renowned 2ND Field Regiment of the Artillery on 11TH June 1967. It needs to be mentioned that this Regiment has had the exceptional honour of contributing two Army Chiefs of opposing armies i.e. General Tikka Khan of Pakistan, and General P.P. Kumaramangalam of India! During his long and illustrious career, Major General Sandhu has held varied command, staff and instructional assignments, and has done all the prestigious military courses i.e. Long Gunnery Staff Course, Defence Services Staff College Course, Higher Command Course as well as the National Defence College Course. He saw action in the Punjab sector in the 1971 Indo-Pakistan War, and has also served in the operationally vital regions of Jammu & Kashmir and Ladakh, during the critical periods of the Siachen Conflict and Operation Vijay (Kargil conflict), and was decorated for rendering Distinguished Services of a very high order in both the assignments. He has the distinction of several "firsts" for an Indian Army Officer-he was selected on merit to be a member of the 'first' Indian Army Training team sent to train the Botswana Defence Forces. He also had the unique honour of becoming the 'first' Indian Artillery Officer to be posted as a Brigade Major of an Armoured Brigade.

The Generals

Ardaman Jit Singh Sandhu, Major General (Cont.)

Later, when it was decided to open up the Indo-US military-to-military cooperation in 1992(as an outcome of the 'Kicklighter Proposals'); he was the first Officer to be selected to attend a Military Seminar hosted by the US pacific Command in Honolulu.

Major General Abdo Sandhu has commanded 2ND Field Regiment and 261 Artillery Brigade. As Brigade Commander, during the Yamuna floods in Delhi in September 1995, he was responsible for the successful evacuation of over 500 stranded persons to safety without any loss of life. He has been Instructor at the School of Artillery, Army War College as well as at the Defence Services Staff College. He was Brigade Major of 1st Armoured Brigade, GSO 1 Operations of 3RD Infantry Division, Col General Staff of 29TH Infantry Division and Brig –In- Charge Administration of 16TH Corps. His last appointment was at the Army Headquarters, where he served as Additional Director General of Artillery, and from where he retired in 2004 after rendering over 37 years of Distinguished Service. During his career, Major General Sandhu was awarded the Vishisht Seva Medal, Chief of Army Staff's Commendation Card as well as the Northern Army Commander's Commendation Card (twice).Ardaman Jit is married to Ameeta Harsh .They have two children Karan (married to Priajit Brar) and Aditya (married to Shreya Budhraja), and two grand children Meher and Adhiraj.

MS Shergill, Lieutenant General, VrC

Lieutenant General M.S. Shergill graduated in June 1962 from the Indian Military Academy and was commissioned in 7TH Light Cavalry in the same year. At the Academy, he was awarded blue*s* in hockey and polo and was also captain of the teams. He was awarded a Vir Chakra during the Indo-Pak war of 1971 as a Squadron Commander in the Shakargarh Sector. He was Commandant of 7TH Light Cavalry from 1981 to 1984 and later Colonel of this Regiment. Lieutenant General M.S. Shergill retired on July 31ST, 2001 and held the appointment of Director General, Mechanized Forces at Army HQs before hanging his spurs.

The Generals

BS Dhillon, Major General, VSM

Major General B.S. Dhillon, born on 4TH November 1946, joined the National Defence Academy in January 1963 and was commissioned in 16TH Battalion of The Maratha Light Infantry on 25TH December 1966 from the Indian Military Academy, Dehradun. Major General Dhillon belongs to an Army background, as his Father was in the Army and on top of the Dhillon Family Tree is Jai Singh, Kumedan (General) in Maharaja Ranjit Singh's Army. Mrs. Brenda Dhillon, wife of Major General Dhillon, is the daughter of Colonel L.T. Fernandez of Artillery. Major General Dhillon is a Graduate of the National Defence College, New Delhi, Defence Service Staff College, Wellington and Post Graduate from Chennai University. He has attended the Higher Command Course at Army War College, Mhow (MP) after successfully commanding 16TH Maratha Light Infantry for four and half years. He has held the appointments of Brigade Major of a Brigade deployed in Mizoram and Colonel Q (Operations and Maintenance) at Headquarters Southern Command, Pune. He has held Instructional Appointment at the National Defence Academy, Khadakwasla and has been a Directing Staff at Army War College, Mhow in Junior and Senior Command Wings. He has served in various capacities in Jammu and Kashmir on the line of control in the anti infiltration, counter insurgency and counter terrorism roles in the difficult terrain and hostile weather conditions. He served in Naugam Sector as a young Officer from October 1967 to June 1970 as a Captain / Major. He again served as a Major in active operation in the very sensitive area of Uri Sector from July 1973 to July 1974. He was the Brigade Commander of 93RD Infantry Brigade in Poonch Sector in Counter Insurgency operations on the line of control from February 1994 to January 1996 and was awarded the Vishist Seva Medal (VSM) by the President of India for Distinguished Service of very high order on 26TH January 1997. He took an active part in the Indo-Pak conflict of 1971. He was awarded Army Commander's Commendation Card for devotion to duty as Colonel 'Q' (Operations and Maintenance) at Headquarters Southern Command, Pune on 26TH January 1993. He was a Member of the Indian Delegation to United Nations Conference on prohibition of Land Mines and Laser Weapons at Vienna (Austria) in 1995. He was awarded Army Commander's Commendation Card in January 1999 for his dedication in imparting innovative and realistic training to recruits as Commandant of The Maratha Light Infantry Regimental Centre.

The Generals

BS Dhillon, Major General, VSM (Cont.)

Major General B.S. Dhillon, VSM took over as the General Officer Commanding of 11TH Infantry Division on 20TH December 1999 on completion of NDC course. During the tenure of his Command, the Division was extensively employed for operational tasks in Rajasthan and Gujarat Sectors. He articulated coordinated and institutionalized employment of various agencies in Rann of Kutch i.e. Army, Navy, Air Force, Civil Administration, Police and Para Military. He handled and supervised the massive operation in aid to civil authorities in the aftermath of the earthquake in Gujarat on 26TH January 2001. Major General B.S. Dhillon, VSM took over the Command of Training Centre, National Security Guard, Manesar, and Gurgaon on 7TH September 2001 as Inspector General. He retired from the Army on 30TH November 2004 and is settled at Gurgaon (Haryana).

Baljit Singh Grewal, Major General, VSM

Major General Baljit Singh Grewal was commissioned into the Cavalry Regiment Hodson's Horse on 14TH November 1971. He is an Alumnus of Yadavindra Public School, Patiala National Defence Academy, Khadakwasla and Indian Military Academy, Dehra Dun. He is a winner of the Silver Centurion on his YOs course and also the Vijay Sachar Trophy on JC (Armour) course. Baljit Singh has commanded his Regiment Hodson's Horse, and Independent Armoured Brigade in the desert and an Armoured Division. He has held prestigious staff appointments in various ranks including Brigade Major of an Infantry Brigade, Assistant Military Secretary, Colonel General Staff of an Infantry Division in Jammu and Kashmir, Deputy Military Secretary and Brigadier General Staff of a Strike Corps. As a Captain and Major he has been an Instructor at the Armoured Corps Centre and School. In the rank of Colonel he has been a Directing Staff at the Defence Services Staff College at Wellington. He has also been the Commander of the Higher Command Wing at the Army War College, Mhow and the Deputy Commandant and Chief Instructor at Armoured Corps Centre and School. In the rank of Major General he has been the Deputy Commandant and Chief Instructor at the National Defence Academy, Khadakwasla for two years. During this period he made a significant contribution towards improving the training of cadets and for his Distinguished Service in this appointment he was awarded the Vishist Sewa Medal in 2010. He retired from the Army on 30TH June 2010.

The Generals

Dalbir Singh Major General, PVSM

The passing away of Major General Dalbir Singh (Retd) at his farmhouse in Ambala brings back to memory the honour that he earned for his formation of 9TH Infantry Division, the Army and the country in the 1971 war. On December 6TH, Dalbir Singh's Division was given the task of advancing along the axis of Bojra-Jessore-Khulna to capture Jessore and Khulna. The former was not only heavily fortified and well defended by a brigade-size force but it also housed Headquarters 9TH Infantry Division of the enemy, commanded by Major General Idris. Expecting stiff resistance from the enemy, the General planned to punch a hole through Jessore's defences at Durgabati, 15 km west of the former. The Indian Division moved so swiftly that by December 8TH, Jessore was captured. This brought to Dalbir Singh the title of the "Hero of Jessore". Thereafter, the enemy fell back in great confusion to Khulna, 40 km south-east of Jessore. Moving on the heels of the enemy, 9TH Infantry Division captured Khulna on December 16TH and on December 17TH, the Pakistani Brigade Commander surrendered to Major General Dalbir Singh. Major General Dalbir Singh's action in the Bangladesh War brought him the Param Vashisht Seva Medal (PVSM). He also commanded the famous 1ST Jat (Light Infantry) Regiment. He retired in August 1976

Gurbaksh Singh Badhani, Major General, VrC

Gurbaksh Singh joined the Military Academy, Dehradun in 1936, and after successful training, was appointed 2ND Lieutenant. After Distinguished Service at various military stations he had attained the rank of Major General. During the 1965 Indian-Pakistan war Major General Gurbaksh Singh, General Officer commanding a Mountain Division, was responsible for the military operations in the Khem Karan sector. Although the enemy force was numerically superior, the troops under the command of Gurbaksh Singh, not only held their position, but practically decimated the famous First Armoured Division of the Pakistan Army. This was the most critical time, when the Indian Army Commander in Chief, had panicked and insisted on withdrawal against the enemy. Generals Harbakhsh Singh and Gurbaksh Singh had disobeyed the orders and instead smashed the units of the Pakistan Army. Major General Gurbaksh Singh was awarded the Mahavir Chakra for his gallant leadership, when leading from the front. He retired from the Army in 1967, after a splendid military career. He died in September 1995.

The Generals

Gurbaksh Singh Reen, Major General

Gurbaksh Singh Reen was born on July 26TH, 1923 in Rawalpindi, now in Pakistan. His Father was a Deputy Controller of Military Accounts. Gurbaksh Singh graduated from Garden College, Rawalpindi, now in Pakistan in 1942. He joined the British Indian Army in 1943 as Second Lieutenant and served in Malaya during the Second World War. At the Indo-Pakistan partition in 1947, he moved to India and took part in the war against Pakistan in October-November, 1947. He fought in 1962 against China. In 1963, he completed a Command and General Staff Course in United States of America. In 1971, he fought against Pakistan on the Punjab border. Gurbaksh Singh retired as Major General in 1977 after serving 34 years in the Indian Army.

Gurcharn Singh Sandhu, Major General, PVSM

Major General Gurcharn Singh Sandhu was commissioned into 18TH King Edward's Own Cavalry in 1945 and saw military service during World War II on the Northwest Frontier. In 1948, he attended the first Staff College Course at Wellington. As a Staff Officer at HQ1 Armoured Division he took part in the Hyderabad Police Action in 1948. In 1959 he was selected to attend a year-long Armour Officer's Advance Course at the US Armor School at Fort Knox. Soon after the 1962 Indo-China War he was posted as Military Assistant to the Chief of the Army Staff, and continued in that appointment during the 1965 Indo-Pak War. He raised an Armoured Brigade at Siliguri before the 1971 war with Pakistan and took part in operations against the Pakistan Army in the Northwest sector of erstwhile East Pakistan (now Bangladesh). After a course at the National Defence College, he commanded another Armoured Brigade followed by the command of an Infantry Division. His last appointment in the Indian Army was as Head of the Director, Armoured Corps at Army Headquarters, from where he retired early in 1978. He was awarded the Param Vashisht Sewa Medal in 1976 for 'Distinguished Service of the most exceptional order' including Operational Service during the 1971 Indo – Pak Conflict. He is a Graduate of both the Defence Services Staff College and National Defence College. He holds a Masters Degree from Government College, Lahore and is the author of the Histories of the Indian Cavalry and of the Armoured Corps.

Harkirat Singh, Major General

Major General Harkirat Singh was granted the King's Commission in Madras Sappers from the Royal Military Academy, Woolwich U.K in 1933. After having served in various parts of the world and India, he was appointed the Chief Engineer of the Southern Command in 1947. Subsequently, he served as the Chief Engineer of the Western Command and yet again the Chief Engineer of the Southern Command. He commanded an Infantry Brigade, thus distinguishing himself as an outstanding Engineer and an eminent Soldier. During his three tenures as Command Chief Engineer, he played a leading role in the Post –War re-organisation of the Corps of Engineers and execution of a large number of construction projects for the Army, Navy, and Air-Force. Later, he was appointed as the Commander of the College of Military Engineering and was one of the main pillars in the growth of this premier institution of the Corps. He was elected President of the Institute of Engineers (India) for two consecutive terms. Of all his outstanding achievements, perhaps the most crucial was his compilation of the first National Building Code which covered the entire gamut of administrative, financial, construction, and technical aspects. The monumental publication was his personal handiwork and has been adopted by major construction departments of the Central and State Governments. In recognition of his crusading zeal and valuable contributions in the field of standardisation, the General was awarded the Moudgil Prize in 1970. Like a true General, he could asses who could be the right person for any job and likewise, he selected a team of competent people to design and execute the project for the Hemkunt Trust. Whenever the Trust was in need of his guidance he would always come to their rescue by helping them out on technical matters and advising them on the necessary personnel. As mentioned before, the General was a man of rare vision and had influenced the developing society of the country by his valuable contributions through various organisations. A man, who made sure he completed what he began with dedication. General Harkirat Singh gave his best both to public and private sectors. He was a man for all seasons-always enthusiastic, ever encouraging and endearing himself to all and sundry through his large hearted virtues. The General was a person who epitomised the saying of 'living life to the fullest'. A remarkable man with a varied spectrum of talents and achievements, he was undoubtedly one of the tallest figures of the Corps of Engineers.

The Generals

Himmat Singh Gill, Major General, VSM, AVSM

Himmat Singh Gill was commissioned in the Armoured Corps. He assisted in the Delineation of the LOC in Jammu and Kashmir after the 1971 war, while posted in the Military Operations Directorate at that time. He also assisted in the higher planning and execution of the successful war in Bangladesh in 1971, while posted in the crucial Military Operations Directorate of Army Headquarters at Delhi. Himmat Singh assisted in the raising of the Army Aviation Corps and the Directorate General Mechanized Forces at Army Headquarters in 1986-88. He conducted military level Border meetings with the Chinese Armed Forces in Bumla in Arunachal Pradesh as part of the CBMS in 1991-92. He worked as Deputy Director, Perspective Planning at Army HOS for Strategic Planning of the Indian Army dealing with Threat Perception, Force Levels Internal Security and Terrorism, Advance Strategic Planning and NBRC Warfare. He had served in senior and crucial commands at the higher level in Ladakh and Kargil along with the LOC and along the Macmohan Line in the Northeast. As the General Officer Commanding at Shillong, he has handled the counter-insurgency operations against the ULFA and the Bodos. He was considered an expert on Mountain Warfare and High Altitude Operations and Logistic Planning. He was awarded the 'Vashisht Sewa Medal' in 1982 for the furthering of Indo-Afghan relations, when posted as the Military Attaché from 1978 to 1982 at the Embassy of India, Kabul. He was also awarded the 'Da Sha Khidmat ke Khatir' Medal by the President of Afghanistan. For his Distinguished Services, he was awarded the Ati Vashisht Sewa Medal in 1984 for his leadership in pioneering effective defences on the border with China. Major General Gill sought voluntary retirement and left the Indian Army in 1993. Major General Gill is a highly decorated soldier, world traveller and a successful diplomat, having recently been assigned on a diplomatic mission to the USA, along with a former Foreign Secretary of India, in the wake of the Kargil War by the Government of India. He is a former diplomat, a novelist, commentator, columnist, short-story writer, defence analyst, book reviewer, expert on Pakistan-Afghanistan and Iranian affairs, and his résumé emphasis world traveller. Major General Himmat Singh Gill passed away on 25TH November 2008.

The Generals

Hardev Singh Kler, Major General, KC, AVSM

Major General Hardev Singh Kler was commissioned in the Indian Army on 17TH, June, 1973. He has a rare and exceptional service career profile. He is the only Officer in his batch to have taken "Command and General Staff Course" from USA and obtained Master's degree in Military Arts and Science (Strategy), USA, Research Fellowship (Strategy) and IDSA (a leading think – tank of India). He has served in both the prestigious Directorates of Military Operations and Perspective Planning. He has also served as Brigadier General Staff of a Corps and is presently, a Major General, General Staff of a Command. As head of the General Staff, both at Corps and Command, he has been responsible for a vast number of subjects pertaining to operations (war plans), intelligence, training, etc. Besides, he has written a paper on "Command and Control (Strategic Forces)", which laid the foundation for evolving organisation of Strategic Forces Command of India. The petitioner has written another paper on "Battle Field Transparency" and done research work at IDSA, which was forwarded to the Ministry of External Affairs because of its importance to south Asia.

Jaswant Singh, Major General

Major General Jaswant Singh was commissioned into the Corps of Signals on 1ST June 1941. Having served during the Second World War, he commanded 1ST Armoured Divisional Signal Regiment from 24TH November 1947 to 7TH December 1948. He was responsible for providing signal communications for the speedy march of the Division and other Indian Forces, which liberated the State of Hyderabad. The General was subsequently Chief Signal Officer 11TH Corps from 10TH June 1953 to 12TH December 1956. Chief Signal Officer Southern Command from 26TH May 1960 to 18TH July 1962 and then Chief Signal Officer Western Command, from 9TH April 1963 to 1ST June 1965. He retired from Service on 26TH June 1972. As can be seen from the appointments he held, he had vast experience in planning and providing Signal Communications at all levels. The Family has the proud privilege of having another Major General in the Corps, Major General Surjit Singh (2ND IMA Course), younger brother of Major General Jaswant Singh. Major General Jaswant Singh passed away on 23RD November 2007, at Bangalore, after a brief illness. He celebrated his 90TH birthday in May 2007.

The Generals

Joginder Singh, Major General

Major General Joginder Singh was commissioned in 5TH Battalion 14TH Punjab Regiment in 1937. He saw action in military operations against the Frontier tribes in the late 1930s. During the Second World War he was engaged in the bitter fighting against the Japanese in the Far East. After the war he attended the 1945 Army Staff Course at Quetta, served in various Command and Staff Appointments, including a stint at the Indian Ministry of Defence, command of an Infantry Battalion (7TH Punjab), Commander 80TH Brigade-Nowshera Sector, Deputy Commandant Infantry School, Brigadier General Staff 15TH Corps during the Sino-Indian War, GOC 5TH Infantry Division and Chief of Staff of the Western Command under three successive GOC in Chiefs. The last assignment included 1965 War, after which Joginder finally retired in 1967.

Kulwant Singh, Major General, UYSM

President of the Division of Enlightened Defence at the Institute for Development of Enlightened Arts and Sciences Inc. Major General (Dr.) Kulwant Singh (Retd.) received his Ph.D. and M.Sc. in Defence Studies from Chennai University. He also has a Postgraduate Diploma in Human Resource Development from Indira Gandhi National Open University in New Delhi. Dr. Singh has a Postgraduate Diploma in Management from the Regional College of Management and Technology. He qualified for the prestigious Higher Command Course at the College of Combat and is a Graduate of the Defence Service Staff Collage. Major General Singh is a veteran of two wars with Pakistan (1965 and 1971). He commanded two active combat formations: a Division deployed along Indo-China border, and a Brigade deployed on line of control against Pakistan in Jammu and Kashmir. Major General Singh had significant experience fighting terrorism at the levels of execution, planning and concepts in Sri Lanka and in India, in extremely challenging and hostile environments. He was awarded the Uttam Yudh Sewa Medal, the second highest decoration for Senior Officers during operations in Sri Lanka as part of the Indian Peace Keeping Force. Major General Singh was the Director of Maharishi Institute of Management at Noida, and Vice Chancellor of Maharishi University of Management and Technology, located at Bilaspur in Chhttisgarh (Central India). Today he is leading an international group of Generals and Defence Experts that advocates Invincible Defence Technology. Dr. Singh lives in New Delhi, India.

The Generals

Kuldip Singh Bajwa, Major General

Major General Kuldip Singh Bajwa was commissioned into the Indian Army on 22ND December 1946. He had the rare distinction of having served in the Engineers, the Infantry, and the Artillery, three of the premier fighting arms of the Army. He graduated from the Defence Services Staff College, Wellington in 1959. In February 1972, he was selected to command Infantry Formations. He had held a variety of Command and Staff Appointments and took part in all the military operations from 1947 to 1971. After leaving Service on 1ST November 1979, he became a widely read Defense Columnist, an objectively critical Military Analyst, and an accurate Military Historian. His four earlier books, the Falcon in My Name-A Soldiers Diary, Jammu and Kashmir War 1947-48: Political and Military Perspective, The Dynamics of Soldiering, and India's National Security-The Challenges and Responses have become a must read inside, as well as outside, the Military circles.

Kuldip Singh Sindhu, Major General

The General Officer is an Alumnus of St George's College, Mussoorie and subsequently graduated from the National Defence Academy, Kharakvasla and later from the Indian Military Academy, Dehradun. He was thereafter commissioned into the Poona Horse, one of the illustrious Regiments of the Armoured Corps. The General Officer is a Post Graduate of the prestigious Defence Services Staff College, Wellington and has held various illustrious appointments during his 37 year career, including Command of an Armoured Regiment, an Infantry Brigade and an Infantry Division. He also held the post of Defence Attaché in an Indian Embassy in the Middle East, besides holding an important instructional appointment in Higher Command Wing, Mhow. Prior to this new assignment, the General Officer was the Managing Director of the Ex-servicemen Contributory Health Scheme, Army Headquarters. Major General Kuldip Singh Sindhu took over the appointment of Director General Resettlement, Ministry of Defence in 2004.

The Generals

Lachman Singh Lehl, Major General, PVSM, VrC

Major General Lachman Singh Lehl was commissioned in the Regiment of Artillery in 1943 and retired from the Army in 1978. He was an Instructor Gunnery from the School of Artillery and is a Graduate of the Defence Services Staff College and the National Defence College. He is, at present, the Vice-President of the War Decorated Association. He served with the Punjabi Mussalman troops till the partition of Indian and saw active service in Burma in the Second World War. In the Jammu and Kashmir 1947-48 operations, he took part in the battles of Chhamb, Naushera, Jhangar, Rajauri, Uri and Zojila, where he was wounded. He was awarded the Vir Chakra for Gallantry in the battles for the recapture of Jhangar. He has held important command and staff appointments and was General Staff Officer Grade I in the Military Operations Directorate during the 1965 Indo-Pak war. In 1971, he commanded a Mountain Division in Bangladesh and was awarded the Param Vishisht Seva Medal for outstanding leadership in battle. His book Indian Sword Strikes in East Pakistan gives detailed accounts of the operations of his Division and the over all campaign for the liberation of Bangladesh, while his other book titled Missed Opportunities gives an extensive account of the Indo-Pak War of 1965.

Lakhwinder Singh, Major General

Major General Lakhwinder Singh is a Decorated Officer of the Indian Army with over 40 years of experience in the world's largest army. Major General Lakhwinder Singh's innovative use of howitzers during the Kargil war was one of the factors which helped the Army repel intruders from the steep mountain peaks. Major General Lakhwinder Singh says his name was cleared for promotion as Lieutenant General twice, by two special selection boards, the first under the Chief of Army Staff General N.C. Vij and the second under General J.J. Singh. Yet he was not promoted. All these years of hands on man management and strategic planning have honed his executive skills to perfection. He founded SNG Security and Placement in 2008, post retirement.

The Generals

Mander PS, Major General, YSM

Major General P.S. Mander is an Alumnus of National Defence Academy, Pune. He was commissioned into 3RD Punjab Regiment in December 1978. He is a Graduate of Defence Services Staff College, Wellington. He has done all important courses including the prestigious Long Defence Management Course. He has wide ranging experience of various Command and Staff appointments. He has commanded 25TH Punjab Regiment and 10TH Assam Rifles in intense counter insurgency operations. On Staff, he has served as BM of a Mountain Brigade, Colonel GS of Infantry Division and Dy QMG at Integrated Headquarters of MoD (Army). Besides this he has been an Instructor at The National Defence Academy, Khadakvasla (Pune) and The Infantry School Mhow. He has also done tenure as a Directing Staff in Army War College, Mhow. He was awarded the Yudh Seva Medal for his Distinguished Service while commanding the Assam Rifles. The General is married to Mrs Sharanjit and they have two sons. The General Officer took over as Additional Director General, (ADG) NCC Directorate Punjab, Haryana, Himachal Pradesh and Chandigarh on 1ST February, 2012.

Manmohan Singh, Major General, AVSM

Major General Manmohan Singh (Retd.) was the 40TH Colonel Commandant of the Corps of Signals. An alumnus of National Defence Academy, the General Officer is a Graduate of Defence Service Staff College, Wellington. He has also attended National Defence College in New Delhi and Higher Command Course at College of Combat, Mhow. He holds a Masters Degree in Business Administration and is a Fellow of the Institute of Electronics and Telecommunication Engineers. Major General Manmohan Singh has been a General Staff Officer (operations) in an Infantry Division and at a Command Headquarters. He has also been a Deputy Commander of an Infantry Brigade in Western Sector. He commanded a Mountain Division Signal Regiment in high altitude in Sikkim and was instrumental in planning and restoration of communication during the flood which struck Mangan district in August 1983. He was appointed Additional Director General Personnel Services at Army Headquarters. Prior to this, he was Chief Signal Officer of Southern Command. He was Operational Logistics analyst at Army Training Command. Major General Manmohan Singh is a recipient of the Ati Vhishisht Seva Medal. Now after retirement he heads the AWES, Army Welfare Education Society.

The Generals

Mohindar Singh Chopra, Major General

Major General Mohindar Singh Chopra was from one of the first batches of King's Commissioned Indian Officers of the Indian Army, having graduated from the Royal Military College at Sandhurst in England in 1928. Born in 1907 in Amritsar, he did his schooling at the Prince of Wales Royal Indian Military College at Dehra Dun before being selected for Sandhurst. After first attachment with 1ST Royal Fusiliers at Ambala and Kasauli, he transferred to 1st Rajputs before becoming the first Indian Officer to join the famous 6th Royal Battalion of 13TH Frontier Force Rifles at Hanguin 1932. He thus became a Piffer (the elite Frontier Force) of the Army. Many years were spent on active duty on the North West Frontier Province before he was selected to become the first Indian Officer for the Advance Course of the Army School of Physical Training at Aldershot in England. He graduated from the Staff College at Quetta in 1941 and served both with the Iraq-Persia (Paiforce) and in the Burma Theatre during the Second World War. In 1946 he was promoted to Lieutenant Colonel and took over as the first Indian Commanding Officer of 1st Assam Regiment in Shillong. In late 1947 he took over command of 123RD Infantry Brigade at Amritsar, charged with the onerous responsibility of not only defending hundreds of miles of turbulent frontier but also of evacuating safely nearly two million refugees during the partition of the sub continent. In late 1949 he was promoted to Major General and given the responsibility to resurrect the famous 5th Infantry Division, then scattered along most of north and eastern India. The 5th Division was built up into a formidable fighting force and mobilised twice for the border crisis of 1950-51. In 1950 he was given the singular honour of being appointed Colonel-in-Chief of 5TH Royal Gurkhas Rifles (Frontier Force) being then and remaining the senior Piffer in the Sub-Continent. In 1953 he took over as GOC 20TH Infantry Division, the last Division to have troops stationed in Tibet. Retiring from the Army in 1955 he became India's first Ambassador to the Republic of the Philippines, a post he held until 1959. On return to India, and few years of civilian life, he was appointed the Director, National Institute of Sports at Patiala, a post he held until 1968. He passed away in 1990.

The Generals

Narinder Singh, Major General

Major General Narinder Singh, who held the key appointment of Director-General, Military Operations, during the 1965 Indo-Pak war, passed away on 10TH October 2005. He was 86 and was a witness to some of the most decisive moments in the history of the Army. He was born in October 1919, to a middle class agricultural family in Thatta village, in Chabhal district Amritsar. He passed his intermediate from Khalsa College, Amritsar, and was commissioned in the Indian Army in June 1942. He joined 8TH Cavalry and later commanded 20TH Lancers. He saw active service during World War II. Also took part in the Indo-China war in 1962 and the Indo-Pak war in 1965 and 1971. He held various staff appointments, including the command of 163RD Infantry Brigade in Ladakh, GOC of 19TH Infantry Division and GOC of Srinagar Sector. General Narindar Singh was awarded the Presidents Medal for Meritorious Service in the Indian Army. After retirement from the Army in 1974, he was seconded to the newly raised Border Security Force. He served as the Inspector-General, Operations at Border Security Force Headquarters. Later, he served as the IG Kashmir with the Border Security Force. He was also an active member of the Cavalry Officers Association and used to attend social functions regularly. For his condemnation of Blue Star, General Narinder Singh was held in prison for two years under 'The Terrorist and Disruptive Activities Act' - TADA. General Narinder was a Member of the Human Rights Organization and the Committee on Disappearance of Youth in Punjab, which investigated the cases of all those cremated as "unclaimed" by Punjab Police in Amritsar district during the militancy period. He was actively involved in the investigation of these cases and the publication of the report "Reduced to Ashes" vol I. He also took active part in the rehabilitation of victims of the 1984 Delhi riots and Sikh soldiers who left their barracks in protest against Blue Star and were imprisoned or discharged. On the education side, General Narinder is a founding Member of Sikh Education Society based in Chandigarh. This Society runs four institutions in Chandigarh and two in Punjab. He served as local Secretary for five years and now is a Member of the Executive Committee. Since 1980, he has been a Member of the Government body of Bir Baba Budha College near Chabhal in district Amritsar. He is also a Member of the Institute of Sikh Studies Chandigarh. He was a Trustee of Guru Asra Trust, which looks after Sikh orphans of militants and others killed by the Punjab Police.

The Generals

Pannu RS, Major General

Major General R. S. Pannu, fondly known as Raghoo Pannu, was commissioned in the Indian Army's Tank Corps where he ultimately rose to the rank of Major General. After leaving the Military, he shifted to the Voluntary Sector where he has had a brilliant career as Chief Executive of Help Age India. He took the helm of this six-year old NGO working in the field of age care and put it on the map as India's leading charity during his 12-year tenure. He conceived and executed a 10-year plan that brought more than 430 NGO's under Help Age India's umbrella. Fundraising techniques implemented by General Pannu included direct mail campaigns, corporate fundraising and payroll giving, special events, greeting card sales, sponsored events in schools, collection boxes and cause-linked fundraising campaigns. Welfare projects managed by Help Age India included community development projects, as well as the more traditional assistance for nursing homes, day care centres, cataract operations, mobile Medicare units, and research and training. General Pannu recently retired from Help Age India to take on an advisory role internationally in the Voluntary Sector. He has served as Treasurer General and Vice President (Asia) for IFA. He has been on the Governing Board of the World Fundraising Council (USA), as well as the Founder-Chairman and Trustee of the South Asian Fundraising Group. He was also on the visiting faculty of the International Fundraising Group (London) and was a much sought after speaker. He was a special invitee to the United Nations General Assembly Session on Ageing and is also the recipient of the "Distinguished Leadership Award for Outstanding Contributions to Contemporary Society" from the American Biographical Institute. AARP (USA) has extended Honorary Membership to him. He was the Patron of Rehabilitation India and a Member of the Governing Body of Community Aid Sponsorship Program. As a soldier, Major General Pannu had witnessed pain, suffering and death during the 1971 Indo-Pak war, when he commanded a Brigade in Bangladesh. A retired Cavalry man is in a better position to understand the suffering and pain of a human being when he is shot at and, on most occasions, dies in pain due to lack of care. Cancer patients in India face the same fate, a slow and a painful death due to lack of care and absence of a scientifically proven cure and lost courage to fight the pain. This scantiness led to the establishment of GCCI by Major General R.S. Pannu. Major General R. S. Pannu passed away on 9TH October 2003.

The Generals

Rajinder Singh Sparrow, Major General, VrC and Bar

Rajinder Singh was commissioned in the Army in 1937. He saw service in the North West Frontier Province for a year with a British Unit. After that he joined 7th Light Cavalry and subsequently became its Commander. When India became independent on 15th August 1947, Pakistani-backed regulars, irregulars and tribesmen invaded the state of Jammu and Kashmir on October 22nd. Hopelessly outnumbered the Indian troops had to withdraw to Naushera, and Jhangar was occupied by the Pakistanis. In May 1948, as the Pakistanis were poised to attack Naushera, Lieutenant Colonel Rajinder Singh, leading a force named "Chita Force" attacked Asar Kadala, the Pakistani base for operations against Naushera, and completely annihilated the enemy. During the battle for recapture of Jhangar in March 1948, Rajinder Singh was commanding two Squadrons of light tanks. The main road from Naushera to Jhangar is of an extremely poor class and completely dominated and flanked by precipitous hills. Twelve days of incessant rain had literally turned the Naushera Jhangar valley into a bog. The enemy, previous to the rain, had carried out extensive mining of the routes leading up to Jhangar. These mines had got completely covered and camouflaged when the rains ceased. Lieutenant Colonel Rajinder Singh led his tanks with great dash and élan, without regard to his personal safety. One tank was blown up over approximately three mines and rendered completely useless. It was a hazardous task removing this tank from the route; it was completely blocking the only passage and the area was under heavy fire from the enemy. Undaunted by innumerable difficulties, Rajinder Singh led his armour onwards. His selfless devotion to duty and his untiring zeal were one of the major factors, which made 7th Light Cavalry enter Jhangar ahead of all other troops, and thus led to the successful finish of this battle. In the battle of Jhangar Rajinder Singh was awarded the most coveted Gallantry Award, the Mahavir Chakra. Major General Rajinder Singh was the first soldier to receive the Mahavir Chakra non–posthumously. He made armour history at the Battle of Zojila November 1st, 1947, when he led 7 Stuart tanks to support an attack by 77th Parachute Brigade. His Stuarts were brought from Srinagar using deception, across bridges that were too light to support the tanks. The last part of the journey was over a mule track that was hastily improved. The Zojila Pass lies at an altitude of 3900-meters. The assault began on November 1st and the bewildered Pakistanis were hunted down and decimated.

The Generals

Rajinder Singh Sparrow, Major Genera, (Cont.)

Until then nobody could have imagined that tanks could be deployed at such a high altitude. He then led the tanks and cleared the road to Ladakh. He was credited with the most spectacular success against the Pakistan Army and is also responsible for destroying the largest number of Pakistani Patton tanks and other equipment, and making the deepest salient into Pakistani territory. Major General Rajinder Singh "Sparrow" also commanded the First Armoured Division, in the Sialkot Sector. In the battle of Phillaura, troops under General Rajinder Singh destroyed as many as 77 enemy tanks in a single day. This has eclipsed Rommel's record of destroying 70 tanks in the famous battle of Knight's-Bridge. As against Rommel's 30 tanks, General Sparrow's men lost only six tanks of their own in the process. In the short spell of 15 days, the First Armoured Division destroyed 250 enemy tanks and the Division fought continuously for 15 days, thus setting a record again, for the tank formations pulled back after four or five days of fighting. Throughout these operations, Major General Rajinder Singh displayed conspicuous bravery and leadership of a very high order, in the best traditions of the Indian Army, for which he was awarded the Bar to his Mahavir Chakra. He retired from the Army in 1966. The General died in April 1994. The citation for his Gallantry Award reads; "In 1948, Lieutenant Colonel. Rajinder Singh was in command of 7TH Light Cavalry in Jammu and Kashmir. His bold and imaginative employment of tanks materially changed the course of events in that theatre, earning him the Mahavir Chakra. During the 1965 Indo-Pakistani War, Major General Rajinder Singh led his formation into battle against numerically superior and better-equipped armoured forces in the Sialkot Sector. Inspired by his tactical ability and leadership, his troops inflicted heavy tank casualties on the enemy armoured forces. By his presence in the thick of the battle, in utter disregard for his personal safety, Major General Rajinder Singh inspired the tank crews to engage the enemy forces closely. He commanded the highly complex armoured formation in an outstanding manner, and established such moral ascendancy over the enemy that in the latter stages of the campaign the enemy tanks avoided battle and had to be sought out to be destroyed."

The Generals

Rawind Singh Grewal, Major General, MC, VSM
Major General Grewal was commissioned in the Indian Army in 1937. He served in South East Asia Command during World War Two and was awarded the Military Cross, and mentioned in despatches on two occasions. He was transferred to the Army Ordnance Corps in 1951 and held the appointment of Brigadier Ordnance Corps Western Command. He was then transferred to the Infantry in July 1958, and posted as Provost Marshal at Army Headquarters. He held command of various Infantry Brigades in Jammu and Kashmir before being promoted as General Officer Commanding an Infantry Division. After taking command of a Brigade in Ladakh, in December 1960, he carried out a number of reconnoitring operations in difficult terrain, under extreme climatic conditions. His personal example, cheerfulness and courage, infused in his troops the determination to maintain their position in difficult conditions. His conduct has been a model of sacrifice, courage and devotion to duty.

Sandhu PJS, Major General
Major General P.J.S. Sandhu was commissioned into 8TH Light Cavalry on 15TH June 1966 and later commanded 47TH Armoured Regiment. He retired from the Army as Chief of Staff, 1ST Corps on 31ST July 2003. Presently, he is working as Deputy Director and Editor at USI since 1ST May 2007.

Satbir Singh, Major General, Sena Medal
Major General Satbir Singh, Sena Medal is a Lumina of National Defence Academy. He was commissioned in the Regiment of Artillery in June 1966. Having held many distinguished appointments in the Army, he has the privilege of being Instructor at four premier Institutions of the Army. He has been trained at the College of Defence Management in HRM & HRD and also trained as Interviewing Officer at the Defence Institute of Psychological Research (DIPR). He was Senior Fellow at the Institute of Defence Studies and Analysis (IDSA). Major General Satbir Singh, SM has served as Commandant Services Selection Centre and President of Services Selection Board. He has also been Examiner of PhD. thesis in Security & Defence Studies at a reputed Indian University. He has over seen approximately 40000 SSB interviews during his tenure of three years at the Services Selection Centre. Major General Satbir Singh retired from the Army on 31ST March 2003.

The Generals

Shabeg Singh, Major General, AVSM and PVSM

In 1940, an Officer's Selection Team visiting Lahore colleges were looking for fresh recruits to the Indian Army Officer's cadre. Out of a large number of students, who applied, Shabeg Singh was the only one to be selected from Government College and sent for training in the Officer Training School. After training he was commissioned in 2ND Punjab Regiment as a Second Lieutenant. Within a few days the Regiment moved to Burma and joined the war against the Japanese, which was then in progress. In 1944 when the war ended he was in Malaya with his Unit. After partition, when reorganization of the Regiments took place, he joined the Parachute Brigade as a Paratrooper. He was posted to 1ST Para Battalion, in which he remained until 1959. He was an Instructor in the Military Academy at Dehra Dun and held a number of important staff appointments in various ranks. In the Army he had a reputation of being a fearless Officer and one who did not tolerate any nonsense. People either loved him or dreaded him, because of his frank and forthright approach. During the course of his service in the Indian army, Shabeg Singh fought in every war that India participated in. In 1947, he was at Naushera in Jammu and Kashmir fighting against the Pakistan Army. Because of his knowledge of military science and excellent grasp of military operations, he was appointed a Brigade Major of 166TH Infantry Brigade, a crack formation. In 1962 during the India-China war, he was in Northeast Frontier Agency as a Lieutenant Colonel in HQ, 4TH Corps, where he was GSO-J (Intelligence). In the 1960's operations against Pakistan, he was in the Haji Pir Sector in Jammu and Kashmir, commanding a Battalion of Gorkha troops. He commanded 3RD Battalion, 11TH Gorkha Rifles with distinction and was mentioned in dispatches for the capture of important enemy positions on the Haji Pir front. A few days before the Battalion he commanded was to launch an attack, he received a telegram from his mother informing him that his father had expired. He quietly put the telegram in his pocket and no one in his Battalion even knew that the Commanding Officer had lost his father on the eve of battle. Only when the operations were over, did he apply for leave and perform his duty of consoling his mother and family. His mother, Pritam Kaur, never asked why he had not been reached for performing the last rites. Everything was understood. The call of duty to defend the Nation's frontiers was of primary importance. Soon after the 1965 operations, Shabeg became Colonel G.S. of an Infantry Division, after which he was given command of the crack 19TH Infantry Brigade in Jammu Sector.

The Generals

Shabeg Singh, Major General (Cont.)

When the Eastern sector of India was becoming deeply involved in Naga anti-insurgency operations, he was posted as Deputy GOC of the largest Indian Division, 8TH Mountain Division which had nearly 50,000 troops under command. With his leadership qualities and employment of daredevil tactics, he was greatly successful in handling the counter-insurgency operations in that region. In 1971, when the political turmoil in East Pakistan (now Bangladesh) started and the Bengalis declared their intention to separate, the Yahya Khan Government cracked down on the Bengalis, forcing them to flee to neighbouring Indian States. India decided to intervene and in 1971 started the clandestine insurgency operations in East Pakistan. The Indian Army Chief Field Marshal Manekshaw specially selected Shabeg Singh, then a Brigadier, and made him in-charge of Delta Sector with lead Quarters at Aggartala. He was given the responsibility of planning, organizing and directing insurgency operations in the whole of Central and East Bangladesh. Under his command were placed all the Bangladesh Officers that had deserted from the Pakistan Army. These included Colonel Osmani, as adviser, Major Zia-Ur-Rehman and Mohammad Mustaq. Zia Ur Rehman later became the President of Bangladesh while Mustaq Mohammed became Bangladesh's Army Chief. Starting from about January to October 1971, the insurgency operations gradually grew to such intensity that by the time war started, the Pakistan Army in East Bengal had completely lost their will to resist. The Indian Government did not want the world to know that the Indian Army was training and directing the Bengali insurgents, so all activities were very secret. Shabeg was so thoroughly involved in these clandestine operations that for five months from December 1970 to April 1971, his family had no news about his whereabouts. They believed he was still in Nagaland and wondered why he did not write because he had always been regular in writing home to his wife. In April 1970, the first letter was received from the civilian address of a merchant shop in Aggartala and his name was written as S.Baigh, such was the nature of secrecy maintained of the Army's involvement in the insurgency movement. The wife was quite confused and the family wondered what was going on because the letter was very brief and just said, "don't worry I am ok." Meanwhile as the Mukti Bahini got bolder, the Pakistani Army in the East began to grow demoralized due to the onslaught.

The Generals

Shabeg Singh, Major General (Cont.)

The Pakistani Army got so widely dispersed in trying to contain the 'Mukti Bahini' that when the Indian Army launched its operations in November, 1971, they were able to walk through to Dacca, virtually unopposed. Over one hundred thousand enemy troops with the complete General Staff surrendered, leading to the emergence of Bangladesh. The credit for this great achievement was mainly due to the efforts of Shabeg Singh, who spent day and night organizing, motivating and training young Bengali youth to fight for their land. Such was the motivation of a Bengali youth force known as Mukti Bahini and so perfect the direction of their operation, that no Senior Administrative Officer felt safe in Bengal. Guerrilla strikes were launched on five star hotels and on ships in Chittagong harbour to show the extent of power which the Mukti Bahini wielded. Strategic bridges were destroyed, factories closed and movement within Bangladesh restricted, resulting in a paralysis of the economy. No doubt it was a cakewalk for the Indian Army when the actual operations were launched. The Indian Government promoted Shabeg Singh to the post of Major General and awarded him the Param Vishist Sewa Medal in recognition of his Services. He had earlier been awarded the Ati Vishist Sewa Medal also. He was made General Officer Command of MP Bihar and Orissa. The Jaya Pyakash Narayan movement had started during 1972-73 and became a serious threat to the Indira Government. Police were sympathetic with JP and his followers, so the Government decided to use the Army. General Shabeg was asked to arrest JP and take some harsh measures against his followers but he refused saying this was not his job. The result was that the Congress Government later instituted a CBI inquiry to harass him on cooked-up charges and he was posted out of the area. After the Indo-Pak war, all the Pakistani POWs were under his jurisdiction. Due to jealousy of certain Senior Army Officers, he was not given the command of a Division, which was a move of the Army for denying him promotion. Here was a Field Commander with so much war experience, denied command of a Combat Formation. Why so? Only to deny him promotion when his name came up. While he was posted as GOC of the UP Area HQs, in whose jurisdiction the Kumaon Regimental Centre is placed, it was found that the Commander of the Kumaon Military Farm had given a large sum of money to the Chief, General Raina, who was himself from the same Regiment.

The Generals

Shabeg Singh, Major General (Cont.)

A Court of Inquiry discovered that General Raina (a Kashmiri Brahmin), had received over two hundred thousand rupees from the Kumaon farm to meet expenses for his daughter's marriage. When this information was brought to the notice of the General Office Commanding, Shabeg Singh; he told General Raina about the findings of the Court of Inquiry and requested the Chief to return the amount, as the Military farm of the Kumaon Regiment was already running at loss. The result was that General Shabeg was promptly posted out of the indiscretion and the inquiry hushed up. The forthwith posting was an unprecedented action because peacetime postings are never conducted on such emergency basis. Soon after that the Army instituted a Court of Inquiry against General Shabeg Singh, which dragged on for one year until the date of his retirement on May, 1ST 1976. The main charge against the General was that he had accepted a plaque costing Rs 2500 as a gift on his positing out of Jabalpur area HQs. Even though a similar present had been accepted by his predecessor, and it is common for Senior Officers to accept such gifts. However, in the case of General Shabeg it became an offence. Some other flimsy charges were also made, like allowing his official house land to be used for cultivation purposes and permitting sale of goods purchased from customs in the area HQs Canteen. These practices had been in vogue even before the General had taken command of the area in 1972. The vindictiveness of the Indian Government and the Army Chief was made obvious, when one day prior to General Shabeg's retirement, on April 30TH, 1976 the hero of Mukti Bahini, a highly decorated General with PVSM and AVSM, who had been actively involved in every operation that the Indian Army had fought since his joining Service and who spent the major portion of his life in field areas separated, at the cost of his wife's health and the education of his children, was dismissed from the Army. Such was the treatment meted out to a brave Soldier and an outstanding General, a leader of men, whom the Indian Government and some senior Army officers in 1984, after Operation Blue Star, dubbed as 'disgruntled' and frustrated because he was loyal to his community and fought for its honour and to protect the Golden Temple against the Army attack. He died protecting the Golden Temple.

The Generals

Surjit Singh, Major General, AVSM, VSM, FNAE

Major General Surjit Singh was commissioned in the Army through the National Defence Academy in December 1961. He is a post Graduate in Electronics from the IIT Delhi and has participated in several Research and Development projects pertaining to missile systems and computer based training simulators. He is one of the few Military Officers who have been admitted into the Indian National Academy of Engineering (INAE). He was a Member of the Pay Cell formed by the Army Headquarters for 4TH Pay Commission during 1983-87 and was the Chairman of 5TH Pay Commission in 1996-97. After retirement, he served with Ashok Leyland for over five years and has since then been undertaking teaching assignments in several education institutions. Writing has been his passion all through his life. He published his first novel in 1965 and has since written four more books, including one on Salary Structures. It is his belief that with a bit of planning, soldiers can effectively contribute to society by converting their military experience into civilian success.

Surat Singh Sandhu, Major General

Major General Surat Singh Sandhu is an International Consultant based in India. Born in Malaysia he completed his schooling there and then moved to India, where he completed his Graduation. He joined the Indian Army where he did his Masters Degree in Defence Studies and Business Administration. He speaks English, Punjabi, Hindi and a little Malay. After a successful career spanning 34 years in the Army, General Sandhu took premature retirement to be the Chief Executive of a leading National Charity, Help Age India. During his four-year tenure General Sandhu raised the profile of the charity to make it a household name and tripled the fundraising. He also started his own consultancy and has worked with organizations in India, Kenya, Nigeria, Sri Lanka and the UK with services ranging from management to fundraising consultancy. He was Chair of South Asian Fundraising Group (2005-2009), New Delhi when he successfully raised the profile of Fundraising in developing countries. His consulting clients included PATH and Kusuma Foundation in India, and Plantation Human Development Trust in Colombo and Oxfam in the United Kingdom. He has helped plan strategies and implements fundraising for many major NGOs in South Asia.

The Generals

Amar Singh Lieutenant General, PVSM, AVSM

Lieutenant General Amar Singh was born on March 1ST, 1923, in a Jat Sikh family in a small village of erstwhile Garhshankar Tehsil, now Nawanshahr district, He was commissioned in 1942 soon after he graduated from Forman Christian College, Lahore. He served in Waziristan in North-western Frontier Province, now in Pakistan, and thereafter in Java and Burma during World War II. After several Regimental, Staff and Instructional assignments, he was posted in 1975 as Major General, ASC, at Headquarters Northern Command. In 1977, he took over the post of the Corps Director, Supplies and Transport, at the Army Headquarters, New Delhi. He retired on February 28TH, 1981, from the post of Director Supplies and Transport, DST. He passed away on December 23RD 2005.

Amarjeet Singh Chabbewal, Lieutenant General YSM

Lieutenant General Amarjeet Singh Chabbewal, YSM, an Alumnus of the National Defence Academy, was commissioned into the Armored Corps in June 1974. A Graduate of Defence Service Staff College, the General Officer has also attended the prestigious Higher Command Course at Army War College and Executive Course in Hawaii, USA. He is a Master of Science (Defence Studies) and Master of Philosophy (Defence and Management Studies).He has been an Instructor at Officers' Training Academy at Chennai and held coveted staff appointments including Brigade Major at Headquarters of an Independent Armored Brigade and Colonel General Staff at the Headquarters of a Mountain Division during Op Rakhshak and Op Vijay. He also tenanted the appointments of Colonel General Staff (Operations) at Headquarters Western Command during Op Parakram and Deputy Military Secretary at Headquarters Southern Command. He also held the prestigious appointment of Defence Attaché, Embassy of India in Moscow, Russia. The General Officer has commanded an Armoured Regiment and an Armoured Brigade. He subsequently took over as General Officer Commanding of a Mountain Division along the Line of Control in Jammu & Kashmir. The General Officer has been Commandant; Armoured Corps Centre and School, Ahmadnagar prior to taking over as General Officer Commanding of a Strike Corps. The General Officer was awarded the Yudh Seva Medal during Op Vijay.

The Generals

Amarjeet Singh Sekhon, Lieutenant General, YSM, AVSM

Lieutenant General Amarjeet Singh Sekhon was commissioned into the Infantry in June 1970. He has attended all prestigious courses like Defence Services Staff College, Higher Command and National Defence College and has seen active service in all theatres, in both Regimental and Staff appointments, including the Indo-Pak conflict 1971. Having commanded his unit in North East and Punjab, the General Officer went on to command an Infantry Brigade along the sensitive Line of Control in the State of Jammu and Kashmir, where he was decorated with `YSM' for his Distinguished Service during Operation VIJAY in 1999. In addition to Command, the General Officer has held a number of important Staff and Instructional appointments including instructional tenures at National Defence Academy and Army War College. The General Officer has been Brigade Major of an Infantry Brigade in High Altitude Area, Deputy Military Secretary and Brigadier General Staff (Operations) in Command Headquarters. After the National Defence College course, the General Officer went on to hold the appointment of Deputy Director General at the Directorate General of Military Operations. The General has had the distinction of commanding Infantry Division in Jammu and Kashmir and was awarded the AVSM for his Distinguished Service along the Line of Control. He has also held the appointment of Additional Director General of Perspective Planning. He has been posted as Director General of Military Operation after completion of a successful command of 15TH Corps in the North Sector. During his command at 15TH Corps, the violence levels in the Kashmir valley have dropped significantly during the current year. Considerable attrition on the terrorist cadres was ensured by the Army with 337 terrorists killed in action in 2006. Besides, 566 terrorists were apprehended during 2006 and 2007. At the same time the local terrorists were motivated to surrender to own forces and 195 terrorists have surrendered to own troops since January 2006. Lieutenant General Amarjeet Singh Sekhon was appointed Director General Military Operations (DGMO) at New Delhi in 2007.

The Generals

Arvinder Singh Lamba, Lieutenant General
PVSM, AVSM, VSM

Lieutenant General Arvinder Singh Lamba, a Senior Artillery Officer with commando training, took over as the Army's Vice Chief on 6TH December 2010. An Alumnus of the Khadakvasla-based National Defence Academy, Lamba was commissioned into the Regiment of Artillery in June 1997 and is the Senior Colonel of the Regiment. An Ati Vishisht Seva Medal awardee, his operational experience includes participation in the 1971 Indo-Pak War in the eastern as well as the western theatres. He has had vast exposure to counter-insurgency operations over several years both within and outside the country. His Command assignments encompass that of a Rocket Regiment, Mountain Brigade in counter-insurgency operations and commanded Operation Parakram in 2001-02. He also commanded an Infantry Division on the western sector, and an elite Strike Corps in the southern theatre. He was Commander-in-Chief of the Army's Training Command at Shimla prior to taking over as the Army Vice Chief. This tenure at the training command drew the General's focus on the imperative transformation in training to meet the postulations of emerging security and technological challenges. His priorities were articulation of the Army Doctrine, Information Warfare, Review of Training, Simulation, War Gaming, Human Resource and Leadership Development and Inter-Service Joint-man ship. Lamba's staff experience includes Brigade Major with Indian Peace Keeping Force (IPKF), Colonel Administration in Counter-insurgency and Brigadier General Staff of a Corps in the eastern theatre. Appointments at the Army Headquarters include Additional Director General Operational Logistics Directorate, Deputy Director General Strategic Planning Group in Perspective Planning Directorate, Director Operational Logistics and Colonel General Staff Army Standing Establishment Committee. He has been a Directing Staff at Defence Services Staff College as also at the Indian Military Academy. His professional courses include Defence Services Staff College at Wellington, Higher Command Course at Army War College in Mhow and the prestigious Royal College of Defence Studies in United Kingdom.

Currently Serving Army's Vice Chief.

The Generals

Avtar Singh, Lieutenant General, PVSM, VSM

Lieutenant General Avtar Singh was born on 13TH March 1946 to Major Ranjit Singh at Ludhiana (Punjab). His family has been serving the Indian Army, more specifically the Jat Regiment for three generations. Lieutenant General Avtar Singh did his schooling from Sherwood College, Nainital before joining the National Defence Academy in December 1961. He passed out from there in December 1964. He was commissioned into the Army on 25TH December 1965 after successful training at the Indian Military Academy. He was posted to 3RD JAT in the Lahore Sector. During his tenure with the Unit, he served in insurgency areas of Nagaland and Mizoram, as well as high altitude areas in North East Frontier Agency. He captured a Pakistani post in the Rajasthan Sector in 1971 Indo-Pak war. He served as Brigade Major Independent Armoured Brigade, even though he was an Infantry Officer, after completing the DSSC Course. He commanded 17TH JAT in the Eastern Theatre. For his outstanding leadership during command he was awarded the Chief of Army Staff's Commendation Card. After which he was posted to DSSC as an Instructor. He was selected for the Higher Command Course and then served as Defence Advisor in the Indian Embassy in Addis Ababa (Ethiopia) for four years. On his return to India, he commanded 104TH Infantry Brigade on the LC in Jammu and Kashmir, at the peak of insurgency. After which he was selected for the NDC Course. Following this he was posted as BGS Operations, Northern Command, where he coordinated the successful conduct of Parliamentary and Legislative Elections in Jammu and Kashmir, after 10 years of insurgency. Thereafter, he assumed command as GOC 15TH Infantry Division at Amritsar Sector for 3 Years, after which he was appointed as Joint Secretary, Military, with the Ministry of Defence. On promotion, as Lieutenant General, he commanded 33RD Corps in the Eastern Sector. After this tenure he was appointed as Deputy Chief of Integrated Defence Staff and Director General Defence Intelligence Agency, before retiring on 31ST March 2006, after over 40 years service. For his Meritorious Service of an exceptional order he was awarded the VSM and PVSM by the President of India.

It must be pointed out that very few, if any; Generals of his time would have had such wide exposure with the Foreign Service as Military Attaché, administrative Service as Joint Secretary and Inter Service as Director General Defence Intelligence Agency.

The Generals

Avtar Singh Lamba, Lieutenant General
As a young second lieutenant in 1971, Lamba became a war veteran within weeks of being commissioned as India had plunged into what is now called the Bangladesh Liberation War. After the war, Lamba, who was commissioned in the Gorkha Rifles, converted to the Parachute Regiment. He has combat experience during counter-insurgency operations in Nagaland and Manipur, and with the Indian Peace Keeping Force (IPKF) in Sri Lanka in the late 1980s. He later commanded a mountain brigade, 16TH Infantry Division, the elite 21ST Corps Strikes Formation and the Shimla-based Army Training Command. Lieutenant General Avtar Singh Lamba retired in October 2011 after 40 years of service.

Avtar Singh Lamba, Lieutenant General
Lieutenant General Avtar Singh was commissioned into the JAT Regiment in 1965. He participated in 1965 and 1971 operations in the Western Sector. He commanded a strategically important Brigade in Jammu and Kashmir and a Frontline Division in the Western Theatre. He was Brigade Major of an Independent Armoured Brigade, Brigadier General Staff (Operations) in Northern Command, Instructor at the Defence Service Staff College and College of Combat. He served as Military Naval and Air Attaché in Ethiopia. He was Director-General of Rashtriya Rifles and on 14TH September 2002, he took over as General Officer Commanding of 33RD Corps in the Eastern Sector. Prior to his retirement in 2009 he was Chief of the Defence Intelligence Agency.

Balraj Singh Takhar, Lieutenant General, VSM
Lieutenant General Balraj Singh was commissioned into 17TH Horse of the Armoured Corps on December 25TH, 1965. A Graduate of Defence Services Staff College, Wellington, he also attended National Defence College, Delhi. He has held many Staff and Instructional Appointments, including command of 17TH Horse, an Armoured Brigade, an Armoured Division and a Corps in the Western Sector. He has also held appointments as Instructor, DSSC and Additional Director General, Military Operations at the Army Headquarters.

Currently GOC-in-C, Southern Command

The Generals

Bhalla PS, Lieutenant General, AVSM

Lieutenant General P.S. Bhalla is an Alumnus of National Defence Academy, Pune. He was commissioned into 64TH Cavalry in December 1973. He is a Graduate of Defence Services Staff College, Wellington. He has done all important courses including the prestigious Long Defence Management Course and Advance Programme on Public Administration from the Indian Institute of Public Administration, New Delhi. He is also accredited with higher qualifications and is a Master of Philosophy in Social Science from Punjab University, Chandigarh. He has wide ranging experience of various high profile Command and Staff Appointments. He has commanded 64TH Cavalry, 88TH Armoured Brigade and 20TH Mountain Division. On staff, he has served as Dy GOC of Victor Force responsible for Counter Terrorist Operations in Southern Kashmir, COS of HQ 4TH Corps and ADG WE at Integrated Headquarters of MoD. He was awarded the Ati Vishisht Seva Medal for his Distinguished Service while serving as GOC 20TH Mountain Division. P.S. Bhalla took over as Director General National Cadet Corps on 21ST February 2011.

Bikram Singh, Lieutenant General, PVSM

Lieutenant General Bikram Singh was commissioned from Officer Training at Sandhurst in the Army in 1933. He took part in various operations on the North West Frontier Province and went on to serve in Iraq and Iran. He saw active service in the Middle East during the Second World War. During a long and distinguished career, he held a number of important appointments which included command of Assam Area and of Division in Jammu and Kashmir. In July 1961, he was appointed to command a Corps in Jammu and Kashmir in the rank of Lieutenant General. As Corps Commander he was responsible for organizing the integrated defence of Ladakh. He is held in the highest esteem for his record in defending Ladakh and Chushul during the critical period of Chinese aggression in 1962. On 16TH November 1963 he was promoted to the rank of Army Commander, Headquarters Western Command and was to take over command from Lieutenant General Daulat Singh. On his visit to the forward areas in Jammu and Kashmir sector he died when the helicopter of the Indian Army crashed on 22ND November 1963 near Poonch city. He is considered the bravest and most efficient General of the Indian Army. Lieutenant General Daulet Singh also died in the crash. In memory of this Great Sikh General a Chowk of Jammu city has been dedicated in his name.

The Generals

Bikram Singh, Lieutenant General, PVSM, UYSM, AVSM, SM, VSM, ADC

General Bikram Singh is the current Chief of Army Staff of the Indian Army (2012). He is the second Sikh to be CoAS, the first having been General J. J. Singh. An alumnus of the National Defence Academy, Lieutenant General Singh was commissioned into the Sikh Light Infantry Regiment on 31ST March 1972. He was adjudged the 'Best Young Officer' at the Young Officer's course at the Infantry School. He was awarded both the Commando Dagger for being the best commando and the 'Best in Tactics' trophy. He later was an Instructor at the Commando Wing of the Infantry School. He has done the Higher Command Course at Mhow and the US Army War College, Pennsylvania. After completing the Higher Command Course, he served his first tenure as a Director in the Military Operations (MO) Directorate. The tenure coincided with the Kargil war and he was the official spokesperson of the Army during that period. He went on to serve four important tenures at Army HQ: an additional tenure in the MO Directorate as the Deputy Director General, two tenures in the Perspective Planning Directorate, as the Deputy Director General of Perspective Planning (Strategy) and later, as the Additional Director General. He was posted back to the Army HQ as a Lieutenant General to serve as the Director General Staff Duties (DGSD). With over 38 years of active service, he has held a number of important Command and Staff Appointments. He commanded an Infantry Battalion in the northeast and along the Line of Control in Jammu and Kashmir. He was the Corps Commander of the prestigious 15TH Corps in his last command tenure. Lieutenant General Singh has also served in three United Nations (UN) peacekeeping missions. In his last UN assignment, he was the Deputy Force Commander and GOC of a multinational division in Africa, comprising officers and troops of 48 nationalities. He has been awarded the Uttam Yudha Seva Medal (UYSM), Ati Vishisth Seva Medal (AVSM), Sena Medal and Vishisht Seva Medal (VSM) for his Meritorious Service so far. He has also held some important Staff Appointments at Army Headquarters, which include two tenures each in the Directorate General of Military Operations and the Directorate General of respective Planning. He has held positions of GOC-in-C Eastern Command, GOC 15TH Corps, GOC Rashtriya Rifles and GOC of Eastern Division in the Democratic Republic of Congo. He was wounded while posted as a Brigadier in Jammu and Kashmir, where he has spent much of his service.

Indian Army

BS Dhaliwal, Lieutenant General

Lieutenant General B.S. Dhaliwal (Retired) is a Decorated Soldier with a distinguished and chequered career, spanning 41 years, in the Corps of the Engineers of the Indian Army. Possessing eminent self-motivation, the General Officer has made a difference, wherever he has served, with a remarkable aptitude for pragmatic, intuitive and logical deduction. His deeds and out-of-box ideas have left an indelible mark in all appointments he has served in. Throughout his service, he has utilized his engineering knowledge and skills, with a capability and capacity to endure and to accomplish tasks, in a time-bound manner, during peace and war and in all terrains. One notable example, worth bringing to the notice of the audience, was in the terminal phase of 'Operation PARAKRAM', when a strategic relocation of forces was ordered in India. He employed innovative and unconventional drills oblique procedures to complete de-mining operations in record time, without a single fatal casualty. In India, one of the roles of the Corps of Engineers, in peacetime, is to assist in Relief Operations when disasters occur. The General Officer, with his tremendous experience and expertise combined with visionary ideas, has been at the forefront in providing succour to the people of his Country in all disaster relief operations – whether floods, snow and avalanches, earthquakes or tsunami. As the Commandant of the College of Military Engineering, he is remembered even today for blazing new trails and revitalizing the Institution, advancing in pace with technology but never losing sight of the basics. As Engineer-in-Chief of the Indian Army, his contribution has been un-fathomable. Besides operational achievements, he rejuvenated the ethos and functioning of the organization. His visionary zeal and sheer effort gave a huge fillip to the use of non-conventional energy sources. In the field of eco-conservation, he ensured that the Armed Forces include waste water re-cycling plants and rainwater harvesting schemes into all major projects coming up in the country. The General Officer has lectured extensively on Environment and Ecology, an issue very close to his heart. In recognition of his endeavours, he was awarded the 'Golden Peacock Award for Eco-Innovation' by the World Environment Foundation. The General Officer is a member of a large number of professional societies. He has published a number of Papers in technical journals of repute, two of which have been conferred with prestigious awards.

The Generals

Charanjit Singh, Dr. (Major General) AVSM, VSM, MD, DM
Charanjit Singh is a Director Cardiac Sciences. He has an extensive experience of more than three decades in supervision and administration of Medicine and Cardiology Departments. He is an eminent Cardiologist of the Armed Forces with vast experience in Cardiology and was Professor Cardiology at the Armed Forces Medical College, Pune for five years. He also worked as Departmental Head of Medicine and Cardiology at Military Hospital, Jalandhar Cantonment; Associate Professor at the Army Hospital (Research and Referral), Delhi Cantonment. 2500 Cardiac procedures, including interventions, were done by him during the tenure at Cardio Thoracic Centre and AFMC.

Daljeet Singh, Lieutenant General
Lieutenant General Daljeet Singh was the General Officer Commanding the Western Command in Chandimandir Cantonment. Prior to taking over the reins of the Western Command, Lieutenant General Daljeet Singh was the General Officer commanding 3RD Corps. Commissioned in June 1967 into 8TH Light Cavalry, he is a product of the National Defence Academy and the Indian Military Academy. He attended the prestigious Defence Service Staff College, the Higher Command Course at the Army War College and the course at the National Defence College; he is also a Graduate of the Command and General Staff College Fort Leavenworth (USA) and the School of Infantry, Warminster (UK). During a career spanning 38 years, the General Officer has held Staff and Command Appointments in all the theatres of the Indian Army. Lieutenant General Daljeet Singh passed away on August 16TH 2011.

Daulat Singh, Lieutenant General
In the Indo-China war of 1962, the Western Army Commander, Lieutenant General Daulet Singh, bitterly criticised the Government's 'Forward Policy', which would sacrifice his troops in a gamble that he saw as irrational and hopeless. Singh's warning, like those of many other Senior Officers, was ignored. He consequently resisted tactically unwise pressure from his COAS, General Thapar, thus saving Ladakh from being overrun by the Chinese. He died alongside Lieutenant General Bikram Singh when their helicopter crashed near Poonch city on 22ND November 1963. It is said that the helicopter accident maybe a conspiracy, to be rid of two outspoken Sikh generals.

Indian Army

Devinder Dayal Singh Sandhu, Lieutenant General, PVSM, ADC, (DR.)

Lieutenant General D.D.S. Sandhu is an Alumnus of National Defence Academy, and was commissioned in 1967. He is a Graduate of Defence Services Staff College, Wellington. The General has done his post graduation in Defence studies from Madras University and M. Phil in Defence & Management Studies from Devi Ahilya Bai University, Indore. He has an inclination towards research on vital issues of military logistics and has acquired his Doctorate in "International Marketing of Indian Defence Products" from Punjabi University, Patiala. He holds a MBA Degree and a Masters Degree in Materials Management. He is a Fellow of British Institute of Management and a Member of the Board of Studies of IIMM. The General is an expert in the Ammunition and Armament subjects of the Army. He has served as the "Ammunition Quality Controller" in the Nigerian Army. His forte is "Management" and "Automation" and he is qualified on various courses of management and automation. He has had long exposures as a System Analyst, Senior System Analyst and later as Director, Computerised Inventory Control Project. This is an automation project that is going to help the Army Ordnance Corps in meeting the logistic challenges of future. The General Officer has held various prestigious appointments. He has been Commandant of Central Ordnance Depot, Delhi Cantonment which is one of the biggest logistics depots of the Army Ordnance Corps. As a Major General D.D.S. Sandhu was a pivotal functionary of the logistics support system of one of the operational commands of the Indian Army. Lieutenant General D.D.S. Sandhu retired from the Army as the Director General of Ordnance Services and Senior Colonel Commandant, Army Ordnance Corps in January 2008. He is the only serving Defence Officer to have been awarded a 'D. Litt' (Honoris Causa**).** Currently he is Vice-Chancellor, Kurukshetra University, Kurukshetra. Under his guidance, the College had witnessed unprecedented advancement in all facets of functioning and specially made tangible strides in the field of Automation and Academics. He is widely travelled and has participated in various seminars. He has been a Member and Leader of numerous important studies in the Army on issues relating to Management and Automation.

The Generals

Dhaliwal B S, Lieutenant General, PVSM, AVSM, VSM

General B. S. Dhaliwal, a second generation Army Officer, was commissioned into the Corps of Engineers as a Bengal Sapper on 25TH December 1966. In his 41 years of Commissioned Service in the Corps of Engineers, he has held the key appointments of Engineer-in-Chief, Commandant College of Military Engineering, Chief Engineer Southern Command, Director General Works, Chief Engineer Project Beacon (Border Roads) and Chief Engineer Bhatinda Zone. The General Officer has made a difference, wherever he has served. His deeds and out-of-box ideas have left an indelible mark in all appointments he has served in. Throughout his Service, he has utilized his engineering knowledge and skills, with a capability and capacity to endure and to accomplish tasks, in a time-bound manner, during peace and war and in all terrains. One notable example was in the terminal phase of 'Operation Parakram', when a strategic relocation of forces was ordered in India. He employed innovative and unconventional drills; oblique procedures to complete de-mining operations in record time, without a single fatal casualty. As the Commandant of the College of Military Engineering, he is remembered even today for blazing new trails and revitalizing the Institution, advancing in pace with technology but never losing sight of the basics. As Engineer-in-Chief of the Indian Army, his contribution has been un-fathomable. Besides operational achievements, he rejuvenated the ethos and functioning of the Organization. His visionary zeal and sheer effort gave a huge fillip to the use of non-conventional energy sources, environment and ecology. In recognition of his endeavours, he was awarded the 'Golden Peacock Award for Eco-Innovation' by the World Environment Foundation in 2007. The General Officer is a Member of a large number of professional societies. He has published a number of Papers in Technical Journals of repute, two of which have been conferred with prestigious Awards. He is a voracious reader and a teacher of "Rapid Reading." He is also a Postgraduate in Human Rights. A keen sportsman, he has excelled in Rowing and has been awarded the 'Admiral Kohli Trophy' for lifetime achievement in Sailing. For his outstanding contribution to Humanity through Engineering, he was conferred the Engineer of the Year 2011 by the Federation of Engineering Institution of Asia and Pacific. The Corps of Engineers describe him as a man with epic fortitude and sense of rationale who by his deeds has left an undying mark in the records of the Sappers.

The Generals
Dhaliwal Bachittar Singh, Lieutenant General (Cont.)
Engineer of the year award 2011
(The first Indian and Army Officer to receive this recognition)

"Lieutenant General B.S. Dhaliwal, PVSM, AVSM, VSM, is a Decorated Soldier with a distinguished and chequered career, spanning 41 years, in the Corps of Engineers of the Indian Army. Possessing imminent self-motivation, the General Officer has made a difference, wherever he has served, with a remarkable aptitude for pragmatic, intuitive and logical deduction. His deeds and out-of-box ideas have left an inedible mark in all appointments he has served in. Throughout his service, he has utilized his engineering knowledge and skills, with capability and capacity to endure and accomplish tasks, in a time- bound manner, during peace and war and in all terrains. One notable example, worth bringing to the notice of the audience, was in terminal phase of 'Operation Parakram', when a strategic relocation of forces was ordered in India. He employed innovative and unconventional drills oblique procedures to complete de-mining operations in record time, without a single fatal casualty. In India, one of the roles of Corps of Engineers, in peacetime, is to assist in relief operations when disasters occur. The General Officer, with his tremendous experience and expertise combined with visionary ideas, has been at the forefront in providing succour to the people of his country in all disaster relief operations-whether floods, snow and avalanches, earthquakes or tsunami. As the Commandant of the College of Military Engineering, he is remembered even today for blazing new trails, and revitalizing the Institution, advancing in pace with technology but never losing sight of basics. As Engineer-in- Chief, of the Indian Army, his contribution has been un-fathomable. Besides operational achievements, he rejuvenated the ethos and functioning of the organization. His visionary zeal and sheer effort gave a huge fillip to the use of non-conventional energy sources. In the field of eco-conservation, he ensured that the Armed Forces include waste water re-cycling plants and rainwater harvesting schemes into all major projects coming up in the country. The General Officer has lectured extensively on Environment and Ecology, an issue very close to his heart. In recognition of his endeavours, he was awarded 'Golden Peacock Award for Eco-Innovation' by the World Environment Foundation. The General Officer is a member of a large number of Professional Societies."

The Generals

Dhaliwal Bachittar Singh, Lieutenant General (Cont.)

Lieutenant General B.S. Dhaliwal has published a number of Papers in technical journals of repute, two of which has been conferred with prestigious awards. He is a voracious reader and a teacher of 'Rapid Reading'. He is also a post graduate in Human Rights. A keen sportsman, he has excelled in Rowing, and has been awarded the 'Admiral Kohli Trophy for lifetime achievement in sailing'. As they say a soldier never retires. Immediately after his superannuation in August 2007, the General Officer was picked up as Advisor (Technical) to the Honourable Chief Minister of Punjab. In the past three years, with his meticulous sense of professional organization, he has revamped the system to bring in much greater transparency and accountability. By initiating a number of steps in quality control, he has ensured timely completion of projects with least time and cost over runs. Striving for perfection, in this age of mediocrity, his mode of leadership and supervisory qualities are manifest and conveyed by example. He has always encouraged an environment that promotes leadership and initiative at all levels, open to ideas, and focusing on results and managing-rather than avoiding risk-giving greater flexibility in managing resources and priorities. To sum up, the FEIAP Engineer of the Year – 2011 is a Soldier and Gentleman, and above all, an Engineer par excellence."

Grewal SS, Lieutenant General, PVSM, AVSM, SM, VSM

Lieutenant General S.S. Grewal, Adjutant General at Army Headquarters retired after putting in forty years in the Army. An Alumnus of Rashtriya Indian Military College, Lieutenant General Grewal was commissioned into 5TH Battalion, the Jammu & Kashmir Rifles in June 1962 and participated in the 1965 and 1971 Operations. He Commanded Ladakh Scouts at Partapur and on promotion to Brigadier commanded an Infantry Brigade in the Western Sector. He was awarded the Sena Medal for the Flood Relief Operation undertaken in the Punjab in the year 1989. As a General Officer, he commanded a Division in the Kashmir Valley and Corps in the Eastern Sector. Lieutenant General S.S. Grewal was appointed as Adjutant General at Army Headquarters in the year 1998 and was Colonel of Jammu & Kashmir Rifles and Ladakh Scouts. He is also the Colonel Lieutenant. General S.S. Grewal is decorated with the Param Vishisht Seva Medal, Ati Vishisht Seva Medal, Sena Medal and Vishisht Seva Medal.

The Generals

Gurbachan Singh Buch, Lieutenant General, VSM

Gurbachan Singh Buch was born on January 1ST 1922 at Narangwal. He joined the Army as Gentleman Cadet in 13TH Lancers. In 1942 he was posted in the Guide Cavalry. During the Second World War he was with 19TH Lancers and served in Arakan and Malaya. When the war was over, he was posted in the North West Frontier Province and Waziristan and served there until the Independence of India in 1948. After that he went to England to get training in the Gunnery Course at Royal Armed Corps. On his return he was appointed Commanding Officer of the Gunnery Wing in the Armed Corps Centre. He graduated in 1952 from Defence Service Staff College, Wellington, and was posted as Brigade Major in the Armed Brigade and eventually appointed as General Staff Officer in the Infantry Division in the Eastern Sector. In 1960 he was promoted as Lieutenant Colonel in 20TH Lancers. With 13 tanks under his command, he was posted to Ladakh. This was considered a stupendous and formidable task but under his leadership, the Regiment performed this difficult task most successfully. He was posted to North East Frontier where he was given the command of Mountain Brigade. After that he served as G.O.C. in Jammu and Kashmir. He was at that time Chief of Staff in the Northern Command with the rank of Major General. Soon he was promoted to Lieutenant General and awarded the Vishist Sewa Medal for his Outstanding Services to the Army. He settled in Patiala after his retirement from the Army. Lieutenant General passed away at the age of 76 on the 19TH July 1998.

Gurbaksh Singh Sihota, Lieutenant General, PVSM, AVSM, VrC, VM.

Gurbaksh Singh Sihota joined the Regiment of Artillery, and topping the Young Officer's course, was awarded the prestigious Silver Gun. Having been posted to the elite 7TH Field Regiment, he participated in the 1965 war with 1ST Battalion, The Sikh Regiment in Jammu and Kashmir's Tangdhar sector. In 1966 he went on to be an Air Op Pilot, after attending flight training at Flying Training Club at Patiala; he was awarded Silver Pushpak for standing first on the course. He went to attend Staff College in United Kingdom at Camberley, and Nuclear, Biological, and Chemical course in USA. He has been conferred with many Gallantry and Distinguished Service Awards. He is a recipient of Mentions-in-Despatches in 1965 war, a Vir Chakra and a Vayu Sena Medal in 1971 war in Bangladesh.

The Generals

Gurbaksh Singh Sihota, Lieutenant General, PVSM, AVSM, VrC, VM. (Cont.)

Gurbaksh Singh Sihota had been awarded Ati Vishisht Seva Medal as a Major General Commanding Victor Force of Rashtriya Rifles in Jammu and Kashmir. On promotion to the rank of Lieutenant General he was given command of Strike Corps, a rare honour for an Artillery Officer. After that he was appointed Director General Military Operations at the Army Headquarters and awarded the Param Vishisht Seva Medal. He took over as GOC-in-C of Southern Command (SC), the largest Army Command, in October 2000. After serving 40 years of Meritorious Service he retired on February 29TH 2004.

Gurdeep Singh, Lieutenant General, PVSM, AVSM, VSM, ADC.

Lieutenant General Gurdeep Singh was born at Jalandhar City. He left school in June 1968 (Bhagat House). He passed out of 40 National Defence Academy with a Silver Medal (First in order of Merit) and was commissioned on 31ST March 1972 to the Regiment of Artillery. He was awarded the Silver Gun on the Young Officers Course (Best Young Officer). He then qualified as a Helicopter Pilot of Army Aviation and attended the Long Gunnery Staff Course of Artillery at Defence Services Staff College. He also attended a Higher Command Course and National Defence College. He topped all courses attended, including Staff College and LGSC. He was an Instructor at the School of Artillery and Staff College and a Qualified Instructor on Bofors Guns from Sweden. He commanded the only Heavy Regiment of the Indian Army and the Artillery Brigade in the crucial Punjab Sector during Op Parakram. His important appointments include: Brigade Major of Mountain Brigade in High Altitude Area, Colonel Administration of an Infantry Division, Brigadier Admin of a Strike Corps in the Deserts, Major General Admin of a Command in Western Sector, Additional Director General Assam Rifles in North East in Counter Insurgency Operations, Director General Financial Planning at Army Headquarters. . Presently he is Commandant of the School of Artillery.

The Generals

Harbakhsh Singh, Lieutenant General, VrC, Padma Bhushan, Padma Vibhushan

Lieutenant General Harbakhsh Singh was commissioned into 5TH Sikh Regiment in 1935. He was a Graduate of the 1ST course at Indian Military Academy. He had a year's attachment with a British Battalion, The Argyll and Sutherland Highlanders, wherein he saw active service on the north-west frontier. He commanded a Company of 5TH Sikhs in 1942 in Malaya against the Japanese. Severely wounded in the head, a steel plate, which he carried to his last day, was a constant reminder. He was in a Military Hospital when General A.E. Percival, Allied Field Commander, surrendered to the Japanese. He spent three years of a miserable existence, in a Japanese Prisoner of War camp. Released at the end of the war in 1945, he remained in a military hospital for some months. Posted as Second-in-Command of 4TH Sikh Regiment on release from hospital, he was perhaps the only Deputy ever to ride a horse on parade in an Infantry Battalion, as he was too weak to march. We now come to three episodes in his brilliant military career which make him stand out as one of the outstanding Commanders in modern Indian history. India became independent on 15TH August 1947, and Pakistani-backed regulars, irregulars and tribesmen crossed into the state of Jammu and Kashmir on October 22ND. In spite of a determined effort by the Jammu and Kashmir State Forces and by the initially inducted Indian troops, the enemy reached the outskirts of Srinagar on November 20TH and the fall of the capital city was imminent. On November 21ST, reports came in of a concentration of around 3,000 enemy troops on the outskirts of Srinagar at Shalateng, just 4 miles from the city centre, preparing to attack the city. Colonel Harbakhsh Singh, then Second-in-Command of the newly inducted 161ST Brigade was given the task of conducting the battle. He attacked Shalateng on November 22ND with two Infantry Battalions, 1ST Sikh and 1ST (Para) Kumaon with a troop of armoured cars of 7TH Cavalry and, in a brilliantly planned and executed operation, routed the enemy leaving 472 enemy dead on the field. He was promoted to command 163RD Brigade, on 17TH May 1948, to clear the enemy out of the Jhelum Valley, up to Muzaffarabad and Domel. While 161ST Brigade was held up near Uri, Brigadier Harbakhsh Singh's offensive, as discussed by General Birdwood in his book; 'A Continent Decides' was a triumph.

The Generals

Harbakhsh Singh, Lieutenant General (Cont.)

"Pakistan's situation was now grim, and had India only used air supply more aggressively to maintain the impetus of this outflanking success, her forces would so severely have threatened Muzaffarabad as to force a Pakistani withdrawal from the whole of the northern sector. Luckily for Pakistan, they paused." Tithwal fell on May 23RD. In six days, Brigadier Harbakhsh Singh had in a lightning move secured all territory starting from Handwara to the Kishanganga over the Nasta Chun Pass and Tithwal after fighting aggressive battles. Finally after commanding 5TH Division and 4TH Corps for a while, during the Chinese Operations of 1962, where many soldiers believe that had he been allowed to command the Corps during the second phase of the battle by the Chinese, which started on November 20TH, the situation would have been quite different in NEFA. Sadly for the Corps, their old GOC, Lt. General B.M. Kaul, was sent back to command, from a sick bed in Delhi, by Krishna Menon, the then Defence Minister. Lieutenant General Harbakhsh Singh was then given command of 33RD Corps at Siliguri and he finally took over as the Western Army Commander in November 1964. War clouds gathered once again in 1965. Pakistan took the offensive in April in Kutch and was successfully repulsed. In August, Kashmir became the target and on September 6TH, India went to war. The Western Army offensive across the Punjab border, which started at 4:30 a.m. on September 6TH, went well till Pakistan counter attacked 4TH Division on the 11TH Corps left flank at Khem-Karan. The 4TH Division comprising 62ND and 7TH Brigades, a strength of 6 Infantry Battalions, had not quite recovered from the drubbing it received in 1962 at the hands of the Chinese, lost two-and-a-half Battalions in a matter of hours, less through enemy action more by desertion, and was virtually overrun. The situation on the 7TH afternoon was grim, while the Division fell back to the village of Asal Uttar and hurriedly prepared a defended sector based on the surviving three-and-a-half battalions and 2ND Armoured Brigade. On the 9TH, Pakistan's 1ST Armoured Division, whose existence was not known, attacked the Division. Their operational order was captured. The plan was to attack and overrun the weak 4TH Division, while a strong combat group was to cut the lines of communication of both 4TH Division, 7TH Division on the Barki Axis and finally to cut the GT Road at the Beas Bridge, effectively sealing off 11TH Corps HQs and Corps troops at Raya, and the LOFC of 15TH Division in one sweep.

The Generals

Harbakhsh Singh, Lieutenant General, (Cont.)

The situation was extremely grim and as a consequence Delhi panicked. Having returned to HQ Western Army at Ambala from 4TH Division at midnight on the 9TH and after a visit to the operations room, the Army Commander retired for three hours rest before leaving at four o'clock the next morning. At 2:30 a.m. the Army Chief, General J.N. Chaudhari, called and spoke to the General and after a heated discussion centred around the major threat that had developed, the Chief ordered the Army Commander to withdraw 11TH Corps to hold a line on the Beas river. General Harbakhsh Singh refused to carry out this order. The next morning, 4TH Division stabilised the position and when the Chief visited Command Headquarters at Ambala that afternoon, the 10TH, the crisis was over and the subject was not discussed. Had the General carried out these orders, not only would half of Punjab been under Pakistani occupation but the morale of the Indian Army would have been rock bottom, affecting operations in other theatres as well. He retired at the end of September, 1969. He passed away on 14TH November 1999. (Amarinder Singh)

Hardev Singh Lidder, Lieutenant General, UYSM, YSM, VSM

Lieutenant General Hardev Singh Lidder assumed charge as the third Chief of Integrated Service Command on 2ND March 2006. A fourth generation Army Officer, he was a recipient of the Sword of Honour for the best all-round performance at the Indian Military Academy. He was commissioned into the Deccan Horse, one of the oldest Regiments of the Armoured Corps, in July 1967. A Graduate of the Staff College at Camberley in Britain, he has served in Jammu and Kashmir and as an Instructor with the Indian Military Training Team in Bhutan. He also served as the Commander-in-Chief of the tri-services Andaman and Nicobar Command. He has held several prestigious appointments at Army Headquarters, New Delhi and was also the Military Attaché in the Indian Embassy in the United States for three years. He retired from the Indian Army on 1ST October 2008.

The Generals

Harbhajan Singh Banga, Lieutenant General, PVSM, VSM

Lieutenant General Harbhajan Singh Banga, (Born – 24TH September 1924, Died – 22ND December 2011) it is sad news for all of us in olive green that we have lost one more of that rare breed of Gentlemen-Soldiers. General Banga came from an illustrious family. His father, Dr. Gyan Singh was an eminent doctor. Following in the foot steps of his elders, General Banga excelled in both professional and academics front. He began his military life as the course topper in the First Technical Graduates course in December 1948. During his career spanning more than four decades, he attended most of the prestigious courses. He firstly attended the course in UK when he was Captain in 1959. As a Major and Lieutenant Colonel he was posted to 512 ABW, where the technical acumen of General Banga was appreciated by one and all. For his Distinguished Services in the Armoured Division during the 1965 war, he was awarded Visisht Seva Medal. In 1970 he served as Dy DEME as Brigadier and subsequently participated in 1971 war in the Eastern Sector. General Banga was the Director General of Corps of EME from March 1978 to March 1982, when he was decorated with the Param Vishisht Seva Medal. After retiring from the Army in 1982, he joined Ashok Leyland and served for about seven years as Plant Director first in Alwar (Rajasthan) and then in Hosur (Tamil Nadu). Thereafter, General Banga was head of the administration of Hindujas hospital in Mumbai and became the first non-medico to be the CEO. During his decade long service with the hospital, he acquired so much knowledge of the medical science, that he was often invited to preside over seminars and discussions. General Banga was the epitome of professionalism, both while in Service and in Industry. General Banga is survived by his wife Mrs. Jaswant Banga, their two sons Manvinder and Ajaypal and their daughter Deepa. General Banga enjoyed an illustrious career even after leaving uniform. His memory will be cherished by the EME fraternity.

The Generals

HRS Kalkat, Lieutenant General, VSM, AVSM

Born in 1942, Lieutenant General Kalkat was commissioned into the Infantry in June 1962. General Kalkat is a Graduate of the Defence Service Staff College and the National Defence College, and holds a Post-Graduate Degree in Military Service. He is a veteran of the 1971 Indo-Pakistan war. He commanded a Company in Nagaland and was awarded the Vishist Seva Medal (VSM). As a Major General he commanded Assam Rifles, Rashtriya Rifles and BSF in Nagaland and was successfully able to bring a cease fire in 1997 which is still holding. He was awarded the Ati Vishist Seva Medal (AVSM) for his Operational Success and Outstanding Achievement. Prior to his retirement, General Kalkat was the top General in charge of the eastern command in India. He is known for his expertise in mountain warfare and exceptional organizational skills. He also served as the Military, Naval and Air Adviser of the south Pacific region and was posted to Australia from 1982-86.

Inder Singh, Lieutenant General

Lieutenant General Inder Singh was born in 1913 at Maymyo (Burma) Having graduated in 1936 from the University of Rangoon, between 1936 and 1940 he attained further qualifications in London, Edinburgh and Glasgow. In 1940 he was commissioned in the Armed Force's Medical Services and had a long distinguished medical career holding many important academic and administrative posts. From 1949 to 1951 and from 1958 to 1961 he held the appointments of Professor of Clinical Medicine and Professor of Medicine respectively at the Armed Forces Medical College, Pune, and a prestigious institute of the country. Between 1954 and 1958 he served as Assistant Director of Medical Services of the Ministry of Defence. In 1961 he became Consultant in Medicine to the Armed Forces. He was promoted to the status of Senior Consultant in 1966 and then occupied the office of the Chief Consultant till he retired in 1972 with the rank of Lieutenant General. In recognition of his achievements he was ordained as the Scientist Emeritus to the Armed Forces. A cruel fate deprived the scientific community of this legendary figure. General Inder Singh died on 9TH November, 1980 at the age of 67.

The Generals

Inderjit Singh Gill, Lieutenant General, PVSM, MC

Inderjit Gill was born in Madras, Southern India, in 1919, the son of a Royal Medical Corps Officer, who later became Inspector General of Prisons in the province. After schooling in Madras, Gill went to England to study but ended up joining the Royal Engineers. He was posted to 142ND Royal Engineer Officers Course Training units in Aldershot in October 1941. On 5TH April 1942, he was granted a Regular Army Emergency Commission, and 2ND Lieutenant Inderjit Singh Gill was posted to 274TH Field Company, 51ST Division Royal Engineers, which embarked for Egypt on 15TH June 1942, arriving at their destination almost two months later on 12TH August. Inder's war had begun. Volunteering for Operation 'Harling' Inderjit Gill was part of a campaign to formant resistance against the Axis powers in Greece and to cripple their transport arteries by blowing up key bridges. 'Harling' was the first major operation outside Western Europe by the Special Operations Execute (SOE) that Britain had formed to, in Churchill's words, 'set Europe ablaze.' During the operations in Greece, Inderjit Gill was awarded the Military Cross for his Conspicuous Gallantry. The British Military Mission's work in Greece between November 1942 and November 1944, when the last German pulled out of Greece, there were several successes that all the officers involved with 'Harling' had reason to be proud with.

Greece, for its part, never forgot what had happened at the Gorgopotamos Bridge and the fuse it lit to bring the Resistance movement to life. Early in 1982, Inder, who was by then retired and settled in Madras, received a telegram from George Gennimatas, the Greek Minister for the Interior. It read:

It was November 25TH, 1942, when one of the most significant destruction operations against the Axis forces in Europe took place. This happened at the Gorgopotamos Bridge in Greece and you had personally participated. The Greeks who fought with you in those days and also all the Greek people of today will never forget the heroism, sacrifices and struggles you offered for our National Liberation Effort. But for one more reason those common struggles do rest unforgettable in our memory to remind us that people when untied write brilliant pages of heroism in the book of history. Today, 40 years after this great event, the Greek Government will officially celebrate this anniversary of Gorgopotamos Bridge destruction and at the same time this is also in honour for the epic struggle of our national resistance.

The Generals

Inderjit Singh Gill, Lieutenant General (Cont.)

You are cordially invited to the celebration which will take place at Gorgopotamos Eria on November 25^{TH,} 1982 at 10.30 am. We would be very much moved by your presence at the ceremony which will give us also the opportunity to honour you and your fellow fighters of those days, Greeks and foreigners, who have been invited of the Greek Government.' (S. Muthia.2008, p 54)

Leaving Greece, Inder served with the Royal Engineers on the slog from Cassino to Bologna in Italy, where he was injured twice in explosions, shrapnel from which he carried in his body for the rest of his life.

English Patient

Lieutenant Kip Singh, the Sikh soldier with a talent for defusing bombs, who finds a romantic connection with co-star Juliet Binoche- the English patient's nurse- in the Academy Award-winning romantic epic, Michael Ondaatje's 1992 novel "The English Patient". It is believed that Lieutenant Kip, the Sikh Sapper is modelled from real life exploits of Inderjit Singh Gill the WW II British Sapper demolition expert in Greece, 1942.

Gill returned home just before Independence in 1947 and nine years later commanded the elite 1ST Para Regiment which was part of the United Nations Peacekeeping contingent in Egypt and the Sinai. During the second war with Pakistan in 1965 Gill, then commanding a Parachute Brigade used his Second World War experience as a guerrilla fighter to track down hundreds of Pakistani infiltrators in Kashmir. Twenty four years later, as the Indian Army's Director, Military Operations, Gill, then a Major-General, once again displayed the same soldierly qualities and blunt reasonableness by planning and executing the defeat of the Pakistani Army in 1971. He never left his Operational Headquarters for the fortnight-long war that ended with the capture of over 91,000 Pakistani soldiers and the formation of Bangladesh. A few months later he was responsible for delineating the line of control that divided the northern disputed Kashmir state between the rival claimants, India and Pakistan. Gill was a dedicated, principled Officer and a Gentleman, who shunned fame or media plaudits for his brilliant Military Career, and who many thought should have made it to the post of Army Chief.

Lieutenant General Inderjit Singh Gill PVSM, MC, passed away on May 30TH, 2001.

The Generals

Jagjit Singh Aurora, Lieutenant General, PVSM, PV

Jagjit Singh Aurora was commissioned into 2ND Punjab Regiment in 1939, after his graduation from the Indian Military Academy, and went on to command it during the 1947-1948 hostilities with Pakistan in Kashmir. He had reached the rank of Brigadier by the time he was involved in border hostilities with Chinese troops in 1961. In 1971, Aurora was made commander of Indian forces in the east, and he was responsible for hostilities in East Pakistan. In less than two weeks, months of guerrilla warfare were ended and Pakistan split in two, losing 55,000 square miles of its territory and 70 million of its people, in an operation meticulously prepared months in advance by Aurora and others. Aurora had also been closely involved in training and equipping the Mukti Bahini, a ragtag group of freedom fighters who were transformed into an effective guerrilla force that harassed and demoralised the Pakistanis. This softened up the Pakistanis in readiness for India's strike, which was launched after Pakistan carried out bombing raids on several Indian airfields on December 3RD, 1971. These had been preceded by several Pakistani attacks on Mukhti Bahini camps inside India. War was now inevitable. Aurora had helped to oversee the logistical preparations for the coming battles, including the improvement of roads, communications and bridges, as well as the movement of 30,000 tons of supplies close to the border of East Pakistan. Even so, the Indian Army could never have anticipated how quickly the Pakistanis would be routed. Instead of attacking Pakistani positions head-on, Aurora ordered his troops to bypass them wherever possible and head straight for Dhaka. The key breakthrough came when thousands of forces succeeded in crossing the Meghna River, which the Pakistanis had left unguarded, having blown up the only bridge. Local people ferried the Indian troops across in huge numbers of small boats under cover of darkness: "That was the turning point," Aurora later recalled. On December 16TH, 1971, a day familiar to every Bangladeshi, Aurora accepted the surrender of Pakistani forces led by General Niazi. After signing the document at about 4.30pm, the Pakistani Commander handed over his Personal Pistol and Lanyard to General Aurora and removed his badges of rank. With that a cheer went up in the Dacca race course and Dacca became the free capital of a free country, Bangladesh.

The Generals

Jagjit Singh Aurora, Lieutenant General (Cont.)

Earlier Lieutenant General Aurora inspected a combined Guard of Honour offered by local Pakistani troops, as well as the Indian Army troops which had come into Dacca. This was the first time such an event had occurred in History. Lieutenant General Aurora was accompanied by his wife.

The signing of the document ended the war, and led to the formation of Bangla Desh, the name of the new country was used in the instrument of surrender, which declared: "The Pakistan Eastern Command agree to surrender all Pakistan armed forces in Bangla Desh to Lieutenant-General Jagjit Singh Aurora, General Officer Commanding-in-Chief of the Indian and Bangla Desh forces in the Eastern Theatre."

Aurora accepted the surrender without a word, while thousands cheered. He was hoisted on soldiers' shoulders amid shouts of jai Bangla (victory to Bangla). Niazi then had to be swiftly spirited away when crowds began calling for him to be lynched. Back home, he was widely criticised for submitting to such humiliation. More than 90,000 Pakistani fighters were taken prisoner after the ceremony. The total number of uniformed personnel consisted of about 79,676 of which 55,692 were Army, 16,354 of Paramilitary and 5,296 Civilian Police personnel, in addition to about 800 Pakistan Air Force and 1000 Pakistani Navy personnel. In honour of his contribution to Bangladesh liberation, he was awarded the 'Bir Pratik' Gallantry Award by the newly formed Bangladesh nation. After his retirement Aurora spent several years as an MP in the Rajya Sabha (Upper House of Parliament) for the Sikh party, the Akali Dal. He fiercely opposed the 1984 Army attack on the Golden Temple in Amritsar, the Sikhs' holiest shrine, to flush out armed Sikh militants who had taken up positions inside. He was also a leading activist on behalf of the victims of anti-Sikh riots in Delhi in 1984, which followed the assassination of the Prime Minister, Indira Gandhi, by her Sikh bodyguards. He died on May 3RD, 2005, aged 89. He is survived by a son and daughter. After his death, the eternal gratitude of Bangladesh to General Aurora was emphasised in a message to India, from Morshed Khan, the Bangladeshi Foreign Minister, stating: "Aurora will be remembered in the history of Bangladesh for his contribution during our war of liberation in 1971, when he led the allied forces." The site of the Pakistani surrender is being converted into what will be called Independence Square, with an eternal flame.

The Generals

Jaswant Singh, Lieutenant General, PVSM, VSM

Lieutenant General Jaswant Singh was a very distinguished and celebrated Indian Sikh General, who rose to become the Vice Chief of Army Staff in the Indian Army. His military accomplishments ranged from taking part in active combat in three full scale wars, running a self-conceived refugee camp during the bloodbath of the Partition, as well as fighting an intense insurgency environment in the North East.

Lieutenant General Jaswant Singh was born in Sialkot (Undivided India) on 10TH March 1925. His father Subedar Sohan Singh was then serving in $2^{ND}/8^{TH}$ Punjab Regiment. Sohan Singh had a very distinguished service and showed extreme courage and bravery on more than one occasion: he was "Mentioned-in-Dispatches" for his Exceptional Gallantry in a battle against the Turks, in the First World War by Lieutenant General F.P.Maude, the Supreme Commander of Allied Forces in Mesopotamia; (the Certificate was signed by Sir Winston Churchill, who was then Secretary of State for War). Later, Sohan Singh was also awarded the "Force Commander" Certificate "for bravery during operations in Waziristan", and was also a recipient of the "Jangi Inam" by the British Government.

Lieutenant General Jaswant Singh was educated initially at King George's Royal Military School (Jalandhar), where he became the Head-boy and also stood first in Class 10; and later at Kitchener College, Nowgong. He joined the Indian Military Academy, Dehra Dun, from where he was commissioned into $7^{TH}/15^{TH}$ Punjab Regiment on 16TH January 1944. After a few months he was transferred to $6^{TH}/15^{TH}$ Punjab where he saw active combat in Burma.

Lieutenant General Jaswant Singh had a very illustrious career during which he actively participated in three major wars, and the very bloody and intense Mizo Insurgency. He also held many prestigious Command, Staff and Instructional assignments. During his varied assignments he was Brigade Major of an Infantry Brigade(twice), served in the prestigious Military Operations Directorate (twice, including one under Brig(later Field Marshal) Sam Manekshaw),was Instructor in Defence Services Staff College, Brigadier General Staff of 11TH Corps and Chief of Staff of 1ST Corps. He commanded 7TH Punjab Battalion, 61ST Mountain Brigade and 10TH Infantry Division.

The Generals

Jaswant Singh, Lieutenant General, PVSM, VSM (Cont.)

Lieutenant General Jaswant Singh is perhaps one of the very few Officers of the Indian Army who have held Command Appointments from the Platoon to Division level, in active operations i.e. he commanded a Platoon and Company in Burma in the Second World War (1944-45), a Company again along the Chinese Border (1958-59) during which he led a long-range patrol inside Tibet for strategic military reconnaissance, a Battalion during the 1965 Indo-Pakistan War, a Brigade in Mizo Hills in its peak insurgency period in 1966-68, and later a Division in the crucial Chhamb Sector in the 1971 Indo-Pakistan War. Some of the highlights of his Military Career are mentioned below. As a young Platoon Commander in Burma in 1944, Jaswant Singh conducted an audacious "ambush operation" of the Japanese forces by operating behind enemy lines and causing numerous casualties, for which he was recommended for a Military Cross. On return from Burma, he was posted to Special Selection Boards in Bareilly and Yol Camp to screen War Commissioned Officers for permanent commission into the Indian Army. Later, during the communally disturbed and riotous period of the Partition of India while on leave, as a young Captain, Jaswant found himself on the wrong side of the Border. He saw that there was great insecurity amongst the non-Muslim population due to the bloodshed and massacres which were taking place. On his own initiative, young Jaswant single-handedly conceived and set up a "Refugee Camp" for Hindu and Sikh families of nearby villages in Daska, (Sialkot District) and successfully evacuated close to one lakh people to India. He, along with his family, was the last to cross over. For this exemplary act in true Military tradition, he was awarded the "Commander in Chief's Commendation Certificate" by India's C-in-C, Field Marshal KM Cariappa. On return to India, he was posted to Special Selection Boards in Bareilly and Yol Camp, which were set up to screen the War Commissioned Officers for permanent commission to the Indian Army. In 1951 he passed the entrance examination to attend the Indian Staff Course obtaining a competitive vacancy, and was the youngest Officer to do the course at the age of only 26 years! Many years later in 1960) he was selected on merit to attend the Joint Services Staff College Course in Latimer (UK). During the 1965 Indo-Pakistan War, as Commanding Officer of 7TH Punjab Battalion, he led his Unit to capture the formidable Lchhogil Canal (along with 3 Pakistani tanks), after two other Battalions had failed to do so.

The Generals

Jaswant Singh, Lieutenant General, PVSM, VSM (Cont.)

For this action he was awarded the Vishisht Seva Medal, while the Battalion received 42 gallantry awards, which was a record for a single action in the 1965 War! As a Brigadier he was selected to command 61ST Mountain Brigade in the Mizo Hills, in its most active insurgency period, during which he survived a helicopter crash, and hostile fire from the Mizo insurgents on many occasions; he was once again recommended for a Gallantry Award. As a Major General, he commanded 10TH Infantry Division in the strategically important Chhamb Sector during the 1971 Indo-Pakistan War and was responsible for thwarting what was the biggest Pakistani offensive of that War, despite the last minute orders to cancel their offensive plan, and lack of air support in the first three critical days of the war. The importance of this offensive to Pakistan can be gauged from the fact that Pakistan employed much more artillery guns to support this thrust towards Jammu, than it had in support of its entire Eastern Command in East Pakistan! In fact Prime Minister Mrs. Indira Gandhi, in a meeting with General Jaswant shortly after the war, acknowledged it to be the "toughest battle" of the War. In an article on the war titled 'From the Western Front' by Jay Inder Singh Kalra, published on 9TH Jan 1972, the famous Illustrated Weekly of India printed a photograph of General Jaswant Singh with the caption " The Saviour of Chhamb", and quoted a Senior Staff Officer from HQ Western Command saying that Jaswant "fought a grand battle ". It is also noteworthy, that during the 1971 Indo-Pakistan War, 6 persons from the same family, four of whom were brothers, were fighting for the nation on the western and eastern fronts i.e. Jaswant was a Division Commander, Harbhajan was a Brigade Commander, Upkar was a Battalion Commander, Mohinder was a Flight Commander, Ardaman Jit was an OP Officer and Sarabjit was an Engineer Platoon Commander!).

Lieutenant General Jaswant Singh became a Lieutenant General at a very young age of 50 years. He served as the Deputy Chief of the Indian Army, and also commanded 1ST Corps. He was also the 'Colonel' of the Punjab Regiment. Later, he was promoted as Vice Chief of Army Staff of the Indian Army, wherein he died in harness on 30TH March 1980 at the age of 55 years. Had his life not been cut short abruptly, he had a very good chance of becoming the first Sikh Chief of the Indian Army. During his long and very Distinguished Service, Lt. General Jaswant Singh was awarded the Param Vishist Seva Medal, the Vishisht Seva Medal as well as the C-in-C's Commendation Card.

The Generals

Jasbir Singh Lidder, Lieutenant General, UTSM, AVSM

Lieutenant General Lidder (Retd.) was born in 1949. He was commissioned as an Infantry Officer in the Grenadiers Regiment of the Indian Army, following four years of training at the National Defence Academy, Khadakvasla and the Indian Military Academy, Dehradun. General Lidder is a recipient of numerous Gallantry and Distinguished Service Awards. As a Company Commander, he received the Army Commander's Commendation for Gallantry. He has been awarded the Uttam Yudh Seva Medal by the President of India, for Distinguished Service of Exceptional Order in Combat and Ati Vishisht Seva Medal, for Distinguished Service of Exceptional Order for directing Counter-insurgency/terrorism operations in Jammu and Kashmir. Through effective orchestration of the Ceasefire structures, he managed to conduct major separation and re-deployment of the opposing forces, integration of the Other Armed Groups (OAGs), deployment and development of the Joint Integrated Units (JIUs) and diffusing tribal violence. Previously, he was the Commanding Officer of an Infantry Division from 2002 to 2004. Between 2000 and 2002, he was Brigadier General Staff of an Army Corps. He has served as Chief of Staff of the United Nations Peacekeeping Force in Mozambique from June 1994 to January 1995. Lieutenant General Lidder has served most recently as the Commandant of an elite Infantry School. Prior to this, he served for more than two years as the Force Commander to the United Nation Mission to the Sudan.

Jasbir Singh, Lieutenant General, VSM, AVSM

Lieutenant General Jasbir Singh Chief of Staff of the Northern Command is an Alumnus of National Defence Academy. He was commissioned into the Dogra Regiment on March 31ST, 1972. He is a Graduate of Defence Services Staff College, Wellington. He has attended the prestigious Higher Command and NDA courses. His key command assignments are that of an Infantry Battalion in counter-insurgency environment in Jammu and Kashmir. An Infantry Brigade in active operations in India's Western Theatre of operations and an Infantry Division in counter insurgency. For Counter Terrorism operations in Jammu and Kashmir he was awarded the prestigious VSM and AVSM. He has also been Colonel Administration of an Infantry Division and Brigadier General Staff of a Corps deployed in super high altitude terrain. He has been the Defence Attaché in Myanmar for three years.

The Generals

Jasbir Singh, Lieutenant General (Cont.)

He assumed charge of the Northern Command Headquarters at Udhampur, after having relinquished the distinguished post of Director General of Infantry at the Army Headquarters in New Delhi. He holds the coveted appointment of the Colonel of the Dogra Regiment and Dogra Scouts and heads the Fraternity of the Distinguished Dogra's as their Colonel Commandant. Lieutenant General Jasbir Singh retired from the Service in July 30TH 2011.

Joginder Jaswant Singh, General

General Joginder Jaswant Singh assumed charge of the Indian Army, as the 22ND Chief of Army Staff, on 31ST January 2005. He is an Alumnus of the National Defence Academy and was commissioned into 9TH Maratha Light Infantry on 2ND August 1964. He received the Colour of the Battalion from President Dr. Zakir Hussain at the Investiture Parade in 1968. Hailing from a family of warriors, he is a third generation Soldier. Born on 17TH September 1945 in Bahawalpur (now in Pakistan), his family migrated to India (Patiala, Punjab) after partition in 1947. His grandfather served in 67TH Punjabis during the First World War in Mesopotamia and Kut-al-Amara (present day Iraq) along with 103RD, 105TH, 110TH, 114TH and 117TH Mahrattas. These five battalions subsequently joined the Maratha Light Infantry; the same Regiment General Singh was commissioned into 50 years later. His father, Colonel Jaswant Singh Marwah, served in the Electrical and Mechanical Engineers from 1943 to 1973 and is also a veteran of the Second World War. During his tenure with 7TH and 9TH Maratha Light Infantry and also while on Higher Command and Staff appointments, General J.J. Singh has served in Jammu and Kashmir, Nagaland, Arunachal Pradesh, Sikkim and Joshimath in Uttranchal Pradesh. He was awarded the Vishisht Seva Medal during his command tenure of 9TH Maratha Light Infantry in Arunachal Pradesh. He later commanded 5TH Maratha Light Infantry at Hyderabad in the rank of Colonel. A consistent front runner, he was the youngest and one of the first in his batch to attend Staff College, Senior Command, Higher Command and National Defence College courses. He has contributed articles for Regimental and other Professional Journals and his Thesis on 'Sino-Indian Border Dispute' and 'Strategy to Boost Defence Exports' has been highly acclaimed. He has the honour of being India's first Defence Attaché to Algeria (1987 - 1990).

The Generals

Joginder Jaswant Singh, General (Cont.)

After returning from Algeria, he successfully commanded 79TH (Independent) Mountain Brigade in the Baramula Sector, Jammu and Kashmir, during the peak of insurgency there in 1991-92. During this tenure, he was gravely wounded in action, in a fierce engagement with terrorists infiltrating across the Line of Control (LoC). For that operation, he received the War Wound Medal and was awarded the Chief of Army Staff's Commendation. He was nominated to attend the prestigious National Defence College (NDC) course in 1993. He was posted as Deputy Director General Operational Logistics in Army HQ after the NDC Course and later commanded 9TH Infantry Division from 1996 to 1998. General Singh was then selected for a key appointment as the Additional Director General Military Operations (ADGMO) at Army HQ, Military Operations Directorate. During his tenure as ADGMO, he contributed positively towards evolving India's policy on the Sino-Indian border issue and visited Beijing as part of the Joint Working Group. He was also part of the Ministry of Defence team for talks with Pakistan on the Siachen and Sir Creek issue in 1998. He visited Sierra Leone with the Defence Minister, where an Indian contingent carried out successful operations as part of the UN Mission. As the ADGMO, he became the Indian Army's public face during the 1999 Kargil conflict. He was decorated with the Ati Vishisht Seva Medal in recognition of his Services in the Planning and Execution of the war. General Singh assumed command of the elite 1ST 'Strike' Corps at Mathura. He successfully coordinated the Corps level exercise (Poorna Vijay) in May 2001 in the deserts of Rajasthan. He subsequently led 1ST Corps during Operation Parakram, the military standoff against Pakistan, from December 2001 to December 2002. He was then appointed as the General Officer Commanding-in-Chief of the Army Training Command in January 2003, where he was credited with drafting a new doctrine for the Indian Army. He was instrumental in giving the Command a distinctly discernable and widely appreciated thrust towards modernisation. After his stint at ARTRAC he stated, "Every assignment has its own importance, but the one at ARTRAC, the think-tank of the Army, has been quite different as it plays a crucial role in preparing the Army for future challenges in a constantly changing battlefield milieu. The responsibility involved development of new concepts and doctrines at the strategic and operational levels for the emerging security environment"

The Generals

Joginder Jaswant Singh, General (Cont.)

He was awarded the Param Vishisht Seva Medal (PVSM) on 26TH January 2004 for his Distinguished Services of the Highest Order. General Singh took over as the GOC-in-C Western Command on 1ST February 2004 and his tenure at this elite Command, provided an opportunity to put into practice the concepts and doctrines evolved at ARTRAC and he refined operational planning by co-opting the battle winning role of Revolution in Military Affairs (RMA). And provided focused direction based on the recently released 'Doctrine for the Indian Army' having earlier been its architect. He simultaneously gave training a visionary direction in conjunction with principles of synergetic cohesiveness at all levels. His tenure at Western Command also saw a quantum leap in the implementation of the Ex-servicemen Contributory Health Scheme (ECHS). He was also appointed as Honorary Aide-de-Camp (ADC) to the President of India on 1ST February 2004. On assuming the office of the Chief of Army Staff on 1ST February 2005, General Singh stated in a message, "We stand poised at a critical juncture in the timeline of history. Having left behind us the vagaries of the past, we purposefully stride towards economic growth, social harmony, peace and prosperity. Simultaneously and seamlessly, we are also making the transition to a highly motivated and modern Army, driven by the engines of high technology and Revolution in Military Affairs. I assure our countrymen that the Army will remain at the service of the nation, at all times, ready and eager to take on any challenge with determination and resolve to emerge victorious." He is widely considered to be a thinking soldier and is a thorough professional. Affectionately known as General JJ within army circles, he was appointed Colonel of the Maratha Light Infantry on 10TH October 2001. He is an ace shooter and plays basketball, squash and golf. He is also a keen mountaineer who has trained under the late Tenzing Norgay at Himalayan Mountaineering Institute, Darjeeling. He is married to Mrs Anupam Singh and they have a son and a daughter. He is fluent in both Arabic and French, the widely spoken languages in Algeria. [3]

---

[1] Lieut-General Joginder Jaswant Singh was the first Sikh Officer to become the Chief of the Indian Army Staff on February 1ST 2004. Though the Sikhs have formed the bulwark of the Indian Army since its inception, this is the first time that a Sikh Officer has been named to the top post.

The Generals

Joginder Singh Dhillon, Lieutenant General,

Lieutenant General Joginder Singh Dhillon was first, in 1933, in the all India entrance examination to the Indian Military Academy, and then won both the coveted Gold Medal and the Sword of Honour, before joining the Bengal Sappers on February 1ST, 1936. Graduating in 1939 with Honours from Rookie's Thomson Civil Engineering College, he was soon sent overseas for the first four years of World War Two. He saw active service in Iraq, Iran and Burma and, after a stint in the Staff College, Quetta, was again sent to command a Field Company in Malaya (1945-46), then onto Sourabaya (Indonesia) where he commanded 2ND Field Company, before returning home. From 1946 to 1947 he was Staff Officer in the E-in-C's Office Army HQ, then went to Quetta as Garrison Engineer, before taking over as GSO1 in the E-in-C's Branch from October 1947 to February 1948 in the rank of Lieutenant Colonel. Dhillon was handpicked to take charge of the Regimental Centre at Roorkee. In the two years after taking command in February 1948 of what was left of the centre, after the division of the Indian Army at the partition of the subcontinent, Dhillon turned the challenge of resurrecting it into a personal triumph that left everyone breathless. Combining organisational skill with drive, determination and steel, he rehabilitated the Centre, streamlined its training and administration and integrated it into an efficient and war-worthy team. A change of profound importance introduced at the Centre, which the newly independent Nation's Army as a whole eventually adopted, was that whilst hitherto several messes for the other ranks had cooked food in each Unit for a particular caste, Colonel Dhillon decisively ended this outdated practice. He decreed a single integrated mess would serve food to all men and not their caste. Another thing, according to a retired Sappers Officer, Colonel Chanan Singh Dhillon, the dynamic Commandant did was demolish the wall that separated the centre's Gurdwara and Hindu temple and build a platform instead, so that gatherings of both denominations could jointly celebrate their special days. When Prime Minister Jawaharlal Nehru visited the centre in 1949 he was so impressed by what he saw that he extended Jogi Dhillon the singular honour of selecting him to command India's first Republic Day parade in 1950. After command of the Bengal Sappers, Dhillon commanded two Infantry Brigades in succession, before his appointment, in 1956, as Director of Technical Development in Army HQ. He then served as Director, Weapons and Equipment, before being promoted to Major General in December 1957.

The Generals

Joginder Singh Dhillon, Lieutenant General (Cont.)

He was Chief of Staff, Western Command, at the time of his selection to attend a course at the Imperial Defence College in the United Kingdom, from where he returned to an appointment in the National Defence College, before assuming command of a Division in August 1960. His next job was as Deputy Chief of the General Staff at Army HQ, then promotion to Lieutenant General and posting as GOC, XI Corps in Punjab. The posting would be the culmination of everything that had gone into the making of this exceptional Soldier. When on the morning of September 6TH, 1965, war with Pakistan broke out, with the XI Corps launching a massive retaliatory attack across the border in Punjab on several fronts at 4 am; the aim was to teach Pakistan a lesson for its unprovoked attack on India in the Chhamb sector a few days earlier. It is not possible to describe this 17-day war here but the decisive tank battle of Assal Uttar, near Khem Karan, on September 10TH does bear telling. Indian units hid their Sherman tanks 500 metres apart in a U-shaped formation in tall and un-harvested sugarcane fields, and snared the enemy's vastly superior Patton tanks into this ambush, annihilating them to the last tank and deciding the outcome of the war. The destruction of Pakistan's armoured pride and the casualties it suffered, including an Artillery Brigadier and many other Senior Officers killed or surrendered, destroyed the enemy's morale. In recognition of his role in the 1965 war, the President of India invested Dhillon with the Padma Bhushan in August 1966 and also appointed him GOC-in-C Central Command, from where he retired on August 4TH, 1970. When the army bade farewell to its distinguished Comrade in Delhi on November 21ST, 2003, six Generals acted as pallbearers and the COAS, General N.C. Vij, flew in for the funeral from Hyderabad. This reaffirmed that the Indian Army stands steadfast on some of its finest traditions. On a more personal note, Jogi Dhillon was married for 62 years to Minnie, who survives him, and to whom he was as devoted as she to him. He is also survived by his three daughters, Kiran, Komal and Kamal: an architect, airline executive and head of her own consultancy firm; each as individualistic as their indomitable parents.

The Generals

JP Singh, Lieutenant General, PVSM, AVSM

Lieutenant General J.P. Singh is a distinguished General Officer who retired from Service on 30TH September 2011. He has analysed the existing, as well the emerging International Scenarios, evaluated the National Defence Technological Absorption and Production Capability, evolved long-term Perspective Plans (upto 2027) for ensuring effective Organisational Structures, Equipment Profile, Capability Development and Financial Management of the Indian Army, in order to meet the complete range of threats and eventualities of both external and internal nature. He was also responsible for 'Face Structuring', 'Technological Capability Development Strategy', induction of complete spectrum of equipment and systems, dynamically managed the implementation of acquisition Management Plans and Dynamic Financial Management of the Army Budget for the FY 2010-11. He was responsible for Military Diplomacy with a large number of Developed Nations, has visited almost all major international industries, steered numerous bilateral Indo-Foreign Committees and evaluated their technological capabilities. Having worked closely with the Apex Level Leadership of the Department of Defence, Department of Defence Products the Defence Acquisition wing, the Defence Finance and the Land System Management, he is endowed with in-depth knowledge and extensive experience of the strengths, procedures and processes involved at the Apex Level Defence Capability Development Mechanism. During his tenure at the Defence Headquarters, he had been responsible for evolution of the long-term plan involving approx Rs 30 Lakh Crores, the five year Plan for the Indian Army involving approx Rs 8 Lakh Crores and three annual plans involving 7-9000 Crores each. In view of his sound knowledge of the strategic scenarios, capability status, understanding of technological intricacies and conviction of the highest order, he was also responsible for getting the highest value contract for the Army signed with BDL for approx Rs 15000 Crores and has ensured procurement of high tech Equipment Systems to the tune of nearly Rs 58,000 Crores, an unprecedented landmark. He has closely worked with DRDO, Ordnance Factories and almost all Defence related Public Sector Undertaking for technology development, capacity enhancement, technology absorption, selection of Production Agencies and forging of joint ventures. He has imparted a new thrust to indigenization, increasing the share of indigenous procurement and introduction of new categories for Indian manufacturers.

The Generals

JP Singh, Lieutenant General, PVSM, AVSM (Cont.)

For his Distinguished Services of most Exceptional Order he was awarded the Param Vishist Seva Medal on 26TH June 2011. His visionary approach, diplomatic skills and understanding of the overall Defence Strategy led him to be selected as Deputy Chief of Integrated Defence Staff in Charge of Perspective Planning and Force Development. During his Chairmanship of SCAPCC for over a year he has steered the critical initial stages of the acquisition process of 'Acceptance of necessity' and 'categorization'. The General Officer was selected to command the most prestigious Armoured Division and the Strike Corps, both large fighting formations. He has been awarded Ati Vishist Seva Medal during the command of the first T- 90 Armoured Division wherein he showcased to an international defence forces audience the manoeuvres and live engagement by the Armoured Division in a net enabled environment. His conceptual clarity had been the basis for his selection as an Officer in Charge for Evolution of Doctrines for the Indian Army at the Army Training Command. The General Officer has throughout his career been a meritorious Officer which led to his being selected for all the competitive training courses viz the Defence Service Staff College, Combat Group Commander, Senior Command, Higher Command and the most prestigious National Defence College, wherein at each such occasion he has attained the highest grades/ results. He was commissioned into 2ND Lancers in June 1971 and has held numerous Command, Instructional and Staff Assignments, including command of an Armoured Brigade, being an Instructor at Armoured Corps Centre & School and Defence Service Staff College. He was an Instructor and Chief Advisor to the Zambian Army. He saw action on the Western Front in Fazilka Sector during the 1971 operations. In 1976, he was part of the select team to raise 82ND Armoured Regiment, which he later commanded. Presently he is the Colonel of 6TH Lancers, 82ND Armoured Regiment, 85TH Armoured Regiment and Defence Security Corps.

The Generals

Jatinder Singh, Lieutenant General, AVSM and Bar

Lieutenant General Jatinder Singh, is an Alumnus of the National Defence Academy and was commissioned into 1ST Guards (2ND Punjab) Regiment of the Indian Army on June 13TH 1973. He is a Graduate of the Defence Services Staff College, Wellington and Higher Command Course (Air) at College of Air Warfare, Secunderbad. He has operational experience of commanding from a Company to a Division in the counter-insurgency environment. He also held the position of Chief of Staff of the Desert Corps and Director General of Rashtriya Rifles. Lieutenant General Jatinder Singh has been awarded Ati Vishisht Seva Medal (AVSM) in recognition of his Devotion to Duty and Distinguished Service. The Bar to AVSM means the General Officer has bagged the AVSM for the second time. Prior to his retirement in June 2012, he was Commandant of the National Defence Academy.

Kalwant Singh, Lieutenant General

As the natural outcome of the policy of satisfying Indian political aspirations stimulated by the grant of the constitutional reforms of 1919, a scheme of 'Indianisation' was introduced in the Indian Army. In February, 1923, eight Units were selected to be officered by Indians. Amongst these was 2ND Battalion of 1ST Punjab Regiment. Indian Officers holding commissions in the Indian Army were to be gradually transferred to these Units, and the process of Indianisation was to continue as these Officers gained seniority and fitness in other respects to hold senior posts. 2ND Lieutenant Kalwant Singh was one of the first Indian Officers to join the 2ND Battalion in 1926. 2ND Battalion spent practically the whole of the period between the two World Wars on the North-West Frontier. During the Second World War, with surprising rapidity and masterly skill, the Japanese had pushed back the Allied Forces in Burma to the Indian border. It was not only essential to stop the Japanese from invading India, but also imperative to regain Burma. The 2ND Battalion was mobilised in February, 1942 as a part of 47TH Brigade and joined 14TH Indian Division on April 5TH. In October, 1942, 14TH Division mounted offensive operations against the Japanese in the first Arakan campaign and recaptured Donbaik and Hitzwe. At Buthidaung Major Sarbjit Singh Kalha took over the command of the Battalion. He was the first Indian to command a Battalion of the Regiment. Meanwhile, in November, 1943, now Lieutenant Colonel Kalwant Singh took over the command of 7TH Battalion stationed at Razmak.

The Generals

Kalwant Singh, Lieutenant General (Cont.)

He was the Senior Serving Officer of 1ST Punjab Regiment. In September, 1944, 7TH Battalion, preparatory to moving to operational area in South-East Asia, left Razmak for Risalpur. However, their share of fighting was dashed by the sudden surrender of the Japanese in August, 1945. The Battalion was stationed in Singapore at the time of the Partition of India. Between the end of July and the end of October, 1947, the old Indian Army ceased to exist and the Sikhs formed part of the Army of the Republic of India. At the conclusion of the First Anglo-Sikh War (1845–46) Gulab Singh became the first Maharaja of the newly formed princely state of Jammu and Kashmir. Before and after the withdrawal of the British from India in 1947; the princely state of Kashmir and Jammu came under pressure from both India and Pakistan to agree to become part of one of the newly independent countries. As the Maharaja of Kashmir, Hari Singh acceded to India; the Pakistani Army backed infiltrators, invaded the Kashmir Valley. Immediately the Indian troops were sent to the state to defend it. On 8TH September 1947, Jammu and Kashmir forces Headquarters was set up in Jammu under the command of Major General Kalwant Singh. In April 1948 the forces in Jammu and Kashmir were re-organized and Major General Kalwant Singh was appointed Chief of Staff of the Corps. India airlifted troops and equipment to Srinagar, where they reinforced the princely state forces, established a defence perimeter and defeated the tribal forces on the outskirts of the city. The successful defence included an outflanking manoeuvre by Indian armoured cars. The defeated tribal forces were pursued as far as Baramula and Uri and these towns were recaptured. In the Poonch valley, tribal forces continued to besiege state forces. Indian forces ceased pursuit of tribal forces after recapturing Uri and Baramula, and sent a relief column southwards, in an attempt to relieve Poonch. Although the relief column eventually reached Poonch, the siege could not be lifted. After capturing Mirpur on 25TH of November 1947, the tribal forces attacked and captured Jhangar. In the south a minor Indian attack secured Chhamb. By this stage of the war the front line began to stabilize as more Indian troops became available. The Indians held onto Jhangar against numerous counterattacks, which were increasingly supported by regular Pakistani Forces. In the Kashmir Valley the Indians attacked, recapturing Tithwal. The Indians continued to attack in the Kashmir Valley sector driving north to capture Keran and Gurais. They also repelled a counter attack aimed at Tithwal.

The Generals

Kalwant Singh, Lieutenant General (Cont.)

In the Jammu region, the forces besieged in Poonch broke out and temporarily linked up with the outside world again. During this time the front began to settle down. The siege of Poonch continued. An attack was launched to capture Zojila La pass. Stuart light tanks of 7TH Cavalry were moved in dismantled condition through Srinagar and winched across bridges, while two Field Companies of the Madras Sappers converted the mule track across Zojila La into a jeep track. The surprise attack on 1ST November by the Brigade with armour supported by two Regiments of 25 pounders and a Regiment of 3.7 inch guns, forced the pass and pushed the tribal/Pakistani forces back to Matayan and later Dras. The Brigade linked up on 24TH November at Kargil with Indian troops advancing from Leh, while their opponents eventually withdrew northwards toward Iskardu. The Indians now started to get the upper hand in all sectors. Poonch was finally relieved after a siege of over a year. The Indians pursued the Pakistanis as far as Kargil before being forced to halt due to supply problems. The Zojila La pass was forced by using tanks and Dras was recaptured. At this stage Indian Prime Minister Jawaharlal Nehru decided to ask the UN to intervene. A UN cease-fire was arranged for 31ST December 1948. A few days before the cease-fire the Pakistanis launched a counter attack, which cut the road between Uri and Poonch. After protracted negotiations a cease-fire was agreed to by both countries, which came into effect. General Kalwant Singh was not in favour of cease-fire. Nehru ignored his request to capture Muzaffarabad. Both differed on Kashmir policy. He retired as Lieutenant General from the Army and was the first Sikh Officer to be bypassed and superseded. He was senior to next Army Chief General J.N. Chaudhary. His last posting was as General Officer commanding Western Command. He retired from the Army on 15TH May, 1959. Lieutenant General Kalwant Singh passed away on 21ST January 1966 at Delhi.

The Generals

Kartar Singh Gill, Lieutenant General, PVSM

Lieutenant General Kartar Singh Gill was an Instructor, Grade One, Defence Services Staff College, Wellington, Tamil Nadu, and India from October 1971 to March 1974. He taught military strategy and tactics at the premier think-tank of the country. Students consisted of middle level Officers (12 to 14 years service) from 30 foreign countries, including the US, UK, Africa, Iran and Iraq. He served as Brigade Commander, Infantry and Artillery Brigades, Northern India from October 1978 to May 1982. He commanded two Brigades in sensitive border areas in Northern India. He was General Officer Commanding, Infantry Division (Desert), Gujrat-Rajasthan sector, western India from June 1982 to May 1984 and commanded and trained an Infantry for war in the desert. He was Additional Director General of Military Training, Indian Army, in New Delhi, June 1984 to December 1986. He started work on modernizing training establishments, published pamphlets on new tactics for desert and plains warfare, recognized war games and rationalized officer training career courses. Supervised and improved technical training and encouraged Officers to obtain civil professional degrees to improve technical skills. He was a Senior Member, Foreign Ministry Delegation to Islamabad, Pakistan. January – February 1987 and Selected as senior most Defence Member of the Delegation led by the Foreign Secretary to resolve the border crisis with Pakistan. He played a key role in protracted talks both in New Delhi, India and Islamabad, Pakistan. This resulted in diffusion of tension between the two countries. He was Director General of Military Training, Indian Army, New Delhi, India. January 1987 to July 1988. He guided over 150 training establishments and modernized training aids with a crash course. He computerized major training and teaching methods and obtained major financial allotments from the Defence Ministry. He organized and conducted India's most comprehensive field exercise 'Brass-tacks' in 1986-87, involving four Corps, over ten Divisions and about a half million troops.

Lieutenant General Kartar Singh Gill studied Intermediate Science, at Punjab University, Chandigarh, India in 1946. He holds Ph. D., in International Relations. He was admitted to George Town University, Department of Political Science, Washington, DC, in the fall of 1991. He obtained M. Sc., Defence Studies, Madras University, Madras, India in April, 1987.

The Generals

Kartar Singh Gill, Lieutenant General, PVSM (Cont.)

Kartar Singh Gill was awarded 'Distinction' in the Master's Thesis of; "Air Power in the Middle East: Lessons for India." A Study of the Israeli and Arab armed forces, with special reference to air power. The Study analyzes the importance of air power in the 1967 and 1970 Arab-Israeli conflicts, followed by recent trends of air power in South Asia. The study then highlights the lessons learned in conflicts in the Middle East and their applicability in the South Asian theatre. He had work experience as Principal, Mata Jai Kaur Public School, Delhi, India from July 1988 to June 1990. He headed the premier private higher secondary school with 100 teachers and approximately 2000 students. He was elected Executive member of National Public Schools Conference and organized four seminars on current problems in the Indian School system. The school's academic and sports results improved by 100 percent during his tenure. He was a Member of the Committee to review Officers Training of the Three Armed Services. He authored and reviewed papers on Pre-commission Training, Management and Staff Training, Tactical Courses and National Strategy at Senior Levels. He travelled and examined curricula in over 50 civil and defence institutions in India and presented reviews to the Defence Minister. Some of the changes proposed have already been implemented. Published 10 volumes for 'Army of the Future' Lieutenant General Kartar Singh Gill is a retired, Director General of Military Training of The Indian Armed Forces, New Delhi, India. On retirement he has turned to seriously uplift the educational needs of Punjab's rural areas. Along with partners, he has founded a Degree/Vocational College at Gurney Kalan in Distt. Sangrur. Co-Convener and Secretary General of the "International Sikh Confederation" Chandigarh which came into being after the World Sikh Council went defunct. The International Sikh Confederation also supports the needy students who enter professional institutes through competitions. The organization ensures the proper utilization of Central and State financial aid to minorities in Schools and Colleges with particular stress on Rural Areas.

General Kartar Singh Gill was awarded the Param Vashisht Seva Medal, the Indian Armed Forces highest peace time award for Distinguished Services of Exceptional Order. January 1987.

The Generals

Khem Karan Singh Lieutenant General, MvC 'Padma Bhushan'

Lieutenant General K.K. Singh graduated from St. Stephen College, Delhi and was commissioned in the Indian Army. He took part in the Hyderabad police operations. During the 1962 Indo-China War, General K.K. Singh was Commander at Tezpur Headquarters. When the Deputy Commissioner of Tezpur fled, General K.K. Singh asked the SDM to perform the duty, and helped maintain the morale of the civilians. During the 1965 India-Pakistan War, then Brigadier K.K. Singh, commanded Armoured Brigade in action in the Sialkot Sector from 6TH September to 22ND September. In addition to his own Brigade, Brigadier Singh was given command of additional Tank Units in order to cope with the enemy tanks, which were superior both in numbers and quality. The force under Brigadier Singh destroyed over 75 enemy tanks. This was possible due to his able leadership and by his being in the thick of the battle in his own tank. Brigadier K.K. Singh fought the battle of Phillora for three days and nights. Finally because of his superior leadership, better tactical and technical performance, the enemy forces were defeated and thrown out of this important communication centre. He was given the task of destroying as much enemy tanks and equipment as possible. Just a few days before ceasefire the enemy commanders were so demoralized that they avoided combat. Brigadier Khem Karan Singh displayed outstanding skill, high tactical ability and great devotion to duty, for which he was awarded the Maha Vir Chakra in September, 1965. During the 1971 India-Pakistan war, the newly promoted Lieutenant General K.K. Singh was the GOC of 1ST Corps. He was given the job of removing the threat to Punjab and the vital communication lines to Jammu and Kashmir. The enemy in that sector had a well developed, fully prepared system of defences protected by extensive minefields in depth. General K.K. Singh, showing great professional ability and planning, pressed on with his offensive in the Shankargarh Sector, inflicting great losses to the enemy. He forced the enemy to commit its Armor to battle and caused heavy attrition to the enemy. He showed devotion to duty and leadership of exceptionally high order for which he was awarded the 'Padma Bhushan'. After 32 years of Meritorious Service he retired from the Indian Army to his farm in the village of Amarpur.

The Generals

Kuldip Singh Brar, Lieutenant General, AVSM, PVSM, VrC

Kuldip Singh Brar was born into a military family in 1934. His father, D S Brar, served in World War II and retired as a Major General. Kuldip Singh Brar joined the Maratha Light Infantry in 1954 as a Lieutenant. During the Indo-Pakistani War of 1971 Kuldip Singh Brar commanded an Infantry Battalion, and was in the first batch of troops who entered Dhaka (now the capital of Bangladesh) on the morning of 16TH December 1971. He won the Vir Chakra for the battle fought at Jamalpur on the night of 10TH December 1971. His Battalion was pitted against 31ST Baluch of the Pakistani Army. The Baluch Regiment launched continuous attacks against Brar's Battalion. His soldiers had to move across the river Brahmaputra, at a location where no bridges existed. Therefore, they were able to carry only limited weapons on a man-pack basis. Brar moved from Company to Company in the midst of the battle, motivating his soldiers to continue the fight despite the lack of sufficient weapons. In the years following the 1971 Indo-Pak war, Brar was involved in anti-insurgency operations in Nagaland and Mizoram states of India. In June 1984 he commanded the highly controversial Operation Blue Star, an attack on the Golden Temple complex. General Brar's troops using tanks and causing extensive damage to the Golden Temple complex were finally successful in removing the militants from the Akal Takht. Operation Blue Star was militarily successful, but it is criticized by many for being badly planned. It is considered to be a political disaster and an unprecedented act in modern Indian history, and was followed by events like the assassination of Indira Gandhi, the subsequent 1984 anti-Sikh riots, and the Punjab insurgency. At the time of his retirement, General Brar was commanding the Eastern Theatre of India (the borders with China, Nepal, Bangladesh and Myanmar), and was also responsible for the defence of Bhutan. He was also involved in the counter-insurgency operations in North-East India. After his retirement, General Brar had to reside in the heavily guarded cantonment area of Mumbai. There have been attempts on his life, but none have yet succeeded.

The Generals

Malvinder Singh Shergill, Lieutenant General PVSM, AVSM, VRC

Lieutenant General Malvinder Singh graduated from the National Defence Academy Kharakvasla in June 1961. Then he went to the Indian Military Academy, Dehradun. He was commissioned into 7TH Light Cavalry in June 1962 in the footsteps of his father Major General Rajinder Singh, MVC and Bar. He saw extensive tenures in field and operational areas of NEFA, Nagaland (twice) and Jammu and Kashmir (thrice) His Regiment participated in the Sino-Indian war of 1962 and also took part in both wars against Pakistan in 1965 and 1971. He was awarded the Vir Chakra for Gallantry in the Shakararh sector of 1971 war. He was a Squadron Commander in this sector. He was Commandant of the Regiment from 1981 to 1984. Whilst commanding an Infantry Division on the line of control with Pakistan, he was awarded the Ati Vishisht Sewa Medal. He was Colonel of the Regiment from 2000 to 2001. He retired in July 2001.

Maninder Singh Buttar, Lieutenant General

Lieutenant General Manjinder Singh Buttar was commissioned in December 1972 into the Regiment of Artillery. His long and illustrious career spanned 37 years. The General has held various prestigious Instructional, Staff and Command Appointments. He commanded an Artillery Regiment in Basoli and was Commander of a Mountain Brigade before commanding an Infantry Division in the State of UP. The Instructional and Staff appointments include Instructor in the School of Artillery, Brigade Major of an Infantry Brigade, Defence Attaché in the High Commission of India in Nigeria and stints at the Army HQs among others. He is a Graduate of the Defence Services Staff College, Wellington and has also done a tenure as the Directing Staff in the Defence Services Staff College, Wellington The General Officer has participated in Op Meghdoot in Siachen and Op Rakhshak in J&K and was awarded the coveted Chief of Army Staff Commendation Card for his role in Op Meghdoot in the Year 1988. The General Officer was again awarded the Chief of Army Staff Commendation Card in the year 1993 for his stellar contribution towards Indo-US Army to Army Cooperation. Lieutenant General Buttar was Chief of Staff of a prestigious Corps in the Northern Command before taking over his present appointment as the Chief of Staff of Headquarters Western Command.

The Generals

Manjit Singh Bhullar, Lieutenant General, VSM, PVSM

Lieutenant General Manjit Singh Bhullar retired after 39 years of Service to the Nation. Commissioned into the Sikh Regiment, he has had the distinction of holding various prestigious posts including Staff, National and International Assignments. Lieutenant General Bhullar commanded 9TH Sikhs in counter-insurgency operations in Nagaland from 1977 to 1979 and later an Infantry Brigade and an Infantry Division as part of a strike formation. His last command assignment was that of 16TH Corps on the Line of Control in Jammu and Kashmir from mid 1994 to 1997. During this tenure he was also the Security Advisor to the Government of Jammu and Kashmir. His last appointment was the Quartermaster General at Army Headquarters, which he had the distinction of holding for about three and a half years. Lieutenant General Bhullar was awarded Vishisht Seva Medal in 1980 and Param Vishisht Seva Medal in 1998.

Mohan Singh, General

Mohan Singh, famous for his part in the Indian National Army for the liberation of India from British rule, in which he held the rank of a General, was born the only son of Tara Singh and Hukam Kaur, at Ugoke village, near Sialkot. He joined 14TH Punjab Regiment of the Indian Army in 1927. Mohan Singh had been promoted Captain when his Battalion left for Malaya on 4TH March 1941. Japan entered the War with her surprise attack on the American air base at Pearl Harbour, Hawaii, on 7TH December 1941 and overran the entire South East Asia within a few weeks. The British force in the northern part of the Malaya Peninsula, including Captain Mohan Singh's Battalion, was fleeing towards the south. Mohan Singh, with some of his men, was a straggler in search of the main body of his troops. An Indian troop, headed by Giani Pritam Singh, had on 4TH December 1941 entered into an agreement of collaboration with a Japanese Officer, Major Fujiwara, Head of Field Intelligence section in the region. Captain Mohan Singh contacted this group near Alor Star and surrendered to the Japanese on around the middle of December, 1941. All Indian prisoners of war and stragglers were placed under his charge, and he was asked to restore order in the town. Kuala Lumpur fell on 11TH January 1942 with 3,500 Indian prisoners of war and Singapore on 15TH February with 85,000 British troops, of whom 45,000 were Indians. Mohan Singh asked for volunteers who would form the Azad Hind Fauj (Free India Army) to fight for liberating India from the British rule.

The Generals

Mohan Singh, General (Cont.)

A large number of men, mostly Sikhs, came forward to join what came to be termed as the Azad Hind Fauj (National Army of Independent India). The new setup came into being on 1ST September 1942, by which time the strength of volunteers had reached 40,000. Mohan Singh was appointed Commander in Chief of the "Army of Liberation for India," i.e. the Indian National Army. General Mohan Singh was soon disenchanted regarding the intentions of the Japanese who, it appeared, wanted to use the Indian National Army only as a pawn and who were deliberately withholding recognition and public proclamation about its entity as an independent Liberation Army. On 29TH December 1942, General Mohan Singh was removed from his command and taken into custody by the Japanese military police. It was only after the arrival of another Indian leader, Subhas Chandra Bose, from Germany to the Far Eastern front in June 1943, that the Indian National Army was revived and Mohan Singh reinstated to his former command. The Indian National Army participated in the Japanese offensive on the Indo-Burma front in 1944 and gave a good account of itself. But the British forces withstood the offensive and in fact launched a counterattack during the winter of 1945. The Japanese, as well as the Indian National Army, retreated fast, and the war ended with Japan's surrender on 14TH August 1945. Even before that, during May/June 1945, most officers and men of the Azad Hind Fauj (I.N.A.), numbering about 20,000, including General Mohan Singh, had been made prisoners by the British and brought back to India. They were all set free during 1945. General Mohan Singh and his comrades of the Indian National Army were everywhere acclaimed for their patriotism. Mohan Singh's dream of liberation was realized with India's Independence on 15TH August 1947, but this was accompanied by the partition of the country into India and Pakistan. Nehru, in 1948, refused to readmit the men of the INA to the Indian Army after Independence. Also, although Nehru promised pensions, the men of the INA were, however, not eligible for the Freedom Fighters Pension until 1972.

General Mohan Singh entered politics and joined the Indian National Congress. In and out of Parliament he strove for the recognition of the members of his *Azad Hind Fauj* as "freedom fighters" in the cause of the nation's liberation. General Mohan Singh died at Jugiana on 26TH December. 1989.

The Generals

Mohinder Singh Wadalia, Lieutenant General

Lieutenant General Mohinder Singh Wadalia passed away on May 20TH, 2001. He was 93 years old. Draped in the Tricolour, he was cremated with Full Military Honours at the Cantonment Cremation Ground, Delhi. The Last Post was also sounded. Those who turned up to give him a touching farewell and place wreaths included many of his colleagues, friends and old soldiers. Born in 1908, Lt Gen Wadalia belonged to Sialkot district and came from a land-owning family. Commissioned in 1929 from Royal Military College, Sandhurst as a KCIO, he was initially posted to $4^{TH}/19^{TH}$ Hyderabad Infantry (later 4TH Kumaon). Some years later, he got himself transferred to 16TH Light Cavalry. He was appointed Adjutant of the Regiment at Peshawar during 1940-41 when the Regiment was still having a few British Officers who held mostly war time/temporary commissions. The Regiment, then being a Horsed Cavalry Regiment, helped him excel in equestrian sports and to become an excellent polo player. His love for horses saw him setting up his own stud farm after his retirement. He was a man of exceptional patience and ability whose wonderful character aroused affection and esteem in all who knew him. After Partition in 1947, he got rapid promotions and became the Indian Army's Chief of General Staff and later Deputy Chief (known today as Vice Chief of Army Staff) Amongst important appointments held by him were Adjutant and Second-in-Command of 16TH Light Cavalry, Military Adviser to the Indian High Commissioner in UK, BGS at HQ Eastern Command (then located at Ranchi), Commander 1ST Armoured Brigade, Commandant of Indian Military Academy, Dehra Dun, GOC 1ST Armoured Division and Deputy Chief of Army Staff before he finally retired. Though he never commanded 16TH Light Cavalry or Deccan Horse, he loved both Regiments equally and endeared himself to the men of both Units. He donated money equally to both Regiments and will be remembered fondly by all those who knew him. He was Colonel of Deccan Horse from 1949 to 1964 until his retirement.

He is survived by his wife, Aruna and his daughter, Tara. With his passing away, an era has passed into history.

The Generals

Narinder Singh Brar, Lieutenant General, AVS, VSM

Lieutenant General Narinder Singh Brar is an Alumnus of the Rashtriya Indian Military College, Dehra Dun and National Defence Academy, Khadakwasla, Pune. He was commissioned into the Regiment of Artillery in 1969. He is an experienced Army Aviation Helicopter Pilot and a Qualified Instructor in Gunnery. A veteran of the 1971 war, he has commanded an Artillery Regiment in North Sikkim, a Brigade in counter-insurgency operations in Manipur and Nagaland and a Division in Punjab. He retired as the Commander of Chetak Corps at Bhatinda.

Paramjit Singh, Lieutenant General

Lieutenant General Paramjit Singh was commissioned in December 1968 into the Infantry - Garhwal Rifles. A Graduate of Defence Service Staff College and National Defence College, he attended the Higher Command Course. He has held various Staff, Instructional and Command Appointments in his long career. He has the distinction of commanding 2ND Garhwal Rifles and Infantry Brigade in Jammu and Kashmir on the Line of Control. He has also been Instructor at the Indian Military Academy, Dehradun. Currently he is Chief of Staff, Headquarters Western Command at Chandimandir.

Pawar B.S., Lieutenant General, PVSM, AVSM

Lieutenant General Pawar was commissioned into the Regiment of Artillery on June 9TH, 1968. He is an Alumnus of Rashtriya Indian Military College and National Defence Academy, Khadakwasla, Pune. He has attended all the prestigious courses including Long Defence Management Course. Lieutenant General Pawar has held a number of prestigious Staff Appointments including Brigade Major of an Infantry Brigade and a Mountain Brigade, Director General, Staff (Perspective Planning) at Army Headquarters, Brigadier Aviation and Major General Artillery at Command Headquarters. The General Officer is a keen flier and a qualified Flying Instructor with four years of instructional flying. He has a rich and varied experience of flying in all terrains/areas and has 4000 hours of flying to his credit. Currently Lieutenant General Pawar is the Commandant of School of Artillery, Deolali.

The Generals

Punita Arora, Lieutenant General

Lieutenant General (Mrs) Punita Arora of the Army's Medical Corps was the first woman Lieutenant General of the Indian Army. Arora graduated from Armed Forces Medical College (AFMC), Pune. She did her post - graduation in Gynae and Obst from AFMC and was awarded the Gold Medal for standing first in Pune University. During her service she worked as Gynaecologist at various prestigious Armed Forces Hospitals like Head AFMC and Army Hospital. She studied in Sophia School in Saharanpur till 8TH grade. After that she moved to Guru Nanak Girls Inter-College. In 11TH Standard while getting admitted to Government School for Boys she decided to take science as a career. She joined Armed Forces Medical College, Pune in 1963 which was the second batch of the AFMC and she turned out to be the topper of that batch. Punita was commissioned in January 1968. Before becoming Vice Admiral of the Indian Navy she was Commandant of AFMC. She took the charge of Commandant of Armed Forces Medical College in 2004 thereafter becoming the first woman Officer to command the Medical College. Before that she was co-ordinating Medical Research of the Armed Forces at the Army Headquarters as additional Director-General of Armed Forces Medical Services (Medical Research).She moved from the Army to the Navy as the AFMS has a common pool which allows Officers to migrate from one service to another depending on the requirement. Punita Arora was awarded the Sena Medal by the President of India for establishing Gynae Endoscopy and Oncology facilities in Armed Forces Hospitals. She was awarded the Vishisht Seva Medal by the President of India for the efficient and prompt treatment provided to the victims of Kalu Chak terrorist attack, under her leadership while commanding Military Hospital, Jammu. Lieutenant General (Mrs) Punita Arora was appointed as Commandant, Armed Forces Medical College, Pune. Lieutenant General Punita Arora is the first woman in India to attain the second highest rank i.e. Lieutenant General of the Indian Armed Forces and the first Vice Admiral of the Indian Navy.

The Generals

Prem Singh Gyani, Lieutenant General, PVSM, OBE

Lieutenant General Prem Singh Gyani was born on 17TH July 1910. In the competitive combined examination for admission to Sandhurst, Woolwich and Cranwell in November 1929, Prem Singh Gyani was the highest-scoring candidate and opted for the Artillery. He was commissioned in the Regiment of Artillery on 27TH January 1932. After serving a period of attachment with the Royal Artillery he was posted to A Field Brigade, Indian Artillery. He attended the Staff College Course in 1941. During World War Two he served in Burma with various units and formations, and was awarded O.B.E. (an honorific title which he ceased to use after India gained Independence) He was the first Indian Commanding Officer of 2ND Field Regiment, which he took over in November 1944. He led the Indian Artillery contingent at the Victory Day Parade at London in 1946. He attended the Long Gunnery Course in the U.K. in 1947. He became the first Indian Commandant of the School of Artillery when he was promoted as Brigadier in October 1947. He was also the first Indian Director of Artillery from December 1947 to December 1950. In 1951 he attended the Imperial Defence College, London. During 1952-54, he commanded 7TH Infantry Brigade and 81ST Independent Brigade Group. In July 1954, he was sent as Alternate Delegate (Military) too the International Commission for Supervision and Control for Indo China. Promoted as Major General in April 1955, he was appointed Commandant of the Defence Services Staff College, Wellington. He took over as the Director of Artillery in March 1959. Shortly afterwards in June 1959, he was appointed GOC of 4TH Infantry Division. He was sent as the Commander of United Nations Expeditionary Force for Gaza as a Lieutenant General in January 1960. He took over as Head of the UN Force in Cyprus in 1963, an assignment which he relinquished in July 1964. General Gyani retired from service on 3RD October 1964. He was Colonel Commandant of the Regiment of Artillery form 4TH October 1954 to 3RD October 1964. The PVSM was awarded to the General Gyani sometime after Independence and prior to 1974, exact dates not known. Lieutenant General Prem Singh Gyani passed away at Chandigarh on 3RD June 1988.

The Generals

Rajinder Singh Sujlana, Lieutenant General, PVSM, AVSM, VSM

Lieutenant General Rajinder Singh Sujlana, Commandant, Indian Military Academy Dehradun, retired on pension on June 30TH 2011, after completing 40 years of Dedicated Service in the Army. He has been the Commandant of the Indian Military Academy for the past two years and eight-months. He has an outstanding record of service throughout his career and has been instrumental in bringing many positive changes in the organisation. During his tenure in the Indian Military Academy, he brought many changes in infrastructure, such as a state of the art Hoshyiar Singh gymnasium, central Gentlemen Cadet mess; living accommodation for GCs was established. His focus of training was on improving the quality and content of the training. He strongly believed in the phrase "knowledge is power" and motivated Gentlemen Cadets to enhance their knowledge in every sphere of life and guided them to mould their personalities as per the requirement of the organisation. General Sujlana is a keen sportsman and plays hockey, basketball and golf. He played a vital role in introducing mountaineering (mount black peak) and cycle expeditions organised by Hercules India. As part of his extracurricular activities his interests are in Philately, Angling and Environment Related aspects. General Sujlana was born on June 5TH, 1951 at Ambala and obtained a Masters Degree in Defence Studies from Madras University. He is a third generation Army Officer. Continuing the family tradition, the Officer commanded the same Infantry Battalion as his father. Alumni of the National Defence Academy, Kharakvasla and the Indian Military Academy, General Sujlana was commissioned into 9TH Battalion the Sikh Regiment in June 1971 and as a young Officer took an active part in the 1971, Indo-Pak war. The Officer has had five tenures in active counter insurgency/terrorist operations in Jammu and Kashmir and North East. He has undergone various prestigious Army Courses at the Infantry School, Defence Services Staff College, Wellington, Army War College, Mhow and National Defence College, New Delhi. He was decorated with the Vishisht Seva Medal on Republic Day 2003 for his commendable role during Operation Parakram and was again decorated with the 'Ati Vishisht Seva Medal' for his Distinguished Service to enhance the image of the Indian Army while serving as Additional Director General of Public Information with Army Headquarters and the 'Param Vishisht Seva Medal on the occasion of Republic Day 2010.

The Generals

Ranjit Singh Dyal, Lieutenant General

Lieutenant General R. S. Dyal was born on 15TH November, 1928. His father was Sardar Bahadur Risaldar Ram Singh Dyal, who had settled in the village Tukar Bodhni, Kurukshetra district, Haryana. Lieutenant General Dyal graduated in 1942, and four years after his graduation, was selected for the Indian Military Academy. He was commissioned in the Indian Army in Punjab Regiment (Para) and assigned to 1ST Battalion. This battalion was part of 50TH Independent Parachute Brigade during the 1948 Indo-Pak War. He was posted as Instructor at the Indian Military Academy Dehradun (Uttranchal) in 1956. Later he was selected to serve with the United Nations Emergency force, Gaza (Egypt) to supervise the withdrawal of Israeli forces. He returned with the Battalion and served in the NEFA Sector from 1959 to 1962. On successful completion of Defence Services Staff College, he was posted as Brigade Major to the 50TH Independent Para Brigade. After his Staff tenure, he joined his Battalion, 1ST Para, as Second in Command in the Uri Sector of Jammu and Kashmir. Later he commanded 1ST Para from 1965 to 1968 in Jammu and Kashmir and again as part of 50TH Independent Para Brigade at Agra, (Uttar Pradesh). 1965 India-Pakistan War: On the night of the 25/26th August, 1965, Major Ranjit Singh Dyal led an assault on Sank in Jammu and Kashmir, which was stalled by heavy enemy fire. Major Dayal managed to extricate his Company intact and on the following night managed to capture Sank. He pursued the fleeing Pakistanis and captured Ledwali Gali on 27TH August, 1965. Thereafter, marching at night through very difficult terrain, he took the enemy by surprise and on 28TH August, captured the Haji Pir Pass. In this operation, one Pakistani officer and 11 soldiers were taken prisoner. On the following morning, Major Dyal deployed a Platoon to capture yet another feature. When this Platoon came under enemy fire, he launched a lightening attack with his two Platoons, as a result of which the enemy fled in utter confusion. Throughout this operation, Major R. S. Dyal displayed Outstanding Leadership and Courage in the best tradition of the Indian Army. On 28TH August 1965, Major Ranjit Singh Dyal was awarded the Maha Vir Chakra, the second highest Bravery Award in the Indian Army. He went on to serve the Army with distinction, and rose to the rank of Lieutenant General before retiring. In 1984, Ranjit Singh Dyal was appointed the Security Advisor to the Governor of Punjab for Operation Blue Star. He passed away on 29TH January 2012.

The Generals

Samer Pal Singh Dhillon, Lieutenant General, VSM, AVSM

Samer Pal Singh Dhillon passed out from the Scindia School in 1965. He was commissioned into the Regiment of Artillery on December 21ST 1969. During his ensuing distinguished career, he has risen to the rank of Lieutenant General and the appointment of Deputy Chief of the Army Staff. He has the distinction of being appointed Colonel Commandant of the Regiment of Artillery, a rare honour in the Indian Army. Samer Pal Singh Dhillon has held important Command, Staff and Instructional Appointments. He has commanded a Field Artillery Regiment and an Infantry Brigade in Jammu and Kashmir, the famous 'Bison Division' and the elite 'Desert Corps'. His Staff assignments include tenure in the Directorate General of Military Operations in Army Headquarters and as Major General Staff in Headquarters, Northern Command. He has played a key role in the modernization of the Indian Army and in advising the Chief of the Army Staff on United Nation Troops deployment. He has a brilliant academic profile. He has attended the Long Gunnery Staff Course at the School of Artillery, at Deolali, the Defence Services Staff College at Wellington, and Higher Command Course at Mhow and the National Defence College at New Delhi. He has also attended the prestigious Command and General Staff course at Fort Leavenworth, USA. The General has been an Instructor at the School of Artillery, Devlali, Defence Services Staff College, Wellington and the National Defence College, New Delhi. Samer Pal Singh Dhillon has been actively involved in Disaster Management Activities at the time of earthquakes in Uttarakhand and Jammu and Kashmir, Tsunami in Southern India and floods in Rajasthan. He is a recipient of the coveted Lengtaigne Memorial Medal. The President of India has conferred on him the Vishist Seva Medal and Ati Vishist Seva Medal for Distinguished Services. A good athlete and sportsman and an avid golfer, Samer Pal Singh, a man of many facets, inspires the men he leads and unites them in a team. He is well known among his friends and associates for his wit, sense of humour and leadership qualities. Samer Pal Singh Dhillon, by his outstanding contributions to the Indian Army, has distinguished himself as an Old Boy of The Scindia School. The Scindia School confers on Samer Pal Singh Dhillon the Madhav Award, as an Old Boy of Eminence for the year 2008.

The Generals

Sandhu DDS (Dr.) Lieutenant General

Lieutenant General (Dr.) D.D.S. Sandhu is currently the Director General of Ordnance Services and Senior Colonel Commandant, Army Ordnance Corps. Lieutenant General Sandhu, an Alumnus of National Defence Academy was commissioned in 1967. He is a Graduate of Defence Services Staff College, Wellington. The General has done his post graduation in Defence Studies from Madras University and M. Phil in Defence & Management Studies from Devi Ahilya Bai University, Indore. He has an inclination towards Research on vital issues of Military Logistics and has acquired his Doctorate in "International Marketing of Indian Defence Products" from Punjabi University, Patiala. He holds a MBA Degree and a Masters Degree in Materials Management. He is a Fellow of the British Institute of Management and Member of the Board of Studies of IIMM. The General is an expert in the Ammunition and Armament subjects of the Army. He has served as the "Ammunition Quality Controller" in the Nigerian Army. His forte is "Management" and "Automation" and he is qualified on various courses of Management and Automation. He has had long exposures as a System Analyst, Senior System Analyst and later as Director, Computerised Inventory Control Project. This is an Automation Project that is going to help the Army Ordnance Corps in meeting the logistic challenges of the future. The General Officer has held various prestigious appointments. Besides being Commandant of Central Ordnance Depot, Delhi Cantt, which is one of the biggest logistics depots of the Army Ordnance Corps, he has been Deputy Director of Ordnance Services of a Strike Corps of the Indian Army. As a Major General he was a pivotal functionary of the logistics support system of one of the operational commands of the Indian Army. The General, as Commandant of College of Materials Management, had brought about radical improvements in the pedagogy, training curriculum and infrastructure at the College. Under his guidance, the College had witnessed unprecedented advancement in all facets of functioning and specially made tangible strides in the field of Automation and Academics. He is widely traveled and has participated in various seminars. He has been a Member and Leader of numerous important studies in the Army on issues relating to Management and Automation. The General during his tenure as Commandant, College of Materials Management, had organized a two day National Seminar "Logiminds 2006" on Supply Chain Management.

The Generals

Sartaj Singh, Lieutenant General, Padma Bhushan

Lieutenant General Sartaj Singh was commissioned into the British-Indian Army's Regiment of Artillery in April, 1940. He had, as a young Officer posted with an Anti-Tank Regiment in Ceylon, won the George Medal for Outstanding Gallantry and Initiative. After completing his Long Gunnery Staff Course in UK, he was appointed the first Indian Chief Instructor of the Field Wing of the Deolali-based School of Artillery in 1947. After a stint as an Instructor at Defence Services Staff College, Wellington, and Commander 4TH Artillery Brigade, he attended the first course at the National Defence College and was later detailed for a special mission to the Congo. During the 1965 Indo-Pak war, he commanded a Mountain Division in the north-eastern theatre and then took over as Director General Military Operation in 1966. In the 1971 war, India was under the impression that Pakistan had only one Brigade earmarked for the Chhamb-Jaurian sector, whereas during the operations, it was discovered that there were five Brigades under the Pakistani 23RD Infantry Division operating against the Indians. Pakistan started its offensive on the night of December 3RD. After a fierce battle in the Chhamb sector, in which both sides suffered heavy casualties, the Indians had to withdraw to the east of Manawar Tawi on the night of December 6TH. The Pakistani's then started its operations east of the Tawi in a bid to capture Akhnur. And it was on the night of December 9TH that the enemy launched a determined attack to dislodge the Indians from east of the Tawi. Reacting to this, the GOC of Indian Division started considering the withdrawal of two Brigades to the depth positions. It was at this time that the late Lt-Gen Sartaj Singh, the then GOC 15TH Corps, flew into the sector, rejected the plan of withdrawal, assumed control of the sector, reorganised the forces and ordered a counter-attack, which met with success. Thus General Sartaj Singh saved the Honour of the Country. General Sartaj Singh, known to be one of the most determined Field Commanders of his time, retired as GOC-in-C Southern Command in 1974 and passed away on April 23RD, 1998.

The Generals

Sant Singh, Lieutenant General
Lieutenant General Sant Singh did his Officer Training Course at Sandhurst in U.K. and was commissioned in the Indian Army and joined 2ND Bihar Regiment. During the Second World War, he saw action with the Regiment in Operation Zipper for the reoccupation of British Malaya. At the time of India's Independence he was commanding the Bihar Regiment. As a Brigadier he commanded 43RD Army Brigade. Thereafter, he participated in the undeclared war in the Kashmir Valley during 1948-49. As Major General he took over the command of the famous 4TH Infantry Division at Ambala. In 1951 he was promoted to Lieutenant General and appointed G.O.C. Eastern Command. He was commanding non-bifurcated Eastern Command at the time of his retirement in 1957. He passed away in November 1996.

Sarabjit Singh Dhillon, Lieutenant General, PVSM
Lieutenant General Sarabjit Singh Dhillon, is the Indian General Commander of Kashmir (GoC) since 2005, and is Master General of the Ordnance of the Indian Army. He is one of the most respected Generals currently serving in the Indian Army, and it is widely believed that he will be a future Chief of Army Staff of India. He is a veteran of the Indo-Pakistani War of 1971 and has held several important Command and Staff Appointments at various levels of his career. An Alumnus of the prestigious Rashtriya Indian Military College, Dehradun, and the National Defence Academy, Khadakwasla, Pune. Lieutenant General Dhillon was commissioned to the Grenadiers Regiment in 1968. He attended the Defence Services Staff Course, Wellington, Senior and Higher Command Courses at the Army War College, Mhow, and also the National Defence College in New Delhi. Currently Serving Master General of the Ordnance of the Indian Army.

The Generals

Sarvjit Singh Chahal, Lieutenant General, PVSM, AVSM, VSM

Opting for a career in the Indian Army, Sarvjit Singh Chahal was selected for the National Defence Academy, Poona in 1961. In June 1965, he was commissioned into 1ST Sikh, the most highly decorated Battalion in the Commonwealth of Nations. Immediately on joining his unit in Jammu and Kashmir, he saw action in the Tithwal Sector across the Cease Fire Line against Pakistan. This baptism of fire moulded his approach to a military career spanning 40 years. The first hand experience gained, prepared him to handle all operational assignments including the insurgencies in Nagaland, Mizoram, Tripura, Assam, Punjab and the proxy war in Jammu and Kashmir. He had the distinction of commanding 1ST Sikh Battalion in "Punjab" through the tumultuous period straddling the assault on the Golden Temple, the holiest of Sikh shrines in 1984. Promoted to the rank of Brigadier in July 1992, he successfully tackled the uprising in upper Assam. In October 1996, he was elevated to the rank of Major General and given the command of one of the most sensitive sectors on the Line of Control in Jammu and Kashmir. On successful command of his Division, he did a stint as Chief of Staff of a Corps, deployed on the disputed Sino-Indian Border in the Eastern Theatre, before being promoted Lieutenant General in October 2001. On promotion, he assumed the most prestigious appointment of Director General Military Operations of the Indian Army. In this assignment, he successfully handled the largest mobilization of the Indian Armed Forces, post the attack on the Indian Parliament on 13th December 2001. In his chequered career, he held important Staff assignments and instructed at the Indian Military Academy, Dehradun and the Defence Services Staff College, Wellington. Besides this, he was a Member of the Indian Delegation to China for the Joint Working Group set up to untangle the vexed boundary issue, chaired meetings of the Indo-US Steering Group on military to military cooperation and also chaired the ASEAN Regional Forum of the Heads of Defence Universities. His last assignment was Commandant of India's National Defence College, New Delhi, from where he retired on 30th June 2004. For Distinguished Services of an Exceptional Order, the President of India awarded him the PVSM, AVSM and VSM. His Regiment too honoured him by unanimously electing him as Colonel of the Sikh Regiment from 2000 to 2004. Post retirement, he has been intimately involved with the Private Security Sector.

The Generals

Sidhu Dalbir Singh, Lieutenant General, VSM

Meet General D.S. Sidhu who is the last man standing of this illustrious family, sharing his thoughts and experience with Society. Like his glorious family history, the four walls of the room of his house in Lodhi Estate in Delhi are also covered with pictures. Wondering does one remember all the stories behind every photo? Some of them are so old that with all possible ways it has been preserved. Then there comes Lieutenant General Dalbir Singh Sidhu all dressed up in Army uniform with his better half Mrs. Jaspreet Kaur Sidhu, elegant in a pale yellow sari. If looks can be deceptive, he is totally different than what he looks like, all smiles and soft spoken, not at all like an army man. As they settle down in the sofa, we are ready to glance into the past. Did he join the Army by his choice or to keep the family tradition alive? After all that's the first thing that comes into the mind. "It was my choice. In fact I never thought about any other profession or job. I was inspired by my father, grand father and by all the people before them." Suddenly there is a change in his tone, "But I must share that as a young child my first impression was to become a nuclear physicist. I don't know why. But very soon I realized that I was not cut out for that. After that there was nothing else in my mind other than the Army," says the General. "From the day one, when I joined the Army it was like home coming. My grand father and one of my uncles were in the same Regiment where I was going to join," he continues. But the sad part of the story is that after five generations this lineage is going to end here. As his son Karan (29) is into documentary film making and daughter Nimrata (25) is a lawyer with a private firm. "Well to be honest, when they were born I wanted them to be in the Army. But as they grew up and have their own aspiration, I realize it's their life. And I supported them in whatever career they choose. We are going to take a temporary break after five generations. But I can't say about the future generation," says the 59 year old father. He has two younger brothers who are settled in America, one is Merchant Navy and other one is working with a shipment company. Going back to his glorious past, "On my maternal side, my grand father Tara Singh Bal was commissioned in 1929 and he joined 7th Calvary. After the Second World War he went to Poona Regiment. He commanded 19TH Infantry Brigade and went on to command One Armor Brigade; he was the first Indian to do so. Then came as GOC Delhi area and was Theatre Commander J&K with local rank of Lt Gen from 1949 to 1953. Then he represented India in International Control Commission in China. He was Ambassador in Argentina, Uruguay and Paraguay.

The Generals

Sidhu Dalbir Singh, Lieutenant General, VSM (Cont.)

His ancestors were also in Calvary from Central India Horse who was decorated by Order of British India second class. Both my maternal uncles, elder one Late Major MS Bal lost his life just thirty minutes before the ceasefire in 1965 war. And the younger late Brig. AS Bal won his Mahavir Chakra in 1971. He was in the same tank with Col. Tarapur where he (Tarapur) won his Param Vir Chakra in 1965," says the solider with a pride. If you think that's over, it's just half of the family and the history. Getting a bit relaxed in his seat he continues. "On my parental side, my father was the first to join the Army. He was a Doctor and during Second World War he was decorated with the Military Cross for Gallantry and retired 1972 as Commandant, Army Hospital. And my uncle, Lt. Gen. KS Randhawa was the DGMF from 1986 to 1989. A large number of my uncles have done well in the Army." After all the above, he comes in the line. He is Director General Mechanized Forces. He has been decorated with the Vishist Seva Medal (VSM) for his Distinguished Service while commanding and Ati Vishisht Seva Medal (AVSM) for his Distinguished Service while commanding 33RD Corps. Just give a thought how it must be when all the family members come down together? "It is very interesting and some times very intense. There is good old banter and exchange of information and how the things have been. And it sometimes gets intense when each one talks about his Unit. How his Regiment has performed and which one is better." Seriously it must be more like an Army gathering. "So it is great fun but at the same time a lot of competition spirit is displayed, even between us," says candidly the Army man. Till now as a good wife she was quietly listening and smiling to the conversation. According to the Mrs. Sidhu, "the best part of being an Army man's wife is that you get to meet lot of different people of different backgrounds. And you get to see many beautiful places which one never heard of, like Tanga in Arunachal Pradesh." And there comes out secrets about him, "Being in the army he is not fussy at all about the foods and also he never enters the kitchen," sharing a glance with him. "And we have to remind him that when he is at home and not wearing uniform, he can act normal. But he is an Army man at home also." In a way what can one expect from a person whose family is in Army for generations? That's how he is! Lieutenant General Dalbir Singh Sidhu former Director General Mechanised Forces retired from the army in October 2012.

(Posted by N. Khayi, January 31ST 2012)

The Generals

Surjit Singh Sangra, Lieutenant General, PVSM, VSM

Lieutenant General Surjit Singh Sangra was commissioned in 1961. He is a Graduate of the Defence Services Staff College, Wellington, and has done the Long Defence Management Course (LDMC) at the College of Defence Management, Secunderbad. He has also attended the prestigious National Defence College, New Delhi. Having held coveted Command and Staff Appointments, General Surjit Singh has gained wide experience at all levels. He commanded a Corps in the western theatre, was Chief of Staff at the Southern Command, after which he took over as GOC-in-C, Central Command. On October 1ST, 2000, General Sangra was posted as GOC-in-C Western Command. General Sangra was Mentioned-in-Dispatches in the 1965 war and was later awarded the Vishisht Seva Medal. In 1998, he was awarded the Param Vishisht Seva Medal for his Distinguished Services. He was Chief Instructor at the Defence Services Staff College and has also done tenure with the Indian Military Training Team in Bhutan. General Sangra is Colonel of the Dogra Regiment and the Dogra Scouts. General Sangra rose to become Army Commander and would have become Chief but the government extended the retirement age of Lieutenant Generals and he did not make it as a result.

Surjit Singh, Lieutenant General, PVSM, VSM

Lieutenant General Surjit Singh joined the National Defence Academy Kharagwasla, Pune in May 1957. He was commissioned into the Army in 1961. He is an Alumnus of three of the most prestigious institutions of the country namely; The Defence Services Staff College, Wellington College of Defence Management, Secunderbad and the National Defence College, New Delhi. He was a Chief Instructor at the Defence Services Staff College, in addition to tenure with the Indian Military Training Team abroad. His service career profile spanning almost 41 years in the Army has been highly distinguished and varied, covering wide ranging operational, administrative and teaching assignments. During 1965 Indo-Pak war, he was Mentioned in Despatches and later awarded the Vishist Sewa Medal for his Distinguished Services to the Army and the Nation. While in command of the Central Army Lucknow, the General spearheaded the Army's relief and Rescue operations in the Malpa Land Slide Tragedy in Kumaon Hills and later the Tragic Cyclone of Orissa. Lieutenant General Surjit Singh, one of the most experienced and successful General Officers of the Indian Army, retired on 31ST March 2002 as Chief of the Western Army from Chandimandir.

The Generals

Tejinder Jit Singh Gill, Lieutenant General

Commissioned in June 1963, the Lieutenant General is a skilled Paratrooper. As a young Officer, he had participated in the 1971 operations as part of the Paratrooper Brigade. He took part in the battle of Haji pir Pass and the assault at Tangail. He has held various prestigious appointments. As a Major, he was the Deputy Assistant Adjutant and Quarter Master General of the Paratrooper Brigade. He has the rare distinction of commanding a depot in a foreign army and also served as an adviser to the Federal Government of Nigeria. He has held key appointments in Area Headquarters and Strike Corps. During operation, Vijay he was the Major General, Army Ordnance Corps of the Northern Command. Lt Gen Tejinder Jit Singh Gill took over as the Director General, Ordnance Services and Senior Colonel Commandant of the Corps. Prior to his present appointment, he was the Commandant, College of Materials Management in Jabalpur.

Currently Director General, Ordnance Services

Tejinder Singh Shergill, Lieutenant General, PVSM

Lieutenant General, Tejinder Singh Shergill, sibling of Lieutenant General Malvinder Singh, served as General Officer Commanding in North East India and Commander, Senior Command Wing of Jammu and Kashmir, India. Early in his military career the General saw battle in two wars and later, commanded a Division and then a Corps both in counter-insurgency operations that included development of terrorist prone areas and where he had several medical establishments under command. For four years, he served as Defence Attaché' in the USA and Canada. He has taught at the Defence Services Staff College and the Army War College. His abiding interests in history and spiritual matters inspired him to introduce 'The Code of the Warrior' at the Indian Military Academy where he was the Commandant; it is now the 'Code' of the Indian Army. He graduated from the National Defence Academy, India, first in order of merit and with four 'blues'. He received his M.Sc in Defence Studies from Madras University, India, and MAMS from North Central Association of Colleges, USA. Lieutenant General Shergill has 40 years of experience in the military and has experience in teaching assignments and as a Diplomat. On retirement from the Army Lieutenant General Shergill has been Non-Executive Independent Director of Fortis Healthcare Limited since April 21ST, 2005.

INDIAN NAVY

The origin of the Indian Navy goes back to the English East India Company which set up the force and named it the Honourable East India Company's Marine, after they encountered and defeated the Portuguese at the Battle of Swally off Diu. The first fighting ships arrived on 5TH September 1612. This force protected merchant shipping off the Gulf of Cambay and the rivers Tapti and Narmada. The ships also helped map the coastlines of India, Persia and Arabia. In 1686, with most of English commerce moving to Bombay, the force was renamed the Bombay Marine. The Bombay Marine was involved in combat against the Marathas and the Sidis and participated in the Anglo-Burmese Wars. The Bombay Marine recruited many Indian lascars but commissioned no Indian Officers until 1928. In 1830, the Bombay Marine became Her Majesty's Indian Navy. The British capture of Aden increased the commitments of Her Majesty's Indian Navy, leading to the creation of the Indus Flotilla. The Navy then fought in the China War of 1840. Her Majesty's Indian Navy resumed the name Bombay Marine from 1863 to 1877, when it became Her Majesty's Indian Marine. The Marine then had two divisions; the Eastern Division at Calcutta and the Western Division at Bombay. In recognition of the services rendered during various campaigns, Her Majesty's Indian Marine was titled the Royal Indian Marine in 1892. By this time it consisted of over 50 vessels. In the wake of World War I, Britain exhausted in manpower and resources, opted for the expansion of the RIM. Consequently, on 2ND October 1934, the RIM was reincarnated as the Royal Indian Navy (RIN) and all ships were prefixed with HMIS. RIN became the Indian Navy on Independence Day 1950 but continued to have a British Royal Navy Admiral as the CNS till 1958.

During WW1, when mines were detected off the coasts of Bombay and Aden, the Royal Indian Marine went into action with a fleet of minesweepers, patrol vessels and troop carriers. Besides patrolling, the Marine ferried troops and carried war stores from India to Iraq, Egypt and East Africa. The first Indian to be granted a commission was Sub Lieutenant D.N Mukherjee who joined the Royal Indian Marine as an Engineer Officer in 1928.

At the start of the Second World War, the Royal Indian Navy was very small and had five sloops, one trawler, one survey ship and one patrol craft. It had 114 Officers and 1732 Ratings. Prior to the Second World War, Britain's Royal Navy was responsible for the overall maritime defence of India.

Indian Navy

The Royal Indian Navy (RIN) was responsible for coastal defence only. It had one naval base at Bombay and training establishments scattered in many regions of India. The onset of the war led to a rapid expansion.

The sloops HMIS Satluj (U95) and HMIS Jumna (U21) played a key role in Operation Husky – the invasion of Sicily. In 1945 when the war ended, the Navy had seven sloops, four anti submarine frigates, eight corvettes, fourteen minesweepers, sixteen trawlers, one survey ship, two depot ships, thirty auxiliary vessels, one hundred and fifty landing craft, two hundred harbour craft and forty five harbour defence launches. The number of personnel had risen to 3014 Officers and 27,433 Ratings, most of who served in shore establishments. Several new naval base establishments and training establishments had come up all along the West and East coasts.

Indian sailors started a rebellion also known as The Royal Indian Navy Mutiny, in 1946 on board ships and shore establishments, which spread all over India. A total of 78 ships, 20 shore establishments and 20,000 sailors were involved in the rebellion. This mutiny hastened the progress to Indian Independence. On partition in August 1947, the RIN comprised four Sloops, two frigates, one Corvette, twelve coastal minesweepers, one survey ship, four trawlers, four motor minesweepers, one motor launch, four harbour defence motor launches and landing craft. In 1954, agreements were signed for the acquisition from Britain of eight new frigates and that marked the renaissance of the Indian Navy.

Independent India's first naval offensive was the Junagadh operation, which was executed during the month of October,1947 after the Dewan of the Princely State of Junagadh, much against the will of her people and adjoining neighbours, signed an instrument of accession to Pakistan that led to political turmoil in the Kathiawar region. Codenamed Exercise Peace, India's RIN was tasked with the planning and execution of the mission to land troops and equipment on the Kathiawar Coast along with ground forces. The amphibious landings were carried out by RIN ships Kistna, Jamuna, Cauvery, Konkan and some landing craft, in three phases and the Navy stayed on till a civil administration was set up in the state, thereby ensuring stability in the region.

The Portuguese continued to repress the people of Goa and in November 1961, there were two acts of aggression by Portuguese soldiers garrisoned on Anjadip Island off the Karwar coast. These incidents led to the execution of Operation Vijay. The main thrust of naval operations was the capture of Anjadip Island in an amphibious landing by a platoon of seventy five sailors in a daring mission.

Indian Navy

The extraordinary courage and fortitude of these men forced the well-entrenched enemy to surrender. It also witnessed a furious gun battle between the Portuguese warship Alonso de Albuquerque and Indian frigates Betwa, Beas and Cauvery. After an intense gun battle, the Albuquerque hoisted the white flag of surrender, turned towards the harbour and beached herself. Meanwhile the land offensive raged at Diu with INS Delhi being tasked to provide gunfire support to the army units. Delhi's guns obliged, concentrating a withering volume of fire on target until the Old Fort was captured and the Indian flag hoisted by the Army at Diu. Operation Vijay was concluded in less than forty hours, and liberated all Portuguese territories in India

In the 1965 Indo-Pak war, the Indian Navy was instructed to maintain a defensive posture in order not to escalate the conflict, which was the stated policy of the Government at the time. The Government felt that the presence of the Indian Fleet was required in the Andaman's as there was intelligence of a joint offensive by Pakistan and Indonesia on the Andaman and Nicobar Islands. Government instructions required that the Indian Navy was not to proceed more than 200 miles beyond Bombay nor north of the parallel of Porbandar. On the start of hostilities, the Indian Fleet was ordered back to the West Coast from the Bay of Bengal. In the meantime PN ships had bombarded Dwarka. Subsequently IN patrolled the Arabian Sea to prevent any Pakistani offensive action

The Indo-Pak War of 1971 has many firsts to its credit for the Indian Navy. It was the first major war in which the Indian Navy was fully involved and the role it played tilted the balance of power in favour of India. The aircraft carrier INS Vikrant was strategically employed in the Eastern theatre to launch offensive operations against Pakistani ports and units in East Pakistan. The luring and sinking of the Pakistani submarine PNS Ghazi by an innovative combination of deception and manoeuvre marked the high point of operational art. Action in the Bay of Bengal led to the total isolation of East Pakistan from any possible reinforcements. On a sadder note, the Indian Navy lost one of its frigates, INS Khukri and part of her crew in the attack by the Pakistani submarine PNS Hangor. The Navy's innovative employment of missile boats INS Nirghat, INS Nipat & INS Veer to carry out lightning strikes on Karachi led to destroying not just her men-of-war and merchant ships but also her national will and morale to fight. The daredevil missile attacks on the night of December $3^{RD}/4^{TH}$ on Karachi harbour, called Operation Trident, is celebrated every year as the Navy Day.

Indian Navy

This operation was closely followed by another successful attack on Karachi, codenamed Operation Python four days later. On 10TH December 1971, America announced that American Naval Task Group 74, consisting of the aircraft carrier Enterprise, an amphibious assault ship, four guided missile destroyers, a guided missile frigate and a landing ship was heading towards the Bay of Bengal. Whilst India prepared to counter the TF, US announced its withdrawal and warded off an unpleasant incident.

Kargil War 1999. The Pakistan Army's misadventures in the frigid heights of Kargil and Drass Sector, on the Indian side of the Line of Control from early May till their eviction in July led to one of the most fiercely fought land wars by the Indian Army. INs reaction, Operation Talwar was swift and comprised aggressive manoeuvring and posturing in the North Arabian Sea and ready to strike both Pakistani naval ships and their ports of Karachi and Qasim. This action resulted in Pakistani naval units being bottled up close to home ports evading action and resulting in the conflict coming to an early close.

The 1988 Maldives coup d'état, whose rescue efforts were code-named Operation Cactus by the Indian armed forces, was the attempt by a group of Maldivians led by Abdullah Luthufi and assisted by armed mercenaries of a Tamil secessionist organisation from Sri Lanka, the People's Liberation Organisation of Tamil Eelam (PLOTE), to overthrow the peace and harmony in the island republic of Maldives. The coup d'état failed due to the acts of valour by the Maldivian Army and with assistance of the Indian Army.

The Indian paratroopers immediately secured the airfield, crossed over to Male using commandeered boats and rescued President Gayoom. The Paratroopers restored control of the capital to President Gayoom's Government within hours. Some of the mercenaries fled toward Sri Lanka in a hijacked freighter. Those unable to reach the ship in time were quickly rounded up and handed over to the Maldives Government. Nineteen people reportedly died in the fighting, most of them mercenaries. The dead included two hostages killed by the mercenaries. The Indian Navy frigates Godavari and Betwa intercepted the freighter off the Sri Lankan coast, and captured the mercenaries. Swift operation by the military and precise intelligence information successfully quelled the attempted coup d'état in the island nation.

THE ADMIRALS

Pritam Singh Mahindroo, Rear Admiral
By Rear Admiral Satyindya Singh

Rear Admiral Mahindroo was the first Sikh Rear Admiral of Indian Navy, loved and respected by the whole service. He left a lucrative career in Merchant Marine Service to join R.I.N. following the outbreak of World War Two in 1939. Initially denied entry because, being a Sikh, he refused to cut his hair; he soon earned respect for his splendid turbaned Sikh persona, and rose to be a Rear Admiral. We condole his passing away in October 1999 and pray for the peace of his soul. It has been said that old soldiers never die, they just fade away. In the case of sailors, when they pass into maritime history they continue to navigate the ethereal seas. For that is where Admiral Pritam Singh Mahindroo now is. He passed into history at Chandigarh on 8TH October, 1999. This legendary mariner commanded destroyers and cruisers. He brought home our first aircraft carrier Vikrant, in 1961. A British paper thus recorded the event: "A hymn composed to Aditi, the Indian god of eternity, figured in the commissioning ceremony of the Indian Navy's aircraft carrier Vikrant. The four verses of the hymn were recited by the resplendent figure of Captain P.S. Mahindroo. He spoke in Sanskrit, the language in which the hymn was originally written. The ceremony formally commissioning the ship was a mixture of East and West. The drill and marching of a guard of honour and the playing of the ship's small band was of a standard which could not have been bettered by the Royal Navy." On 31ST January 1997, Vikrant passed into history at a solemn ceremony at Naval Dockyard, Bombay, and the decommissioning ceremony was, significantly, also performed by the eighty-year old Admiral Mahindroo. Admiral Mahindroo held important operational and administrative appointments during his distinguished career. His service in World War Two extended to Atlantic Ocean and beyond. "Peter" Mahindroo - as he was affectionately known to many of us was the Chief Instructor at the Defence Services Staff College, Wellington. He was a 'guru' to many of us 'chelas' now residing in many parts of the globe.

The Admirals

Pritam Singh Mahindroo, Rear Admiral (Cont.)

An incident which brings out his seasoned, mature and non-flamboyant leadership needs to be told. Peter was commanding the cruiser Delhi forty years ago. It is graphically recorded by the then Lieutenant Hugh Gantzer (the well known travel writer) in the Naval Archives: "Every year, after the monsoons ships of the Royal Navy, the Pakistan Navy, the Royal Ceylon Navy and the Indian Navy used to meet in Trincomalee for joint exercises. There under the watchful eye of a British Admiral we exercised for a week. We got to know each other's strengths and weaknesses, matched our performance against our neighbour's and those of the RN, and renewed old acquaintances. Fighting men generally have a strange empathy that crosses international borders. Or rather that is the theory. The exercises concluded without any mishaps or frayed tempers and all we had to look forward to was the Jet Hockey match. As usual, we were pitted against Pakistan. It was a sultry evening on the Jet grounds, and our boys and the Pakistanis had turned out in full force. The clock moved towards half time and no goal had been scored. We began to get bored. And then, quite unexpectedly, one of the Pakistani's rushed forward with the ball almost glued to his stick. Terence Duckworth, our star player, was taken by surprise and rushed the Pakistani player. The man had just crossed the half line when he saw Duckworth bearing down on him; he stopped, looked around for a team mate to pass the ball to, and finding no one, took an almighty swipe that sent the ball racing down the field towards the goal. Terence Duckworth, amused at the man's panicked reaction turned around and called out, "leave it" he yelled. The back stepped aside, grinning letting the ball roll past. The balls speed fell over the uneven field. And we watched it trickle slowly towards our goal. Gracefully, and with mock courtesy, our goalie moved out and bowed the ball in, showing his contempt for the player who shot from outside the D. The ball its force almost spent rolled very slowly into the goal. We filled the air with our derisive laughter. But our laughter turned to abject dismay when the soccer trained RN referee blew a shrill sharp goal! When the match was over, we trooped back to our ships, but the Pakistanis took out a triumphant procession through the streets of Trincomalee. And, that night they circled our ships with their boats, and blaring through their loudhailers, hurled the choicest Urdu (Punjabi?) abuses at us."

The Admirals

Pritam Singh Mahindroo, Rear Admiral (Cont.)

"And from their ships, searchlights lanced out and criss-crossed us in searing contempt, while more abuses thundered and boomed across Trincomalee Bay. At about midnight the Sikh sailors from INS Delhi came in a delegation to their Captain. They wanted to lower boats and tackle the Pakistanis. I saw them approaching and I knew that they meant business. But the moment they reached the Commanding Officer's door, it opened, and Captain Pritam Singh Mahindroo stood before them. He was dressed in shorts and a shirt, and his hair was tied in a knot at the top of his head. A Sikh sailor who worked in my office said: "They are humiliating us, Sir. This is war!" Captain Mahindroo looked at his men, listened to the yowling invective of the Pakistani sailors. And then he said: "Dogs do not humiliate men". He paused, smiling grimly. "When the time comes to fight as warriors, I will lead you". And then his lips curled in contempt. "For tonight", he said softly, "let the dogs bark". So there was no war, and the Pakistani Commander apologised, the next morning. We learnt later that in every Pakistani ship, the sailors had locked their officers below deck and taken the law into their own hands". Admiral Mehindroo's ashes have been immersed in a small river which is a tributary of a bigger river which finally carries its waters to the ocean. This is what he would have liked. As the late American President John F. Kennedy said in 1962: "We all come from the sea, all of us have in our veins the exact same percentage of salt in our blood that exists in the ocean... we are tied to the ocean, and we go back to the sea, whether it is to sail or to watch it, we are going back from whence we came".

A Victory parade was held in London on June 8TH, in which representative of the three Indian Armed Forces participated. Naval Contingent was led by Lieutenant P.S. Mahindroo. In keeping with the inter- Service in which the Navy was the senior service, the parade was led by the Naval Contingent. Rear Admiral Mahindroo reminisces on the occasion, "Needless to say, that as turbaned officer leading the Naval Contingent, I was most prominent and I must have given hundreds of autographs amongst thousands of spectators who probably slept on the pavement for one or two nights to witness this historic parade."

Rear Admiral Pritam Singh Mahindroo passed away on 8TH October 1999.

The Admirals

Satyindra Singh, Rear Admiral AVSM - A Son's Homage

By Lt. Col. Premendra Singh

Rear Admiral Satyindra Singh born at Lahore on 23RD May 1920. He joined The Royal Indian Navy in 1941 and served on the active list of the Indian Navy for 36 years. He wrote two books on the History of The Indian Navy at the instance of Government. He was a regular columnist in newspapers and journals for over twenty years and was on the Editorial Board of The Indian Defence Review and The Sikh Review. He worked on the making of films on Robert Clive and Jawaharlal Nehru with the British author and actor Kenneth Griffith, and advised on a film "The Sea Wolves". Notably he took up the case for Defence Pensioners with bulldog tenacity - right to the Supreme Court - and, with a favourable judgment, won the regard and respect of the military establishment and all army, navy and air force ex-servicemen. He was married to Mrs. Haridarshan Kaur, grand daughter of Bhai Kahn Singh of Nabha. Grandson of Subedar Sant Singh of the 23RD Sikh Pioneer Regiment, father kept his grandfather's original medals with him, with considerable pride; the medals include the 1860 China Medal with clasp, Peking and Taku Forts, awarded when the regiment was sent by the British and attacked and occupied nine square miles of Peking in that year; the Abyssinia (Africa) medal of 1867. The Afghanistan campaign medal of 1878-79-80 with clasps, Kabul and Ali Musjid and the Kabul to Kandahar Star of 1880. The British gave Subedar Sant Singh extensive land and a village Santpura (on the Lahore-Amritsar road) was named after him. His father, Sardar Amar Singh served for a short while in the army and then established the Model Press at Lahore in 1911, which functioned until the partition of the continent. It was only natural that the military, as also literary work, were father's twin interests. He studied at Forman Christian College, Lahore, where he was the Editor of the College Magazine 'Folio' (One of his old classmates, a retired defence officer, told me a few days ago that the magazine was adjudged the best college magazine of its time (we have with us a photograph of the young Editor with his staff). After graduation, he planned to go to Oxford University to study history, but then the Second World War caused him to abandon plans, and he joined the Armed Forces. Commissioned in the Royal Indian Navy Volunteer Reserve in June 1941, he was seconded to Royal Indian Navy, later Indian Navy.

The Admirals

Satyindra Singh, Rear Admiral AVSM (Cont.)

Before Indian independence, he was specially selected to assist Admiral Sir Geoffrey Miles and earned praise for his cool and measured response to problems that beset that office at Partition of the Indian subcontinent. Later he became secretary to the Fleet Commander Admiral Dickinson. In the Navy, he served on the warships - the cruisers INS Delhi, INS Mysore and the aircraft carrier, INS Vikrant, and various shore establishments, including INS Hamla. He was posted at the Indian High Commission in London in the period 1949 to 1951 when Krishna Menon was High Commissioner. In 1953 he went for the Coronation Review to UK and was one of the only two Indian Naval officers to be awarded the Coronation medal. He qualified at the prestigious inter - services Defence Services Staff College Course in Wellington and also the National Defence College Course. For 11 years, till retiring in 1977, he held senior appointments in the military and intelligence wing of the Cabinet Secretariat and later became member secretary of the Joint Intelligence Committee. The JIC was established in the early 1960's as the nodal body for collating information gathered by security agencies and drawing up six monthly security projections for the government with a 30 day warning of imminent hostilities. He put life into this one -time sinecure organisation and got it out of its slumber to take on the tasks of the break-up of Pakistan, the formation of Bangladesh and the 1971 war. After his 36 years of distinguished military service, he retired and tended to his gardening - he managed to grow grapes and lemons and figs and curry plant and papaya and miniature oranges and all manner of vegetables and plant silk cotton trees in the middle of his Delhi colony - generating a verdant green - frequented by birds, joyfully barked at by Dad's handsome Alsation dog Simba. Relatives from mother's small town and villagers from Punjab were amazed to find green pigeons in the trees around our house - they were a rarity in Punjab having been hunted down. Possibly they learnt a thing or two about conservation from him. Soon the Navy called Dad again, this time with official sanction to write two volumes of History of the Indian Navy. This he did with meticulous detail, verve and style; both volumes are well researched and immensely readable accounts of the Navy's history. These volumes are (a) Under Two Ensigns (The Indian navy 1945-1950) published by Oxford and IBH Dec. 1985, released by President Zail Singh and then P.M.

The Admirals

Satyindra Singh, Rear Admiral AVSM (Cont.)

Father wrote steadily and strongly on matters of Defence and State interest in front rank English language newspapers and journals. He was on The Sikh Review's Editorial Advisory Board. He was always interesting to read - the ultimate accolade for a writer who must be read and remembered. He also appeared on various TV panel interviews and also on Air where he put across his views very forcefully. This uncommon man with common touch was always ready to help anyone for anything - any injustice irked him. He turned his pen scathingly against the insincere and dishonest politician and bureaucracy, and in that he was ahead of his time in knowing where the evil in Indian society lay - the Greeks, he said knew that a fish rots from the head.... Never one to be cowed down by injustice he took up the cause of ex-servicemen for one-rank one-pension and, with bulldog like tenacity, single-handed fought the establishment for years, right to the Supreme Court, got a favourable judgment so that now the injustice of unequal pensions is well tackled. His last article published on 1ST August 2000 (after he passed away) in The Hindu newspaper was on the military - titled "Ex Servicemen - Children of a Lesser God". The Sikh Review featured his article 'Blind Men of Hindustan': remembering Operation Bluestar in its August, 2000, issue, which turned out to be his parting gift. A short while before he passed away he was asked to join the Justice Nanavati Commission of Inquiry on 1984 Anti Sikh Riots. He did attend a meeting on this issue on 7TH July 2000 and also tendered written advice to the committee on 16TH July on a course of action. He was asked by the Government to join the deliberations of the Arun Singh Committee on Higher Defence Management, which he declined.

Courage: In 1984 in Delhi when the anti Sikh riots rocked the city, he refused to be cowed down and defiantly went about his work, despite desperate warnings by well wishers.

Religion and Tolerance: Dad's religious beliefs were intensely personal; he enjoyed listening to early morning Kirtan on TV or radio daily. He had no fears or prejudices - He felt that probably the best cure for intolerance is education, trust in one's own core spiritual values - and humour. At Chief Minister Parkash Singh Badal's advice he was nominated as a member of the SGPC to contribute his balanced and educated views. He passed away in July 2000.

The Admirals

Kirpal Singh, Rear Admiral, AVSM, ADC

Kirpal Singh studied at Khalsa High School in Rawalpindi in Punjab. He joined Indian Mercantile Marine Training Ship "Dufferin" at Bombay in January 1940 and passed out in December 1942 with an Extra First Class Certificate. In 1943 he was selected for the Royal Indian Navy and was sent to England for training with the Royal Navy during 1944-45. He served as Midshipman onboard Royal Navy Battleships H.M.S. Anson and King George V. He saw active service in World War Two, first in the Atlantic and Arctic Oceans against Germany and later in the Pacific Ocean against the Japanese. On return to India he served in several ships and establishments and later commanded Indian Naval Ships Ganga, Tir, Brahmaputra, Beas, the aircraft carrier Vikrant and the Western Fleet. His shore appointments included: A.D.C. to the first Indian Governor General, C. Rajagopalachari, Officer in Charge Gunnery School, Battalion Commander at the National Defence Academy, Khadakvasla (Pune), Deputy Naval Adviser to Indian High Commissioner to U.K., Chief of Personnel at Naval Headquarters, Commodore in Charge Naval Barracks at Bombay and Director General Naval Dockyard Expansion Scheme, Bombay. He is a Graduate of the Defence Services Staff College, Wellington, Nilgiris, the Joint Services Staff College, U.K. and the prestigious Royal College of Defence Studies, London. He was awarded the Ati Vishisht Seva Medal for his contribution to the Human Resource Development in the Indian Navy. He retired from the Indian Navy on 31ST March 1977, in the rank of Rear Admiral.

Harinder Singh, Vice Admiral, PVSM, AVSM

Harinder Singh was born in Lahore in September 1942 and belonged to one of the illustrious and well-known families of the Punjab. His Grandfather was the senior most Indian Police Officer in undivided Punjab and had been awarded the OBE and the title of 'Sirdar Bahadur' by the British. His father, Dr Partap Singh was a renowned Surgeon who was amongst the first few Indians to earn an FRCS and MRCP in England early 1930s. He was a KCIO having commissioned in 1933 and participated in WW2 and finally commanded the Dacca Group of Hospitals as a Lieutenant Colonel towards the end of WW2 and was the recipient of several Medals. Harinder received his early education in Bishop Cotton School, Shimla, Convent of Jesus and Mary, Ambala and RIM College, Dehra Dun before joining the National Defence Academy, Kharakvasla in the 21ST Course.

The Admirals

Harinder Singh, Vice Admiral, PVSM, AVSM (Cont.)

In the Navy, he joined the Executive Branch, specialized in Anti Submarine Warfare and rose to become the first Sikh Naval Officer to become the Commander in Chief of a Naval Command (the highest rank but for the Navy Chief). He was married in 1972 to Meena H Singh and has two children. Amongst the major courses he attended were a Special Course in the then Soviet Union (1967-69), advanced Anti Submarine Warfare Course (1970), tri service Defence Service Staff Course, Wellington (1975) and the prestigious National Defence College, New Delhi (1990). He did unusually long tenures in sea Commands and his important sea appointments included those of Commanding Officer, INS Nipat (1974), Executive Officer, INS Himgiri (1976-77), Chief Staff Officer, INS Agnibahu (1977-79), Commanding Officer, INS Shakti (1984-86) and Commanding Officer INS Rajput (1989-90) where he was also deployed for the Sri Lanka Ops and later was appointed as the Flag Officer Commanding Eastern Fleet. He also did many noteworthy appointments ashore and these included those of Joint Director Naval Intelligence (1982-84), Officer Commanding, National Defence Academy Wing, Pune (1986-87), Deputy Director General, Defence Planning Staff, Ministry of Defence (1989) and Director of Combat Policy and Tactics (DSR) (1991-92). As the DSR he was responsible for the operation, maintenance of all currently held weapons and sensors, drawing up staff requirements for futuristic weapons and sensors, their acquisition and for initiation, supervision and follow up all Research and Development Projects for the Indian Navy. Harinder Singh became a Rear Admiral in 1992 and was appointed as Joint Secretary, Military Wing (1992-93), Ministry of Defence and Secretary to the Chiefs of Staff Committee. He interfaced between Ministry of Defence and Services Headquarters on all substantive matters, was the Secretary to the three Chiefs of Staff and co-coordinated highest level administrative functioning between the three Armed Forces. He then moved as the Flag Officer Commanding, Eastern Fleet (1994-95) to command India's Eastern Fleet; the sea based deterrence based at Visakhapatnam and was charged with the Maritime Defence of India's East Coast. During this period he also led many good will missions to East Asian countries.

The Admirals

Harinder Singh, Vice Admiral, PVSM, AVSM (Cont.)

After successful command of the Fleet was appointed as the Assistant Chief of Personnel (HRD) (1995-96) and his responsibilities involved managing the entire cadre strength of Indian Navy covering promotions, transfers, education, training and manpower planning and successfully brought in far reaching changes. On promotion to the Rank of Vice Admiral he was appointed as the Fortress Commander (1996-99), Andaman and Nicobar (now renamed as the Far Eastern Command). An operational Tri Service Command charged with the defence of the Andaman and Nicobar Islands and during his tenure a very large number of infiltrators and poachers were interdicted and many operations carried out against them. During this period he also had a tiff and disagreements on operational and other matters with his boss, the Chief of the Naval Staff. Consequent to his representations to the Government his point of view was upheld and this finally led to the dismissal of the Chief of the Naval Staff by the Government. He then took over as a Principal Staff Officer at NHQ as the Deputy Chief of Naval Staff (1999-2000) and his responsibilities included overseeing all aspects of all offensive and defensive Naval Operations - on the surface, in the air (naval aviation) and underwater (submarine assets) and all aspects of the functioning of Naval Aviation (force planning, force structure, logistics, procurements, training, operational readiness et al for about 175 aircraft), National Hydro-graphic Service and managing Intelligence and Diplomatic matters with Foreign Embassies. During this period he also oversaw Kargil Operations-2000 in entirety as the single point responsibility including interface with the highest level in the Government of India. On the last leg of his naval journey he was appointed as the Commander–in-Chief, Southern Naval Command (2000-2002) and became the first Sikh Officer to hold this rank. His responsibilities included the Maritime Defence of South India and the Training and Education of the entire Naval Community of about 100,000 Service and civilian personnel throughout the entire country. He also oversaw several capital projects involving large outlays that included the new Naval Academy, Estimable Project. During this period he had also taken in hand and overseen an unusual program, that of reconstruction of Moda Village in Gujarat, that had been completely destroyed during the major earthquake of 2001. The reconstruction of the village with a novel design and about 500 houses of various sizes, was completed in a record time, the first such NGO project to be completed and that too, to the entire satisfaction of the villagers.

The Admirals

Harinder Singh, Vice Admiral, PVSM, AVSM (Cont.)

No better reward for the project was possible than the renaming of the newly rebuilt village as 'Navy Moda' by the villagers. Simultaneously, village development in the form of adult literacy, training of artisans and imparting skills was also undertaken under his supervision. As a part of his duties he also served as Director on the Board of Hindustan Aeronautics Ltd and as a Member of the National Shipping Advisory Board in 1999-2000. For his Outstanding Service to the Nation he was given the National Awards of Param Vishisht Seva Medal (2001) and Ati Vishisht Seva Medal (1993) by the President of India. Post his retirement in 2002 he ran a Wealth Management Service for NRIs and joined the Boards of some Finance Companies including as Director, Delhi Stock Exchange Ltd, Chairman, and DSE Financial Services etc. Simultaneously he also took up as the President of Navy Foundation, New Delhi (an NGO) an appointment he held for 6 years till 2012 and was in the forefront in fighting for the rights of the Naval Veterans. He loves to play Bridge, Golf and Badminton and he and his wife have settled down in Noida near Delhi.

Birinder Singh Randhawa, Vice Admiral, AVSM, VSM

Vice Admiral B.S. Randhawa was born on 14TH December 1948, at Bombay, the youngest of four children of Commander (later Rear Admiral) Balwant Singh and Rani Kaur. The family had roots in the Amritsar area with strong military tradition. After initial schooling at Bombay and Delhi, he joined the Rashtriya Indian Military College at Dehra Dun, from where he completed the Indian School Certificate in the 1ST division and thereafter entered the National Defence Academy, Khadakvasla, with the 32ND course. On passing out in 1967, he joined the Indian Navy's training ship 'INS Tir', where he was awarded the 'President's Telescope' being adjudged the 'Best all round Cadet' and also the 'Binoculars' for standing first in the order of merit in the passing out examinations. He opted for the Engineering branch of the Navy and underwent training at the Naval College of Engineering at INS Shivaji, Lonavla, from where he stood first in the Marine Engineering Specialisation Course. He went on to qualify in the Advanced Marine Engineering Course and the Engineering Management course at the Royal Naval Engineering College, at Plymouth, UK. Subsequently, he also obtained an MBA Degree from the Faculty of Management Studies at Delhi University.

The Admirals

Birinder Singh Randhawa, Vice Admiral (Cont.)

In his early Naval Career from 1971 to 1988, he served at sea on five different warships, the last three appointments being as the Head of the Engineering Departments. He also served at sea as the Fleet Engineer Officer of the Western Fleet. His early shore appointments included tenures in the Design Directorate, where he was part of the team entrusted with preparing the design to install guided missiles on the frigate 'INS Trishul'. He also held appointments as Directing Staff at the Institute of Armament Technology, Pune, at the Naval Dockyard at Mumbai and a Staff Appointment at Naval Headquarters. He was decorated with the Vishisht Seva Medal in 1985 for Distinguished Service. He underwent the Naval Higher Command Course in 1998 and thereafter held the appointments of Director, Indian Naval Ship Maintenance Authority, Director of Marine Engineering and Director of Ship Production. He was selected for the prestigious National Defence College course in 1995 and was promoted to the rank of Rear Admiral in 1998, in which rank he headed the Defence Machinery Design Establishment at Secunderbad, entrusted with developing machinery for the strategic submarine "Arihant". He also served as the Assistant Chief of Material at Naval Headquarters, entrusted with coordinating maintenance and support of all ship and submarine assets, and with creation of support infrastructure. In his Command Appointment as Admiral Superintendent of Naval Dockyard, Visakhapatnam, he was instrumental in completing the first ever major refit of the 'Kilo' class submarine in India, a major landmark in achieving self sufficiency. He was decorated with the Ati Vishisht Seva Medal in 2002. He was promoted to the rank of Vice Admiral in 2005 and appointed as the Controller of Warship Production and Acquisition. During his tenure the tempo of production and acquisition of ships and submarines gained great momentum, and an unprecedented number of units came into the pipeline, greatly adding to the Navy's capability. The first-ever ship acquisition from the United States, that of the Landing Platform Dock 'INS Jalashwa' was also undertaken at record pace. In 2007 he was appointed as a Principal Staff Officer at Naval Headquarters in the post of Chief of Materiel, the highest post that can be held by an Officer of the Technical Branches of the Navy. For his Outstanding Distinguished Services he was decorated with the Param Vishisht Seva Medal. He retired from the Navy on 31ST December 2008, after an achievement filled career spanning 40 years in commission and has settled in New Delhi.

The Admirals

Hari Simran Malhi, Vice Admiral, AVSM, VSM (Retd)

Rear Admiral Malhi was commissioned in the Indian Navy on 1ST July 1972. He is an Alumnus of the National Defence Academy, Khadakvasla. During his distinguished career, he held various appointments onboard ships with Steam, Gas Turbines and Diesel propulsions. He has also been the Commanding Officer of INS Shivaji, Warship Production Superintendent - Mumbai, General Manager Refit - Naval Dockyard, Visakhapatnam and Director of Defence Machinery Design Establishment, Hyderabad. During his nine months tenure at Naval Dockyard, Visakhapatnam, he is credited with improving productivity, implementation of numerous welfare measures for the workforce and leveraging Information Technology for various processes. For his Distinguished Service, has also been awarded the Ati Vishisht Seva Medal and Vishisht Seva Medal. Vice Admiral Malhi then opted to leave the Navy and go to Mumbai and take over as the Chairman and Managing Director of Mazgon Docks Ltd. He has since completed this task and retired in 2010.

Anup Singh, Vice Admiral, PVSM, AVSM, NM, ADC

Vice Admiral Anup Singh, Flag Officer Commanding in Chief Eastern Naval Command retired from the Navy on 31ST October after 38 years of illustrious service. Commissioned into the Indian Navy in July 1973, Admiral Anup Singh has commanded four ships of different classes and capabilities. The Admiral also had the distinction of being the Commissioning Commanding Officer of INS Veer, a missile vessel and INS Delhi, the first indigenously designed and built destroyer of the Indian Navy. The Admiral was commanding the Western Fleet when he led 'Operation Sukoon', involving evacuation of civilians from war-torn Lebanon in July 2006. His other important assignments include being Chief of Staff of Western Naval Command and Chief Instructor (Navy) at the Defence Services Staff College, Wellington. Vice Admiral Anup Singh was the Sailing Master of the first ever square-rigged Sail Training Vessel 'Varuna' in 1980-82. He also skippered the Naval Yacht 'Samudra' for the Pacific crossing during her round-the-world voyage in 1989.

He subsequently successfully commanded the Eastern Naval Command and retired after Meritorious Service in 2011 and has now settled down in Greater Noida, near Delhi

The Admirals

Jagjit Singh Bedi, Vice Admiral, PVSM, UYSM, AVSM, VSM, ADC

Vice Admiral Jagjit Singh Bedi is an Alumnus of the National Defence Academy and was commissioned in the Indian Navy in July 1969. The Admiral is a specialist in Communication and Electronic Warfare. He has held a number of coveted appointments, both afloat and ashore and has the distinction of having commanded a ship at every rank. His Sea Commands include command of Seaward Defence Boat 'Atul', Ocean Going Minesweeper 'Bedi', Leander Class Frigate 'Udaygiri', Guided Missile Destroyer 'Ranvir' and the Aircraft Carrier 'Viraat'. He has served as the Chief Instructor and Officer-in-Charge of the Signal School, Directing Staff at the College of Naval Warfare (CNW), Commanding Officer of the Naval Academy at Goa and Director of Naval Plans at Naval Headquarters. On promotion to Flag Rank, the Admiral was appointed as Assistant Chief of Naval Staff (Policy and Plans) at the Naval Headquarters. He has the distinction of being the Chief of Staff, Western Naval Command at Mumbai during Operation 'Vijay' and eventually spearheaded the operations of the Western Fleet, the premier sword arm of the Navy, during Operation 'Parakram' as the Fleet Commander. On promotion to the rank of Vice Admiral, he held the appointment of Controller of Warship Production & Acquisition followed by Deputy Chief of Naval Staff at the Integrated Headquarters. Prior to taking over the reins of Western Command, he held the appointment of Flag Officer Commanding-in-Chief, Southern Naval Command based at Kochi. He is an Alumnus of the Royal Naval Staff College, Greenwich (UK) and the Naval War College, Rhode Island (USA). He is a recipient of the prestigious Param Vishisht Seva Medal (PVSM), Uttam Yudh Seva Medal (UYSM), Ati Vishisht Seva Medal (AVSM) and Vishisht Seva Medal (VSM) for Meritorious and Distinguished Service. He retired in 2006 and has settled down in Pune.

The Admirals
Inderjit Singh Khurana, Vice Admiral PVSM, ADC

Admiral Khurana was born to an illustrious family in April 1930 and was commissioned in the Indian Navy in 1948. He obtained his basic five years training at the British Naval Institutions in the United Kingdom. He is a Graduate of the Defence Services Staff College, where he subsequently served as the Chief Instructor (Navy). His career profile in the Navy comprised of numerous Command, Administrative and Staff Assignments. Vice Admiral Khurana retired from the Indian Navy after 39 years of unblemished and Distinguished Service for which he received the Highest Service Award of the Param Vishist Seva Medal. In the last decade of his Service he held top managerial posts both afloat and ashore. He retired as the Director General Coast Guard. Prior to this appointment he commanded both the Eastern and Western Fleets of the Indian Navy, in succession, a rare distinction in itself. His other assignments in Flag rank was that of Chief of Staff, Eastern Naval Command where he was charged with the responsibilities of development of shore support facilities and administration and training of a large number men. In February, 1985 he was appointed as the Director General Coast Guard. He was instrumental in the induction of a number of vessels and aircraft and commissioning of Coast Guard shore and air stations, thus making the Indian Coast Guard a strong and viable para-military force with an all- India capability. During the tenure as Director General Coast Guard, he was appointed as the Honorary ADC to the President of India. He twice served as Director in Naval Headquarters and performed the duties of planning futuristic projects and establishment of civil and harbour works ashore. From 1973 to 1977 he was posted as India's Naval Attaché, Embassy of India in Moscow and concurrently accredited to Poland as Naval Attaché; he established close personal rapport with Senior Defence Officers, especially Senior Soviet Naval Officers, in the Ministry of Defence and the State Committee of Economic Relations of the then USSR government. In charge of his official duties he has had frequent interaction with top Soviet entrepreneurs, designers and manufacturers of defence equipment. This coupled with his knowledge of Russian language, helped the Indian Navy a great deal in successful procurement of ships, aircraft, submarines, equipment and critical spares from the erstwhile USSR. He was responsible for training there of Indian Naval personnel in the repair and maintenance of Soviet ships and submarines. He also co-ordinated completion of Naval Dockyard facilities at Visakhapatnam. He is now happily settled with his wife and family in New Delhi.

The Admirals

M. M. Singh, Commodore

Commodore M.M. Singh joined Khalsa College at Jullunder and completed B.Sc first year before joining the Naval Academy in 1973. He specialised in Anti–submarine Warfare along with flying. He also opted for the observer cadre in flying. Observer is akin to a navigator but with a much bigger role. In the course of flying he piloted Alize, a carrier borne aircraft, Russian helicopter Kamov 25, another ship borne aircraft. He has commanded naval ships and Coast Guard vessels at sea, been a Commanding Officer of a Naval Air Station at Port Blair (farthest frontiers in the east coastline) and been a part of the A and N Command (a tri-service command of the Armed Forces). Before retiring in November 2009, he was a Member of NSEC, the Committee looking after the staffing pattern of Naval Units and Establishments.

Gobind Singh, Rear Admiral

Gobind Singh was born in Lyallpur now called Faisalabad (now in Pakistan) in October 1943. His father, Sardar Shumsher Singh, was on attachment to the Indian Government from the Burmese Government where he was appointed as an Entomologist. In due course Sardar Shumsher Singh was transferred permanently to the Indian Government. Gobind Singh moved over the next 15 years with his parents from Harbanspura near Lahore to Calcutta, to Kanpur, New Delhi, Ranchi Lucknow, Kanpur, and Calcutta and finally to New Delhi. He changed a number of schools ranging from Delhi Public on Mathura Road; his first, to Loreto (used to be a co-ed), La Martiniere, Christ Church and finally Colvin Taluqdar from where he joined the Engineering College Birla Institute of Technology in Mesra Ranchi. Gobind Singh was selected to join the Engineering Branch of the Navy while in College and actually joined in 1966. After a delayed start in his training in Venduruthy, Cochin, INS Shivaji and watch keeping on board the Grand Old Cruiser INS Delhi, Gobind Singh opted to join the Naval Aviation branch. He had obviously got tired of the perennial leaking steam and the strong pungent smell of the FFO. The training in Aviation was with the Indian Air Force at Jallahalli Bangalore for 18 months. His first meaningful appointment was in the 310 Alize anti submarine Squadron, which was Carrier borne. Having completed his tenure for 2 years, he was moved out during the war with Pakistan in 1971 and had to be satisfied by providing the war requirement of aircraft from balmy Goa.

The Admirals

Gobind Singh, Rear Admiral (Cont.)

He was married soon after to Manorita Kalha, daughter of Colonel R.S. Kalha. A daughter was born while serving in the Naval Air Technical School in Cochin in December 1975. Soon after, he moved as part of a Project for acquiring Long Range Maritime Patrol Aircraft IL 38 from the Soviet Union for training in Riga, Capital of Latvia for 11 months. He was appointed the First Squadron Engineer of INAS 315. In due course he was appointed as Station Air Engineer of Hansa- the Naval Air station in Goa, and in charge of Russian aircraft maintenance and finally to Cochin as Superintendent of the Naval Aircraft Yard, where all the aircraft other than those of Russian origin are overhauled. By 1993 he was appointed as the Director of Naval Air Material in Naval Headquarters. By now he had completed all the possible appointments an Air Engineer could hold in the Navy. The powers that be, thought it otherwise and in November 1994 he was appointed as Project Director, Ship Building Centre in the rank of a Rear Admiral which opened up a totally new dimension in his career. In SBC he managed to put in place a magnificent shipyard for building the ultimate submarine and the support structure. He retired in October 2001 and settled down in Gurgaon.

Balwant Singh Rear Admiral, PVSM

Rear Admiral Balwant Singh was commissioned in the Royal Indian Navy in September 1942. He was born in the village Pandoori Ran Singh, one of the historic five Pandoori villages founded by Baba Buddha Singh Randhawa, in Tarn Taran, district Amritsar. Belonging to a family with an Armed Forces heritage going back several generations, he was the son of a World War 1 veteran, Sardar Surain Singh Randhawa, who had served in various campaigns on the North West Frontier, in Mesopotamia, and Europe. On completion of his schooling in Penang, where he excelled as a bright student and in athletics, as a fast bowler and as a hockey centre forward, he graduated from the Panjab University and thereafter was selected for Commissioned Officers' Training for the Indian Army, in the Indian Military Academy at Dehra Dun. While he was under training, the Government issued a call for volunteers for commission in the Royal Indian Navy, which was being expanded to meet the war plans of the Allied powers. He volunteered and thereafter never had time to look back.

The Admirals

Balwant Singh, Rear Admiral, PVSM (Cont.)

Immediately on commissioning in 1942, while WW-II was in full spate, he was appointed to sea on HMIS Barracuda, a light Frigate deployed in the Bay of Bengal for keeping the sea route open for Calcutta. While on patrol duties he saw action against Japanese air strikes. For these active war operations he received the George VI 39-45 Medal, the Burma Star, and the 1939-45 Star. After the war he was appointed to the Naval Establishment HMIS Hamla at Bombay and was one of the few Indian Officers, serving alongside many British counterparts. The Naval Sailors Mutiny erupted on 18TH February 1946 as a consequence of poor service conditions, the racially biased behavior of some British Officers and the delays associated with demobilization and resettlement of Indian Sailors after WW-II. During this critical situation, with nationalist sentiments also running high, (then) Lieutenant Commander Balwant Singh played a pivotal role in calming and re-assuring the agitated Indian Sailors of HMIS Hamla by winning their confidence, preventing escalation of the situation and restoring order, thereby avoiding harm to British personnel and their families. However, while deposing before the commission set up to determine the cause, extent and consequences of the Naval Mutiny, he had the courage of conviction to state that there were innumerable cases of racial discrimination in the RIN which made the lot of Indian Officers serving under some British Officers very miserable. Events moved rapidly towards independence of the country, and Indian Naval Officers took up the challenge to fill the places vacated by the British Royal Navy Officers. In 1946, he was appointed as Officer-in-Charge, RIN Pay Office, at a time when post-war demobilization and settlement of accounts was at its peak. He was promoted to the rank of Commander in 1948, and being the first 'turbaned' Sikh Officer to rise to that rank; he played a leading role in designing the "brass hat" for the "naval turban badge". In 1952, he was appointed as the Supply Officer of the Indian Navy's flagship, INS Delhi. He was jointly the Flotilla Supply Officer, and was responsible for all the logistic, secretarial, financial and legal matters of the entire Fleet. He was also a Member of the Indian contingent at the Coronation of Queen Elizabeth II and received the Queen Elizabeth II Coronation Medal. In 1955, after an attachment with the British Admiralty at UK, he was promoted to Captain and appointed as Director of Stores at Naval Headquarters, New Delhi, being the first Indian incumbent.

The Admirals

Balwant Singh, Rear Admiral, PVSM (Cont.)

Rear Admiral Balwant Singh was instrumental in laying the foundation of the Naval Stores Organization and in this capacity he put into place the organization and procedures for provisioning, procurement, and supply of Naval and Air stores, after obtaining approval of the Government. In 1962 he was selected to undergo the prestigious National Defence College course, after which he was appointed as the Director of Supply Branch at the Naval Headquarters. In March 1968, the Western Naval Command was created, with the Western Fleet integral to it. Commodore Balwant Singh was appointed as the first Chief Staff Officer, Personnel and Administration, to the Flag Officer Commanding-in-Chief, Western Naval Command. In February 1969, he was promoted to the rank of Rear Admiral and appointed as the first incumbent to the newly created Principal Staff Officer post of Chief of Logistics at Naval Headquarters. He set the course for the new organization, putting in place effective processes and methods for efficient functioning and meeting the needs of a growing Navy and was decorated by the President with the Param Vishisht Seva Medal for his Distinguished Services. He retired from service in 1970, and settled in New Delhi and was on the UN panel of experts. He passed away in February 1985, after a brief illness. His naval legacy is carried on by his son, Vice Admiral Birinder Singh Randhawa, PVSM, AVSM, VSM, who joined the Indian Navy and rose to become the Chief of Material of the Indian Navy.

Malvinder Singh Bedi, Rear Admiral, AVSM, VSM

Rear Admiral M.S. Bedi was born in 1945. He did his education at Sherwood College, Nainital. He is a Graduate of the National Defence Academy, Pune, and was commissioned in the Executive branch of the Navy in 1967. He is also an MSc in Defence Studies from The Royal College of Defence Studies, UK for which he was deputed by the Navy in 1991. He was a Gunnery and Missile specialist and had the distinction of serving in both the Indian Navy's Cruisers and was commissioning crew for two Frigates. His commands at sea include a front line Missile Corvette and a large Missile Destroyer. He has held a variety of Operational and Administrative Appointments ashore which include Chief of Staff in the tri- service Andaman Command and Asst Chief of Naval Staff (Operations) at Naval Headquarters. He has had command of the Naval Officers Training Academy at Goa.

The Admirals

Malvinder Singh Bedi, Rear Admiral, AVSM, VSM (Cont.)

Rear Admiral M.S. Bedi was the Deputy Commandant and Chief Instructor at his alma mater, the National Defence Academy, Pune. He was also the Director at Naval Headquarters responsible to conceive, plan and steer the project for the new Naval Academy that has since been set up in Kerala. The work included the identification of requirements, planning the training curriculum up to BTech level and complete spatial and infrastructural provisions, including finalisation of the architectural plans, for a military training campus spread over 1200 acres for over 1600 trainees. Earlier in his career, he was deputed to the Government of Mauritius and helped set up the Police Marine Wing and laid the foundations for the Mauritian Coast Guard Service as also the joint Mauritius / French Navy Search and Rescue Organisation (SAR) for the Mauritius /Reunion Indian Ocean Island Territories. He received a commendation from the Mauritian Government for his work. Rear Admiral Bedi was twice decorated with AVSM and VSM Awards by the President of India. Rear Admiral Bedi was selected to command the Indian Navy Eastern Fleet, which he declined for personal reasons and took premature retirement in 1998. He worked for a while with a private firm and has now settled down in Gurgaon.

Madanjit Singh, Vice Admiral, PVSM, AVSM

Madanjit Singh was commissioned into the Indian Navy in January 1966 and has specialized in Gunnery and Missiles. He has held various appointments both afloat and ashore. Madanjit Singh has had the unique distinction of having commanded five ships including the Frigate INS Ganga and the Aircraft Carrier INS Viraat. Earlier, he looked after Policy and Tactics and was the Director of Staff Requirements at Naval Headquarters for two stints. The Officer was also the Leader of the IN Team in Nigeria from 1980-83 for setting up an Officers Training Academy at Port Harcourt. An Alumnus of the National Defence Academy, Pune, he graduated as the Best Naval Cadet. He did the Staff Course at the DSSC Wellington in 1977. Later, he graduated from the National Defence College; New Delhi in 1991. He was promoted to Flag rank in March 1993 when he took over as the Chief of Staff, Western Naval Command. Thereafter, he was Assistant Controller, Warship Production as Acquisitions at Naval Headquarters before being appointed as Fleet Commander, Western Fleet in 1996-1997.

The Admirals

Madanjit Singh, Vice Admiral, PVSM, AVSM (Cont.)

On completion, he took over as the Assistant Chief of the Naval Staff (Information Warfare and Operations) at Naval Headquarters. Madanjit Singh was promoted to the rank of Vice Admiral in April 1998. He carried out the duties of Deputy Chief of the Naval Staff till March 1999 and as Director General Defence Planning Staff till March 2001. He thereafter headed the Implementation Cell in the MOD wherein he steered all issues relating to restructuring of the Higher Defence Organization within the Ministry of Defence as also with other Ministries. He was appointed as COP in October 2001 and was also the Flag Officer Commanding-in-Chief, Southern Naval Command. His final appointment was of Flag Officer Commanding-in-Chief, Western Naval Command. Vice Admiral Madanjit Singh is a recipient of the PVSM and AVSM for Distinguished Services of an Exceptional Order. He has settled down in Mumbai after his retirement in 2004

Cheema SPS, Vice Admiral, PVSM, AVSM, VSM

Vice Admiral Cheema took over as the Chief of Integrated Defence Staff to the Chairman, Chiefs of Staff Committee (CISC) on 31ST August, 2012. Vice Admiral Cheema was commissioned into the Indian Navy on 1ST January, 1977. He is a Graduate of the National Defence Academy (NDA), Khadakwasla, the Defence Services Staff College (DSSC), Wellington and the College of Naval Warfare (CNW), Mumbai. A specialist in Missile and Gunnery, he has spent the majority of his time on 'afloat' appointments. He was the Commissioning Commanding Officer of Missile Boat INS Nishank, Mauritian Coast Guard OPV Vigilant and the Stealth Frigate INS Trishul. He also commanded Missile Corvette INS Khanjar and India's only Aircraft Carrier INS Viraat. His appointments ashore include the Commandant of the Naval Academy and Commanding Officer INS Mandovi. He also has the unique distinction of wining both the Lengtaigne and Scudder Medal at DSSC. He was awarded the Nau Sena Medal Gallantry when Commanding INS Nishank, when in Command of INS Viraat. A keen sportsman, he plays Squash and Golf.

INDIAN AIR FORCE

The Indian Air Force (IAF) has come a long way from its modest beginning to become one of the finest Air Forces in the world, renowned for its professionalism and competence. The IAF came into being on October 8TH, 1932, and the first Flight was formed in 1933. At that time, there were only six Officers, five Pilots and one Equipment Officer, apart from 19 Havai Sepoys (air soldiers) and its aircraft inventory comprised four Westland Wapiti biplanes at Drigh Road (now in Pakistan). The outbreak of the Second World War resulted in the expansion of the IAF. By the end of 1941, the IAF had three Squadrons and five Coastal Defence Flights. The Japanese occupation of Burma brought the war to India's doorstep and in December 1942, the IAF was inducted into Burma for the first Burma Campaign. In recognition of the services rendered by the Indian Air Force during the war, the Service was bestowed with the prefix "Royal" on 12TH March 1945 and was then known as the Royal Indian Air Force (RIAF). In 1946 it consisted of 8 Fighter and 2 Transport Squadrons with modern aircraft. On the division of the country into the two Dominions of India and Pakistan, the Dominion of India received 7 Fighter Squadrons and 1 Transport Squadron as its share. The RIAF lost many permanent bases and other establishments as a result of the division of the country. It had virtually no breathing space to recover from the surgery that had accompanied the partition. Tribal raiders, clothed, fed and armed by Pakistani military commanders, raided Kashmir in October 1947. On October 26TH, the same year, the Maharaja of Kashmir signed the Instrument of Accession as per the requirements of the partition process and asked for military help. The next day, the RIAF flew to Srinagar, carrying the first contingent of the Indian Army in three DC-3 Dakotas of 12 Squadron. A couple of days later, the Spitfires from Ambala reached Srinagar and were soon engaged in strafing the raiders beyond Pattan. Within a week, the Tempests of No 7 Squadron were playing a decisive role in the battle of Shelatang and had halted the movement of the insurgents. The fighting continued for 15 months and the RIAF was involved throughout the operations. In January 1950, India became a Republic within the British Commonwealth and the Indian Air Force dropped its "Royal" prefix. At this time, it possessed six Fighter Squadrons of Spitfires, Vampires and Tempests operating from Kanpur, Poona, Ambala and Palam, one B-24 Bomber Squadron, one C-47 Dakota Transport Squadron, one AOP Flight, a Communication Squadron at Palam and a growing training organisation.

Indian Air Force

The real test of the IAF's airlift capability came in October 1962, when an open warfare erupted on the Sino-Indian border. During the period, October 20TH to November 20TH, pressure on the Transport and Helicopter Units was intense, troops and supplies having to be flown to the support of the border posts virtually round-the-clock and at high altitudes. The helicopters had to constantly run the gauntlet of Chinese small arms and anti-aircraft fire, while operating on tricky helipads in the mountains. Many notable feats were performed by the IAF during this conflict, including the operation of C-119 Gs from airstrips 17,000 ft AMSL in the Karakoram Himalayas and the airlifting by AN-12Bs of two troops of AMX-13 light tanks to Chushul, in Ladakh, where the small airstrip was 15,000 ft AMSL. On September 1ST, 1965, Pakistan launched a massive attack in the Chhamb sector of India. In response to the urgent requests for air strikes against Pakistani armour advancing in the Chhamb-Jaurian sector, IAF fighters went into action. Vampires of No 45 Squadron undergoing operational training at a forward base mounted their first sorties at 17.45 hrs on the first day of the conflict and on their heels came the Mystere of Nos 3 and 31 Squadrons operating from Pathankot. IAF Gnats proved their mettle in shooting down several PAF F-6 Sabres in this sector, the first aerial victories being notched up by Nos 23 and 9 Squadrons. Full-scale war broke out on September 6TH all along the international border between West Pakistan and India. Pakistan attempted a pre-emptive strike on the same day, attacking IAF bases at Adampur, Halwara, Pathankot, Srinagar, Jamnagar and Kalai Kunda. On the following day, the IAF retaliated with air raids and shot down a PAF star fighter in air combat in Sargodha. The IAF provided close air support to the Indian Army in the famous battle of "Assal Uttar" in Khem Karan sector. In this battle, the thrust of Pakistani Armoured Division was beaten back. The IAF also interdicted Pakistan's railway network, successfully hitting at the Pakistani forces as well as their stores of necessary war-material and also their lines of communication and supply by blowing up trains carrying these goods. With the assistance of the IAF, India's Ground Forces advanced to the outskirts of Lahore. A cease-fire was shortly declared.

As the political situation in the sub-continent deteriorated, the load of ten million Bangladeshi refugees in India was too much for a weak Indian economy. The IAF was alerted to the possibility of another armed conflict.

Indian Air Force

For some weeks in November, both Indian and Pakistani governments protested violations of national airspace along the western border, but aerial conflict between the respective air arms began in earnest on 22ND November, preceding full-scale warfare between India and Pakistan within 12 days. At 14.49 hours, four Pakistani Sabres strafed Indian and Mukti Bahini positions in the Chowgacha Mor area, and 10 minutes later, while engaged on a third strafing run, the Sabres were intercepted by four Gnats from No. 22 Sqn, a detachment of which was operating from Dum Dum Airport, Calcutta. During the ensuing melee, three of the Sabres were shot down, all Gnats returning to base unscathed. The first blood of a new Indo-Pakistan air war had been drawn. Other encounters were to follow over the next 10 days, within both Indian and Pakistani airspace, before full-scale war began on 3RD December. On December 3RD, 1971, pre-emptive strikes were launched by the Pakistani Air Force against the IAF bases at Srinagar, Amritsar and Pathankot followed by attacks on Ambala, Agra, Jodhpur, Uttarlai, Awantipur, Faridkot, Halwara and Sirsa. In response to these strikes, the IAF carried out some 4000 sorties in the west from major and forward bases in Jammu, Kashmir, Punjab and Rajasthan while, in the east, a further 1978 sorties were flown. It was in the western theatre that the MiG-21 was employed in Pathankot in the north to Jamnagar in the southwestern area. The MiG-21 mounted combat air patrol missions over vital points and vital areas, flew escort missions for bombers and strike-fighters, and were continuously scrambled to intercept hostile intruders. The first aerial victory was on December 12TH, 1971, when MiG-21s of No 47 Squadron shot down a PAF F-104 over the Gulf of Kutch. This was followed by three more victories in quick succession on December 17TH when MiG-21s of No 29 Squadron escorting Maruts, shot down intercepting F-104s near Uttarlai in Rajasthan desert in gun-missile encounters while a third F-104, on an intruding mission, was shot down by another MiG-21 of No 29 Squadron. This singular contribution by the IAF resulted in a decisive victory for India that resulted in the birth of an independent state of Bangladesh, with the unconditional surrender of 90,000 soldiers of Pakistan's armed forces.

THE MARSHALS

Arjan Singh, Marshal of the Air, DFC

Marshal of the Indian Air Force Arjan Singh, DFC, was one Pilot who grew up in the annals of the Air Force as the first Chief for leading the force into war. He was Chief of Air Staff when the Indian Air Force saw action in its first combat in 1965. He was hardly 44 years of age when entrusted with the responsibility of leading the Indian Air Force. A responsibility he carried with considerable flamboyance and élan. Arjan Singh was born on 15TH April 1919, in Lyallpur, completing his education at Montgomery. He was 19 years of age in 1938, when he was selected for the Empire Pilot Training Course at RAF Cranwell in England. His first posting on being commissioned was flying Westland Wapiti biplanes in the North Western Frontier Province as a member of the No.1 IAF Squadron. Arjan Singh flew against the tribal forces, before he was transferred for a brief stint with the newly formed No.2 IAF Squadron. Later he moved back to No.1 as a Flying Officer, when the Squadron re-equipped with the Hawker Hurricane. Promoted to Squadron Leader in 1944, Arjan Singh led the Squadron against the Japanese during the Arakan Campaign. Flying close support during the crucial Imphal Campaign and later assisting the advance of the Allied Forces to Rangoon, Burma. For his role in successfully leading the Squadron in combat, Arjan Singh received the Distinguished Flying Cross (DFC) in 1944. He was given command of the IAF Display Flight, flying Hawker Hurricanes after the war, which toured India giving demonstrations. On 15TH August 1947, he had the unique honour of leading the fly-past of over a hundred IAF aircraft over the red fort in Delhi. Promoted to Wing Commander, he attended Staff College at UK, and immediately after Indian independence became the AOC, Ambala in the rank of Group Captain. In 1949, promoted to Air Commodore, Arjan Singh took over the Air Officer Commanding of Operational Command, which later came to be known as Western Air Command. Arjan Singh had the distinction of having the longest tenure as the AOC of Operational Command, from 1949-1952 and again from 1957-1961. Promoted to Air Vice Marshal, he was the AOC-in-C of Operational Command. Towards the end of the 1962 war, he was appointed the DCAS and became the VCAS by 1963. He was the overall Commander of the joint air training exercises "Shiksha" held between the IAF, RAF and RAAF. On 1ST August 1964, Arjan Singh took over as the Chief of Air Staff in the rank of Air Marshal, which became the pinnacle of this career.

The Marshals

Arjan Singh, Marshal of the Air, DFC (Cont.)

Arjan Singh was the first Air Chief who kept his flying category till his CAS rank. Having flown over 60 different types of aircraft from Pre-WW-2 era biplanes to the more contemporary, Gnats & Vampires, he also had flown in transports like the Super Constellation. Arjan Singh's testing time came in September 1965, when the subcontinent was plunged into war. When Pakistan launched its Operation Grand Slam, in which an armoured thrust targeted the vital town of Akhnur, he was summoned into the Defence Minister's office with a request for air support. With a characteristic non-chalance, he replied "...in an hour." And true enough, the Air Force struck the Pakistani offensive in an hour. He led the Air Force through the war showing successful leadership and effort. Though at a certain level, mistakes were made and planning could have been better, in all fairness, it must be said that the credit for thwarting Ayub Khan's grandiose plans to capture Kashmir is shared by the Indian Army and the Indian Air Force, and Arjan Singh for leading the Air Force through the war. Arjan Singh was awarded the Padma Vibhushan for his leadership of the Air Force, and subsequently in recognition of the Air Force's contribution in the war, the rank of the CAS was upgraded to that of Air Chief Marshal and Arjan Singh became the first Air Chief Marshal of the Indian Air Force. He retired in August 1969, thereupon accepting ambassadorship to Switzerland. He remained a flyer to the end of his tenure in the IAF, visiting forward Squadrons & Units and flying with them. Arjan Singh was a source of inspiration to a generation of Indians and Officers. In recognition of his Services, the Government of India conferred the rank of the Marshal of the Air Force onto Arjan Singh in January 2002 making him the first and the only 'Five Star' rank Officer with the Indian Air Force.

Marshal of the Air, Arjan Singh

The Marshals

Dilbagh Singh, Air Chief Marshal, PVSM, AVSM, VM

Dilbagh Singh was the second Sikh Chief of Air Staff the Indian Air Force had, after Marshal of the Air Force Arjan Singh. Born in Punjab on 10TH March 1926, Dilbagh took an interest in flying at a very early age. He joined the Indian Air Force in 1944 at the height of World War Two and was posted to the No.1 Squadron flying Hurricanes at Kohat in 1945. When the tribal invasion of Kashmir began in October 1947, Dilbagh Singh was actively involved in the operations. He was one of the first to fly operations in a Spitfire from Srinagar. Later he joined No.10 Winged Daggers Squadron and flew sorties against the raiders in the Hawker Tempest aircraft. For his role in the operations, Dilbagh Singh was Mentioned-in-Dispatches. After the Kashmir Operations, he was deputed to attend Flying Instructors Training after which Dilbagh Singh was involved in training Afghan Air Force cadets. Promoted to Squadron Leader in 1954, he assumed the responsibilities of Officer In charge of Flying at the Ambala Air Base. Command of a Squadron came his way in August 1955, when he took over No.2 Squadron flying Spitfire XVIIIs. Dilbagh did not stay with No.2 Squadron for long; he handed over command in February 1956 and went to France to get trained on the Mystere IV-A fighter. After returning from France, Dilbagh took over as the CO of No.1 Squadron flying the Mystere IV-A at Kalaikunda. He also undertook the first official 'Supersonic Bang' over India in New Delhi when the Mystere IV-A was showcased to the Nation. After four years of operational flying, Dilbagh Singh went to Jamnagar as the Chief Instructor at the Armament Training Wing. Dilbagh shot into the limelight in late 1962, when he was selected to be trained on the MiG-21F, which was being acquired by India from the USSR. He led the first batch of seven "chosen" Pilots and 15 Engineers for training at Lugovya, an airbase in Kazakhstan in the erstwhile USSR for training on the MiG-21F fighter. After undergoing training for five months, the team came back to India to form the core of the first supersonic squadron, No.28 First Supersonics Squadron. Dilbagh Singh raised the Unit in Chandigarh with an order of battle of six MiG-21s in early 1963. In May 1965, Dilbagh handed over the command of No.28 Squadron to Wing Commander M.S.D. Wollen (later Air Marshal) and joined Air Headquarters as Deputy Director (Weapons). He was holding the Staff job until the end of the 1965 war with Pakistan, when he took over command of Halwara AFB in the rank of Group Captain. His Services were recognised with the award of the Vayu Sena Medal in 1966.

The Marshals

Dilbagh Singh, Air Chief Marshal, PVSM, AVSM, VM (Cont.)

At the outbreak of the 1971 War, Dilbagh Singh was under Central Air Command, as Air Officer Commanding of Lohegaon AFB, near Pune. From his base, No.35 Squadron flying Canberras struck Karachi Oil Tanks and Harbour Installations. Dilbagh's responsibilities included providing facilities to aircraft of the maritime air operations. Dilbagh became the Senior Air Staff Officer in the Western Air Command in 1976 and finally became the Air Officer Commander in Chief (AOC-in-C) of Western Air Command in 1978. In 1979, he received the Param Vishist Seva Medal for Distinguished Service. In 1981, Dilbagh Singh became the Chief of Air Staff, in the rank of Air Chief Marshal. His tenure lasted three years until 1984, in which time the IAF saw the induction of the MiG-25, MiG-23 and the selection of the Mirage 2000. He was also the Commodore Commandant of No.28 Squadron. Dilbagh Singh laid down the office of CAS in 1984, by which time, in a career spanning four decades, he had about 5000 hours of flying on different types of aircraft, was decorated by the Government for Distinguished Service thrice. Dilbagh Singh passed away in the city of Dehradun on February 11TH, 2001.

Bajwa Singh (Dr.) Air Marshal, PVSM

Air Marshal Bajwa was born on October 25TH 1925. Dr. Bajwa joined King Edward Medical College, Lahore in 1942. He was able to finish his Medical Studies and pass his final M.B.B.S. exam from Amritsar Medical College in 1948. He joined the Indian Army in September 1948 as a Lieutenant, and then transferred to the Indian Air Force after one month. Dr. Bajwa's final promotion was to the rank of Air Marshal (a three-star General rank) in October 1984 as Director, Medical Services of the Indian Air Force, which is the highest military rank available to Physician Officers. During his final postings in Delhi Dr. Bajwa was an Honorary Physician to the President of India. He retired as Air Marshal in 1985. Air Marshal Bajwa received India's Param Vashist Seva Medal in January 1985. The PVSM award is India's highest Military Decoration for Distinguished Peacetime Service. Dr. Bajwa passed away on Monday, November 30TH 2009.

The Marshals

Darshan Singh Basra, Air Marshal, VSN, AVSM, PVSM

Air Marshal Darshan Singh Basra says that the determination and dedication he learnt as a young lad in Punjab helped him reach this pinnacle in the Indian Air Force. "It is primarily the rich spirit of Punjab which taught me that one can achieve anything if one sets his heart and soul on it," the Air Marshal told The Tribune in an exclusive interview. Beginning his career as an engine fitter as a 17-year-old, Air Marshal Basra is one of the few Officers to have reached the top echelons from the very bottom. Recounting his days spent in the Air Force, Air Marshal Basra said, "I was always interested in flying and had performed well in my school examinations. My family members were keen that I pursue a career in medicine but I thought otherwise and joined the Air Force, as an airman." He has since kept his ambitions soaring in the sky by logging more than 3700 hours as a Fighter Pilot and has flown a variety of fighter aircraft, including MiG 21, MiG 23, MiG 25, Jaguar, Mirage and F-86 (Sabre). After joining the Air Force in the ranks, Air Marshal Basra went on to distinguish himself sufficiently to be awarded a commission in 1962 and then rose steadily to become an Air Marshal. Air Marshal D. S. Basra was born in the village of Basrai of Gurdaspur district on August 20TH, 1940. His father, a traditional Jat farmer, stood proud in his village for his three sons were in the service of the country in the Armed Forces that had the rare distinction of fighting all three wars of 1962, 1965 and 1971. The eldest son had fought in World War II and was a prisoner of war in Japan for three years. The family tradition continues as many of his nephews and nieces have joined the Armed Forces or the Police. "My family background imbibed in me a strong sense of patriotism which led to my joining the Services," he recollected. Both the children of Air Marshal Basra are in the Services. His son Squadron Leader H. S. Basra, a Fighter Pilot with A2 Instructor's category flies the Mirage 2000 while his daughter, Captain Manpreet Basra, is a Doctor in the Army Medical Corps. "I told my son to pursue the career of his choice but he opted for the Air Force and today he is a Fighter Pilot like me. It is a matter of pride," he said. In his 36 years of Commissioned Service, Air Marshal Basra has served in important Command and Staff Appointments. He received his initial combat training on T-33 and F-86 (Sabre) in the USA. His final command was Air Officer Commander-in-Chief Southern Air Command.

Air Marshal Darshan Singh Basra retired in August 2000

The Marshals

Harjinder Singh, Air Vice Marshal, MBE, PVSM

Harjinder Singh was born on 4TH February, 1909, in Sirhala-Khurd village in the District of Hoshiarpur, Punjab. Having joined the Indian Air Force as a Hawai Sepoy (Air Soldier), a rank lower than that of a Soldier, Harjinder Singh rose to become an Air Vice Marshal. He dominated the technical side of the Indian Air Force's earlier years and made the Indian Air Force the only Air Force in the world to undertake manufacture of aircraft.

In India of the late twenties, there remained many sceptics who were dubious of India's ability to raise and run an efficient Air Force. The key to an effective fighting air arm would not only be the aviators but aircraft, men, mechanics and technical tradesmen who would constitute its backbone. To the good fortune of the future Indian Air Force, amongst the first to apply were a number of well educated, highly motivated and patriotic individuals who sacrificed better emoluments in order to join what they felt was an important contribution to a future free India. One of them was Harjinder Singh, then studying at the Maclaghen Engineering College, Lahore but for some time obsessed with joining the Air Force. He was amongst the first nine Engineering Students to be selected in November 1930. He joined the 1ST Squadron, Indian Air Force, in January, 1931, at Karachi. In the years 1933 to 1937 the Squadron trained for its primary role of Army Co-operation from Drigh Road, Peshawar, Chaklala and Sialkot. As a Non Commissioned Officer, Harjinder Singh saw extensive service in continuous operations against hostile tribesmen in the North West Frontier Province. On 3RD September, 1939, Harjinder Singh was offered a commission in the Royal Air Force, so he could command 500 Indian non-Combatant Section personnel working for the Royal Air Force. He declined the offer. 'I felt too strongly the esprit de corps of our fledgling Service to desert them for the sake of a Commission'. On 1ST November, Harjinder Singh was promoted to the rank of Sergeant (Hawai Havildar)

In November 1941, the Squadron moved en masse for an air display to Calcutta. On their return, when they had touched down at Lahore to refuel, Harjinder saw a damaged Lysander of No. 28 Squadron RAF classified as Category 'E'; that is beyond repair. 'I told Majumdar (Squadron Leader) that I would go on ahead to Lahore and repair the crashed Lysander: then when our Squadron passed through Lahore, it could pick up the aircraft as a moral claim and just annexe to our Squadron!' Harjinder picked up the wrecked Lysander and repaired it as their 13TH aircraft!

The Marshals

Harjinder Singh, Air Vice Marshal MBE PVSM (Cont.)

December 1941 saw the outbreak of the war in the Far East. On 1ST February 1942, No. 1 Squadron moved to Taungoo, Burma. Warrant Officer Harjinder Singh, who had improvised a wooden tail wheel for the Lysanders when the spares ran out, was appointed Member of the Order of the British Empire for his imaginative improvisation and for maintaining very high aircraft serviceability in spite of poor logistic backing. Harinder Singh was commissioned as Flying Officer in the Indian Air Force on 3RD September 1942 and rose to become Air Vice Marshal. A Pilot as well as an Engineer, he was a compatriot of the Marshal of the IAF Arjan Singh and IAF's legend, Baba Mehar Singh. He was an engineering genius who had a vision ahead of his time. AVM Harjinder Singh's vision to produce the first transport aircraft within the country led to IAF, Indian Airlines and a few other operators using aircraft made indigenously. It also led to the creation of HAL's Transport Aircraft Division, which later made many more aircraft – AVRO 748, Dornier 228, HPT-32 and Ardhra gliders. This is a fantastic legacy we owe to Air Vice Marshal Harjinder Singh's drive and dedication. Maintenance Command was formed at Kanpur on 26TH January 1955, with Air Vice Marshal Harjinder Singh as its first Air Officer Commander-in-Chief. Kanpur was the core centre of maintenance activities even before Independence. A unit called Aircraft Manufacturing Depot was subsequently added to undertake manufacture of AVRO aircraft. As Kanpur alone was not able to absorb the futuristic industrial activities, Nagpur was eventually selected as the new site for setting up Maintenance Command Headquarters. Maintenance Command was set up to provide maintenance support to operating bases both by undertaking service and repair of aircraft, aero engines, ground equipments, radars and missiles and warehousing of stores required during peace and war. These works are undertaken by Base Repair Depots, Equipment Depots and Air Storage Parks. These units have the most modern and state of the art equipment to undertake repair and service of various weapon systems.

Harjinder Singh retired as AOC-in-C of the Maintenance Command in 1964 and then served as Technical Adviser to the Punjab and Haryana Governments on a token salary of just Re 1. He died in November 1971. An entire colony in Kanpur has been named as Harjinder Nagar after him.

The Marshals

Jagjit Singh Sandhawalia, Air Marshal, PVSM, VSM

Air Marshal Sardar Jagjit Singh Sandhawalia was born in 1928. He was educated at Government College Lahore and attended the Mclagan Engineering College in Lahore. He went on to train at the Government Engineering College, Roorkee and was admitted to the Air Force Technical College at Jallahali and the National Defence College. He qualified as a Mechanical Engineer in 1949, and became a Pilot Officer, Indian Air Force (Technical Branch) 1950. He was promoted to Squadron Leader in 1960. He became Commanding Officer Technical Branch at Chushul (Ladakh) 1960-1963, and went on to serve in the Chinese confrontation of 1962. He was promoted to Wing Commander in 1965. He served as Deputy Air Attaché Moscow in 1965-1968. He was Senior Maintenance SO Western Air Command and Training Commander to 1978. He was promoted to Air Marshal in May 2012 and took over as the Director General (Aircraft) at the Air Headquarters in June 2012.

Kanwar Dalinderjit Singh, Air Marshal, AVSM

Air Marshal Kanwar Dalinderjit Singh (Retd.) graduated from the National Defence Academy in December 1968 and was commissioned as a Fighter Pilot in June 1970. He is an Alumnus of Defence Services Staff College, Wellington and National Defence College New Delhi. He has the unique experience of being a Forward Air Controller with the Indian Army during the liberation of Bangladesh in 1971. He has flown Hawker Hunter and MiG 21 variants among other fighter and trainer aircraft. He is a Qualified Flying Instructor with an A2 category and was deputed to the Iraqi Air Force as an Instructor for two years in 1982. He has commanded a front line Fighter Squadron. He has been Chief Operations Officer of a Fighter Base and later Chief Instructor (Flying) at the Air Force Academy. The Air Marshal has the experience of commanding two Air Force Stations. He has held important Staff Appointments at the Air HQ. The Air Marshal was holding the appointment of Assistant Chief of Air Staff (Personnel Officers) at Air HQ Vayu Bhavan, New Delhi and later as Senior Air Staff Officer, Central Air Command Allahabad, before taking over as Air Officer Commander-in-Chief, South Western Air Command on 1ST May 2007. He was awarded the Ati Vishist Seva Medal for Exceptional Devotion to Duty. Air Marshal K.D. Singh retired in 2010.

The Marshals

Lal Singh Grewal, Air Marshal, VrC, AVSM, PVSM

Air Marshal Lal Singh Grewal (Retd.) joined the last Indian Air Force formation raised during World War Two, No.10 Squadron, with whom he flew Hurricane IICs in the Arakan in 1944-45. After the war, and conversion to multi-engine aircraft, he was amongst the first to fly troops into the Vale of Kashmir in October 1947. In November 1948, he formed No.5 Squadron, Indian Air Force's first Heavy Bomber Unit with B-24 Liberators. He had several important appointments in various Air Force Units and has also attended important courses both in India and abroad. In 1960, in view of the threat of the Chinese aggression, it was considered necessary to send a large number of troops to Ladakh area. This involved increase in tonnage to be airlifted. He was Wing Commander at that time and by his professional skill and initiative and despite many hazards made several trials and ultimately succeeded in landing at Chushul with a Packet Aircraft. He flew nearly 700 operational hours in 20 months. In 1963, and in the aftermath of the frontier war with China, Lal Singh was handpicked to establish the Aviation Research Centre (ARC) for special operations, about which very little has still been revealed. Air Marshal Lal Singh Grewal later rose to be the Vice Chief of Air Staff.

He was awarded the Vir Chakra in 1950 and the citation reads:-

"During 1947-1948 Indo-Pakistani conflict, Flight Lieutenant Lal Singh Grewal made a number of landings by day and night at Poonch while it was under enemy fire. He also dropped supplies of ammunition and rations in inclement weather to the garrisons in Kotli and Mirpur when these places were subjected to heavy enemy fire. He also captained aircraft during night bomb sorties. On 21ST March 1948, when Poonch was being shelled heavily by the enemy, he made two hazardous landings there, one by day and another by night, without any landing aids to deliver urgently required heavy guns and ammunition to the troops. He also flew in regularly the much-needed supplies to Leh."

The Marshals

Manjit Singh Sekhon, Air Marshal, PVSM, VrC, SC, VM

Manjit Singh was commissioned in the Indian Air Force in 1962. He immediately flew sorties during the Indo-Chinese war of 1962, evacuating casualties and carrying ammunition and supplies to the Indian troops. He was transferred to helicopters, and flew extensively in Eastern India, in support of the Indian Army, Police and Para Military Forces. While on a mission of causality evacuation as a co-pilot evacuating injured patients of the Indian Army, the helicopter engine failed near the China border and the aircraft crashed at the altitude of 8700ft. and five patients died on the spot. He pulled the other seven badly injured patients from the burning helicopter. He then walked for seven days, surviving on grass and jungle berries and managed to reach Jorhat Hospital on the 8TH day. He assisted in recovering the surviving patients on the eleventh day. He was posted to Jorhat- Dinjan- Chabua in the Eastern Sector for six years and saved nearly 400 casualties, troops and civilians from remote areas of Nagaland, Mizo Hills, Arunachal Pradesh, Tripura, Tirip, Meghalaya, Sikkim, and Bhutan. During the 1965 Indo- Pakistan war, he was awarded Vayu Sena Medal for Exceptional Devotion to Duty. He was posted to 121 Vampire Squadron of the World War Two fame. During the 1971 war his Unit was in Srinagar. His Senior Officers were reluctant to fly operational sorties on this vintage aircraft but he volunteered to almost all sorties and destroyed enemy bunkers, dumps and war support machinery in Kargil and Leh sectors. He was awarded the Vir Chakra for most daring attacks in Poonch, Haji Pass and Pir Pass, Tangdhar, Tithwal, Kargil Heights, Chlunka, Thang, Kharmang, and Khapulu. He then raised and commanded a Helicopter Unit for two and half years. For gallant search and rescue operation at night in saving two aircraft pilots from crashed aircrafts near Pathankot–Passur border, beyond the normal call of duty, he was awarded the Shauriya Chakra on February 25TH, 1975. He went on to command a Fighter Squadron of MIGS very successfully and was awarded commendations by Chief of Air Staff. During the Kargil war of 1999, as an Air Marshal he flew seven sorties, night and day and contributed greatly to the victory of the Kargil war. He has flown about 50 types of aircraft, including all types of Fighter Aircraft, Transport Aircraft and Helicopters, on the inventory of the Indian Air Force, Navy and Army. In the infamous Purulia Arms Drop case, he played an exceptional role with sound professional knowledge and tactics. He single-handedly caught and force landed Pakistani linked transport aircraft at Bombay, which is still in Indian custody.

The Marshals

Manjit Singh Sekhon, Air Marshal (Cont.)

Air Marshal Manjit Singh was an Alumnus of National Defence College. While holding various Staff Appointments at Air HQ, he made meaningful contributions in Operations, Flight Safety, Training, Induction of Women Officers in the Indian Air Force and in various other operational fields. As Air Defence Commander and officiating Senior Air Staff Officer, South Western Air Command, he made commendable contributions in reorganising and relocating Units, Radars, Flight Safety in concepts of Control and Reporting Centre, Mobile Pulse Doppler Radar Busting, Special Heliborne Operations and Photo Reconnaissance. As SASO HQ, Eastern Command, and later as SASO HQ Western Air Command, he improved the overall Operational, Flight Safety and Air Defence Environment of the area. All air maintenance tasks, flood relief, causality evacuation, counter insurgency operations and tasks given by Air HQ were achieved in the most professional manner. As Air Officer Commander in Chief, Southern Air Command, he brought about remarkable improvement in the field of operations, maintenance and administration, and succeeded in achieving some of the tasks pending for more than ten years. As an AOC-in-Chief, he brought up Car Nicobar and Port Blair Air Force Station operationally and administratively improved the quality of life. For his most Devoted Services to the Nation, Dedication and Exceptional Contribution of the Highest Order, the President of India awarded him the Param Vishist Seva Medal on 9TH October 2002. He has been awarded three Gallantry Awards of Vir Chakra, Saurya Chakra, Vayu Sena Medal and PVSM. After flying as a Pilot for 41 years, he was forced to retire a year before the scheduled time, for the inadvertent letter he wrote to Mr. Parkash Singh Badal, the then Chief Minister of Punjab.

The citation of the Vir Chakra awarded to Manjit Singh Sekhon reads:-

"During the 1971 Indo-Pakistani War, Flight Lieutenant Manjit Singh Sekhon was commanding a detachment of a frontline fighter squadron. He flew 14 missions at a low height in very difficult terrain of Jammu and Kashmir and caused extensive damage to several enemy bunkers, vehicles, guns mortar position, petrol and ammunition dumps. He carried out these missions in the face of heavy ground fire. He substantially contributed to the success of the ground forces in Kargil, Tithwal, Poonch, and Uri Sectors."

The Marshals

Paramjit Singh Bhangu, Air Marshal, VSM, AVSM

Air Marshal Bhangu was commissioned in the Indian Air Force as a Fighter Pilot on January 22ND, 1972. He had more than 4000 hours of combat flying experience and commanded a Front Line Air Base. A qualified A2 Category Flying Instructor and a Fighter Combat Leader, he has served as Commanding Officer of a Fighter Combat Squadron and the Tactics & Air Combat Development Establishment (TACDE). He is an Alumnus of Defence Service Staff College, Wellington. Besides Staff Appointments at Air Headquarters as Joint Director Air Defence and Principal Director Flight Safety, the Air Officer had a flying instructional tenure of two years in a friendly country and also a diplomatic tenure in the Embassy of India Moscow, Russia as an Air Attaché for over three years. He had also held the appointments of Director General, Air Force Naval Housing Board, Assistant Chief of Air Staff (Personnel Officers) and Assistant Chief of Air Staff (Personnel Airmen & Civilians) at Air Headquarters. Air Marshal Bhangu was awarded the Vayu Sena Medal in 1992 and the Ati Vishist Seva Medal in 1996 for Exceptional Devotion to Duty. He was serving as Senior Air Staff Officer, Western Air Command, and New Delhi before taking over as Air Officer Commander-in-Chief South Western Air Command. Air Marshal Paramjit Singh Bhangu retired on 31ST December 2010.

Prithvi Singh Brar, Air Marshal, AVSM

Air Marshal Prithvi Singh Brar was commissioned in the Indian Air Force on December 15TH, 1960. He retired on superannuation in the year 2000, after forty years of Distinguished Service. Air Marshal Brar had held the key appointments of VCAS and AOC-in-C, Eastern Air Command. Air Marshal Brar also had the distinction of being a Founder Member of the prestigious Tactics Air Combat Development Establishment (TACDE) and having commanded the famous "Thunderbolts", the aerobatics team of the IAF.

The Marshals

Prem Pal Singh, Air Marshal, AVSM, PVSM, MVC

Prem Pal Singh was commissioned in the Indian Air Force on 15TH April 1950. In the beginning he served as a Dakota Pilot but later he switched over to the Canberra aircraft. During the Indo-Pak War 1965, Wing Commander Prem Pal Singh commanded No. 5 "Tuskers" Squadron, stationed at Agra. The Unit equipped with the Canberra bomber, was assigned the triple task of tactical bombing, close support and armed patrolling. Under his able guidance the Squadron carried out tactical bombing of various targets to destroy the Pakistan Air Force on the ground. Led by Wing Commander Prem Pal Singh himself, Pakistani army camp east of Gujarat and airfields at Chaklala, Dab, Murid, Akwal, Risalwala, Wagowal, Sargodha and Peshawar were successfully attacked by his Bombers. The Squadron gave close support to the Army in Kasur, Khem Karan, Pasrur, Chawinda and Sialkot sectors. Bombs were dropped on the enemy concentrations at all these places. During the period of war the Squadron undertook 39 sorties of armed patrolling over Agra, Palam, Ambala, Halwara and Adampur. Most of the operational missions over the enemy territory were carried out during the hours of darkness. The targets were identified in the moon-light. These dangerous operational sorties were undertaken in the face of heavy enemy anti-aircraft fire with exceptional courage and determination. Wing Commander Prem Pal was awarded the Mahavir Chakra for displaying a High Sense of Duty and Gallantry. Wing Commander Prem Pal Singh subsequently rose to the rank of Air Marshal. He was awarded AVSM and PVSM for Distinguished Service. The citation of the gallantry award Mahavir Chakra, reads:-

"During the 1965 Indo-Pakistani War, Wing Commander Prem Pal Singh was the Commanding Officer of an operational Bomber Squadron. He undertook six major offensive and tactical close-support operations which included: reconnaissance over the Sargodha Airfield complex; Dab, Akwal and Murid Airfields; marking of Peshawar Airfield; and bombing of Pakistani troop and armour concentrations in various sectors. Disregarding personal safety in these very dangerous operations in the face of heavy enemy anti-aircraft fire, he led a number of bombing and reconnaissance missions with courage, determination and tenacity. Throughout the operations, Wing Commander Singh displayed a high sense of duty, professional skill and gallantry in the best traditions of the Indian Air Force for which he was awarded the Mahavir Chakra."

Prem Pal Singh retired as an Air Marshal.

The Marshals

Puran Singh Bajwa, Air Marshal, PVSM,

Dr. Bajwa joined King Edward Medical College, Lahore, in 1942. Due to troubles during the partition of India in 1947, Dr. Bajwa was unable to finish his Medical Studies in Lahore. However he gained entry to the Medical College at Amritsar from which he graduated with his M.B.B.S. in 1948. At an early age of about 23 years, Dr. Bajwa joined the Indian Air Force in September 1948 as a Lieutenant. Following a career of much hard work and commitment spanning 36 years, Dr. Bajwa's final promotion was to the rank of Air Marshal, in October 1984, as Director Medical Services of the Indian Air Force, the highest military rank available to Medical Officers. During his final postings in Delhi, Dr. Bajwa was an Honorary Physician to the President of India. He retired as Air Marshal in 1985 at the age of 60. In recognition of his Service and Dedication to his Country and his Profession, Air Marshal Bajwa received India's Param Vashist Seva Medal in January 1985. He has also been a past President and Fellow of The Indian Society of Aerospace Medicine. Air Marshal Puran Singh Bajwa passed away on Monday, November 30TH 2009.

Rajinder Singh, Air Marshal, AVSM, VM

Air Marshal Rajinder Singh was commissioned in the Indian Air Force in December 1974 in the Fighter Stream. An Alumnus of National Defence Academy, he has flown a variety of combat and trainer aircraft during his distinguished career of over 37 years in the Air Force. He has experience of over 3100 hours on Hunter, Marut, all variants of MiG ac and Trainer aircraft Kiran. A qualified Flying Instructor, he is a Graduate of the Defence Services Staff College, Wellington. Air Marshal Rajinder Singh has held a variety of Operational and Staff Appointments during his career. His Operational Assignments include command of a frontline Fighter Squadron and Chief Operations Officer of an Operational Base in the Kashmir Valley. He served as Air Officer Commanding, Air Force Station Palam and Air Attaché at the Embassy of India, Egypt. Senior Personnel Staff Officer at Western Air Command, Principal Director Projects at Air Headquarters, Senior Air Staff Officer at Southern Air Command, Assistant Chief of Integrated Defence Headquarters and Senior Air Staff Officer, Training Command. The Air Marshal is a recipient of the Ati Vishisht Seva Medal and Vayu Sena Medal. He is currently Air Officer Commander-in-Chief, Training Command Bangalore. (2012)

The Marshals

Shivdev Singh, Air Marshal

Air Marshal Shivdev Singh, who died in January, 1994, was the last of the survivors of the batch of 24 Indian Air Force Fighter Pilots who were seconded to the Royal Air Force, as part of the reinforcement the British desperately needed in 1940 to fight the "Battle of Britain". Flying Sterlings over occupied France and Germany - including daring attacks on their submarine pens - he was decorated for Gallantry in a campaign that had many casualties. He was rushed back home when the Japanese conquered Burma and flew the Hurricanes in the Arakan within Burma. One of the pioneers of the Indian Air Force, Shivdev Singh, was responsible for the evacuation of his Squadron from Kohat to Chaklala at the time of Partition in 1947. He later moved to Agra to found the Transport Squadron. Besides flying the political leaders of the day, Shivdev and his men organized the massive airlift to Srinagar in time to save the Kashmir Valley from Pakistani raiders. What makes his contribution to the IAF unique is that he was perhaps the most operationally experienced Commander. He was in charge of the IAF's role in "Operation Vijay" in the liberation of Goa. The IAF Fighter Pilots played no major role in the 1962 Sino-Indian conflict. But the subsequent training for Air Defence Operations named "Operation Shiksha" again had Shivdev Singh in command. The crowning glory was his role as the Vice-Chief, when he master-minded the entire Air Operations in the 1971 Indo-Pak war. Although the Chief, P.C. Lal, was given the credit publically, the man at the head of the operation table was Shivdev Singh. The story going in the IAF circles is that Shivdev Singh almost made it to the top job as Lal's successor. The then Defence Minister, Jagjivan Ram was even supposed to have telephoned him saying, "Let me be the first to congratulate you" - after the appointment had been cleared at the highest level. But things changed overnight for reasons well beyond the reach of the high-flying IAF brass - as often happens in a corrupt India. Shivdev Singh retired - but without any rancour - to his home in Chandigarh, contributing gracefully to Public Service in the Punjab.

The Marshals

Padamjit Singh Ahluwalia, Air Marshal, PVSM, AVSM, & BAR, VM, VSM

Air Marshal Ahluwalia (Retd.) is a Graduate of the National Defence Academy, Defence Services Staff College and National Defence College. A highly decorated Officer, Ahluwalia is held in high esteem within the profession, and is one of only two Indian Air Force Officers to have ever been awarded a bar to his AVSM. The other Officer to have received such recognition was the former Air Chief Marshal L.M. Katre. To date, Air Marshal Ahluwalia has logged approximately 4,000 hours of flying on all types of Fighter Aircraft. Air Marshal Ahluwalia has a mix of crucial Staff and Field Appointments to his credit, along with several professional and diplomatic assignments abroad. He has served in the directorates of electronic warfare, air defence, aircraft induction and concept studies at the Air HQ, apart from performing tours of duty in Japan and South Korea. He has also served a stint as Air Advisor to the Chief of the Air Staff. Air Marshal Ahluwalia is considered to be an Officer with exceptional operational and managerial skills. Currently Air Officer Commander-in-Chief, Southern Air Command, Ahluwalia has earlier served as Director General (inspection & flight safety). It was during his tenure that the Indian Air Force managed to bring down its accident rate of aircraft to all time lows. Earlier, in 1986, as a Wing Commander, Air Marshal Ahluwalia had commanded one of the two Squadrons of the Indian Air Force that were equipped with the newly inducted Mirage-2000s. He was instrumental in the development of tactics for the new aircraft, as well as in the formulation of the syllabus and standard operating procedures for the Mirages. During the Kargil operations in 1999, as the Air Officer Commander of Air Force Station, Gwalior, Ahluwalia, then Air Commodore, undertook several trial runs on the Mirages, which were instrumental in the successful utilisation of these aircraft in Kargil's mountainous terrain.

The Marshals

Jasdeep Singh, Air Vice Marshal

Air Vice Marshal Jasdeep Singh assumed charge of Principal Medical Officer, Headquarters Western Air Command, IAF. (2004) A specialist in Preventive and Social Medicine, he did his Graduation in Medicine from Government Medical College, Patiala. After joining the Army in 1969, he did his DPH in 1976 and MD in Preventive and Social Medicine in 1977 from Pune University. He attended Advance Specialist Course during 1975-77 and stood first in the University. Air Vice Marshal Jasdeep Singh is a Fellow of Indian Society for Malaria and other Communicable Diseases, Fellow of Royal Institute of Public Health & Hygiene, Fellow of Entomological Society of India and a Member of Indian Public Health Association. Besides commanding field ambulances, he has served with the IPKF in Sri Lanka.

Gurnam Singh Chaudhry, Air Marshal PVSM, AVSM, VSM

Air Marshal Chaudhry was commissioned as a Fighter Pilot. He went on to become a fully Operational Air Defence and Strike Pilot, an A Cat Flying Instructor and an Experimental Test Pilot. He commanded a Jaguar Squadron, was Chief Operations Officer at Pune and Commanded Air Base at Tezpur. An Alumnus of DSSC and NDC, he has held a wide variety of Staff and Operational Appointments such as Ops Staff at Western Air Command, Deputy/Joint Director Air Staff Requirement at Air HQ, Instructor at DSSC, founder member of IDS as PD Long Term Force Structure, ACAS (Inspection) and SASO South Western Air Command. He retired as AOC-in-C Training Command. He has written articles and features for magazines like Force (India) and Air Buz by S. P. Publication. His area of expertise is in Long Term & Futuristic Force Structuring. Air Marshal Chaudhry retired as a National Defence Academy Officer.

Jasbir Singh Panesar, Air Vice Marshal

Air Vice Marshal Jasbir Singh Panesar was commissioned in the Fighter Stream of the Indian Air Force in June 1973. He was amongst the first batch of Pilots selected to undergo the Mirage 2000 conversion training in France in 1985. He is an Alumnus of Defence Services Staff College. Air Vice Marshal Panesar has flown about 4,000 hours on various types of aircraft. He was recently Senior Air and Administration Staff Officer of Maintenance Command. Air Vice Marshal Jasbir Singh Panesar took over as Commodore Commander of 15 Squadron, Air Force. (2008)

The Marshals

J.S. Gujral, Air Marshal

Air Marshal J.S. Gujral was commissioned in the Fighter Stream of the Indian Air Force in December 1967. He has flown over 4000 hours of accident-free flying in a wide range of aircraft. A Graduate of Defence Services Staff College, he has also done the Long Defence Management Course and the Higher Command Course. Air Marshal Gujral has commanded various MiG Squadrons and a premier Fighter Base in Eastern Air Command. He was earlier Assistant Chief of Air Staff in the personnel branch at Air Headquarters. He retired on October 31ST, 2006

S.P.Singh, Air Marshal, AVSM, VM

Air Marshal S.P. Singh Air Officer Commander-in-Chief, Southern Air Command, retired on July 31ST, 2012 after a Distinguished Service of 38 years. The Air Marshal took over the reins of Southern Air Command and was instrumental in enhancing the operational capabilities of the Command by ensuring speedy completion of infrastructure works. An Alumnus of Sainik School, Kunjpura, he joined the National Defence Academy in 1970 and was commissioned into the Flying Branch of the Indian Air Force on June 1ST, 1974. He is a Qualified Flying Instructor and has flown over 6,800 hours on various aircraft. The Air Marshal is a Graduate of the Defence Services Staff College, Wellington, Army War College, and Mhow and has an M. Phil. from Indore University in 2002. He has also attended Political and Strategic Higher Studies Course in Brazil. Air Marshal Singh had commanded two premier Transport Squadrons and also served as Chief Flying Instructor at the Flying Instructors' School. The Air Marshal had been Air Officer Commanding of a premier Flying Station, which is the cradle of Transport and Helicopter Fleet Training and also the staging base for the prestigious International Air Show of the country – 'Aero India'. The Air Marshal had held various prestigious posts at Air Headquarters. He has the distinction of being the first Pilot to land AN-32 and IL-76 aircraft at Thoise by night. For his Distinguished Service and Achievements, he was awarded the Vayu Sena Medal for Gallantry during Kargil Operations in 1999 and Ati Vishisht Seva Medal in 2006.

The Marshals

Paramjit Singh Gill, Air Marshal, PVSM, VM

Air Marshal Paramjit Singh Gill took over as the Senior Air Staff Officer (SASO), West Air Command (WAC) (June 8TH, 2012). He is an Alumnus of National Defence Academy and was commissioned in 1975 in the Fighter Stream. The Officer is experienced on the Gnat aircraft and MiG-23 BN. He has more than 1000 hrs of instructional flying and about 4000 hrs of total flying. He is a Qualified Flying Instructor (QFI), holding A2 Instructional Category and served as a Directing Staff at the prestigious Flying Instructors School, Tambram. He was Chief Instructor (CI) at Air Force Stn Bidar, Deputy Commandant and later Commandant at the College of Air Warfare, Secunderbad. He commanded the Tactical Air Centre (TAC) at Ambala; Air Force Station, Wadsar and was Air Officer Commanding, Air Force Station Kalaikunda, a model station for conduct of Air Exercises with Air Forces of friendly foreign countries. He has held appointments of Assistant Chief of Integrated Staff (Joint Operations), ACIDS (Joint Operations), at HQ IDS. He has been Air Officer Commanding, J & K Area and was SASO, CAC since August 2011 before assuming his present appointment as SASO, WAC. He was awarded PVSM and Vayu Sena Medal (VM) for Distinguished Services. He has been instrumental in formulation and planning of policies on Joint Services Operation, National Disaster Management and joint C4I2 architecture, at HQ IDS. He is an Alumnus of Defence Service Staff College, Higher Command and National Defence College.

MM Singh, Air Marshal, VrC

Air Marshal Man Mohan Singh (popularly known throughout the Armed Forces and outside as 'MM') was commissioned in January 1951 into the Fighter Stream. Promoted Wing Commander in 1965 he was Officer Commanding (OC) Flying at Bareilly, then commanded 24 Squadron (Gnats) and later went for training on the Sukhoi Su-7 fighter to the Soviet Union. He then inducted the aircraft into 26 Squadron, the first to fly it in the IAF. After a stint on the staff of HQ Western Air Command as Ops-1, looking after fighter operations, he took over 15 Squadron operating Gnats from Bagdogra. In the pre-December phase of the campaign the unit conducted air patrols to protect own territory as well as discreet incursions into what was then East Pakistan to provide air cover for Mukti Bahini and covert Indian operations.

The Marshals

MM Singh, Air Marshal, VrC (Cont.)

At this stage MM Singh was approved for promotion to the next rank and warned about a fresh posting. However the Gallant Air Warrior preferred to defer his promotion and stay with his Squadron to take them to war. The Squadron conducted its first strikes on enemy positions held by 4TH Frontier Force at Hilli. According to the Army after two strikes by four aircraft each from the 'Fighting Fifteen' the Pakistan Army vacated their defences in the area. The Unit continued to provide close air support in the Northern Bangladesh sector thereafter. Moving to **Dum Dum** on 8th December, the Squadron provided close air support (CAS) to the Army at Khulna, as well as conducting offensive strikes against river shipping, sinking two 10,000 tonnes capacity vessels at Chalna port. The Flying Lances achieved the distinction of operating thereafter from Agartala (from the 13th of December to be exact) till then considered unsuitable for fighter operations because of its short runway, a considerable feat in professional terms. The Squadron supported 57TH Mountain Division's successful heliborne crossing of the Meghna by providing air cover and fire support. The Flying Lances fully lived up to their motto 'Nihantavya Shtravaha' meaning 'annihilate the enemy'. Overall the fighting fifteen flew a total of 250 sorties during the War without losing a single aircraft or suffering any damage, with MM Singh himself flying 20 missions. After the war MM Singh was Station Commander, Tezpur then went to the USSR again, this time to do the training course for the SAM-3 missiles and later put the knowledge gained to good use as Joint Director, Air Defence at Air HQ. Promoted Air Commodore, he was consecutively Station Commander, Srinagar, attended the National Defence College (NDC) course and was Air-1 dealing with operations at HQ Western Air Command. As an Air vice Marshal, he did 3 years as the Senior Air Staff Officer at the headquarters of the newly formed South-Western Air Command at Jodhpur. As an Air Marshal he was once again posted at Air HQ this time as Air Officer in Charge Personnel (AOP) His last posting was as Air Officer Commanding in Chief (AOC-in-C, known colloquially as C-in-C) from where he retired in 1988 to settle in Chandigarh.

The Marshals

Gurinder Pal Singh, Air Vice Marshal, VM

Air Vice Marshal Gurinder Pal Singh (Retd.) is a Graduate from National Defence Academy. He was commissioned on 7TH July 1978 as a Transport Pilot. He has flown over 6000 hrs on Otter, Kiran, HT 2, HPT 32, Avro and An 32 aircraft. In over 31 years of Distinguished Service, he has held several prestigious appointments that include Air Force Examiner on An 32, Avro and Kiran aircraft at Aircrew Examining Board, Commanding Officer HQ CAC Communication Flight, Directing Staff at Defence Services Staff College Wellington, Joint Director Personnel Officers (Transports) at Air HQ, Chief Operation Officer at AF Station Agra, CO 12 Squadron and Chief Instructor at Fixed Wing Training Faculty (FWTF) AF Station Yelhanka, Air Officer Commanding at Air Force Station Jorhat prior to his present appointment as Additional Director General (A) at Dte Gen NCC. The Officer was awarded VM on 26TH January 2008. AVM G.P. Singh is an A2 Flying Instructor. At AF Stn Agra, while commanding an An 32 Sqn he simultaneously performed duties of COO for over a year due to service exigencies. The Officer took over as CI, FWTF on 19TH July 2004. His unflinching passion for excellence and professionalism resulted in award of 'Training Command Flight Safety Trophy' to FWTF for the year 2004–05 and 2005-06, in succession and the 'Best Flying Training Establishment' in 2006-07. As Second in Command at AF Stn Yelhanka his proactive participation in all spheres contributed significantly in smooth conduct of Aero India 2005 and 2007, besides being instrumental in ensuring sound Tarmac Management for over a 100 aircraft and a methodical Aircraft Static Display for both the Air Shows. As AOC AF Stn Jorhat, the systematic and meticulous Officer, demanded high standards and exactitude in all spheres of flying activity that resulted in a first ever An 32 night landing by IAF at an Advanced Landing Ground in Arunachal Pradesh. In spite of the constraints, his professional competence and constant involvement ensured a very high serviceability and availability of An 32 ac that further enhanced the operational preparedness of the IAF in the Eastern sector. Under his command the morale and happiness quotient of the Station, the proactive and willing attitude, especially the professional ego and pride in the uniform exhibited by all the personnel, was praiseworthy. The crowning glory was certainly the award of the 'Best Flying Station in Eastern Air Command' to 10 Wing, AF for the year 2009.

The Marshals

Sukhchain Singh, Air Vice Marshal, VSM

Air Vice-Marshal Sukhchain Singh was commissioned in the Indian Air Force in July 1979. A Post-graduate in Integrated Electronics from IIT Delhi, he has a vast experience in working on various aircrafts, radars and guided weapons systems. He was awarded the Vishisht Seva Medal in 2010. Currently Air Vice - Marshal Sukhchain Singh is a Senior Maintenance Staff Officer (SMSO) at the Gandhinagar based Headquarters South Western Air Command.

Jagjit Singh, Air Vice Marshal, VSM

Air Vice-Marshal Jagjit Singh has been promoted as Air Marshal and will take over as the Director General (Aircraft) at the Air Headquarters on June 1ST 2012. An Electrical Engineering (Hons.) Graduate from Thapar Institute of Engineering and Technology, Patiala, he joined the Indian Air Force in 1977. During his initial years, he served in the Missile Squadrons. For his Distinguished Service, Air Marshal Jagjit Singh was conferred the Vishist Seva Medal in 2007.

Kulwant Singh Gill, Air Marshal, AVSM, YSM, VSM

Air Marshal Kulwant Singh Gill took charge as the new Commandant of the National Defence Academy (NDA) at Khadakwasla in January 2013. The NDA is the only tri-services Academy of its kind in Asia that offers three-year training in Defence and Academics before the Cadets move on to their respective Officers' Training Academies for another one-year course and gets commissioned into the Armed Forces. It is controlled by the Integrated Defence Staff (IDS) and trains more than 2,000 Cadets, including those from friendly countries. Gill was commissioned in the Flying Branch of the Indian Air Force (IAF) in 1977 and has more than 7000 hours of accident-free and incident-free flying experience to his credit. He is also a Qualified Flying Instructor.In his career spanning 35 years, Gill has had the distinction of commanding various frontline bases of the IAF and also has the distinction of being the Contingent Commander for the first United Nations mission to Congo. While commanding the IAF station at Leh, he was instrumental in re-commissioning of two airfields. During his command, Air Force Station Leh was declared the 'Pride of Western Air Command'. Gill is a highly decorated Officer, having received the Presidential award of Vayu Sena Medal (Gallantry) in 1990, Yudh Seva Medal in 2005 and Ati Vishisht Seve Medal in 2010.

The Marshals

Manjit Singh, Air Vice Marshal

Air Vice Marshal Manjit Singh graduated from the Indian Institute of Technology, Kharagpur in 1957. He joined the Indian Air Force in 1959, after working with Krupp-Demag for two years. He served in various projects during his service of 33 years, including Air-to-Air Guided Missile, setting up a Base Repair Depot for Fighter Aircraft, Prithvi Missile, Overhaul of Mi-17 Helicopters. He was selected for the prestigious National Defence College course in 1988. He retired as an Air Vice Marshal in 1992. After his retirement, he took to the study of Consciousness as a serious whole-time hobby.

Jasjit Singh, Air Commodore, AVSM, VrC, VM

Air Commodore Jasjit Singh is former Director of Operations of the Indian Air Force. He joined the Indian Air Force in 1954 and graduated from the Indian Air Force Academy. He was awarded the Sword of Honour' and the Indian President decorated him with three Badges. He also earned the Badge of 'Atay Vitchisit Sifa' for Distinguished Service. Air Commodore Jasjit Singh has served the country at the frontline in many a battle, including in the war with China in 1962. A Decorated Soldier, he was posted at Tezpur in Assam when the war broke out. Post-retirement, he has served as the Director General of premier strategic institutions like the Institute of Defence Studies and Analysis (IDSA). Since 1987, he has been Director of the Institute for Defence Studies and Analyses, New Delhi. Singh is also a Consultant to the Standing Committee of Defence of Parliament; Advisor to the Finance Commission of India; and Member of the National Security Advisory Board. In 1990-91, he served as a Member of the International Commission for a New Asia. Air Commodore Singh has written extensively on strategic and security issues and is Author and Editor of more than two dozen books, including Air Power in Modern Warfare (New Delhi: Lancers International, 1985), Non-Provocative Defence (New Delhi: Lancers International, 1989) and Nuclear India (New Delhi: Knowledge World, 1998). During his Service he served in many key positions, including the Leadership of a MiG-21 Squadron and Director of Aviation Safety and Operations at Air Force Headquarters. Singh retired from the IAF in 1988.

The Marshals

Mehar Singh, Air Commodore, DSO, MVC,

Mehar Singh was selected for the Royal Indian Air Force in 1933 while he was in the final year of B.Sc. During his nearly three years of training at the prestigious Royal Air Force College in England, he impressed the college authorities by his single-mindedness, discipline and spirit of comradeship. His Commandant, Air Vice Marshall H.M. Grave wrote about him: "Keen, cheerful, hardworking and popular. His work compares favorably with that of English cadets. A creditable effort! And exceptionally good pilot, keen on games and has represented the college at hockey of which he is an excellent player." "Mehar Baba", affectionately called so by his colleagues and friends came out with flying colours. This brave, yet unassuming and modest Air Officer won the admiration and affection of his seniors as also of the men under him. Asghar Khan, an Officer under him, who later became Chief of the Air Staff of Pakistan, said about him, "With the solitary exception of Squadron Leader Mehar Singh, a pilot of outstanding ability, no one was able to inspire confidence among us." After his training in England, Mehar Singh joined No 1 Squadron. In the operations in the wild and mountainous North West Frontier Province, he flew in one month as many as a hundred hours. Mehar Singh, being fully adept at piloting Fighters, Bombers and Multi-engine Transport Planes, was asked to rescue women and children from a beleaguered Air Force station of Habbaniyah in May, 1948. He did the job so commendably that the next year he was called upon to evacuate refugees from Burma (Myanmar). In 1942, the Commander-in-Chief presented Mehar Singh a Commendation Certificate in recognition of his operational flying in Sind during the Hur disturbances in that province. A few months later, Mehar Singh accomplished a feat which, as per Air Officer Commanding-in-Chief, "any airman of any air force in the world would be proud to accomplish." Mehar Singh also took over the command of the Arakan area of Burma. There, too, he displayed his unique qualities of leadership and daring. Under the leadership of Mehar Singh, Squadron No 6 with its Hurricanes came to be known as the Eyes of the 14TH Army, commanded by Gen William Slim. After the war, Field Marshall Slim recorded, "I was particularly impressed with the conduct of the Squadron led by a young Sikh Squadron Leader (Mehar Singh). They were a happy and efficient unit." Remembering Mehar Singh, Lieutenant General Harwant Singh (Retd) observed, "Mehar Singh was one of the most celebrated fighter pilots of the Second World War. A pilot par excellence and a dare-devil, once in the cockpit, he became a part of the machinery."

The Marshals

Mehar Singh, Air Commodore, DSO, MVC (Cont.)

For his work in Arakan, which he accomplished with great skill and success, Mehar Singh was awarded DSO in March, 1944. In fact, he was the first and the only Officer of the IAF to have won this award. Soon after the war, Mehar Singh was called upon to assist in the task of reorganising and strengthening of the RIAF and the training of personnel. Promoted as Air Commodore in November, 1947, he took over Command No 1 Operational Group in Jammu and Kashmir. Mehar Singh was deeply attached to the Air Force, which made him an engineer and enabled him to gain experience in administration. He wished to leave it with honour but unfortunately that did not happen. In the interests of the Service, which he wanted to grow from strength to strength, he came to differ with some of his seniors on matters such as purchase of equipment, standard of discipline, programme for effectiveness, appointments, postings, and certain practices and trends in the administration. Instead of getting involved in any controversy or confrontation that might have affected discipline in the Service, he chose to resign. He wished to be considered as one of those several hundreds of Airmen who had joined and served the RIAF and had been written off. At the same time, this Patriotic Air Fighter did not forget his obligation to his motherland. In the event of any emergency, he said, he would like to be the first to offer his services. Thus went away from the Indian Air Force a legendary hero on September 27TH, 1948. When the Gallantry Awards were instituted, MVC (Maha Vir Chakra) was conferred upon Mehar Singh. An honour well deserved, indeed! But unfortunate as it may seem, it is, nevertheless, a fact that this nation soon forgets her sons who play heroic roles. Should not courage and integrity, professional competence and commitment to duty, love of the country and supreme sacrifices to uphold its honour ever remain worthy of grateful recognition and remembrance? What do we really do in this regard is a question to be pondered upon. After his retirement, Mehar Singh was personal adviser of Maharaja Yadvindra Singh (of Patiala), the Rajparmukh of PEPSU. At times he would fly the Rajparmukh to New Delhi and other places for important conferences and meetings. He flew the Rajparmukh to New Delhi for the conference of Governors and Rajparmukh for the last time on March 11TH, 1952. He was to take the Maharaja back to Patiala on March 17TH. An aircraft of the Escorts Ltd. that he was flying from Jammu to New Delhi on the night of March 16TH was caught in a storm, killing Mehar Singh. A worthy life was thus cut short abruptly!

The Marshals

Maverick of the skies

By Lieut-Gen Baljit Singh (Retd)

ONCE the history of any war is diligently imbibed, certain actions and deeds of individuals get imprinted so firmly in memory that they resurface time and again, with the least provocation. So it was that the mere mention of a school child's last name, a few days ago, brought to mind in a flash her late uncle, the indomitable Air Cdre Mehar Singh, D.S.O., M.V.C. Now, Squadron Leader Mehar Singh was conferred the first and the only D.S.O. of the Royal Indian Air Force during World War II. Again, within weeks of India's Independence, Air Cdre Mehar Singh would be marked for the IAF's first Mahavir Chakra. On both occasions, recognition came for gallantry and exceptional leadership on the battlefield in two different wars and under gruelling circumstances. By the time Field Marshal William Slim launched the reinvigorated XIV Army to defeat the Japanese in the India-Burma theatre in 1944, Mehar Singh's actions and deeds had already placed him in the league of legends. His reputation was aptly and amusingly summed up by the Field Marshal in his memoirs, recounting an impromptu visit to No 6 Squadron of the RIAF in the Arakan (Burma): "The last air patrol had run into a bunch of Zeros (Japanese fighter aircraft) and had been shot down. The Sikh Squadron Leader, an old friend of mine, at once took out the next patrol himself and completed the mission. His methods, rumours had it, were a little unorthodox. It was said that if any of his young officers made a bad landing, he would take them behind a *basha* and beat them. Whatever he did, it was effective; they were a happy, efficient and gallant squadron." It was not unusual to find entries in Mehar Singh's log book, flying upward of one hundred hours in a month, time and again. Flt Lieut Asghar Khan, who later became the Chief of Air Staff of Pakistan said: "With the solitary exception of Sqn Ldr Mehar Singh, a pilot of exceptional ability, no one was able to inspire confidence among us." Mehar Singh was probably in the class of born ace pilots but more than that, he was innovative and daring in his modus operandi. Perhaps his calibre as a flyer and leader was best illustrated when one of his pilots crash-landed but survived and walked back to the base. Within minutes of debriefing the pilot, Mehar Singh had the whole squadron airborne. It was an unmitigated tragedy when men of this one subcontinent would now be pitched in battles against each other but as citizens of two different nations. When on January 26TH, 1950, the Republic of India announced its first gallantry awards; Air Cdre Mehar Singh received the IAF's first Mahavir Chakra.

The Marshals
Maverick of the skies

Unlike the foot soldiers, Mehar Singh in his fighter/ bomber aircraft would be dropping bombs in the Poonch-Rajauri area in the west by night, and at dawn, strafing the enemy bunkers in the north along the Zoji La-Amarnath crest line, hundreds of kilometres apart. The moment of his ultimate glory came when he created aviation history by landing the first aircraft on the outskirts of Leh, by the banks of the river Indus. By January 1948, Pakistan's armed misadventure was fully contained in the Jammu region as also in the Srinagar valley. But for Mehar Singh's innovative bombing with Dakotas followed by the landing of the first one at a manually-levelled, mere 600-yard strip at Poonch, that tract of India would have been lost to Pakistan. However, it was the lack of road and aerial access to Ladakh year-long which was now a cause of serious concern. It was evident that for the moment airlift of troops and materials to Ladakh was the only course open. It was equally evident that the only man who could pioneer the aerial landing at Leh was Mehar Singh. In a one-to-one meeting, Major-Gen K S Thimmaya emphasized that "the fall of Leh would be a strategic blow to India. It had to be saved at all cost and that he was prepared to risk his own life with the IAF to save Leh."

Mehar Baba (as the Air Cdre was now affectionately called) explained that "the Dakota was not designed to fly at such high attitude." General Thimmaya knew that Mehar Singh never asked his subordinates to undertake a task that he himself had not first carried out, and so he closed the discussion on a positive note: "I will be on that flight in your cockpit. So let's go!" The stage was thus set for Mehar Baba when, on May 24TH, 1948, he landed the first Dakota at Leh, on an unprepared surface, 11,540 ft ASL. His passenger was Major-Gen K S Thimmaya D.S.O., GOC 19 Div. To land at Leh, one had to negotiate towering mountains in an ancient Dakota with no heating facilities, no pressurization and without any surveyed route map. A great pity that no photo-record was made of the first landing, though the next flight of six Dakotas also led personally by Mehar Baba on May 28TH was fully covered. The aircraft and crews were literally engulfed this time by the astonished Ladakhis. Four months after the Leh landing, Mehar Singh resigned his commission. On March 11TH, 1952, nine days short of his 33RD birthday, he died when the Bonanza aircraft, caught in a freak, sudden storm crashed on the outskirts of Delhi, snuffing out a charmed life.

ROYAL AIR FORCE

'On 1ST August 1940, when the Battle for France had been lost and Battle of Britain was imminent, there were almost one hundred Indian Air Force Volunteer Reserve personnel that reported to the Selection Board at Ambala and were commissioned on the very same day. Of them, 24 were hand-picked for secondment to the Royal Air Force and within four weeks, they had sailed from Bombay on board a P&O liner being used as a troopship to England. The 24 Indian officers, to be known as the IAFVR "X" Squad, were mostly between 19 and 25 years old, having had elementary flying training at various flying clubs in India, a large number of them from Walton, Lahore. The senior most amongst them was the redoubtable Man Mohan Singh who had "won" the Aga Khan Air Race ten years later and pioneered many other flights to other parts of the world and in India. Affectionately known to the IAFVR as "Chacha" (Uncle), Man Mohan was, at 34 years old, the most mature and experienced flyer in the Squad. The Indian contingent had, in fact, arrived at the height of the Luftwaffe's blitz against England and in the midst of what was to be immortalized as the Battle of Britain. The 24 Indians were shortly moved to a Flying School some miles South of Glasgow, in Scotland. After four weeks, the IAFVR 'X' Squad was split into two, young Shivdev Singh being amongst those who started advanced flying training near Liverpool where, once again, the Luftwaffe carried out a bombing raid. After a few more months of training, the Indian Pilot Officers were posted to various RAF squadrons and Shivdev Singh found himself posted to the famous No. XV (heavy bomber) Squadron flying the Short Stirling four-engined bomber aircraft, the very first to be so-equipped in the RAF. Hard flying training followed and Shivdev Singh's "extraordinary performance" got him onto an operational tour very quickly. Raids over Germany included night attacks on the German submarine pens at Kiel, the bombers flying through heavy ack ack fire with searchlights lighting up the night sky. Raids on German industrial centers in the Ruhr were equally tough and Shivdev's Stirling once got battered from flak, losing an engine, with flight controls damaged. Of the 24 Indian pilots who had volunteered to serve with the Royal Air Force in Britain, six did not measure up to standard and were assigned other general duties. Of the 18 who then flew with the RAF, seven were selected as fighter pilots, two of them, Ranjan Dutt and Mohinder Singh Pujji, distinguishing themselves.' (Pushpinder Singh)

Royal Air Force

The Royal Air Force Museum London presents an exclusive opportunity to view a documentary on Sikh fighter pilots, directed by Navdeep Kandola.

"Flying Sikhs - A History of Sikh Fighter Pilots" provides an intimate portrait of the Sikh pilots who contributed so valiantly to British success in World War I and World War II. The history of the Sikhs who flew in the Royal Flying Core, the Royal Air Force and the Indian Air Force has been forgotten, yet their bravery was recognized widely by both the military and the public during the dark days of the Blitz and the brutal Japanese invasion from the East. Drawing on interviews with the last remaining pilots, rare and personal archive materials, and unseen footage, Flying Sikhs pays testimony to the brave and selfless contributions these unsung heroes made to the war efforts across the world. The dramatic and often emotional documentary reveals the pioneering role that Sikhs have played in both introducing and sustaining aviation in India. It was a Sikh - the Maharaja of Patiala, Bhupinder Singh - who procured the first Bleriot monoplane and Farman biplanes in 1910. The first ever Indian pilot to try to enlist as a pilot in WWI was Hardit Singh Malik, the only Indian pilot to miraculously survive the war and later went on to become PM of Patiala and High Commissioner to both Canada and France. The documentary includes first hand accounts taken from the only TV Interview of Sardar Malik and a rare interview with his daughter Harji Malik. Also included are interviews with the last remaining Sikh pilots from WWII, Air Chief Marshal Arjan Singh DFC and Mohinder Singh Pujji DFC, who are both now in their nineties. Air Marshal Arjan Singh led pilots in the Burmese front in the Second World War and later led the Indo-Pak and Indo-China air assaults. Pujji had an impeccable record for bravery and saved a 300 strong battalion of lost American soldiers that were given up for dead in the dense Burmese forests. Although the countless other Sikh pilots from the Great Wars are now deceased, their histories are represented by the recollections of outstanding pilots such as Manmohan Singh, Mehr Singh DSO, Prithpal Singh and Air Marshal Shivdev Singh.

Royal Air Force

Hardit Singh Malik

As described then,"One of the first to be posted to the new squadron was Lieutenant Hardit Singh Malik, a Sikh from Rawalpindi. A keen cricketer and golfer, Malik was one of the most popular officers at Biggin Hill. He staunchly refused to part with his turban and somehow managed to fit over it an outsized flying helmet, earning the affectionate nickname of "Flying Hobgoblin" from the ground crews. Besides Malik the Sikh, the original fighter pilots of Biggin Hill included men from Australia, Canada, New Zealand, Rhodesia, Argentina, as well as the United Kingdom". After the armistice, Hardit Singh was posted to another Brisfit Squadron, No.11, at Nivelles near Brussels, before he finally returned home after the War, a hero in his own right. Hardit Singh Malik was to later join the prestigious Indian Civil Service. As a postscript, this remarkable man's chequered career included assignments as Trade Commissioner in London, Hamburg, Washington and Ottawa. He became Prime Minister of Patiala State and then, Indian High Commissioner to Canada; still later, he was named Ambassador to France. After retirement in 1956, he returned to his first love, golf, becoming India's finest player ever, even with two German bullets still embedded in his leg. Sardar Hardit Singh lived until he was 91, passing away in November 1985.

Man Mohan Singh

Man Mohan Singh was the first Sikh aviator and the first Indian to fly solo in a light aircraft from England to India, and in 1934-35, from England to South Africa. At the outbreak of the Second World War, Man Mohan Singh joined the Indian Air Force Volunteer Reserve as a Pilot Officer. He was selected as leader of an Indian Air Force batch of fliers sent to England for training and active duty. He was later promoted to Flying Officer and assigned operations in the Philippines and Indonesia, and given the command of a Catalina aircraft. Man Mohan Singh was killed in a flying accident in West Australia on 3RD March 1942.

Shivdev Singh, Air Marshal

Air Marshal Shivdev Singh was seconded to the Royal Air Force, as part of the reinforcement the British desperately needed in 1940 to fight the "Battle of Britain". Flying Sterlings over occupied France and Germany - including daring attacks on their submarine pens - he was decorated for Gallantry in a campaign that had many casualties. He was rushed back home when the Japanese besieged the South-East Asian region and flew the Hurricanes in the Arakan within Burma.

Royal Air Force

Mohinder Singh Pujji Squadron Leader, DFC, PCS, BA, LLB

In 1940, Mohinder Singh was one of 18 qualified Indian Pilots who volunteered for the Royal Air Force. Officially he flew just after the Battle of Britain, joining 43 Squadron the formidable 'Fighting Cocks' fighter Squadron. He flew Hurricanes which he preferred to Spitfires, for their relative ease of flying. He was forced down twice; in one instance, his aircraft was disabled over the English Channel by a Messerschmitt, but he managed to coax it to dry land, where he crashed. He was rescued from the burning wreckage and after a week in hospital, Mohinder Singh returned to duty. He was treated well in England, getting preferential treatment at local cinemas and restaurants, often without payment. As a Sikh, he insisted on retaining his Dastar (Sikh headdress), with RAF insignia, even while flying, even carrying a spare, in case it was needed. The Dastar interfered with use of his oxygen mask and resulted in damage to his lungs. After the Battle of Britain, Mohinder Singh was sent to the Middle East where, in 1941, he was forced down, for the second time, in the North African desert and was picked up by British troops. He had dietary problems, as he could not eat the standard issue bully beef for religious reasons. He returned to south Asia and served in Afghanistan and Burma, where was awarded his DFC. After returning to India, Mohinder Singh became a champion air race pilot and held gliding records. He had a career in India as an airline pilot. In 1974, he returned to Britain and became an air traffic controller. Mohinder Singh moved to East Ham after retirement and he became an active member of the local community. Later, he settled in Gravesend, Kent. On 12TH October 2000, he was made an Honorary Freeman of the Borough of Newham. Mohinder Singh Pujji died of a stroke at Darent Valley Hospital on 18TH September 2010, aged 92. The local authority Gravesham Borough Council, celebrated his life and heroism with an exhibition. Despite the high respect that he experienced during the War, Mohinder Singh believed that war films presented a "white-only view of the RAF". He campaigned to have the Sikh contribution to the British war effort, which he believed had been ignored, more widely recognised. He had had no invitations to any of the many events that took place in Britain to mark the 70th anniversary of the outbreak of World War II in 2010, or any other year, he says. He is quoted as saying, "As far as I think, no one in authority remembers that we are here and we were a part of World War II".

SIKH GOVERNORS

In India, Governors are the nominal heads of states with the real power being vested in the hands of the Chief Ministers of the respective states. The Indian Constitution has bestowed similar powers and functions to the Governors of states and Lieutenant Governors of Union territories as enjoyed by the President of India at the Union Level. Governors are appointed in states by the President for a term of 5 years. In the Union territories and in the capital city, Delhi, Lieutenant Governors are appointed by the President for the same period. The Governor is entitled to executive, legislative and discretionary powers. The Governor exercises executive powers in appointing the Chief Minister of the State and his Council of Ministers. He also appoints the Advocate General, the Chairman and the Members of the State Public Commission. The Governor has formal legislative powers over the dissolving of the Vidhan Sabha (Legislative Assembly) and summoning of both the houses of the State Legislature. While exercising these powers the Governor always has to act on the advice of the Chief Minister's Council of Ministers. A bill that has been passed by the state legislature will become a law after the consent of the Governor. Though he cannot reject a money bill, he can send back other bills for reconsiderations. He doesn't have the authority to reject a bill for the second time. The Governor uses his discretionary powers in certain situations. In the Vidhan Sabha elections if no party secures a majority the Governor has the authority to act on his own and ask the leader of the single largest party or the chosen leader of two or more parties to form the government. He then appoints that leader as the Chief Minister. Again when the state machinery breaks down due to improper administration the Governor can send a report to the President and ask him to impose President's Rule in the state. The Governors cannot be impeached from office as the President.

Sikh Governors

Arjan Singh, Governor Delhi
Arjan Singh served as Lieutenant Governor of Delhi from December 1989 to December 1990. He fought three major wars during his tenure with the Air Force and built up the Indian Air Force virtually from scratch. He then went on diplomatic assignments to Switzerland, the Vatican and Kenya. He was a Member of the Minorities Commission; and served as the Heut-Governor of Delhi. The Marshal of the Indian Air Force had managed to live a life in which he incorporated various roles. He had originally received a King's Commission by King George VI to the Indian Air Force, and had gone on to serve Independent India as well. He was honoured by both the British and the Indians.

Buta Singh, Governor of Bihar
Buta Singh was Chairman of the National Commission for Scheduled Castes (NCSC) and an Indian Congress Leader. He has been elected eight times as a Member of Lok Sabha. He is former Union Home Minister under Rajiv Gandhi's Government and more recently Governor of Bihar state, India. He took office on November 5TH, 2004 until his resignation on 29TH January 2006. He was the Home Minister of India during the early 1990s. He was first elected to the Indian Parliament in Sadhna. As the Governor of Bihar, Buta Singh's controversial decision to recommend the dissolution of the Bihar Assembly in 2005 was sharply criticised by the Supreme Court. The court ruled that Mr. Singh had acted in haste and misled the Federal Cabinet because he did not want a particular party claiming to form the Government, to come to power. Mr. Singh however claimed that the party was resorting to unfair means (read horse trading) to secure support to form the Government. On January 26TH, 2006 Buta Singh sent a fax to President Abdul Kalam offering to resign his post. The next day he left office and was replaced by West Bengal governor Gopal Krishna Gandhi

TS Oberoi, Governor of Andaman & Nicobar Islands
Lieutenant General (Retd) TS Oberoi, PVSM, VrC, is a former General Officer Commanding-in-Chief, Headquarters Southern Command, Pune. Former Inspector General, Special Frontier Force. Former Commandant, Headquarters Establishment. Under his able leadership, the Liberation of Bangladesh had commenced in the year 1971 during the Indo-Pak War. He served as Lieutenant Governor of Andaman & Nicobar Islands (December 1985 to December 1989)

Sikh Governors

Gurmukh Nihal Singh, Governor of Rajasthan

Gurmukh Nihal Singh was the first Governor of Rajasthan from 1ST November 1956 to 16TH April 1962. Gurmukh Nihal Singh read for the Bar from Temple Inn after his Masters in Economics from the London School of Economics. Shortly after his return home, his path crossed that of Pandit Madan Mohan Malviya, who was looking for a promising academic to start a Political Science Department in the Banares Hindu University. He stayed on for twenty years to see generations of students pass through the portal of the Political Science Department. Some twenty years later he decided it was time for change. He had not restricted himself to teaching and mentoring an unceasing flow of students who tasted the fruits of scholarship and devotion. He devoted sometime to writing books, including his landmark history of constitutional and political development, which was to become a classic for post-graduate students. Later on he worked on the life and teachings of Guru Nanak. From Banares he moved to Ahmadabad to take up the position of Head Lecturer, a four year stint in the College of Commerce. After a stint as a Chief Minister of Delhi, Gurmukh Nihal Singh consented to be the first Governor of Rajasthan, composed largely of the Princely States that had been brought together in the state's re-organisation exercise. After his one stint in Rajasthan, he was happy to return to Delhi to lead a retired life, given to much reading, some writing and minutely following political developments in the country. He died in Delhi on December 23RD 1969 at the age of 74.

Hukam Singh, Governor of Rajasthan

Sardar Hukam Singh was Governor of Rajasthan from 1967 to 1972. He was an eminent parliamentarian, a noted jurist, a social reformer and an able administrator. He was elected to the Constituent Assembly in April 1948; he was also a Member of the Provisional Parliament (1950-52) and the First, Second and Third Lok Sabhas. Sardar Hukam Singh was elected as Deputy Speaker of Lok Sabha on 20TH March 1956, and he was re-elected to the same post again during the Second Lok Sabha. He had also served as the Chairman of the Committee on Privileges, the Committee on Private Members' Bills and Resolutions and the Committee on Subordinate Legislation during the Second Lok Sabha. Unanimously elected as the Speaker of the Third Lok Sabha, Sardar Hukam Singh endeavored to follow and enforce the rules, procedures, practices and conventions of the House.

Sardar Hukam Singh passed away on 27TH May 1983.

Sikh Governors

Durbara Singh, Governor of Rajasthan

Sardar Durbara Singh was sworn in as Governor of Rajasthan on May 1ST 1998 and died after a short illness on 24TH May 1998. Durbara Singh was born on February 25TH, 1927 in Chak 26 J B Village of Lyallpur district (now in Pakistan). An Engineering Graduate from Punjab Engineering College, Roorkee, he was a Member or Office Bearer of various decision-making bodies, from the Panchayat to the Lok Sabha. He was elected Chairman of the Panchayat Samiti Shahot (Jalandhar-Punjab) in 1964 and became a Member of the Zilla Panchayat the same year. He won the Punjab Assembly elections thrice -- in 1967, 1969 and 1972. He was a Deputy Minister in the Punjab Government from 1968 to 1969. Later he was elected Speaker of the Assembly in 1969. He also won the Lok Sabha election in 1996 from Jalandhar. Apart from politics, he remained very active in fields of education and social work. He was founder president of the Guru Nanak National College for boys and another for girls in Nakodar in Jalandhar district.

In the State elections of 1980, he was elected to Punjab Legislative Assembly from Nakodar, and was appointed as Chief Minister on February 17TH, 1980. The 1980s were a turbulent time in the history of the Punjab, marked by an increase in violence and demand for a separate Sikh homeland. Sardar Durbara Singh remained Chief Minister for three years. During this time his Government was grappling with the rising Khalistan militancy in the state. There was a spate of assassinations, prime among them being the daylight murder of Lala Jagat Narain, Head of the Punjab Kesri group of newspapers of Jalandhar. This was followed by the assassination of DIG of Punjab Police Jalandhar range, Avtar Singh Atwal in the Golden Temple Complex. Due to the increase in terrorist violence, the tenure of the Ministry was cut short and the Durbara Singh Ministry resigned and President's Rule was imposed in the State under Art.356 of Indian Constitution on June 6TH, 1983. Sardar Durbara Singh was then elected to the Rajya Sabha in 1984, and served with distinction in the Council of States being elected the Chairman of the House Committee in 1986. Sardar Durbara Singh made a place for himself as a good Congress party functionary & a good manager of party affairs, having been posted as "Observer" and high command enforcer in different provinces. As a result of his success in managing party affairs he was entrusted with several crisis management assignments within the Congress party.

Sikh Governors

Surjit Singh Barnala, Governor of Tamil Nadu

Surjit Singh Barnala served as Chief Minister of the Punjab from September 29TH, 1985 until May 11TH 1987. He was also Governor of Tamil Nadu, Orissa, Uttarakhand and Andhra Pradesh. He has been a Minister in the Union Cabinet twice and a vice-presidential candidate once. Barnala Singh has been one of the earliest anti-Congress leaders and has contributed a lot to Indian politics. He was also the Party President of Shiromani Akali Dal. Surjit Singh Barnala was born on 21ST October 1925 in Ateli Village, now part of Nabha in Punjab. He was born to a well-to-do family, as his father was a magistrate. After doing matriculation, he went to Lucknow for higher studies. In the year 1946, he received his Degree in Law from Lucknow University. During his stay at Lucknow, in 1942, he plunged into the Quit India Movement. He started his career with practicing Law in District Court at Barnala. But in the late 60's he started his political career vigorously. In the 1952 election, he stood but lost by a margin of four votes. He was elected as MLA from Barnala Assembly Constituency in the year 1967, and thus delineated the Constituency till 1999. In the year1969, he was made the Education Minister of Punjab. And during his tenure, he was played a subservient role in establishing Guru Nanak Dev University in Amritsar. In the year 1977, when he was elected as MP, for the first time he was inducted as Cabinet Minister in Janata Party's Government headed by Morarji Desai. He was given the portfolios of Agriculture, Food, Irrigation and Rural Development. From 29TH September 1985, Barnala has served as the Chief Minister of the Punjab until 11TH May 1987. As the Member of the Sikh political party Shiromani Akali Dal, he was seated at the chair of Chief Minister in a very difficult and turmoil period of the Punjab. It was a period of terrorism in the Punjab. The State at that time, from 1983 to 1985, had been under President's Rule. Barnala was crowded out after nearly two years in office, and the State was put under President's Rule for another three years. Surjit Singh Barnala has served as the Governor of several States since then. From 1990 to 1991, he was first appointed as the Governor of Tamil Nadu. He served as the Governor of Uttarakhand from its formation in 2000 until 2003. After that from 2003 to 2004, he has served as the Governor of Andhra Pradesh. During that period he was also the acting Governor of Orissa. In November 2004, he took up again as Governor of Tamil-Nadu and remained in this position until 31ST August 2011.

Sikh Governors

Dr Shivinder Singh Sidhu, Governor of Manipur

Dr. Shivinder Singh Sidhu was Governor of Manipur from 6TH August 2004 until 23RD July 2008. Dr. Shivinder Singh Sidhu is a political personality and current Governor of Goa. An Indian Administrative Service (IAS) Officer of 1952 batch, Dr Sidhu was born on October 13TH, 1929. He has an MA in Economics from Delhi School of Economics, and Doctor of Philosophy (PhD) in Economics, University of Kanpur. Under the Uttar Pradesh State Government, he served as Secretary to three Chief Ministers of UP, served as District Magistrate, Kanpur and as Divisional Commissioner of Agra. Under the Central Government, he served as the Secretary to Government of India in the Ministry of Health and Family Welfare, Advisor to the Governor of Punjab, Secretary to Government of India, Ministry of Industrial Development, Secretary to Government of India-Ministry of Civil Aviation and Tourism. He has also served as the Chairman of Air India and Chairman of Indian Airlines and as an Advisor to the Governor of Tamil Nadu. Dr Sidhu has also served as the Secretary General, International Civil Aviation Organisation (ICAO), an organ of United Nations, Montreal, Canada-1988-1991. He has held special assignments in Commonwealth Secretariat for evaluation of Commonwealth Fund for Technical Development in Islands of South Pacific Ocean June-August 1994. He headed a non-governmental organisation called 'Foundation for Aviation and Sustainable' from May 1992 until August 4TH, 2004.

Sukhdev Singh Kang, Governor of Kerala

Sukhdev Singh Kang was the fourteenth Governor of Kerala from January 25TH, 1997 to April 18TH, 2002. He served as a Judge of the Punjab and Haryana High Court from February 1979 and was subsequently promoted and transferred as the Chief Justice of the Jammu and Kashmir High Court, a post he held from October 24TH, 1989 to May 14TH, 1993. Following his stint as the Governor of Kerala, he was appointed a Member of the National Human Rights Commission. He has since retired.

Joginder Singh, Sardar, Governor of Rajasthan

Sardar Joginder Singh was Governor of Rajasthan from 1ST July 1972 to 14TH February 1977.

Sikh Governors

Dr. Gopal Singh, Governor Goa

Dr. Gopal Singh (Dardi) (1917-1990), an eminent Punjabi writer, poet, journalist and critic, was born in Amritsar, Punjab. He did his M.A. in English at Khalsa College, Amritsar and for some time edited the weekly magazine Mauji of S.S. Charan Singh 'Shahid' after his death. While working as a Lecturer in D.A.V. and Khalsa Colleges at Rawalpindi, he began to take interest in politics and founded an English weekly paper "Liberator". After partition he also worked for nearly a year and a half as editor in the Publication Bureau of the Punjab University (then named as East Punjab University) stationed at Solan, Shimla. He got his Ph.D. Degree in 1943 from Punjab University, Lahore for his thesis "New Trends in Punjabi Literature". He was nominated to the Rajya Sabha and was then sent as Ambassador to Bulgaria in 1970. Then he was posted as the Lieutenant Governor of Goa, Daman and Dieu. He was honoured by the Punjab Government in 1961 as an outstanding writer of Punjabi. His pen name is 'Dardi'. Basically a poet and a critic, he also wrote biographies of Guru Gobind Singh in 1966 and Guru Nanak Dev in 1969 respectively. His monumental work and the most renowned in the Sikh community is the translation of Sri Guru Granth Sahib into English published originally in two volumes.

Harcharan Singh Brar, Governor Orissa

Harcharan Singh Brar was born on January 21ST, 1922 in the village Sarai Nagar. He graduated from Government College Lahore. He was elected MLA from Muktsar in 1960, again from Muktsar in 1962, Gidderbaha in 1967, Kot Kapura in 1969 and from Muktsar in 1992. An agriculturist by profession, he remained Governor of Orissa and Haryana, Chief Minister Punjab, Minister of Irrigation and Power, Minister of Health and Family Welfare; Deputy Minister from 1961 to 62 in the Cabinet of Late Chief Minister Mr. Partap Singh Kairon. He was a Member of Punjab Legislative Assembly from 1971-72. He was widely travelled to Australia, Singapore, Europe, England, Egypt, and few Middle East countries. He was a keen sportsmen and evinced interest in Cricket, Hockey, Tennis, Riding and Golf. He died in Chandigarh on September 6TH, 2009 after a long illness. He was 86 years old.

Sikh Governors

Ujjal Singh, Governor of Tamil Nadu

Sardar Ujjal Singh (1895-1983), Parliamentarian, expert in Finance and Government, was born on 27TH December, 1895 in Sindhi Sagar Doab of the Punjab (now in Pakistan). His education began in the conventional way. From the Gurmukhi School he went to Makatab madarsa to learn Urdu and Persian. He then went to the Khalsa Collegiate School at Amritsar. He finished his University education at Government College Lahore, where he received his Master's Degree in History. He was elected a Member of the Punjab Legislative Council in 1926. He retained the constituency till after the independence of India. In 1956 he was appointed a Member of the Finance Commission. He also became a Member of the first Shiromani Gurdwara Parbandhak Committee. He was Parliamentary Secretary (Home) in the Unionist Ministry in the Punjab from 1937 to 1942, when he resigned during the Quit India movement. He was nominated as a Sikh representative to the 1ST and 2ND Round Table Conferences held in London to discuss Constitutional Reforms for India, and was also a Member of the Viceroy's Consultative Committee on Reforms, but resigned in August 1932 as a protest against the Communal Award, which had been rejected by the Sikhs because it had ignored their interests as an important minority. Sardar Ujjal Singh was also a Member of the Sikh delegation that submitted a memorandum to Sir Stafford Cripps in March 1942. He was chosen by the Government to be one of the Indian delegates to United Nations' Conference on Food and Agriculture held in Quebec (Canada) in 1945. In 1946 he was elected a Member of the Constituent Assembly for preparing a constitution for free India. As a consequence of the Partition, 1947, S. Ujjal Singh had to abandon his vast estates in Pakistan and cross over to India as a homeless refugee. He was re-elected to the newly constituted Legislative Council of East Punjab and served as Minister of Industries and Civil Supplies, and again as Finance and Industries Minister between 1949 and 1956. He was a Member of the Second Finance Commission set up by Government of India from June 1956 to September 1957, a Member of Punjabi University Commission set up in 1960, Governor of Punjab from 1ST September 1965 to 27TH June 1966 and Governor of Tamil Nadu from 28TH June 1966 to 25TH May 1971. Sardar Ujjal Singh died in his New Delhi residence on 15TH February 1983.

Sikh Governors

Joginder Jaswant Singh, Governor of Arunachal Pradesh

The present Governor of Arunachal Pradesh is retired General Joginder Jaswant Singh. He took the office in 2008 and from then onwards he has been successfully carrying out all the responsibilities of a Governor. The Governor General Joginder Jaswant Singh comes from a family dedicated to the cause of the country. Both his father and grandfather have served in the Indian Army in the World Wars. He is married to Smt Anupama Singh who is an active socialist and works vigorously for the empowerment of women and up-liftment of children. The Governor has led and is still leading an enviable life. He has many feathers on his cap which have turned him into a valuable asset of the country. General Joginder Jaswant Singh was nominated to attend the prestigious National Defence Academy. He has done all the professional courses to include Defence Services Staff Course, Senior Command, Higher Command and National Defence College Courses.

Mrs. Serla Grewal, Governor of Madhya Pradesh

Mrs. Serla Grewal former Governor of Madhya Pradesh and a distinguished Civil Servant, died on January 30TH. 2002. She was 74. She leaves behind her husband, Mr. S.S. Grewal, a former Cabinet Secretary, and two sons. She became the second lady in the country to join the Indian Administrative Service in 1952. She held several important executive positions, both in Punjab and the Union Government. Her tenure as the Deputy Commissioner of Simla is remembered with as much appreciation as the diverse hierarchy of responsibilities shouldered by her in the fields of education, family welfare, food and supplies, and industry in Punjab. Her commitment to health and social growth took her to important forums like the World Health Organization and UNICEF, besides the headquarters of the UN Population Commission in the late '70s and early '80s. She was also associated with the Indian Council of Medical Research. She, as Deputy Secretary of Health in Punjab, played an important role in the setting up of the PGI. Later she became Secretary, Health, Government of India, and served on the Governing and Institute bodies of both the PGI and the AIIMS. She had the reputation of being a strict disciplinarian and an Officer who would not have any target missed. Her approach was that of a hard task master who insisted on propriety being maintained at all times. Subsequently, she became Secretary to the Prime Minister of India, and Governor of Madhya Pradesh.

Sikh Governors

Dr. Iqbal Singh, Governor of Pondichery

Dr. Iqbal Singh (born June 4TH, 1945) is the present Lieutenant Governor of Pondichery, India. He has held that position since July 2009. Dr. Iqbal Singh was born in a Freedom Fighters family, to (late) Shri Lal Singh and (late) Smt. Santokh Kaur. His Father, Shri. Lal Singh was present in Jallianwala Bagh, Amritsar, Punjab, during the Massacre carried out by the British, and it was by fortune that he survived the torment of British bullets on that fateful day. Shri Baba Balwant Singh, Maternal Uncle, also a veteran Freedom Fighter, suffered imprisonment several times for raising voice against the British Regime. Inheriting the spirit of patriotism, Dr. Iqbal Singh has always endeavoured to work for the cause of National Integration. He graduated in B.A. from Punjab University in 1969. Even during his college days, he took keen interest in Politics and took special interest in promotion of Hindi and Punjabi literature. He represented the Indian National Youth Congress in the International Youth Festival, 1978 held at Cuba. He held the position of General Secretary of Punjab Youth Congress and played a pivotal role in bringing the youth of Punjab into the fold of the Congress Party. He is an accomplished businessman. Dr. Iqbal Singh has the distinction of holding several significant positions in the Indian National Congress, including Secretary, All India Congress Committee for 12 continuous years and is a Permanent Member of the Congress Working Committee. As the Member of Parliament of Rajya Sabha from 1992–98, he was a Member of several important Committees, viz., Tourism, Steel, Scout and Raj Bhasha. Dr. Iqbal Singh raised his voice for the welfare of the downtrodden and children in the Parliament and has the unique distinction of having attended all the days of Sittings during Parliament Sessions without a single day's absence. As Chairman of the Committee constituted by the Ministry of Shipping, he received cargo ships "MT Guru Gobind Singh" and "HULL 869" from Korea. He was the Chairman-cum-Secretary of the Transport Committee, for the Satyagraha Centenary Celebration held to spread the message of "Peace, Non-Violence and improvement of Gandhian Philosophy in 21st Century". As a man of principles, he championed human values by organizing Anti Drug Campaigns and Blood Donation Camps. He organized marriages for girls from poor and downtrodden families. He has delivered several keynote talks in visual media and radio on important social issues. He was at the forefront in coming to the aid of Bihar flood victims by mobilizing sizeable aid for providing timely relief to the victims.

Sikh Governors

Gurbachan Singh, Governor of Manipur and Nagaland

Manipur Governor Gurbachan Singh Jagat recently took oath as the Governor of Nagaland at a ceremony in the Raj Bhavan. Born on July 1ST 1942, Governor Gurbachan Singh Jagat is an IPS (Retd) batch of 1966, Punjab Cadre. Among other posts that he held, Governor Gurbachan Singh Jagat was the Director General of Border Security Force from December 2000 to June 2002 and Director General, Jammu & Kashmir from February 1997 to December 2000. He also headed the Intelligence/Security apparatus as DIG (1982 – 1990). Governor Gurbachan Jagat also held the post of Chairman UPSC from April 2006 to June 2007 and was a Member UPSC from August 2002 to March 2006. Governor Gurbachan Jagat, Nagaland's New Governor Gurbachan Jagat is a recipient of Padmashree-1987, President's Police Medal for Distinguished Service–1992, Indian Police Medal for Meritorious Service –1982, J & K Government 'Police Officer of the Year' 2001, Paschimi Star, Sangram Medal, Special Duty Medal (Punjab and J&K), Aantrik Seva Suraksha Medal, Operation Rakhshak & Operation Vijay Medals.

Harcharan Singh Brar, Governor of Haryana and Orissa

Former Governor of Haryana and Orissa Harcharan Singh Brar died on September 6TH, 2009 at the age of 87. He was a Senior Congress Leader and is survived by his widow Gurbinder Kaur Brar. Brar, who remained Governor of Haryana from September 24TH, 1977 to December 9TH, 1979 and that of Orissa for around six months in 1976, was cremated in his native village Sarai Naga. He had taken over as Chief Minister of Punjab on August 31ST, 1995 after the assassination of the then Chief Minister Beant Singh in a bomb blast outside the Punjab and Haryana Secretariat in Chandigarh. He remained Chief Minister until November 21ST, 1996 and was also credited with the creation of Muktsar and Moga districts out of Faridkot district. Born on January 21ST, 1922 in village Sarai Naga to Balwant Singh. Brar graduated from Government College at Lahore and was elected MLA from Muktsar in 1960. He was elected MLA four times from different places including Muktsar in 1962, Gidderbaha in 1967, Kot Kapura in 1969 and from Muktsar in 1992. An agriculturist by profession, he remained Governor of Orissa and Haryana, Chief Minister of Punjab and Cabinet Minister in Punjab on several occasions. He widely traveled to Australia, Singapore, Europe, England, Egypt, and a few Middle East countries and was a keen sportsman and evinced interest in Cricket, Hockey, Tennis, Riding and Golf.

PROMINENT SARDARS

Sir Yadvinder Singh, Maharaja of Patiala

Maharaja Sir Yadvinder Singh Mahendra Bahadur, GCIE, GBE was Maharaja of Patiala from 1938 to 1974. He served in the Patiala State Police and became its Inspector General and served in Malaya, Italy and Burma during the Second World War. He succeeded his father, Maharaja Bhupinder Singh, as the Maharaja of Patiala on 23RD March 1938, but agreed to the incorporation of the princely state into India on 5TH May 1948. He was Rajpramukh of the new Indian state of Patiala and East Punjab States Union until it was merged with Punjab in 1956. Sir Yadavindra served as President of the British Indian Olympic Committee from 1938–1947 and as President of the Indian Olympic Committee from 1947-1960. He was also instrumental in organizing the Asian Games. He founded Yadavindra Public School, a premier public school. Following his accession to the throne of Patiala, Sir Yadavindra pursued a political and diplomatic career, serving as Chancellor of the Chamber of Princes from 1943-1944. In 1947 when India gained Independence he was the Pro-Chancellor of Chamber of Princes, at a special session he said "After centuries time has come when India has gained independence from foreign rule and its the time when we all (princely states) should unite for our motherland" and persuaded many other rulers to join the Indian Union. He continued his career from 1956 onwards, serving as Indian Delegate to the UN General Assembly from 1956–1957 and to UNESCO in 1958. He also headed the Indian delegation to the FAO on and off from 1959-1969. Sir Yadavindra served as Indian Ambassador to Italy from 1965–1966 and as Indian Ambassador to the Netherlands from 1971 until 17TH June 1974, when he died suddenly in office at The Hague from heart failure, aged 61 after a reign of 36 years. On the specific instructions of Indira Gandhi he was cremated with Full State Honours on the longest and hottest day of the year. ***Honours;*** King George V Silver Jubilee Medal-1935, King George VI Coronation Medal-1937, Knight Grand Cross of the Order of the British Empire (GBE)-1942, 1939-1945 Star-1945, Burma Star-1945, Africa Star-1945, Italy Star-1945, British War Medal-1945, India Service Medal-1945, Knight Grand Commander of the Order of the Indian Empire (GCIE)-1946, Indian Independence Medal-1947, Grand Cross of the Romanian order and Grand Cross of the Order of Merit of the Republic of Italy-1966

Prominent Sardars

Giani Zail Singh, President of India

Zail Singh was born on May 5TH 1916 and died on December 25TH 1994. He was the President of India from 1982 to 1987 and the first Sikh to hold India's highest public office and honour. Zail Singh's public life was long and varied. He was a Freedom Fighter, State Congress Leader, Chief Minister and Union Minister. A prominent fighter against principality, feudalism and foreign domination in the pre-independence days, he is also remembered for his campaign against communalism, economic inequality and social injustice in the country.

When he was barely 15 years old, Singh became active in the politics of the Akali Dal, a Sikh organization that opposed British rule. He pursued traditional studies in Sikh holy books and earned the title *Giani* ("Learned Man") for his scholarly mastery of the scriptures. In 1938 he established the Praja Mandal, a political organization allied to the Indian National Congress, in his home district of Faridkot. This insurrectionary act earned him a five-year jail sentence. During his incarceration, he took the name Zail Singh.

After India became independent in 1947, Singh served in Parliament (1956–62) and was Chief Minister of Punjab (1972–77). When Prime Minister Indira Gandhi was voted out of power in 1977, Singh continued to support her. After returning to office in 1980, Gandhi rewarded his loyalty by naming Singh Minister of Home Affairs. He held the post until 1982, when he was named the Congress Party's Presidential Candidate. Many viewed Singh's easy elevation to the Presidency as a way for Gandhi to appease extremist Sikhs in Punjab.

He was an impotent bystander in 1984 when Government troops stormed the Golden Temple in Amritsar, the Sikhs' holiest shrine, in an effort to apprehend militants who were demanding independence for the state of Punjab.

Four months after Government troops stormed the Golden Temple; however, Gandhi was assassinated by her Sikh bodyguards. Zail Singh named Gandhi's son, Rajiv, to succeed her. His relations with Rajiv Gandhi were rocky at best and he soon fell out of favour with the new Prime Minister. Singh further inflamed the Government by refusing to sign into law a 1987 bill permitting official censorship of private mail.

Zail Singh died in 1994 following a car crash.

Prominent Sardars

Dr. Manmohan Singh, Prime Minister of India

Dr. Manmohan Singh is fourteenth Prime Minister of independent India and the original architect of the economic liberalization. Dr. Manmohan Singh is a man of high moral standing and accomplishment. He is also the first Sikh to have reached the country's top legislative position. Singh's rise to the position from humble beginnings and basic simplicity can be described as a rise from the masses. Singh was born in Gah in West Punjab (now in Pakistan) on September 26TH, 1932. Displaced by partition, he came to live in Amritsar along with his parents. He studied Economics in Chandigarh and later went to Cambridge and Oxford UK for higher studies. His qualification reads MA, DPhil (Oxford), DLitt (Honoris Causa). He then taught Economics at the Punjab University, Chandigarh while serving there as a Senior Lecturer (1957-59), Reader (1959-63) and Professor (1963-65). He was Professor of International Trade, Delhi School of Economics, University of Delhi during 1969-71. He was Honorary Professor at Jawaharlal Nehru University, New Delhi, 1976, and at Delhi School of Economics, University of Delhi, 1996. He was Wrenbury Scholar, University of Cambridge, 1957. He was also a National Fellow, National Institute of Education, NCERT, 1986. He was Honorary Fellow at St John's College, Cambridge UK, 1982; Indian Institute of Bankers, 1982; All India Management Association, 1993; and Nuffield College, University of Oxford, Oxford, 1994.

He started his stint as a Civil Servant in 1971-72 when he became Economic Advisor in the Ministry of Foreign Trade. He then served as Chief Economic Advisor, Ministry of Finance during 1972-76. During 1976-80 he served as Secretary, Department of Economic Affairs, Ministry of Finance; Member, Finance, Atomic Energy Commission; Member, Finance, Space Commission; Director, Reserve Bank of India; Director, Industrial Development Bank of India; Alternate Governor for India, Board of Governors, Asian Development Bank; and Alternate Governor for India, Board of Governors, IBRD. He was Member-Secretary, Planning Commission during 1980-82, and Chairman, India Committee of the Indo-Japan Joint Study Committee during 1980- 83.He served as Governor, Reserve Bank of India from September 16TH, 1982 until January 14TH, 1985. During 1982-85, he was also Alternate Governor for India, Board of Governors, and International Monetary Fund. He was Member, Economic Advisory Council to the Prime Minister in 1983-84. He served as President, Indian Economic Association in 1985.

Prominent Sardars

Dr. Manmohan Singh, Prime Minister of India (Contd.)

In August 1987, he became Secretary-General and Commissioner, South Commission, Geneva. In December 1990, he was made Advisor to the Prime Minister on Economic Affairs followed by Chairman of University Grants Commission in March 1991.

When P.V. Narasimha Rao became the Prime Minister, he plucked Dr. Singh from relative obscurity to become Finance Minister in a Congress Party-led Government. Thus, a Professor, Economist and Civil Servant entered Politics. He served the country as Union Finance Minster from June 21ST, 1991 to May 15TH, 1996.

He is credited for ushering in the policy of 'Liberalization, Privatization and Globalization', which has since then changed the face of Indian economy. During his tenure, he nudged India's socialist economic policy down the road of reforms and deregulation, opening up the country for outside investment for the first time.

Though he had entered the post when the Indian economy was stuck in a quagmire with its foreign exchange reserves near rock bottom, and the country close to defaulting on its international debt Singh managed to reverse nearly half a century of socialist planning and excessive bureaucracy. He implemented sweeping reforms ending the "license Raj", the regulations that forced businesses to get Government approval to make nearly any decision. He also devalued the rupee, slashed subsidies for domestically produced goods and privatized some state-run companies.

Dr. Singh was elected to Rajya Sabha from Assam on Congress ticket in October 1991 and was re-elected in June 1995 and June 2001. In March 1998, when the BJP-led NDA formed the Government, he became the Leader of the Opposition, Rajya Sabha. He also served as a Member of several Parliamentary Committees including those on Finance, Rules, Privileges, General Purposes, etc.

In 2004, the Congress Party and its President Sonia Gandhi put faith in him and thus, India got its first economist Prime Minister. Earlier, no Indian could think that a low-profile person like Dr. Singh could ever become the country's Prime Minister. And in 2009, he returned for the second term after successfully completing his first term as the Prime Minister. Singh has a following across party lines, with a clean reputation both as a Politician and as an Economic Reformer.

Prominent Sardars

Sardar Swaran, Foreign Minister of India

Sardar Swaran Singh born on August 19TH, 1907, was an Indian politician and longest serving Union Cabinet Minister. He completed his Intermediate (High school) at Randhir College in Kapurthala. He then joined Government College, Lahore and completed a Degree in Physics with Honors. He then worked as a Lecturer in Physics in Lyallpur Khalsa College. After leaving this job he studied law in Government Law College in Lahore and received his L.L.B in 1932. He started a law practice near his birth village in the nearby town of Jalandhar - he specialized in criminal suits. In 1930s he joined the Akali Dal political party and was a prominent leader in the mid-1940s. He played an important role in the compromise between the Indian National Congress Party and the Akali Dal in the early 1940s. Just before the 1946 elections, the Panthic Party was formed with Baldev Singh as the Leader and Sardar Swaran Singh was elected its Deputy Leader. In 1946 he was elected a Member of the Punjab Legislative Assembly. He then became Parliamentary Secretary to the Punjab Coalition Government. He was a Member of the Punjab Partition Committee where he played an important role. On 15TH August 1947, the day of Indian Independence he was sworn in as Home Minister in the Cabinet of the State of Punjab. At the same time the capital of the Punjab was shifted from Shimla to Jalandhar. On 13TH May 1952 he resigned his position here when Jawaharlal Nehru included him in the Government. He remained in successive Governments until he resigned in November 1975. To this date he is the longest-serving Union Cabinet Minister in India. He is best known for his role as India's Foreign Minister. He was also President of the National Congress in 1969, and 1978. He visited the USSR in July 1966 along with then Prime Minister Indira Gandhi. Sardar Swaran Singh was Chairperson of the Committee entrusted with the responsibility of studying the Constitution of India in 1976 during the national emergency. Soon after the declaration of the national emergency, Indira Gandhi constituted a Committee under the Chairmanship of Sardar Swaran Singh to study the question of amending the Constitution in the light of past experiences. Based on its recommendations, the Government incorporated several changes to the Constitution including the Preamble, through the Forty-second Amendment of the Constitution of India (passed in 1976 and came into effect on 3RD January 1977) He passed away on October 30TH, 1994

Prominent Sardars

Montek Singh Ahluwalia, Civil Servant, 'Padma Vibhushan'

Montek Singh Ahluwalia (born 24TH November 1945) is an Indian Economist and Civil Servant. He is currently the Deputy Chairman of the Planning Commission of the Republic of India. Montek Singh Ahluwalia is Deputy Chairman of the Planning Commission for India. For his outstanding contribution to economic policy and public service, he was conferred the prestigious 'Padma Vibhushan' by the President of India in 2011. He was previously the first Director of the Independent Evaluation Office at the International Monetary Fund. Montek Singh Ahluwalia was born in Rawalpindi, Pakistan. He is Half Bengali and Half Punjabi. He studied at St. Patrick's High School, Secunderbad, Delhi Public School, Mathura Road, and Bishop Cotton School Shimla, and then graduated with a B.A. (Hons) Degree from St. Stephen's College, Delhi, and University of Delhi. He received the BA (Hons) Degree as a Rhodes Scholar from the University of Oxford having studied at Magdalene College, Oxford. He also studied for a BPhil in Economics at Oxford University, which the University later reclassified as an MPhil. While at Oxford, he was the President of the prestigious Oxford Union. The 164-year-old Indian Institute of Technology, Roorkee, conferred him with the Degree of Doctor of Philosophy (Honoris Causa) at the 11th Convocation Ceremony of the Institute held on 12TH November 2011. Ahluwalia, after graduating from the University of Oxford, joined the World Bank during the tenures of Hollis Chenery and Robert MacNamara. At the age of 28, he became the youngest "Division Chief" in the World Bank's bureaucracy. Prior to taking up his position at the IMF, Ahluwalia was a Member of the Planning Commission in New Delhi as well as a Member of the Economic Advisory Council to the Prime Minister. In spite of not being a Member of the Indian Civil Service, he held the following positions of Civil Servants in the Central Government: Secretary, Ministry of Finance Secretary, Department of Economic Affairs Secretary, Ministry of Commerce Special Secretary to Prime Minister Rajiv Gandhi, and Economic Advisor to the Ministry of Finance. In 2007 he became a Member of the influential Washington-based financial advisory body, the Group of Thirty. He has extensively published works on Indian economy. Ahluwalia is married to fellow economist Dr. Ishar Judge Ahluwalia and has two children.

Prominent Sardars

Manjeev Singh Puri, Ambassador

Ambassador Manjeev Singh Puri is India's Deputy Permanent Representative to the United Nations. Prior to taking over his present assignment in New York, Ambassador Puri was Joint Secretary (United Nations – Economic & Social) in the Ministry of External Affairs from March 2005 to March 2009. His charge included dealing with UN and multilateral bodies involved with economic and social issues, including in the areas of development, finance, human rights, migration, humanitarian affairs and UNESCO related matters. Ambassador Puri was also closely involved with the Sherpa negotiations of the G8/G5 Summits from 2005 onwards and other major international forum of which India was a member, including ASEM, IBSA etc. Following the Heiligendamm Summit of 2007, he represented India at meetings of the Working Group on Development and in several meetings on energy and climate issues leading up to the Tokyo G8/G5 Summit in 2008 and thereafter. A key element of Ambassador Puri's charge in New Delhi was climate change and he has been very closely involved with the negotiations on climate change in the context of the G8/G5 Summits and at the UNFCCC. He was a Member of the Indian Delegation at the Conference of Parties to the UNFCCC in Montreal in December 2005, Nairobi 2006 and at Bali in December 2007, where he was among the small group of negotiators in the final rounds of negotiations for the Bali Plan of Action. Ambassador Puri was also the coordinator of India's participation in the Major Economies Meeting and served on the Executive Board of the Asia-Pacific Partnership on Clean Development and Climate. After moving to New York, he has continued his association with climate change and was a Member of the Indian delegation to the UNFCCC Conference of Parties held in Copenhagen in December 2009 where he participated in the high-level negotiations among the select group of countries.

Ambassador Puri is on the Advisory Board of TERI (The Energy and Resources Institute, New Delhi).

He is married (wife: Mrs. Namrita Puri) and has two children.

Prominent Sardars

Hardeep Singh Puri, Diplomat

2008-2009 Secretary (Economic Relations), Ministry of External Affairs, Government of India, New Delhi Ranking Official for Economic Diplomacy responsible for all multilateral economic issues including those relating to the United Nations, WTO and international financial institutions and for trade finance, investment and technology promotion. He coordinated key policy initiatives such as in Energy Security and Food Security. Headed India's Overseas Technical and Development Cooperation Programme - the largest South-South initiative of its kind. 2006-2008 Ambassador of India to Brazil Oversaw transformation of bilateral relations encompassing exponential increase in trade, investment, technological, defence and energy cooperation, political and strategic collaboration, cultural contacts and social sector interaction, and multilateral partnerships including the path-breaking India-Brazil-South Africa (IBSA) initiative and BRICs related dialogue. 2002-05 Permanent Representative of India to the United Nations and other International Organisations in Geneva Proactively negotiated/facilitated first-ever Public Health Treaty - the Framework Convention on Tobacco Control, Outcomes of the two World Summits on Information Societies, UNCTAD XI Conference Outcome – the Sao Paulo Consensus, the establishment of the Human Rights Council, Development Agenda in WIPO. 1999-2002 Ambassador/Deputy High Commissioner of India to the United Kingdom Administrative Head of India's largest diplomatic mission at a crucial phase in bilateral relations; facilitated the establishment of "Friends of India" groups in all major political parties in UK; established institutional frameworks for intensifying India-UK corporate interaction; launched programmes to broad-base bilateral economic ties by reaching out to all regions of UK; structured and enhanced engagement with the Indian Diaspora; Representative of India to The Commonwealth. 1997-1999 Joint Secretary (Europe West), Ministry of External Affairs, Government of India, New Delhi Head of the territorial division; coordinated bilateral relations with Western European countries. Dealt with the EU, EFTA, The Commonwealth. 1994-97 Joint Secretary to the Government of India, Ministry of Defence, New Delhi First Foreign Service Officer seconded to serve as Head of Division responsible for the Indian Navy; Also headed Defence Planning and Coordination division responsible for Army-Air Force-Navy cooperation; Coordinated India's International Defence Cooperation. 1992-94 Joint Secretary (Americas), Ministry of External Affairs, Government of India, New Delhi

Prominent Sardars

Hardeep Singh Puri, Diplomat (Contd.)

Worked on key initiatives that transformed bilateral relations, including the areas of Security and Strategic Cooperation, Human Rights, Science and Technology Cooperation, and Economic and Business Partnerships. Leader of the Indian Delegation to the 2nd and 3rd rounds of Indo-US dialogue on Disarmament and Non-Proliferation. 1991-92 Director (Foreign Secretary's Office), Ministry of External Affairs, Government of India Chief of Staff to the Head of the Diplomatic Service. 1988-91 Coordinator, UNDP/UNCTAD Multilateral Trade Negotiations Project to help Developing Countries in the Uruguay Round of MTNs Provided technical support, capacity-building assistance and advice to developing countries participating in the GATT Uruguay Round resulting in the establishment of the WTO. 1984-88 First Secretary/Counselor (Political), High Commission of India, Colombo. Assisted in the negotiations of the historic India-Sri Lanka Agreement for Peace and Normalcy in Sri Lanka (1987); Political Officer of the Indian Peacekeeping Force. 1981-84 First Secretary, Permanent Mission of India to GATT, Geneva Chairman, Committee on Subsidies and Countervailing Measures. 1979-81 Under Secretary (Foreign Service Personnel), Ministry of External Affairs, Government of India, dealing with human resources management of the diplomatic service. 1978-79 Officer on Special Duty (Press Relations) in the Spokesman's Office, Ministry of External Affairs, New Delhi. 1976-78 Third Secretary (Language Trainee)/ Second Secretary (Political & Commercial), Embassy of India, Tokyo. 1974 Joined the Indian Foreign Service. Obtained his Graduate and Post-graduate Degrees with top honours from Delhi University and spent a year on the teaching faculty of St. Stephen's College, New Delhi (1973-74). Accomplished debater and public speaker, has won many University prizes and was Prime Minister of the Hindu College Parliament (1971-72). Married to Ambassador Lakhmir Puri, also an Indian Foreign Service Officer. They have two daughters. 1982-2007 Experience in International Trade Law and Dispute Resolution Membership and Chairmanship of several GATT and WTO International Trade Dispute Settlement Panels covering key areas of Trade Law. He is former President of the United Nations Security Council and currently he is Chairman of the United Nations Security Council Counter Terrorism Committee.

Prominent Sardars

Kewal Singh, Foreign Secretary

Kewal Singh (1915 - 1991) was an Indian Diplomat, Foreign Secretary and India's Ambassador to the USSR, Pakistan and USA. He was born in 1915 and was educated at the Forman Christian College, Lahore, the Law College, Lahore and at the Oxford University. He joined the Indian Civil Service in 1939 and served in Punjab in various administrative positions until Independence after which he opted for the Indian Foreign Service. Kewal Singh was appointed the first Indian Chief Executive of Pondichery after the French handed control of the territory back to India and later served at Indian missions in Stockholm, London and in Germany. Kewal Singh was India's Ambassador to Portugal in 1962 when India's annexation of Goa led to the breaking off of diplomatic relations between the two nations. A similar fate befell him in 1965 when, as High Commissioner to Pakistan, he had to leave that country after the cessation of diplomatic relations between the two countries following the Indo - Pak War of 1965. He served as India's Ambassador to the USSR from 1966 - 1968 and as Ambassador to the USA from 1976 - 1977. He succeeded T. N. Kaul as Foreign Secretary, serving from November 1972 to October 1976. India took over Sikkim, its protectorate, following prolonged internal disturbances there while Singh was Foreign Secretary. During his tenure, India signed an agreement for demarcating the maritime boundary with Sri Lanka and led a series of talks with the then Pakistani Foreign Secretary Agha Shahi on normalizing communications and travel between the two countries. Following his retirement as the Ambassador to USA, Kewal Singh taught at the UCLA and at Kentucky University's Patterson School of Diplomacy and International Commerce where he was Distinguished World Statesman in Residence until his death in 1991.

Gurdial Singh Dhillon, Minister of Agriculture

Gurdial Singh Dhillon (1915-1992), Parliamentarian, Diplomat and Statesman, was born at Sarhali, in Jalandhar district of the Punjab, on 6TH August 1915. Gurdial Singh was educated at the Khalsa Collegiate School, Amritsar and at Government College, Lahore, from where he graduated in 1935. Gurdial Singh Dhillon was Member of the Legislative Assembly in Punjab from 1952 till 1967, when he was first elected to the Indian Parliament representing Taran Taran Parliamentary Constituency. He was elected Speaker of Indian Parliament from 1969 to 1975 and served as Minister of Agriculture in Indian Government from 1986-1988. He also served as Indian High Commissioner to Canada from 1980-1982.

Prominent Sardars

Navtej Singh Sarna, Diplomat

Navtej Sarna is an Indian author-columnist, and diplomat, who is the present Indian Ambassador to Israel. He was born in Jalandhar, India to noted writer in Punjabi, Mohinder Singh Sarna, and passed out of the 1980 Class of Indian Foreign Service. Before holding this post, he was Joint Secretary for external publicity at the Ministry of External Affairs (MEA), since October 2002, and holds the distinction of being the longest-serving Spokesperson of the Ministry, and served two Prime Ministers, three Foreign Ministers and four Foreign Secretaries, till the end of his term in September, 2008. Previously as a Diplomat he served in Moscow, Warsaw, Thimphu, Geneva, Teheran and Washington, DC.

Navdeep Singh Suri, Diplomat

Navdeep Suri is a Member of the Indian Foreign Service since 1983 and currently heads the Public Diplomacy Division of the Ministry of External Affairs. He has earlier served as India's Consul General in Johannesburg from August 2006 to October 2009 and as Head of the West Africa Division of the Ministry of External Affairs in New Delhi from December 2004 to August, 2006. Mr. Suri's first diplomatic assignment was at the Indian Embassy in Cairo from 1984 to 87, where he also studied Arabic. This was followed by a three-year stint in Damascus before a return to headquarters in New Delhi in early 1991. He moved to the Indian Embassy in Washington DC in 1993 and worked as the Political Counsellor there till his transfer to the position of Deputy High Commissioner at the Indian Mission in Dar es Salaam in 1997. He worked at the Indian High Commission in London from August 2000 to August 2004. Mr. Suri speaks Arabic and French, has a Masters Degree in Economics, and is an Alumnus of the 2010 USC Summer Institute in Public Diplomacy. Navdeep is also co-author of the study *Development Strategy as a Determinant of Foreign Policy: A case study of India and Pakistan*. His authoritative work on Indo-African relations has been published in 'India's Foreign Policy', while his study titled *'Outsourcing and Development'* was presented at the Inter-Government Experts Meeting organized by UNCTAD and has been published in a recent US book on the winners and losers of globalization. He is married, lives in Delhi with his wife Mani and daughters Manveena and Jessleena and is fond of travel, books, cinema, golf and cricket.

MAN ON A MISSION

Narindar Singh Dhesi, Author

The life of Narindar Singh Dhesi has witnessed enormous changes in the fortunes of his people, the Sikhs, and their inextricable links with the United Kingdom and the lands which once constituted its Empire. When he was born to Punjabi parents in Kenya in 1940, the British Empire was still the largest empire that humanity had ever created and a British Viceroy in New Delhi ruled the peoples of India on behalf of a British King-Emperor. Today, India is one of the rising giants of the post-Cold War order, while the UK struggles to decide its place in the world, maintaining huge global commitments with the budget of what is essentially a small European nation. It is the story of the military role of the Sikhs before and throughout this process that Mr Dhesi seeks to tell, and it is his experiences as a young man in the British Army, as well as the memories of his father's fight for justice for Sikh and Indian rights within the Empire, that have impelled him to explore this in his later years and to share it with the reading public. Narindar Singh Dhesi saw at first hand the dismantling of the British Empire as a soldier in Aden, and its subsequent redefinition as just one other member of NATO when he was stationed in Germany. It was when he was on leave from his regimental headquarters in Minden, West Germany, that an episode occurred which stayed in his mind and eventually inspired his present works. Having travelled back to London to spend his leave there, he stayed at the Union Jack club. On the marble walls in the foyer of this institution, he saw inscribed the names of Sikh soldiers who had won the greatest British military honour of all, the Victoria Cross. While he soon travelled back to Germany to resume his military service, the memory of these five valiant men remained in his mind over the subsequent decades. Having achieved promotion to non-commissioned officer in the British Army, Narindar Singh Dhesi returned to the United Kingdom after six years of service and entered the construction industry. It is an irony that in a situation today with people of ethnic minorities being actively targeted for police recruitment, it was only the institutional racism of the British police force in the 1960s that prevented him from continuing to serve his country and perhaps even appear in his third volume *'Sikh Soldier :Policing the Empire'*. After a long career in construction, Narindar Singh Dhesi retired and decided to revisit the memories of his younger days by researching the five Victoria Cross winners.

Man on a Mission

Narindar Singh Dhesi, Author (Contd)

While trawling the archives of the National Army Museum in London to research the citations of these men, Narindar Singh Dhesi encountered a number of retired Sikh military officers. He was shocked to discover that even these men were unaware of the scale of Sikh gallantry within the British and Indian Armed Forces. As he writes: 'One is always tempted to ask why this tiny community has made such disproportionate sacrifices.' It was then that he decided to widen the scale of his research to produce a series of volumes to illustrate to the ordinary reader the huge commitment of the Sikh soldier to the military tradition and to make his mission to record and highlight the most neglected part of Sikh martial heritage.

Narindar Singh Dhesi has since had published four volumes on Sikh Soldier ie *'Sikh Soldier; Battle Honours'*, *'Sikh Soldier; Gallantry Awards'*, *'Sikh Soldier; Policing the Empire'* and *'Sikh Soldier: Warriors and Generals'* which depicts Sikh Sardars, Generals of the Sikh Army, profiles of senior officers of all arms of the Indian armed forces and the military officers of the Sikh Diaspora. He plans to compile a fifth volume, *'Sikh Soldier: At War'*.

Narindar Singh Dhesi has undertaken a highly important task. That so many young, valiant Sikh men fought and died under British and Indian colours is something that should not be forgotten. Whether the mud of Flanders, the shores of Suvla, the deserts of El-Alamein or the hills of Monte Cassino, Sikh soldiers have served with distinction alongside their Imperial and Commonwealth fellow soldiers and they deserve recognition. Nor must it be forgotten that the descendants of these same soldiers at this very moment are in the vanguard of protecting their chosen motherlands, whether in military or police uniform, from British Columbia to Malaysia. It is to share this devotion of the Sikh soldier both past and present that Mr Dhesi seeks to do, and he achieves this task with commitment, tenacity and perspicacity.

SIKH DIASPORA

Singapore Armed Forces

On 15TH February 1942, the British surrendered unconditionally to the Japanese army in Singapore. In the early stages of the Japanese occupation, a programme was initiated by the British for the people of Singapore to facilitate the Japanese administration, in British hopes that the Japanese would treat them humanely. To safeguard their livelihood, the majority of the Sikh police officers retained their employment during the Japanese occupation. The Sikh Police Contingent continued to function and some policemen were sent to Changi Prison to guard the British internees. After the Japanese surrender, Senior British Police Officers who had been made internees during the Japanese occupation in Changi Prison recommended to the British that the Sikh Police Contingent be disbanded. They emphasised that they would not work as Police Officers anymore if the British continued to employ the Sikh Police Contingent. The British Authorities had to accede to their requests, as they needed their services for re-building the Police Force in Singapore. Consequently, the Sikh Police Contingent was disbanded at the end of 1945. However, individual Sikhs were continually recruited in the Singapore Police. The end of the war and the rush to end British rule of the Indian subcontinent raised questions about the future of the Sikh Police Officers in Singapore. India was unlikely to countenance the recruiting of their citizens to uphold British imperialism in Asia. So the Sikh Police Officers became the pioneering Sikh immigrants into Singapore. Their descendants, the Singaporean Sikhs, continue to maintain the Sikh martial tradition in the Armed Forces of Singapore.

Decades after the war saw the rise of anti-colonial and nationalist sentiments. The British, on their part, were prepared to gradually increase self-governance for Singapore and Malaya. On 1ST April 1946, the Straits Settlements was dissolved and Singapore became a separate Crown Colony with a civil administration headed by a Governor. In August 1958, the State of Singapore Act was passed in the United Kingdom Parliament providing for the establishment of the State of Singapore. Elections for the new Legislative Assembly were held in May 1959. Lee Kuan Yew, a young Cambridge-educated Lawyer, became the first Prime Minister of Singapore. British troops remained in Singapore following its Independence, but in 1968, London announced its decision to withdraw the Forces by 1971 and Singapore set out to build its Military, called the Singapore Armed Forces.

Sikh Diaspora

Singapore Armed Forces

Ravinder Singh, Brigadier-General

Brigadier-General Ravinder Singh, a Sikh, was appointed as the Chief of the Singapore Army on March 25^{TH,} 2011. Brigadier-General Ravinder Singh joined the Singapore Armed Forces (SAF) in December 1982. He was awarded the SAF Overseas Training Award (Academic) in 1983 with which he attained a Bachelor of Arts (First Class Honours) in Engineering Science at the University of Oxford (UK) in 1986. He subsequently attained a Master of Arts (Engineering Science) from the University of Oxford in 1992. In 1995, he was awarded the SAF Postgraduate Scholarship and obtained a Master of Science in Management from the Massachusetts Institute of Technology (USA). Brigadier-General Singh earned his commission from the Officer Cadet School at SAFTI Military Institute as a Signals Officer in December 1986. In 1991, he was deployed to United Nations Iraq-Kuwait Observation Mission (UNIKOM) as a Member of the Singapore Observer Team and in 1995; he attended the US Army Command and General Staff College at Fort Leavenworth. Brigadier-General Singh's distinguished military career has seen him hold key appointments in the Singapore Army, SAF, as well as the Ministry of Defence. These include Head System Development Group, Commander 2 Singapore Infantry Brigade, Commander 6TH Division, Chief of Staff-Joint Staff, Deputy Secretary (Technology), and at present, Chief of Army. Brigadier-General Singh's illustrious list of awards is testament to the outstanding contributions he has made to the SAF. He received, among others, the SAF Long Service Award (25 years) in 2008, Public Administration Medal (Silver Military) in 2005, and the United Nations Medal and SAF Overseas Service Medal – both in 1992.

Sarbjit Singh, Brigadier

Brigadier Sarbjit Singh assumed command of Air Power Generation Command (APGC) on 17TH April 2009. Brigadier Sarbjit Singh joined the Republic of Singapore Air Force on 17TH January 1983, attained his Pilot Wings in 1985, and went on to serve as an Operational Pilot on the F-5 and F-16 aircraft. He progressed on to become a Pilot Attack Instructor and an Officer Commanding, before attending the Air Command & Staff College in Maxwell AFB, Montgomery, Alabama, in 1996. On his return, he took over command of 144 Squadron in Paya Lebar Air Base and thereafter became a Branch Head in Ops Planning Group, in Air Operations Department.

Sikh Diaspora

Singapore Armed Forces

Sarbjit Singh, *Brigadier (Cont.)*

In 2002, he attended the Air War College in the USA, and returned in 2004 to assume the appointment of Deputy Head Air Operations (Ops Planning) in Air Operations Department. Subsequently, he assumed the appointment of Deputy Commander Tengah Airbase before becoming the first Commander of UAV Command when it was stood-up in February 2007. Brigadier Sarbjit Singh graduated with a BSc (Political Science) Degree from Auburn University Montgomery, Alabama, USA. He was awarded Summa Cum Laude Honours for his academic achievements. Brigadier Sarbjit Singh has been awarded the Singapore Armed Forces Good Service Medal (5 years), Singapore Armed Forces Long Service and Good Conduct Medal (12 years), Singapore Armed Forces Long Service and Good Conduct Medal (22 years), and The Long Service Medal (Military). In 2008, he was awarded The Public Administration Medal (Bronze) (Military).

Mancharan Singh Gill, Colonel

The late Colonel Mancharan Singh Gill was born in Muar, Malaya on June $28^{TH,}$ 1934. He graduated from the University of Singapore in 1956 with a Degree in Physics, and thereafter commissioned in the Singapore Volunteer Corps in early 1961. During the Konfrontasi (Indonesia–Malaysia confrontation), he saw active service in South Johore and Sabah. In August 1957, after Independence, then Defence Minister, Goh Keng Swee, tasked a young Captain Mancharan Singh Gill, with the responsibility of building up the Singapore Artillery. Mancharan Singh Gill served the Singapore Armed Forces with great distinction and held several key commands. Colonel Gill served as an escort to HRH Queen Elizabeth and HRH Prince Philip on their visit to Singapore in 1972. During his military career; Colonel Mancharan Singh Gill received numerous public awards inclusive of the Public Administration Medal (Silver) (Military) and Public Administration Medal (Gold) (Military) in 1971 and 1982 respectively. He retired from active military service in August 1986, but continued to serve as the President of the Singapore Armed Forces Veteran's League. Colonel Mancharan Singh Gill passed away peacefully on 20TH June 2008.

Sikh Diaspora

Singapore Armed Forces

Jaswant Singh Gill, Lieutenant Colonel

Lieutenant Colonel Jaswant Singh in his own words: "On 15TH May 1923, I was born in Moga, Punjab, into a poor farming family. One of my uncles was educated in English and had obtained a clerical job in Singapore at Police Headquarters. When I was 6 years old, I was packed off to Singapore and my uncle was instructed by the family elders to arrange to give me a good education. I was educated up to a Senior Cambridge and London Chamber of Commerce General Certificate at Raffles Institution. In 1941, I joined the Government General Clerical Service as a Clerk/Stenographer. In 1948, I obtained a transfer to the Ministry of Education as a Trainee Teacher. During the day I taught in school and also attended Teachers Training College. During the evening, I joined the Royal Naval Volunteer Reserve and was trained by the Royal Navy to be a Naval Officer. I qualified as a teacher and also did my Post Graduate Teachers Course and was appointed Principal of Dunearn Secondary Vocational School in 1965.By 1966, I had passed various Naval Exams and has risen to the rank of Commander. After doing some active naval service against the Indonesians, I was mobilized by the Singapore Ministry of Defence in 1966, as Singapore's First Chief of Naval Staff with HQ at Blakang Mati. In 1968, I was appointed Head, Training Department and General Staff Division. In 1971, I was appointed Commander Tengah Air Base. In 1971, I was appointed Commander, Changi Air Base, which was Britain's largest Air Base in the Far East. I retired from Government Service in 1973".

Despite having retired forty years earlier from the Navy, Gill still feels strongly for the Navy and enjoys reading the Navy News. Since leaving the Navy, he has been actively engaged. He taught for 10 years at United World College and went into business after his retirement at 60 years. On 29TH December 2006, he was also recognised for his contributions to the Sikh community at Singapore Khalsa Association's 75TH Anniversary celebrations.

Sikh Diaspora

Singapore Armed Forces

Sukhvinder Singh Chopra, Colonel

Colonel Sukhvinder Singh Chopra joined the Lee Kuan Yew School (LKY) of Public Policy as Director Administration in January 2007. He is responsible for the overall administration of the School and its Research Centres. In this capacity, he is in charge of several key areas, which include Human Resources, Finance, and Corporate Services. Sukhvinder also shares responsibility for the overall strategic management and growth of the School and its Research Centres. He joined LKY School after nearly three decades of distinguished service in the Singapore Armed Forces (SAF), Republic of Singapore Navy (RSN). He is an experienced Operational Leader, Mentor, and Coach for individuals and teams. During his tenure in the SAF-RSN, Sukhvinder held senior leadership appointments, which included the command of a Squadron of the largest modern ships in the Navy and command of the Naval Officers' Advanced School, where he was responsible for training and developing Naval Officers to hold intermediate to command-level appointments. He was the first Senior Officer in the SAF-RSN to be appointed to lead a Task Group for operations in the Gulf to assist rebuild Iraq. For his sterling contributions in service, he is the recipient of Singapore's Public Administration Award. Sukhvinder graduated from the University of Tasmania, Australia with a Masters Degree in Business Administration. He has a Post Graduate Diploma in Change Management, Leading and Sustaining Change awarded by Singapore's Civil Service College. He successfully completed an Executive Programme in International Management that was jointly awarded by the Stanford Graduate School of Business and the National University of Singapore's Business School. In 2008, he achieved a Post Graduate Certificate in Coaching by Lancaster University, United Kingdom, testimony of his belief in people development and continuous learning.

'As the turbaned commander deftly maneuvered the modern warship RSS *Endurance* into the small channel to berth at Green Gate last February, Indian Naval Officers felt pride and admiration. For Lieutenant Colonel Sukhvinder Singh Chopra is Commanding Officer of the Singapore Navy Warship, the first Indian to hold this position. RSS *Endurance* was a part of the recently concluded International Fleet Review. The vessel had berthed to unload humanitarian and relief aid donated by the Singapore public for Gujarat earthquake victims'. (Dharmesh Thakkar)

Sikh Diaspora

Singapore Armed Forces

Sukhmohinder Singh, Colonel

Colonel Sukhmohinder Singh was the Head of the Singapore Armed Forces Centre for Leadership Development. He was a Commando Officer by vocation. He served the Commando formation as a Platoon Commander, Quartermaster, Officer Commanding, and Officer Commanding of the Commando Training Wing. He was also the Head of Operations of the Commando Formation, where he planned and facilitated the execution of Peace Support Operations overseas. He was appointed Commanding Officer 3RD Singapore Infantry Regiment, where the Battalion emerged as the Best Infantry and Best Combat Unit. He was appointed as Aide De-Camp to the President in 1994 and served until 1999. He went on to command 10TH Singapore Infantry Brigade. In 2000, he moved on to command the Army Officers' Advanced School while he was on the Graduate Diploma programme on Organizational Learning by the Institute of Public Administration and Management, Civil Service College. He has also made it a critical feature of leader development for all leaders to be skilled in coaching and facilitating learning, by designing an enduring system for training and operationalisation across the Singapore Armed Forces. Colonel Sukhmohinder Singh assumed the appointment as Head SCLD in January 2003. He was instrumental in setting up the Centre, and growing it from a 12 man team to a 28 man team. As Head of SCLD, he was responsible for formulating the strategies and implementation plans for Leadership Development in the Singapore Armed Forces. He was nominated to be the organizing Chairman for the Organizational Learning Conference in February 2006, where he led a team comprising of Members from 9 Public Sectors. Colonel Sukhmohinder Singh is a certified Executive Coach by Lancaster University. He is also a Certified Trainer for Myers-Briggs Type Indicator Assessment and Fundamental Interpersonal Relations Orientation-Behavior Assessment. He has developed the Leadership Development Master Plan for 2015, as the next lap for the Singapore Armed Forces. Colonel Sukhmohinder Singh retired on 31ST December 2011, after serving 31 years in the Singapore Armed Forces.

Sikh Diaspora

Malaysian Armed Forces

This segment records the contributions of Sikhs, who form a tiny minority of the population of Malaysia. Sikhs played a great part in the history of the Malaysian Armed Forces. The early Sikhs, that joined the Malaysian Armed Forces (then Malayan Army), can be traced to the early 1950s, when General Sir Gerald Templer's twelve selected local cadets were sent to the Royal Military Academy, Sandhurst, United Kingdom for Officer Training. The first Sikh Officer selected was Lakhbir Singh Gill, who formed part of the famous Templer's twelve. From then on there was a gradual recruitment of Sikhs into the Malaysian Armed Forces to this day. Sikhs were part of units and establishments in which they held key appointments and partook in missions/assignments to defeat threats to the country or accomplish set missions. Enlisted Sikhs served with distinction, humility, and compassion. Their sacrifices were justly rewarded in some cases but many went unnoticed and unrewarded. True to the traditions of their forefathers, Malaysian Armed Forces Sikhs served unconditionally – giving their best and expecting nothing in return. Only four Sikh Officers are on record, to have earned some form of Award for Gallantry.

Rajbans Singh Gill, Brigadier General

Brigadier General Rajbans Singh Gill joined the Army in February 1953. He was trained at Eaton Hall, UK in May 1953 and was commissioned on 5TH September 1953. He was posted to 1ST Federation Regiment. He was awarded *"Mention in Despatch"* on 19TH June, 1959, while serving with the UN in the Congo. He commanded 3RD Royal Ranger Regiment May 1970 to January 1971. He was promoted to Brigadier General on 1ST December 1979 (the first Sikh to attain the General rank) and commanded Rejang Area Security Command (RASCOM), a Brigade Group Organization, from January 1980 to February 1981. RASCOM was tasked to eliminate the communist threat (Malayan Communist Party) in the Rejang area of Sarawak. He served as the Chief of Staff General Branch, Army Corps HQ from March 1981 to December 1982 and commanded 10TH Brigade in 1983 to 1985.

Sikh Diaspora

Malaysian Armed Forces

Baljit Singh, Brigadier General

Brigadier General Baljit Singh joined the Army on 2ND February 1953. He first trained at Eaton Hall, UK from 29TH August 1953 to 17th December 1953 and later at RMA Sandhurst from 10th March 1954 to 27TH July 1955. He was commissioned on 28TH July 1955 and was posted to 1ST Federation Regiment. He served with the Malayan Special Force Congo Group (UN) from November 1961 to August 1962. He was awarded *"Mention in Despatch"* for actions in the Congo. He later commanded 1ST Royal Ranger Regiment from April 1971 to January 1973. He served as Defence Attaché to the Republic of Cambodia from January 1975 to January 1976 and New Zealand from October 1976 to December 1977. He later commanded RASCOM from January 1978 to December 1979. He was later the Commandant of the Malaysian Army Combat Training Centre from 1ST January 1981 to 31ST December 1981. He was promoted to Brigadier General on 1ST January 1982 (the second Sikh Officer to be promoted to that rank in the Malaysian Army) and commanded 1ST Malaysian Infantry Brigade from January 1982 to December 1983. He also commanded 10TH Malaysian Infantry Brigade from January 1984 to October 1985. He later was the Commandant of the Malaysian Armed Forces Defence College from November 1985 to April 1986. He retired in January 1988.

Ranjit Singh Ramday, Brigadier General

Brigadier General Ranjit Singh Ramday was trained at the Royal Military College, Kuala Lumpur and was commissioned on 31ST October 1974. He was posted to 3RD Royal Ranger Regiment. Having served in various appointments in the early years, he volunteered to join 8TH Royal Ranger Regiment, the newly formed Malaysian Parachute Infantry Battalion. He served in the Regiment as a Company Commander, Second-in-Command and finally commanded the Regiment from June 1996 until June 1999. He also served with the UN HQ (MONUC) in the Democratic Republic of the Congo from May 2004 to June 2005. He was Directing Staff at the Malaysian Armed Forces Staff College from January 2000 to January 2003 and later at the Malaysian Armed Forces Defence College from July 2007 to February 2011. On 28TH February 2011, he was posted to the Army Training Command as Chief of Staff and was promoted to Brigadier General.

Sikh Diaspora

Malaysian Armed Forces

Ranjit Singh Gill, Brigadier General Dato

Brigadier General Ranjit Singh Gill joined the Royal Military College in February 1968 and was commissioned Pilot Officer in September 1968. He got his "Wings" in January 1970. He was an active Helicopter Pilot supporting ground missions against the Malayan Communist Party in the border regions with Indonesia and Thailand. He rose to become a Pilot Examiner and a Category 'A' Instructor. He had a short stint as a Fixed Wing Pilot flying the Twin-Engine Cessna 402B Transport Aircraft. He commanded the Training Base at Kluang, Johor from 1992 to 1995 and later the Operational Base at Subang, Selangor in 1996 and 1997. He served as the Chief of Staff in No. 2 Air Division in Subang and shortly after set up and commanded the Air Force's Safety, Standards, and Readiness (SSR) Department, which carried out examinations of all Pilots and Cabin Crew. This included the examination and assessment of the Operational Readiness Inspections (ORI) of all RMAF units. Ranjit had the distinction of being the first Sikh General in the Air Force and the third in the Malaysian Armed Forces (MAF) after Brigadier General Rajbans Singh and Brigadier General Baljit Singh. Before his retirement in 2003, he was bestowed with the title of "Dato"[4] by His Royal Highness, The Sultan of Pahang, and the first Sikh in the Malaysian Armed Forces to be granted such an award.

Harchan Singh, Colonel

Colonel Harchan Singh was trained at Eaton Hall, UK from 24TH April 1953 to 22ND August 1953 and at the RMA Sandhurst from 9TH September 1953. He was commissioned on 3RD March 1955 and posted to 1ST Federation Regiment. He served with the Malayan Special Force Congo (UN) from September 1961 to December 1962. He was awarded the *"Mention in Despatch"* in September 1965. He commanded 2ND, 4TH, 5TH, and 9TH Royal Ranger Regiments at various times. He was appointed as Defence Attaché to Vietnam from December 1976 to January 1979. He retired in April 1985 leaving behind the legacy of his command and leadership.

---

[4] 'Dato' is the highest state title conferred by the Ruler on the most deserving recipients who have contributed greatly to the nation or state.

Sikh Diaspora

Malaysian Armed Forces

Baldev Singh Johl, Lieutenant Colonel

Lieutenant Colonel Baldev Singh Johl was trained at the Royal Military College, Kuala Lumpur from April 1969 to April 1971. He was posted into the Royal Ranger Regiment and held several appointments in the various units he served in. In 1974, as the unit Intelligence Officer of 7TH Royal Ranger Regiment, his analysis led to an ambush operation that resulted in the elimination of 5 communist terrorist (CT) of the MCP within a day of execution. In 1977, in a similar ambush operation, a subunit of his Company eliminated 2 CTs in the Malaysia/Thailand border region. He commanded 6TH Royal Ranger Regiment from 1991 to December 1993, during which time the Regiment was involved in a humanitarian effort to rescue the victims of a massive Highland Tower collapse. Later in 1999, while serving with the UN Military Observer group in East Timor, he intervened in a militia raid on refugees, escaping into the UN HQ in Dili. On the night of 10TH September 1999, a militia group was in hot pursuit of refugees escaping into the UN HQ. Colonel Baldev stepped out to halt the militia raid. His timely intervention brought the militia raid to a stop. While negotiating, the militia leader threatened him with two grenades and advised Colonel Baldev to withdraw and go home. The pause in action enabled the refugee group of women and children, to scramble hurriedly through the wire obstacles, into the safety of the UN compound. Lieutenant Colonel Baldev Singh Johl retired on 28TH April 2004, after a good 35 years service.

Lakhbir Singh Gill, Major

Major Lakhbir Singh Gill was one of the twelve potential Officers selected personally by General Sir Gerald Templer, the High Commissioner for the Federation of Malaya, in July 1952, to attend Officer Training at the RMA Sandhurst. The basis for his selection, as Platoon Commander, was to form the first multi-racial Battalion (1st Federation Regiment) for Malaya. It was part of the effort to unite the Malayan people in the fight against the Malaysian Communist Party and to prepare for Malaya's independence. Major Lakhbir was trained from 10TH September 1953 and was commissioned on 3RD February 1955. He was posted to 1ST Federation Regiment. He held various appointments in the Army and was a model Officer for young Sikhs in the Army.

Sikh Diaspora

Malaysian Armed Forces

Dara Singh, Brigadier-General

In 1939, when 4,000 Chinese from Malaya volunteered for service in China, Dara Singh went along with them. "I was the only Indian in the party, but then I knew Chinese." As a Chinese speaking Sikh, called Dara Ah-Leng, in the Kuomintang Army, he had some hard times proving he was as good as his Chinese comrades. However, he succeeded and rose from Sergeant to Colonel in two years and then was personally promoted to Brigadier-General by Chiang Kai Shek in 1943. Later he served with the American forces in Burma and worked closely with General Joseph W. Stillwell, who was commanding Chinese troops against the Japanese. Here he was the General's aide, bodyguard, and interpreter, making good use of the language skills he had nurtured in Malaya and China. He spoke fluent Hokkien and six other Chinese dialects, Malay, English, Hindi, Tamil, Punjabi, and Burmese. Working with General Stillwell then provided the opportunity to work with Lord Louis Mountbatten, the World War Two Allied Chief of Combined Operations, and South East Asia. It was during this period that he rescued Lord Louis from a jeep crash. He had been struck in the eye with bamboo while driving and lost control of the vehicle. Prompt first aid from Dara and then a fast trip to a field hospital with him saved Mountbatten's sight, something acknowledged publicly by Lord Louis at a reception in Malaysia in 1967. When he finally returned to Taiping after the war, the Chinese gave him a hero's welcome and for one year, everything was given free to him and his family as a thank you for what he had done. Free food, accommodation, clothes and more, everything was free! Appointed as Protector of Aborigines (Orang Asli) he made friends with them and their children by handing out used tennis balls no longer required by the clubs. When he left the post he was crowned by the Aborigines "Tata (grandfather) of all Aborigines". He turned down the post of Ambassador to an African country, offered by the Prime Minister Tun Abdul Razak, preferring to stay in Malaysia and live a simple life, working hard, without any form of pension, to ensure his children were educated.

Sikh Diaspora

Malaysian Armed Forces

Wing Commander Jaswant Singh

Jaswant Singh was born in Kuala Lumpur, where he lived all his life.

The young Jaswant, the eldest of three siblings, was educated at the Victoria Institution, the capital's premier day school, but the war years meant that his education would be limited to cycling forty miles most days to buy and sell coconuts and pineapples to occupying Japanese troops. With his Senior Cambridge results received after the war, he joined the newly revived British Civil Service. In 1951, the RAF advertised for volunteers for an Auxiliary Air Force to train local Malayans to empower themselves for national defence. Jaswant, then merely contemplating flying as a hobby, applied along with half a dozen other Sikh friends and was accepted as a Cadet Officer. Thus began an 18-year flying career that would see him become the first local Pilot of the Malayan Auxiliary Air Force, and a pioneer Member of the Royal Malayan Air Force. Early training was in Tiger Moths, Chipmunks and Harvards and by the time he earned his Wings in April 1955 he had done 470 hours, including bombing, gunnery, interceptions and drops, in single and twin-engine aircraft. He clocked the magic 500 two months later as the only local Pilot in the fly past on the 2ND anniversary of the coronation of Elizabeth II.

During the communist insurgency, all through the mid-1950s to mid-60s, Jaswant flew relief and supply missions to Police and Military jungle forts, often putting down his Single Pioneer on postage-stamp sized grass landing strips, earning Mention in Dispatches for Distinguished Service in difficult and dangerous conditions, which saw some of his brave friends, perish. In 1965, Squadron Leader Jaswant became the first Commander of the now Royal Malaysian Air Force's Labuan base off Borneo, where he also served as Senior RMAF Officer for the newly incorporated states of East Malaysia.

With British RAF personnel still holding top positions in the RMAF, Jaswant returned to the peninsula in 1966, and now as Wing Commander, becoming Deputy Commandant of the main Air Force base in Kuala Lumpur, ending there, in December 1969, his Air Force career, at the same place where it all began.

Sikh Diaspora

Canada

Harjit Singh Sajjan, Lieutenant Colonel

Lieutenant Colonel Harjit Singh Sajjan has become the first Sikh in Canada to take command of a British Columbia Regiment. In a historic ceremony, a change of command in the British Columbia Regiment (Duke of Cannaught's Own) took place on September 11TH, 2011, at the Beatty Street Armoury in Vancouver, British Columbia, Canada. Lieutenant Colonel Bruce Kadanoff relinquished command of the Regiment to Lieutenant Colonel Harjit Singh Sajjan, who has taken over as Commanding Officer of the Regiment. Lieutenant Colonel Harjit Singh joined the British Columbia Regiment as a Trooper in 1989 and was commissioned in the Regiment in 1991. He was promoted to Captain in 1995 and to Major in 2005. He has served in Bosnia-Herzegovina as well as three deployments to Afghanistan. Established in 1883, the Regiment is said to be the oldest Military Unit in Vancouver, British Columbia, Canada and has received forty Battle Honours in its history, and has been a formation of the Royal Canadian Armoured Corps since 1942. Lieutenant Colonel Harjit Singh was born in Punjab and moved to Canada with his parents at the age of five. Lieutenant Colonel Harjit Singh's most recent deployment to Afghanistan was in November 2010. In the course of his deployments Lt.Colonel Harjit Singh has been awarded a Mention-in-Dispatches, Commander-in-Chief Commendation, two 'Chief of Defence Staff Commendations', and a US Army Commendation. He is also the recipient of the Deputy Minister's (National Defence) Award. Prior to joining the Army, Lieutenant-Colonel Harjit Singh remained a Police Officer for 11 years with the Vancouver Police Department. He completed his last assignment as a Detective, specializing in organized crime in the Gang Crime Unit. He also spent five years as a certified Technical Search Specialist with Vancouver's Heavy Urban Search and Rescue Team. Father of two children, Harjit Singh is married to Kuljit Kaur, a Medical Physician, and they reside in Vancouver. WSO (World Sikh Organisation) President Prem Singh Vinning, who attended the Change of Command ceremony said, "This is a proud moment for all Canadian Sikhs. Lieutenant Colonel Sajjan is an inspiration to young Sikhs and he shows just how much a part of Canada Sikhs are today."

Sikh Diaspora

United States of America

Gopal Singh Khalsa, Colonel

Colonel Gopal Singh Khalsa joined the U.S. Army in 1976 as a Private, and served in the Special Forces Unit for 10 years on Parachute Status, as a Battalion Commander overseeing an 800-person Intelligence Group, and also received a Meritorious Service Medal with Silver Oak Leaf Cluster Award, amongst many other honours. He is a Graduate of the Army Officer Candidate School in Georgia, and was inducted into the Officer Candidate School Hall of Fame in 2004. Colonel Khalsa currently remains in the Reserve Command, and has therefore served in the U.S. Army for 33 years.

Arjinderpal Singh Sekhon, Colonel

Colonel Arjinderpal Singh Sekhon, a Medical Doctor, served in the Army from 1984 to 2009. During his 25 years of commissioned service, Colonel Sekhon was stationed in multiple cities around the country. During the First Persian Gulf War, he was called to active duty and served stateside as a doctor at the United States Army Hospital in California. He rose through the ranks to Colonel and was given a Battalion Commander position through which he oversaw a unit of 600-700 soldiers. Before ending his career, he was decorated with various awards including a Presidential Unit Citation, Joint Meritorious Unit Award, and an Army Flight Surgeon Badge. During his time of service, Colonel Sekhon's articles of faith never impeded his success. His Sikh identity never interfered with his ability to create strong relationships with his fellow Service Members.

G.B. Singh, Colonel

Colonel G.B. Singh enlisted as a Dentist in the U.S. Army in 1979 and served until 2007. During his 28 year tenure, he was awarded several honours including the (A) Prefix, the highest award a Medical Professional can receive while in the U.S. Army. Colonel Singh was stationed in several areas in the U.S. as well as Korea. Colonel Singh recalls the camaraderie and life-lasting bonds he forged with the Members of his Unit. He remains in contact with many of them. His articles of faith never precluded him from creating strong relationships within the Army, and his superiors never treated him differently.

Sikh Diaspora

United Kingdom

Tarlochan Singh Marwaha, Lieutenant Colonel

Lieutenant Colonel Marwaha was born on 21ST October 1951 in Nairobi, Kenya and moved to Uganda in 1956, where he was raised and educated to the UK 'A' Level standard. He also represented Uganda in hockey at the U21 level. He left Uganda with his family when Idi Amin, the President of Uganda, ejected all Asians from Uganda in 1972, and settled in UK. He furthered his education by reading for an Electrical Engineering Degree at Liverpool University, graduating as a Bachelor of Engineering (Honours) in 1974. After a short stint working in the civilian market he joined the British Army in 1977. As an Engineer he opted to join the Corps of Royal Electrical and Mechanical Engineers (REME). Following a Commissioning Course at the Royal Military Academy Sandhurst he did various postings as a young Officer, serving in Germany with the British Army of the Rhine (BAOR). During that time he was selected to play hockey for both the Army and the REME. On promotion to Major he did various appointments, the highlight of which was commanding the workshop of 16TH Light Air Defence Regiment, Royal Artillery. Following that he attended a Guided Weapons course at the Royal Military College of Sciences at Shrivenham, gaining a Master of Sciences Degree. This led to a job on guided weapons in the Ministry of Defence in London, followed by a Headquarters Staff Appointment in Germany and then promotion to Lt Col. As a Lt Col he did various appointments, some key Staff Appointments in Personnel area and Project Management, and the most enjoyable at the Royal Commissions Board at Westbury, selecting future Officers for the British Army. He finally retired from the Army in April 2012. Throughout his Army career Lt Col Marwaha has also been actively involved in hockey, as a player, coach and in management. He has played for all his Unit sides, the REME, the Army and the Combined Services teams. He captained and coached his Unit and REME teams. He was the Army coach for several years after he stopped playing at that level and then was Chairman of the Army Hockey Association for several years. During this time he also took up the sport of gliding, at which he represented the Army and competed at the National level. He also took on the responsibility of Chairman of the Army Gliding Association for several years.

Sikh Diaspora

Kenya

Gurcharan Singh Chana, Lieutenant Colonel

Lieutenant Colonel G. S. Chana was born in a poor family. Whilst in school it was his desire to become a Pilot. After finishing his education he briefly worked for a bank and at the same time acquired a Private Pilot's License. He then decided to join the Kenya Air Force. He completed his Officer Training with the Royal Air Force in England and on his return he was commissioned by the Late President His Excellency Mzee Jomo Kenyatta. As he progressed in the Air Force, as a Pilot, he was the first Sikh to be awarded the rank of a Lieutenant Colonel in the Kenya Air Force. Subsequently he was the first Kenyan Sikh to acquire the position of Station Commander Kenya Air Force. After serving for 20 years in the Air Force, he retired in 1985. He then joined Kenya Airways as a Pilot and having flown most of the aircraft in Kenya Airways he retired as a Captain and Boeing Instructor. He has flown a total of 15 different types of aeroplanes. He also had a deep passion to go into music and he learned Tabla at the age of 6 years from the great Gurus in India. He practiced regularly and today is regarded as the top percussionist on the Tabla in Africa. He has accompanied the great King of Ghazals Jagjit Singh, Sitar Maestro Ustad Basharat Khan. Ustad Mehdi Hassan and Parvez Mehndi. In addition he has also given numerous musical performances with most of the leading professional artists in the World. Channi, as he is more prominently known, was very close to Jagjit Singh. One of his great moments was when Jagjit Ji came to Nairobi and invited Channi to perform with him on the stage. Channi is married to his charming wife Jaswant Kaur (Jassy). She has been a Head Mistress of various schools and holds a Montessori Diploma. They have two daughters namely Taninder and Maninder and a son Ishwinder, all Southampton University Graduates. Their grand daughter Sahiba who is at the tail end of her higher education is a very talented musician. Both Channi and Sahiba have already produced two CD's and two DVD's. Channi says most people say that Flying and Tabla playing is a very strange combination. It is not, because both Flying aeroplanes and playing Tabla is done with precision.

SOURCES

Bhagat Singh. (1990) *Maharaja Ranjit Singh and His Times,* Delhi.

Bhangu, Ratan Singh. (1962) *Prachin Panth Prakash* [Reprint]. Amritsar.

Chupia, B.R. (1969) *Kingdom of the Punjab*, Hoshiarpur.

Deol, G.S. (1972) *Banda Bahadur*. Jalandhar.

Gopal Singh. (1979) *A History of the Sikh People*. Delhi.

Griffin, Lepel. (1909) *Chiefs and Families of Note in the Punjab*, Lahore.

Griffin, Lepel. (1977) *The Rajas of the Punjab*. Delhi.

Griffin, Sir Lepel. (1890) *The Punjab Chiefs*. Lahore.

Gupta, Hari Ram. (1979) *History of the Sikhs, vol. III.* Delhi.

Gupta, Hari Ram. (1982) *History of the Sikhs, vol. IV*. Delhi.

Harbans Singh. (1995) *The Encyclopaedia of Sikhism*, Patiala.

Harbans Singh. (1980) *Maharaja Ranjit Singh. Delhi.*

Harbans Singh. (1983) *The Heritage of the Sikhs.* Delhi.

Irvine, W. (1922) *Later Mughals.* London.

J.D. Cunningham. (1849) *A History of the Sikhs*, John Murray.

Khushwant Singh. (1963) *A History of the Sikhs*, vol. I. Princeton.

Khushwant Singh. (1962) *Ranjit Singh: Maharajah of the Punjab* 1780-1839. Bombay.

Latif, Syed Muhammad. (1961) *History of the Panjab*. Delhi.

Sinha, N.K. (1933) *Ranjit Singh*. Calcutta.

Smyth, G. Carmichael. (1970) *A History of the Reigning Family of Lahore*. Patiala.

INDEX

Ahluwalia, Jassa Singh Sardar 20
Ahluwalia, Nihal Singh 24
Ajit Singh, Raja 110
Ala Singh, Raja 54
Ali Singh, Sardar 24
Amar Singh Lieutenant General 157
Amar Singh Majithia, Commander 83
Amar Singh Majithia, Governor 83
Amar Singh, Raja 55
Amarjeet Singh Chabbewal, Lieutenant General 157
Amarjeet Singh Sekhon, Lieutenant General 158
Amarjit Singh, Major General 130
Anup Singh, Vice Admiral 232
Ardaman Jit Singh Sandhu, Major General 133
Arjan Singh, Commander 110
Arjan Singh, Governor Delhi 276
Arjan Singh, Marshal of the Air, DFC 244
Arjinderpal Singh Sekhon, Colonel 312
Arvinder Singh Lamba, Lieutenant General 159
Atar Singh Kalianvala, Commander 111
Atar Singh Sandhanvalia, Sardar 83
Atma Singh, Major General 131
Avtar Singh Lamba, Lieutenant General 161
Avtar Singh, Lieutenant General 160
B.S. Pawar, Lieutenant General 159
Bachittar Singh Malvai 84
Baghel Singh, Sardar 25
Baj Singh, Sardar 26
Bajwa Singh (Dr.) Air Marshal 247
Baldev Singh Johl, Lieutenant Colonel 308
Baljit Singh Grewal, Major General 136
Baljit Singh, Brigadier General 306
Balraj Singh Takhar, Lieutenant General 161
Balwant Singh Rear Admiral 236
Banda Singh Bahadur 14
Bedi, Ram Singh, Sardar 27
Bela Singh Mokal, Sardar 114
Bhag Singh, Raja 62
Bhalla PS, Lieutenant General 162

Index

Bhanga Singh, Sardar 28
Bhangi, Bhuma Singh, Sardar 28
Bhangi, Ganda Singh, Sardar 30
Bhangi, Gujar Singh, Sardar 32
Bhangi, Gulab Singh, Sardar 30
Bhangi, Hari Singh, Sardar 29
Bhangi, Jhanda Singh, Sardar 30
Bhangi, Jodh Singh, Sardar 30
Bhangi, Karam Singh Dullu, Sardar 31
Bhangi, Lahna Singh, Sardar 31
Bhupinder Singh, Maharaja 57
Bikram Singh Bedi, Baba 111
Bikram Singh, Lieutenant General 162
Bikram Singh, Lieutenant General 163
Birinder Singh Randhawa, Vice Admiral 230
Bota Singh, Sardar 34
BS Dhaliwal, Lieutenant General 164
BS Dhillon, Major General, 135
Buddh Singh Man, General 112
Budh Singh Sandhanvalia, Commander 84
Buta Singh, Governor of Bihar 276
Charanjit Singh, Dr. (Major General) 165
Charyari Sowars 104
Chatar Singh Attariwala, Sardar 112
Cheema SPS, Vice Admiral 240
Chet Singh, Commander 113
Chuhar Singh, Sardar 31
Churhr Singh, Sardar 70
Dalbir Singh Major General, 137
Daljeet Singh, Lieutenant General 165
Dara Singh, Brigadier-General 309
Darshan Singh Basra, Air Marshal 248
Dasaundha Singh, Sardar 34
Daulat Singh, Lieutenant General 165
Desa Singh Majithia, General 85
Desu Singh, Bhai 68
Devinder Dayal Singh Sandhu, Lieutenant General 166
Dhanna Singh Malvai, Commander 86
Dhaliwal B S, Lieutenant General 167

Index

Dilbagh Singh, Air Chief Marshal 246
Dr Shivinder Singh Sidhu, Governor of Manipur 280
Dr. Gopal Singh, Governor Goa 281
Dr. Iqbal Singh, Governor of Pondichery 284
Dr. Manmohan Singh, Prime Minister of India 288
Durbara Singh, Governor of Rajasthan 278
Fateh Singh Kalianvala, Sardar 87
Fateh Singh Man, Commander 88
Fateh Singh, Commandant 113
Fateh Singh, Sardar 34
G.B. Singh, Colonel 312
Gajpat Singh, Raja 62
Ganda Singh, Commander 114
Ghaiba, Tara Singh, Sardar 36
Giani Zail Singh, President of India 287
Gobind Singh, Rear Admiral 235
Gopal Singh Khalsa, Colonel 312
Gulab Singh Pahuvindia, General 88
Grewal SS, Lieutenant General 169
Gulab Singh, Sardar 35
Gurbachan Singh Buch, Lieutenant General 170
Gurbachan Singh, Governor of Manipur and Nagaland 285
Gurbaksh Singh Badhani, Major General, 137
Gurbaksh Singh Reen, Major General 138
Gurbaksh Singh Sihota, Lieutenant General 170
Gurbaksh Singh, Raja 69
Gurcharan Singh Chana, Lieutenant Colonel 314
Gurcharn Singh Sandhu, Major General, 138
Gurdeep Singh, Lieutenant General 171
Gurdial Singh Dhillon, Minister of Agriculture 295
Gurinder Pal Singh, Air Vice Marshal 264
Gurmukh Nihal Singh, Governor of Rajasthan 277
Gurmukh Singh Lamma, Commander 89
Gurmukh Singh, Sardar 85
Gurnam Singh Chaudhry, Air Marshal 260
Guru Gobind Singh 12
Guru Hargobind 11
Hamir Singh, Raja 64
Haqiqat Singh, Sardar 36

Index

Harbhajan Singh Banga, Lieutenant General 175
Harbakhsh Singh, Lieutenant General 172
Harcharan Singh Brar, Governor of Haryana and Orissa 285
Harcharan Singh Brar, Governor Orissa 281
Hardev Singh Kler, Major General, 141
Hardeep Singh Puri, Diplomat 293
Hardev Singh Lidder, Lieutenant General 174
Hardit Singh Malik 273
Hari Simran Malhi, Vice Admiral 232
Hari Singh Nalwa, General 90
Harindar Singh, Raja 67
Harinder Kaur Sekhon 13
Harinder Singh, Vice Admiral 227
Harjinder Singh, Air Vice Marshal 249
Harjit Singh Sajjan, Lieutenant Colonel 311
Harkirat Singh, Major General 139
Harsa Singh, General 113
Himmat Singh Gill, Major General, 140
Hira Singh, Maharajah 65
HRS Kalkat, Lieutenant General, 176
Hukam Singh Malvai, Sardar 114
Hukam Singh, Governor of Rajasthan 277
Hukma Singh Chimni, Commander 92
Inder Singh, Lieutenant General 176
Inderjit Singh Gill, Lieutenant General 177
Inderjit Singh Khurana, Vice Admiral 234
J.S. Gujral, Air Marshal 261
Jagjit Singh Aurora Lieutenant General 179
Jagjit Singh Bedi, Vice Admiral 233
Jagjit Singh Sandhawalia, Air Marshal 251
Jagjit Singh, Air Vice Marshal 265
Jai Singh, Sardar 37
Jai Singh, Sardar 71
Jasbir Singh Lidder, Lieutenant General 184
Jasbir Singh Panesar, Air Vice Marshal 260
Jasbir Singh, Lieutenant General 184
Jasdeep Singh, Air Vice Marshal 260
Jasjit Singh, Air Commodore 266
Jasvant Singh, Raja 64

Index

Jaswant Singh Gill, Lieutenant Colonel 302
Jaswant Singh, Lieutenant General 181
Jaswant Singh, Major General 141
Jatinder Singh, Lieutenant General 192
Javala Singh Padhania, Sardar 93
Jawahar Singh Nalwa, Sardar 115
Jawand Singh Mokal, Sardar 94
Jhanda Singh Butaua, Commander 94
Jivan Singh Chhachhi, Commander 115
Jivan Singh, Colonel 95
Jodh Singh Rosa, Commander 95
Jodh Singh, Colonel 115
Jodh Singh, Commandant 95
Jodh Singh, Raja 69
Joginder Jaswant Singh, General 185
Joginder Jaswant Singh, Governor of Arunachal Pradesh 283
Joginder Singh Dhillon, Lieutenant General 188
Joginder Singh, Major General 142
Joginder Singh, Sardar, Governor of Rajasthan 280
JP Singh, Lieutenant General 190
Kahn Singh Majithia, General 116
Kahn Singh Man, General 116
Kahn Singh Rosa, Colonel 116
Kahn Singh, Sardar 117
Kalwant Singh, Lieutenant General 192
Kanwar Dalinderjit Singh, Air Marshal 251
Kapur Singh, Sardar 67
Karam Singh, Maharaja 56
Karora Singh, Sardar 37
Kartar Singh Gill, Lieutenant General 195
Kewal Singh, Foreign Secretary 295
Khem Karan Singh Lieutenant General 197
Khushal Singh, Sardar 38
Kirpal Singh, Rear Admiral 227
Kuldip Singh Bajwa, Major General 143
Kuldip Singh Brar, Lieutenant General 198
Kuldip Singh Sindhu, Major General 143
Kulwant Singh Gill, Air Marshal 265
Kulwant Singh, Major General, 142

Index

Lachman Singh Lehl, Major General 144
Lahina Singh Majithia, Commander 97
Lahina Singh, Sardar 96
Lakhbir Singh Gill, Major 308
Lakhwinder Singh, Major General 144
Lal Singh Grewal, Air Marshal 252
Lal Singh Moranvala, General 118
Lal Singh, Raja 108
Lal Singh, Sardar 68
Lang, Hari Singh Sardar 38
Madanjit Singh, Vice Admiral 239
Mahan Singh, Sardar 97
Maharaja Ranjit Singh 72
Maharaja Yadvinder Singh 58
Mahitab Singh Majithia. General 117
Mahtab Singh, Sardar 39
Malvinder Singh Bedi, Rear Admiral 238
Malvinder Singh Shergill, Lieutenant General 199
Manjit Singh, Air Vice Marshal 266
Man Mohan Singh 273
Man Singh, Sardar 118
Mancharan Singh Gill, Colonel 301
Mander PS, Major General 145
Manjit Singh Bhullar, Lieutenant General 200
Manjit Singh Sekhon, Air Marshal 253
Manjeev Singh Puri, Ambassador 292
Manmohan Singh, Major General, AVSM 145
Maninder Singh Buttar Lieutenant General 199
Mehar Singh, Air Commodore 267
Meva Singh Majithia, Commander 98
Mihan Singh, Governor 98
Milkha Singh Thehpuria, Sardar 99
Mit Singh Padhania, Commander 98
MM Singh, Commodore 235
MM Singh, Air Marshal 262
Mohan Singh, General 200
Mohar Singh, Sardar 40
Mohindar Singh Chopra, Major General 146
Mohinder Singh Pujji Squadron Leader 274

Index

Mohinder Singh, Maharaja 57
MS Shergill, Lieutenant General 134
Mohinder Singh Wadalia, Lieutenant General 202
Montek Singh Ahluwalia, Civil Servant 291
Mrs. Serla Grewal, Governor of Madhya Pradesh 283
Nahar Singh, Sardar 118
Nakai, Budh Singh, Sardar 42
Nakai, Hira Singh, Sardar 41
Nakai, Kamar Singh, Sardar 41
Nakai, Ran Singh, Sardar 41
Nanak, Guru 10
Narinder Singh Brar, Lieutenant General 203
Narindar Singh Dhesi, Author 297
Narinder Singh, Maharaja 56
Narinder Singh, Major General 147
Navdeep Singh Suri, Diplomat 296
Navtej Singh Sarna, Diplomat 296
Nawab Kapur Singh, 18
Nidhan Singh Panjhattha, Commander 100
Nihal Singh Attariwala, Sardar 101
Nihal Singh Sodhi, Sardar 101
Nihal Singh, Raja 66
Nirmala, Karam Singh, Sardar 42
Padamjit Singh Ahluwalia, Air marshal 259
Paramjit Singh Bhangu, Air Marshal 255
Pannu RS, Major General 148
Paramjit Singh, Lieutenant General 203
Paramjit Singh Gill, Air Marshal 262
Pawar B.S., Lieutenant General 203
Phula Singh, Akali 102
PJS Sandhu, Major General 151
Prem Pal Singh, Air Marshal 256
Prem Singh Gyani, Lieutenant General 205
Pritam Singh Mahindroo, Rear Admiral 221
Prithvi Singh Brar, Air Marshal 255
Punita Arora, Lieutenant General 204
Puran Singh Bajwa, Air Marshal 257
Raghbir Singh, Raja 63
Rai Singh, Sardar 42

Index

Rai Singh, Sardar 71
Raja, Bhup Singh 43
Rajbans Singh Gill, Brigadier General 305
Rajinder Singh Sparrow, Major General, VrC and Bar 149
Rajinder Singh Sujlana, Lieutenant General 206
Rajinder Singh, Air Marshal 257
Ram Singh Chhapevala, Commander 118
Ram Singh, Sardar 43
Ramgarhia, Jassa Singh, Sardar 44
Ramgarhia, Jodh Singh, Sardar 46
Ranbir Singh, Maharaja 63
Randhir Singh, Maharaja 66
Ranjit Singh Dyal, Lieutenant General 207
Ranjit Singh Gill, Brigadier General Dato 307
Ranjit Singh Ramday, Brigadier General 306
Ranjodh Singh Majithia, Commander 119
Ratan Singh Man, General 119
Ravinder Singh, Brigadier-General 300
Rawind Singh Grewal, Major General 151
Ripudaman Singh, Maharaja 65
S.P.Singh, Air Marshal 261
Sadhu Singh, Akali 97
Sahib Singh Bedi, Baba 47
Sahib Singh, Raja 56
Sahib Singh, Sardar 33
Samer Pal Singh Dhillon, Lieutenant General 208
Sandhu DDS (Dr.) Lieutenant General 209
Sandhu PJS, Major General 151
Sangat Singh Saini, General 100
Sant Singh, Lieutenant General 211
Sarabjit Singh Dhillon, Lieutenant General 211
Sarbjit Singh, Brigadier 300
Sardar Swaran, Foreign Minister of India 290
Sartaj Singh, Lieutenant General 210
Sarup Singh, Raja 63
Sarvjit Singh Chahal, Lieutenant General 212
Satbir Singh, Major General 151
Satyindra Singh, Rear Admiral 224
Shabeg Singh, Major General 152

Index

Shahid, Baba Dip Singh 48
Shahid, Karam Singh, Sardar 49
Sham Singh, Attariwala, Sardar 120
Shamir Singh Thethar 103
Sher Singh Attariwala, Raja 121
Shivdev Singh, Air Marshal 258
Sidhu Dalbir Singh, Lieutenant General 213
Sir Yadvinder Singh, Maharaja of Patiala 286
S.P.Singh, Air Marshal, 261
Suba Singh, General 99
Sukarchakia, Buddha Singh, Sardar 49
Sukarchakia, Charhat Singh, Sardar 50
Sukarchakia, Mahan Singh, Sardar 51
Sukarchakia, Nodh Singh, Sardar 50
Sukha Singh, Sardar 51
Sukhchain Singh, Air Vice Marshal 265
Sukhdev Singh Kang, Governor of Kerala 280
Sukhmohinder Singh, Colonel 304
Sukhvinder Singh Chopra, Colonel 303
Surat Singh Sandhu, Major General 156
Surat Singh Majithia, Sardar 122
Surjit Singh Barnala, Governor of Tamil Nadu 279
Surjit Singh Sangra, Lieutenant General 215
Surjit Singh, Major General 156
Surjit Singh, Lieutenant General 215
Tarlochan Singh Marwaha, Lieutenant Colonel 313
Tej Singh, Raja 109
Tejinder Jit Singh Gill, Lieutenant General 216
Tejinder Singh Shergill, Lieutenant General 216
TS Oberoi, Governor of Andaman & Nicobar Islands 276
Ujjal Singh, Governor of Tamil Nadu 282
Wazlrabadia, Jodh Singh, Sardar 52
Wing Commander Jaswant Singh 310

ABOUT THIS BOOK

The order of the Khalsa, enshrined by Guru Gobind Singh, transformed a lowly man, otherwise an insignificant creature of poor and oppressed society, into a bold Sikh warrior. Narindar Singh Dhesi profiles the Sikh warriors that rose to power and then established and served the Sikh Empire, leading us through to its fall. Having illustrated the Sikh Sardars and Generals who fought and fell in the Anglo-Sikh Wars, he goes on to depict the senior Sikh military leaders of all the armed services of the Indian Armed Forces, as well as the Sikh military officers of the Sikh Diaspora. A well-researched and well-written book, this is a worthy sequel to the author's earlier publications on the Sikh soldiery.

Narindar Singh Dhesi was born in 1940 at Eldoret in Kenya, where his father had migrated from the Punjab. He moved to England in 1957 and joined the British Army. After leaving the armed forces in 1964, he worked in the building and construction industry. He is married with four children and living in retirement at Southend on Sea, England. He is the author of three books on Sikh Soldier i.e. ***Sikh Soldier: Battle Honours (ISBN 978184574891) Sikh Soldier: Gallantry Awards (ISBN 9781845749057) and Sikh Soldier: Policing the Empire (ISBN 9781781519851)*** and are available from the Naval and Military Press.

Any information regarding Sikh Soldier at War, would be most welcome, including any comments and feedback on my earlier books on Sikh Soldier. Please feel free to contact me directly at:

narindardhesi@yahoo.co.uk
(Narindar Singh Dhesi)